全国高等院校法律英语专业统编教材
法律英语证书（LEC）全国统一考试指定用书

法律英语
翻译教程

Legal English
Translation Course

张法连　主编

北京大学出版社
PEKING UNIVERSITY PRESS

图书在版编目(CIP)数据

法律英语翻译教程/张法连主编.—北京:北京大学出版社,2016.9
(全国高等院校法律英语专业统编教材)
ISBN 978-7-301-27519-1

Ⅰ. ①法… Ⅱ. ①张… Ⅲ. ①法律—英语—翻译—高等学校—教材 Ⅳ. ①D9

中国版本图书馆 CIP 数据核字(2016)第 208055 号

书　　　名	法律英语翻译教程 FALÜ YINGYU FANYI JIAOCHENG
著作责任者	张法连　主编
策 划 编 辑	郭栋磊
责 任 编 辑	郝妮娜
标 准 书 号	ISBN 978-7-301-27519-1
出 版 发 行	北京大学出版社
地　　　址	北京市海淀区成府路 205 号　100871
网　　　址	http://www.pup.cn　新浪微博:@北京大学出版社
电 子 邮 箱	编辑室 pupwaiwen@pup.cn　总编室 zpup@pup.cn
电　　　话	邮购部 010-62752015　发行部 010-62750672　编辑部 010-62759634
印 刷 者	北京溢漾印刷有限公司
经 销 者	新华书店
	787 毫米×1092 毫米　16 开本　21.25 印张　680 千字 2016 年 9 月第 1 版　2025 年 1 月第 8 次印刷
定　　　价	56.00 元

未经许可,不得以任何方式复制或抄袭本书之部分或全部内容。
版权所有,侵权必究
举报电话:010-62752024　电子邮箱:fd@pup.cn
图书如有印装质量问题,请与出版部联系,电话:010-62756370

前　言

　　法律英语是法律科学与英语语言学有机结合形成的一门实践性很强的交叉学科，是ESP(English for Specific Purpose)最重要的分支之一。法律英语是以普通英语为基础，在立法和司法等活动中形成和使用的具有法律专业特点的语言，是指表述法律科学概念以及诉讼或非诉讼法律事务时所使用的英语。当今世界的发展日新月异，经济全球化进程突飞猛进，国际交流合作日益加强，涉外法务活动空前频繁。十八届四中全会提出要加强涉外法律工作，运用法律手段维护国家的发展利益。经济全球化过程中我们所面临的很多问题其实都是法律问题，而这些法律问题中的绝大多数又都属于涉外法律的工作范畴，所有这些工作都需要法律工作者通过专业外语完成。国家急需明晰国际法律规则、通晓英语语言的"精英明法"复合型人才，法律英语的重要性日益彰显，掌握专业外语已经成为法律人必备的职业素质。法律英语证书(LEC)全国统一考试的成功推出和中央政法委、教育部"卓越法律人才计划"的顺利启动无疑把法律英语的学习和研究推向了高潮。

　　法律英语是高校英语、法学等专业教学改革的新方向。随着高校英语专业教学改革不断深化，国内许多高校在外语院(系)开设了法律英语课程，设置了法律英语方向，有些高校开始尝试设置法律英语专业，收到了良好的社会效果。2013年高等教育出版社出版发行《法律英语专业教学大纲》，标志着法律英语专业的诞生，给高校外语院系设置法律英语专业指明了方向。本套教材正是以该大纲为重要依据编写而成。

　　本套教材共包括《法律英语精读教程》(上、下)、《法律英语泛读教程》(上、下)、《法律英语写作教程》《法律英语翻译教程》《英美法律文化教程》《法律英语视听说》和《大学法律英语》以及配套学习使用的《英美法律术语双解》。

　　随着全球化进程不断加快，法律翻译变得日趋重要。从文体学角度来讲，法律文件属于公文文体。与其他文体翻译，如文学翻译，新闻翻译一样，做好法律文件的翻译最重要的一点是要遵循翻译的基本原则，在翻译理论的指导下进行翻译实践。我们的前辈创立了一整套的翻译理论：从严复的"信、达、雅"，林语堂的"忠实、通顺、美"，到傅雷的"重神似不重形似"和钱钟书的"化"境，都强调了做好两种语言转换应遵守的重要原则。法律翻译比普通翻译需要遵守更多的原则，这是由于法律翻译的法律框架和法律语言自身的特点所决定的。根据法律语言的特点，我们更强调法律翻译的"信"和"达"。法律翻译其实是两种法律语言的转换过程，要做到目的语准确无误地表达源语的真正含义，无论在用词上及句子结构上都必须做到的准确严谨，这是法律翻译的根本原则。

鉴于法律和翻译在人们生活中的特殊影响和作用，人们对法律翻译的重要性是有目共睹的。但做好法律翻译并不是那么容易的事情。法律翻译不仅涉及两种语言，也涉及两种法律体系、多种法律文化甚至不同的法律观念。在这些复杂条件的限制下，很难寻求完全的统一或对应，这就需要译员发挥创新能力，在允许的范围内灵活机动地解决问题。法律语言中大量存在长句和特有词汇，这在一般翻译中是非常少见的，它特别要求译员具有不凡的语言驾驭能力和理解力。

本书共分九章，在编写上注重理论与实践的结合，从英汉两种法律语言的特点对比入手，介绍了法律翻译的原则和基本技巧，并辅以大量英汉互译的法律例句。诗无达诂，译无定本。书中的例句，尤其是长句，肯定有多种译法，"参考译文"只是编者提供的一种参考标准，未必是尽善尽美，还希望读者能发挥聪明才智，研究出更好的译文。

在编写本书的过程中，我们参考了近二十年来几乎所有的法律翻译方面的论文和著作，在此对原作者表示衷心的感谢，没有他们的研究做基础，就不可能有本书的出现。参加本书编写工作的还有山东大学胡志军教授、中国政法大学王芳副教授，上海大学王颖老师、中国教育科学研究院陈春勇副研究员、甘肃政法大学赵永平副教授、马彦峰副教授、中国石油大学徐文斌副教授、张建科副教授等。感谢法律英语证书（LEC）全国统一考试指导委员会将该套教材指定为复习应考 LEC 的参考用书。

各位教师或同学在使用本书的过程中有什么问题，欢迎及时与编者联系：zhangbook16@163.com。

编者

2016 年 3 月于中国政法大学

目录

第一章　法律翻译概述　001
　　第一节　历史回顾　001
　　第二节　理论建设　003
　　第三节　翻译方法　005
　　第四节　法律翻译问题之所在　005
　　第五节　法律翻译工作者应具备的素质　006

第二章　法律语言的特点　010
　　第一节　法律语言的用词特点　011
　　第二节　法律语言的句法特点　014
　　第三节　法律语言篇章结构特点　021
　　第四节　口头法律语言的特点　026
　　第五节　本章小结　029

第三章　法律翻译的基本原则　033
　　第一节　概述　033
　　第二节　法律翻译的原则　035
　　第三节　本章小结　044

第四章　法律语言词汇的翻译　047
　　第一节　概述　047
　　第二节　法律词汇的特点及翻译　047
　　第三节　本章小结　071

第五章　典型法律句式翻译　076
　　第一节　典型法律英语句式的翻译及解析　076
　　第二节　典型法律汉语句式的翻译与解析　082
　　第三节　本章小结　090

第六章　立法文本翻译　　　　　　　　　　　　　　　　093
　第一节　概述　　　　　　　　　　　　　　　　　　　093
　第二节　语言特点　　　　　　　　　　　　　　　　　104
　第三节　立法文本的翻译分析　　　　　　　　　　　　110
　第四节　本章小结　　　　　　　　　　　　　　　　　134

第七章　国际商务合同的翻译　　　　　　　　　　　　　139
　第一节　国际商务合同翻译原则和方法　　　　　　　　139
　第二节　国际商务合同的词汇特点及翻译　　　　　　　142
　第三节　国际商务合同的句式特点及翻译　　　　　　　152
　第四节　经贸合同基本格式和条款的翻译　　　　　　　160
　第五节　本章小结　　　　　　　　　　　　　　　　　169

第八章　涉外诉讼文书的翻译　　　　　　　　　　　　　173
　第一节　诉讼文书的语言特点及文体风格　　　　　　　174
　第二节　涉外诉讼文书翻译要点　　　　　　　　　　　178
　第三节　常见涉外诉讼类文书样例及翻译　　　　　　　187
　第四节　本章小结　　　　　　　　　　　　　　　　　225

第九章　涉外公证书翻译　　　　　　　　　　　　　　　229
　第一节　概述　　　　　　　　　　　　　　　　　　　229
　第二节　常用涉外公证书的翻译　　　　　　　　　　　237
　第三节　翻译中应注意的问题　　　　　　　　　　　　269
　第四节　本章小结　　　　　　　　　　　　　　　　　277

附录一　合同翻译中的常用词汇　　　　　　　　　　　　280

附录二　中外法律名言英汉对照　　　　　　　　　　　　290

课后习题参考答案　　　　　　　　　　　　　　　　　　307

参考文献　　　　　　　　　　　　　　　　　　　　　　330

第一章

法律翻译概述

社会发展日新月异，人类已进入信息化时代，知识与信息的传播都离不开翻译。当前我国的翻译研究与实务高潮迭起，这次高潮在规模、范围、质量水平和对社会发展的贡献上，都是前几次翻译高潮所无法比拟的；并且这次翻译高潮的重心是科技翻译和法律翻译。近年来，随着依法治国观念的不断深入，中国法制现代化的进程突飞猛进，对外法律文化交流日益增多。每年都有大量的法律文献被译成外文，同时也有大量外国的法律文献被译成中文。为了更好地参与国际社会的政治经济活动，我国也加快了向法律发达国家学习的步伐，其中就包括法律领域的学习和借鉴。因此，法律翻译所承担的功能愈加重要，法律翻译研究的重要性也日益凸显。

第一节 历史回顾

法律翻译由来已久，经历几个历史阶段。1840年爆发的鸦片战争揭开了中国近代史的序幕。在列强的坚船利炮下，中国社会的各个方面发生了深刻的变化。就法律领域而言，在鸦片战争以前，中外虽有少量交流，但一直以天朝大国自居的中华帝国对欧美国家法律（当然还有其他方面）的了解极其有限，甚至可以说根本没有了解的愿望和动机，因而少有翻译。

鸦片战争在中国的开明官僚和学者中引起了极大的震动，他们开始主动了解"西洋岛夷"，去"师夷长技以制夷"。先是师夷之船炮器物，后转向师夷之制度文化，法律即为其中一项重要内容。为师夷之法律，首先需要翻译其法律及其法学著作。客观上，随着各种不平等条约的签订和对外交往的频繁，也需要了解和翻译外国的法律。从鸦片战争到甲午战争以前的翻译活动以传播西学为主，有关法律方面的译著也比较集中，"法学"一词开始从西方文化传入我国。鸦片战争至五四运动这一历史时期，我国上至官方政府、下至民间学者都对外国法律、法学作品进行了大量的译介（国际法以及宪法等公法类著作翻译、法典翻译、法学理论著作翻译、报纸杂志中刊登的法律类译文等等）。这些法律、法学翻译作品不仅推动了我国法制近代化的进程，而且对我国译学的发展也做出了积极的贡献。从鸦片战争至五四运动这一历史时期，我国对西方法律、法学的译介进行了梳理和介绍，并在各学者研究的基础上以时间为序（考虑到法律翻译的特点，鸦片战争以前的内容亦略有涉及），将我国近代法律翻译分为以下几个时期，即近代法律翻译的肇始，洋务运动时期的法律翻译以及变法修律时期的法律翻译。法律翻译的数量不断增加，法律翻译门类日渐齐全（其中宪政类、商法类书籍翻译突出），法律翻译的质量水平不断提高。此外，对几位有影响的法律翻译者、近代法律翻译对法制近代化、译学发展的影响也有涉及。

南京国民政府成立之后，新政权意欲塑造全新的政治形象，逐步完善立法体制。五院制的推行使得立法权形式上取得了与行政权、司法权同等的地位。专业立法人员总结清末以来法制改革的经验，遵循统一的立法精神，按照时代需求，吸收先进国家的最新立法成果，进行了大规模的立法运动。自1927年4月至1937年7月全面抗日战争爆发止，立法者在短短十年时间初步建立了完整的法律体系——"六法"体系，可谓"中华民国立法最盛之时期"。国民政府在立法过程中主要是学习借鉴西方的法律，尤其是日本的法律，另外还吸收了美国、德国和英国的法律。法律翻译在这个过程中发挥了非常重要的作用。当时的主要立法者如王宠惠、石志泉、罗鼎等人都接受过西方良好的现代法学训练，具有广博的学术背景，他们在吸收外国法律进行立法的过程中，对法律翻译也做出了重要的贡献。

新中国成立以后很长一段时间，中国在各个方面都向苏联学习，法律也不例外。在此期间，对苏联法律的翻译占据了重要的地位。其中较为重要的教材和专著有：张君悌译《苏俄刑事诉讼法》（新华书店，1949年）；吴大业译，陈忠诚校《苏联律师制度沿革》（大众法学出版社，1950年）；安·扬·维辛斯基著，王之相译《苏维埃法律上的诉讼证据理论》（人民出版社，1954年）；施夫曼编写，薛秉忠等译《苏维埃刑事诉讼实习教材》（中国人民大学出版社，1957年）；顾尔维奇著，康宝田、沈其昌译《诉权》（中国人民大学出版社，1958年）等等。基本上整个苏联的法律体系及相关的著作都有一定的翻译。抛开其他因素不说，这的确对中国的法律翻译产生了重要的影响，出现了钱育才、陈忠诚等法律翻译大家。

改革开放以后，特别是法制建设的加强和依法治国的基本国策的提出，促进了法律翻译的进一步发展。在此期间，不仅仅是法律翻译实践的发展，大量的相关译著出现，也有不少关于建立法律翻译理论的尝试，部分相关科研成果问世。令人欣喜的是，新世纪以来，有关法律翻译研究的成果正在成比例增加。法律英语证书（LEC）全国统一考试应运而生，它首次科学的设定了考核指标，真实客观地反映出广大法律从业人员的专业英语水平。法律翻译测试是LEC考试的核心测试内容之一，引起了业内人士的广泛关注。因此，我们可以看出学界对于法律翻译越来越重视。这当然也反映出一些问题，比如理论研究欠缺；但法律翻译的研究发展和重要性是有目共睹的。

第二节 理论建设

法律翻译理论建设对于法律翻译实践的指导具有深远的意义。法律翻译者需要一个"有章可循的,前后一致的理论框架,从而使新的研究者比较容易地找到自己的位置,明确自己的研究于他人的研究呈何种关系;也可以使研究者一览不同思路的特点,从而选择合适的路子进行自己的某项特定的研究"(刘润清、胡壮麟,2000:19)。从目前的研究成果来看,法律翻译理论层次的研究亟待加强。有关法律翻译理论的探讨远远滞后于其他研究范畴,法律翻译实践缺乏系统性的理论作指导。其实,这方面的强弱与否在很大程度上直接决定这一学科的发展空间。

要建立系统完善的法律翻译理论,除了要充分认识法律翻译理论的重要性之外,还要实现法律翻译学科的独立性。学科的独立性是其理论发展的前提和基础,没有学科独立的存在,何谈理论?而目前法律翻译缺乏学科建立和学科独立意识。法律翻译曾被错误的定位为科技翻译的一部分。法律翻译涉及三个研究领域的内容:法律理论、语言理论和翻译理论。但是,法律翻译又处于它们的灰色地带。在法律界,法学家和法律工作者对于法律翻译的研究缺乏足够的重视。在语言学领域,法律翻译只是应用语言学的一个分支。当然还有人把法律翻译放在法律语言学中去研究。可见,法律翻译始终隶属于其他学科,没有建立独立的学科,这对法律翻译的发展是极其不利的。针对这种情况,法律翻译研究者应努力找到法律翻译不同于其他学科的特性,从而建立独立的学科,寻求法律翻译的历史合法性,促进法律翻译的全面、有序发展。目前,在法律翻译实践领域,已经存在一些比较有影响力的翻译理论。

从文体学角度来讲,法律文本属于公文文体。各类法律文献,无论是英文还是中文,在用词和句子结构方面都有自己的特点。法律语言自成体系,它要求用词准确、正规、鲜明,并有相当多的专业用语,因此法律语言具有庄重性、权威性、严谨性、准确性和专业性等特点。掌握源语及目的语的上述特点,是翻译法律文本的根本。与其他文体翻译一样,做好法律文本的翻译最重要的一点是要遵循翻译的基本原则,在翻译理论的指导下进行翻译实践。我们在探讨研究法律文件的翻译时,应研究我国翻译界前辈创立的翻译理论,关注近代英语语言学家的理论对翻译学的影响。例如,欧美英语语言学家对结构主义语法体系的研究,为翻译法律文件中那些结构周密严谨的长句提供了原则和方法。翻译的关键在于理解,要读懂原文,然后做好语言的转换,做好从源语转换到目的语。我们的前辈创立了一整套的翻译理论:从严复的"信、达、雅",林语堂的"忠实、通顺、美",到傅雷的"重神似不重形似"和钱锺书的"化"境,都强调了做好两种语言转换应遵守的重要原则,这是我们做好法律文本翻译工作的基础。

陈忠诚先生指出,"法学(律)语言必须精密、规范、符合文法和惯用法"。法律语言有自己鲜明的语言特点。结合法律翻译实践,"准确严谨、清晰简明、前后一致、语体规范"可以作为法律翻译比较全面、适宜的标准。

  法律翻译是一种语言转换,又不仅仅是语言的转换。各国的历史、语言、文化、习俗等的差异导致了法律的差异。在很多情况下,译者不可能翻译出意义相同的平行文本,因此,美国翻译理论家尤金·奈达所提出的等效翻译理论不失为一个更好的翻译方法。他提出,"所谓翻译就是在译语中用最切近而又最自然的对等语再现源语的信息,首先是意义,其次是文体"。也就是说将一篇英语文章译成汉语,或将一篇汉语文章译成英语,其译文能使以汉语为母语的读者和以英语为母语的读者阅读起来,与阅读各自母语的文章所产生的体验、感受、共鸣应该几乎是相同的。所以在法律翻译实践中,译者必须理解的不只是词、句的意思,而且还有其在另一种语言当中具有的法律效力及如何实现这种法律效力。译者的主要任务是在翻译中设法使源语与目的语之间达到几乎完全的等效,即译文能够达到法律功能上的等效。在我国学术界,如何看待奈达的等效翻译理论至今还存在着激烈的争论:一方认为,奈达的理论是西方语言之间的翻译实践的归结,不能指导汉语和西语之间的翻译;更有人认为同语系或同族语的双语转换都不可能等效,不同语言之间的等效根本不可能实现;另一方则认为,译文能对读者产生和原文完全相同的效果,并对它深信不疑。当然源语与目的语之间法律术语之间的差异,句法差异,修辞差异以及法律文化差异等因素都会影响等效翻译的实现。但是,充分认识到这些束缚,能够让我们尽可能的实现等效翻译。在此基础上把握法律翻译等效的基本策略,即忠实于源语内涵(intention),符合目的语的表达习惯,体现法律文本的独特风格,反映出法律语言的权威性、庄严性和规范性。

  20世纪70年代以来,德国功能翻译理论家提出了翻译行为论和翻译目的论,并将此确定为功能翻译理论的核心。翻译目的论认为翻译是一种转换,是一种行为,而任何行为都有一个目标,一个目的,因此翻译应遵循的首要法则是"目的的法则"。翻译行为论则认为翻译行为的参与者不仅包括行为发起者及译者,还应包括翻译译文使用者即信息接受者。此外,翻译活动的环境条件,如时间,地点,媒介等也直接影响翻译交际目的的成功。对于法律翻译,功能翻译理论认为译者的主要任务是翻译出具有同等法律效力的文本,在这种情况下,译者必须理解的不只是词句的意思,而且还有其在另一种语言当中具有的法律效力及如何实现这种法律效力。因此,法律翻译人员必须在翻译实践中充分考虑翻译目的、文本功能、句法结构和用词特点。在这种情况下,功能翻译理论作为一个能从宏观角度指导法律翻译的翻译理论就有其存在的必要性。

  总体来说,法律翻译理论的建设还是不够的,缺乏系统性和学科独立性,远落后于法律翻译实践的发展,需要进一步的加强和完善,以更好地指导翻译实践。

第三节 翻译方法

  法律翻译方法主要是直译、意译或直译意译并用的兼译。至于如何运用,要区别不同情况,因文制宜,因材施法,灵活掌握,该直译的直译,该意译的意译,或需要直译意译并用的兼译。但从实践来看,法律语言的特点决定了法律文件多用直译。法律用词精确正规,具有简明性、准确性和清晰性的特点。法律术语要求统一,法律语言的句式结构严谨,表意清晰,没有歧义。因此从某种意义上说,法律语言近似于数学语言那样的形式语言,这就必然导致直译成为法律翻译的主要方法。但是在法律语言翻译过程中,由于法律文化性差异造成的翻译问题,要求译者有一定的创造性,而此时意译是不可避免的。需要指出的是,由于历史上在翻译方法方面所产生的混乱观念至今还未完全澄清,并对翻译工作继续施加着消极的影响,所以划清直译与死译或硬译、意译与乱译或滥译之间的界限,给直译和意译以完整科学的定义,替它们正名仍是当务之急。

  有关法律翻译的方法论问题在我国也存在着不完全相同,甚至截然相反的观点。由于法律体系之间的差异,大陆法体系中的法律概念与普通法体系中的法律概念并不对等,从事大陆法学研究的学者认为,"应将英美法中的法律概念纳入我国既有的法律体系,使之与我国现行的法律概念相契合"。(王泽鉴,1997)而从事英美法研究的学者则认为,两种不同的法律体系之间的确存在相同之处,如果单凭一两个相同的地方而把一个法律体系中的概念与另一个法律体系中的概念画上等号,很容易就把法律概念在一个体系中的意义带到另一个体系中去,因此,他们主张"只有当两个概念之间的差异在任何情况下都并不具有重要意义时,才可以画上等号,否则宁可生造词汇"(何美欢,1995)。

  总之,法律翻译以直译方法为主,直译与意译相结合,要充分准确把握法律语言的特点,切实做到"忠实准确"。

第四节 法律翻译问题之所在

  近年来,我国法律翻译取得了可喜的成绩,但也存在一些不足之处。总体来说,法律翻译缺乏系统性的研究,有关翻译理论的研究远落后于法律翻译实践的发展,而且多数也仅限于对具体翻译实例的总结性描述或者心得体会的阐发;法律翻译也没有明确的方法论指导,缺乏深入研究的明确目标;正如前面所提到的,法律翻译也缺乏学科建设和学科独立意识,阻碍了法律翻译理论和实践的发展;另外,缺乏法庭翻译的研究,法律翻译的教学资源也相当匮乏。现在的主要任务就是要针对这些问题,在法律翻译所取得的成果之上加强法律翻译的建设和发展。

另外,通过对近些年来我国在法律翻译实践中存在的一些问题进行初步的归纳和总结,法律翻译具体实践中存在的主要问题可以归纳为六种:1.拼写和语法错误;2.省译、增译和望文生义;3.术语翻译不妥;4.译文文体不当;5.对原文理解不透;6.语言修养欠佳;7.法律文化差异引起的错误(金朝武、胡爱平,2000:45—50)。

要避免这些错误,除了翻译人员应加强责任心,不断提高自己的业务水平,加强中英文的语言修养,拓宽自己的知识面,尽量多学相关法律知识,熟悉中外法律文化,充分把握法律语言的特点之外,以下两个方面也应当注意:

首先,要注重培养法律翻译的师资。近年来,国内许多高校都开设了法律外语课程,但大多数的法律外语课程都是形同虚设、名存实无。出现这种现象的主要原因是缺乏师资,这一点不难理解。就法律英语而言,它不是法律与英语的简单结合,能够将两者结合得很好的人,必然要经过长期的英语和法律两方面的知识积累。我们欣喜地看到,中国外语教育研究中心联合中国法律英语教学与测试研究会,已经面向全国组织了几次高校法律英语师资培训,受到广大法律英语爱好者的热烈欢迎。

其次,要充分发挥全国高校中外语院系和法学院系的作用,优势互补,共克时艰。据统计,很多法学教师有留学背景,有的甚至获有美国的JD或SJD学位。所以,外语院系要勇于加强横向联合,和校内法学院系联合起来搞好外语专业本科生的法律外语教学工作,确保法律外语的教学质量。在翻译课教学中增加法律翻译的内容,加强法律翻译学科的建设,提高法律翻译的学科地位,加强法律翻译理论的建设。通过多方面的共同努力,来提高广大翻译工作者对法律翻译的认识,从而进一步提高法律翻译的水平。这不仅对于法律翻译自身的发展十分重要,而且对于加强社会主义法制建设,实现依法治国,减少经济纠纷,促进我国的市场经济建设是具有积极作用的。

第五节　法律翻译工作者应具备的素质

法律翻译同时涉足三个领域,即法律学界、语言学界和翻译界。因此,法律翻译对译者的要求十分苛刻。概括来说,有如下几点:

1. 要具备深厚的语言功底

这里所说的深厚的语言功底,指的是精通源语和目的语。与普通翻译一样,法律翻译同样包括理解和表达两个过程。如果译者不能理解法律原文,就肯定不能表达原文的含义。理解是表达的基础,没有理解,根本就无从谈表达。特别是在英译汉过程中,英语并非是我们的母语,所以在理解英文时就很容易出错。这就要求译者在理解英文原文时要勤查工具书,切不可人云亦云,胡乱猜测。法律翻译又是一种特殊的具有法律含义的翻译。由于中英文在句法结构及法律术语方面有很大的差异,译者必须对这两种语言有很强的驾驭能力。把中文法律文本译成英语时,译者能够充分理解原文的涵义,翻译正确之余,译文的英语语言必须为英语国家的人所说的英语,正式地道的英语,而不是中文式的英语,让外国人读了摸不着头脑。同样的,把英美国家的法律文件翻译成中文时,理解原文是关键,然后再按照汉语的表达习惯,用恰当得体的中文把原文的意思传达给读者。所以,译者必须有较强的理解能力和良好的表达能力:

(1) 较强的理解能力

首先,对于从事翻译的工作者而言,提高语言能力始终是做好法律翻译的基石。对文字的领悟能力固然与天分有关,但后天的努力学习更为重要。提高语言能力并无捷径,必须潜心钻研,多读、多写、多练。要提高法律文件的理解力,最好的方法是研读现有的中英文对照法律文件。目前中国政府颁布的大量法律法规文件都已有英文译本,可供有兴趣的读者研读提高。还有一点也很重要,就是从事法律翻译的人员至少必须熟悉常用的法律专业词汇及基本概念,努力提高法律文件的理解力。如英美法中的 brief(案件辩论书),deposition(庭外采证)和 parity of power and responsibility(权责平衡)等概念和意义在中国找不到对应项。西方法律制度中的"jury(陪审团)"与"impeachment(弹劾制)"等在中国没有参照物。西方审判词中的大量渲染、描述与议论的风格与中国法庭判词中的冷峻、凝重与简约的风格对照鲜明。中国司法体系中的"人民陪审员"和西方国家的"陪审员"意义并不对等。

(2) 良好的表达能力

如前所述,理解是表达的基础。然而为了准确地翻译法律文本,法律翻译者还应当具有深厚的译文功底,即目的语的表达能力。翻译的目的是为了沟通,因此,法律翻译的翻译方法也是直译和意译并用,即能用直译的时候用直译,不能用直译的时候用意译,用意译的时候不能偏离原文的含义。当然,由于法律语言的特殊性,译者在翻译法律语言时,应该尽量接近原文的语言风格和句式结构。

例 1 The purpose of the joint venture shall be to utilize the combined technological, management, operational and marketing **strengths** of the Parties within the approved scope of business of the Company to achieve good economic results and a return on investment satisfactory to the Parties.

参考译文:合营公司的宗旨是结合双方在技术、管理、运营以及营销方面的优势,在合营公司经批准的经营范围内开展业务,以取得良好的经济效益以及令双方满意的投资回报。

译文解析:原文中的 strength 的原意为"实力,力量",但在译文中,为了符合中文表达习惯的需要,它被改译为"优势"。

2. 掌握完备的法律知识

译者从事法律翻译工作时,经常遇到来自不同国家和地区的法律文件,包括不同法系、不同国家和跨国机构的法律文件。平时注重积累法学专业知识并多多研读有关法律文件、多留意国际政治经济新闻。了解比如国际间关于保护知识产权的协定、世贸组织关于成员国市场的协定、国际主要机构的全名和简称等等,将给法律翻译工作带来很大便利。

例 2 With respect to customs duties and charges of any kind imposed on or in connection with importation or exportation or imposed on the international transfer of payments for imports or exports, and with respect to the method of levying such duties and charges, and with respect to all rules and formalities in connection with importation and exportation, and with respect to all matters referred to in paragraphs 2 and 4 of Article III, any advantage, favor, privilege or immunity granted by any contracting party to any product originating in or destined for any other country shall be accorded immediately and unconditionally to the like product originating in or destined for the territories of all other contracting parties. (The General Agreement on Tariff and Trade)

参考译文:在对输出或输入、有关输出或输入及进出口货物的国际支付转账所征收的关税和费用方面,在征收上述关税和费用的方法方面,在输出和输入的规章手续方面,以及在本协定第三条第二款和第四款所述事项方面,一缔约国对来自或运往其他国家的产品所给予的优惠、优待、特权或豁免,应当立即无条件地给予来自或运往所有其他缔约国的相同产品。(关税与贸易总协定)

译文解析:法律文本独特的表达方式以及与日常用语截然不同的法律术语往往构成了法律翻译者正确翻译的极大障碍。如上例的法律文本中,大量使用了术语及专门用语,customs duties(关税)、importation or exportation(输入或输出)、international transfer of payments(国际支付转账)、advantage, favor, privilege or immunity(优惠、优待、特权或豁免)、contracting party(缔约国)、等等,无不是书面语化、规范化、专门化的表达方式,在其他文体中是很少使用的。

一个成功的法律翻译工作者必须是双语语言学家,同时还必须具备充足的法律知识,两者是缺一不可。法律翻译工作者的翻译作品首先必须是规范的法律作品。因此,法律翻译对译者的法律功底提出了较高的要求。

3. 求真务实的态度和高度的责任感

由于法律在调整社会关系中的基础作用,因此,法律翻译的一字一句对于当事人乃至法律文本的读者而言都具有极为重要的影响。而法律文件翻译是法律语言的转换,要做到译入语准确无误地表达源语的真正含义,无论在用词上及句子结构上都必须做到"忠实准确",由此也就对翻译工作者的态度提出了较高的要求——严谨、准确便是法律翻译所应追求的至上目标。在法律翻译史上,因误译而造成重大经济损失时有发生。下面试举一例说明严谨翻译的重要性:

例如,进行法律文件的中译英时,我们常常遇到这样的词语:"应当符合国家有关规定""依照国家有关税收的规定""依照国家外汇管理规定"等等中的"国家有关规定",如按字面含义译成 the relevant state provisions 或 the relevant provisions of the state 显然不正确,这样没有把深层含义译出。按照牛津高阶英汉双解词典的定义,provision〔C〕意为 condition or stipulation in a legal document,比如:"根据协议的规定"可译成 under the provisions of the agreement。把"国家有关规定"译成 the relevant state provisions,把国家与法律文件(a legal document)等同起来显然不妥。那么,"国家有关规定"应怎么理解才能使译文符合原文的含义?首先,我们应清楚,"国家法规"应包括两大部分,即由全国人民代表大会发布的法律(laws)和由国务院及国务院有关部门发布的行政法规(regulations)。故"国家有关规定"一般应理解为"国家颁布的有关法律、法规的规定",译成 the provisions of the relevant laws and regulations issued by the state。然而,"国家有关规定"已成了"国家有关部门的规定"的习惯用语,因此,应译成 the provisions of the relevant regulations issued by the state。

因此,法律翻译需要的是字斟句酌,高度负责,反复推敲。切勿随意化繁为简,主观妄断。一时地贪图方便而舍弃了严谨态度,极易使自己的译文背离原意,从而严重影响翻译质量。译者在翻译法律文件时,不管是立法文本,经贸合同,诉讼文书还是公证书,都应以严谨的态度和高度的责任感来对待这份重要的工作。

 课后习题

1. 国外翻译理论对我国翻译的影响是什么?
2. 我国法律翻译的实践中存在哪些问题亟待解决?
3. 做一名合格的法律翻译工作者应具备的素质条件是什么?

第二章

法律语言的特点

翻译,是指在准确、通顺与贴切的基础上,把源语言(source language)信息转化为目标语言(target language)信息的活动。简而言之,翻译就是把已说出或写出的信息的含义用另一种语言表达出来的活动。翻译的过程是语言转换的过程,通过语言的转换再现原文的信息,因而翻译工作要求翻译人员掌握源语言和目标语言的特点。对于普通的翻译作品,译者如果能够遵循"信、达、雅""顺和通"等翻译原则,那么译文就可称得上是好的作品了。但法律语言作为一门专业性很强的专门用途语言,具有特殊的法律功能和意义,并形成了自身的特点和规律。因此,法律翻译对译者的要求也随之提高,译者在具备精通源语言和目标语言等基本素质以外,还应具有广博的知识,尤其需要掌握相关法律词汇并熟悉相关法律,同时,译员还应具有高度的责任感。法律翻译工作除了对译员及相关的条件提出较高的要求外,还受制于法律语言本身的特点。可见,掌握源语言与目标语言中法律语言的特点和规律对于做好翻译工作也是至关重要的。

法律语言(legal language 或 statutory language)这一术语起源于西方。在英语里,原指表述法律科学概念以及用于诉讼和非诉讼法律事务时所选用的语言或用某一种语种的部分用语,后来亦指某些具有特定法律意义的词语,并且扩展到语言的其他层面。如"法律文句(legal sentence)""法庭诉讼语言(litigious language at law court)""法律用语(legal terms)""法庭用语(language of the court)"等。同其他社会方言一样,法律语言是人们根据社会文化环境和交际目的、交际对象等语用因素,在长期使用中形成的一种具有特殊用途和自身规律的语言功能变体。

法律语言大致分为立法语言、司法语言及法律科学语言三大类和若干小类(见图2-1)。

```
              ┌─立法语言─┬─程序立法语言
              │         └─实体立法语言
              │         ┌─司法文书语言；笔录语言
法律语言──────┼─司法语言─┼─司法谈话；问话语言
              │         └─法庭演讲语言；法庭论辩语言
              │          ┌─法学著述语言；法学论文语言
              └─法律科学语言
                         └─法律史语言；法律哲学语言
```

图 2-1　法律语言分类

由于法学本身的特殊性以及法律长期在人们的政治、经济、科学和文化生活中所发挥的强大的规范和调节作用，使得法律语言在不断发展和完善的过程中形成了一些自身的特征，而对法律语言特点的掌握又是译者能否做好法律翻译工作的决定条件之一。因此，对法律语言特点等相关问题的研究应运而生。

在英语法律语言的研究中，Mellinkoff 针对词语特点做了系统的分析（见 O'Barr 1982:18），Crystal 和 Dave(1969)对法律文本的结构和组织进行了分析总结，他们认为：1.法律语言是工具性语言；2.法律文件具有不同于其他类文本的特征；3.法律英语具有明确的特点；4.法律语言使用了日常英语不采用的语义原则。

中国学者对法律语言的特点也做了一些研究。孙懿华、周广然(1997:58)概括出四类：1.词语的专业性；2.句法结构的模式性；3.表达方式的特定性；4.语体风格的庄严性。

本章将从法律语言的用词特点、句法结构特点、篇章结构特点及口头法律语言特点等方面对法律语言的特点进行分析。

第一节　法律语言的用词特点

法律词语是构成法律语言的基本单位，其运用在法律事件中起着举足轻重的作用。法律语言特点主要体现于其用词的特点。因此，法律用词特点的研究是法律语言特点研究的关键部分。在法律英语语言的特点的研究领域，Mellinkoff(O'Barr 1982:16)列出 9 种情况：

（1）含有法律专业意义的普通词；
（2）来自古英语和中世纪英语的稀有词；
（3）拉丁词和短语；
（4）普通词汇中不包括的法语词；
（5）法律专业术语；
（6）专业行话；
（7）正式词语；

(8) 多义词语;

(9) 极端精确表达词语。

Mellinkoff 列出的 9 种情况中,有的为英语法律语言的独有特点,如第 2、3、4,但其他情况同样适用于汉语法律语言,这体现了不同语言的法律用语有着共同的特点。

中国学者对法律语言的特点也做了相关研究。孙懿华、周广然(1997:58)将其概括为以下三类:1.法律专业术语;2.法律工作常用术语;3.民族共同语中的其他基本词与非基本词。潘庆云(1997)对词语的讨论分成几个部分。在立法部分分为两类:法律词语和普通词语;在立法文书部分识别出四类:法律术语、司法惯用语、文言词语和普通词语。在中外学者对法律词语特点分类的基础上,我们可以将法律语言的基本特点归纳如下:

1. 普通词汇表特殊法律含义

法律语言中有不少词汇是由普通词汇转换而来,和法律专业术语不同,这类词汇看似熟悉,但在法律语境中却有着专业的涵义。准确地掌握这类专业词汇的涵义需要读者对所熟悉词语的法律含义有一定的积累,并且在一定的语境中进行逻辑分析,从而正确地理解。

例如:(1) The man died without *issue*.

(2) Drug testing of employee is a sensitive *issue*.

(3) The statement was *issued* by the Chinese government.

(4) The Company hereby agrees to issue to Consultant one hundred thousand (100,000) shares of the Company's common stock.

以上例句中的"issue",在例句(1)中是法律专业词语的用法,指遗嘱中的"直系继承人"。在例句(2)(3)(4)中分别表达常见的含义"问题""颁布"和"发行"。

2. 古旧词汇的使用

法律语言中的一些词汇自古沿用至今,这种现象存在于各国的法律语言中。人们使用这些旧的法律术语,是因为它们在长期的使用过程中已经形成了为人们所公认的特定涵义,没有必要舍弃它们而另外创造新的法律词语。如我们熟知的法律词汇"自首""诉状""犯罪""原告""大赦"。在法律英语中,古英语(公元约 1100 年以前的英语)和中古英语(公元约 1100—1500 年间的英语)的使用也比较普遍。例如:"whereby(由此)","thereafter(其后)","hereto(至此)","herein(此处)"。

3. 外来词的使用

随着世界各国的交往日益频繁,国家间法律语言的相互借鉴和援引也随之增多,尤其是在国际交往中通用的法律用语。比如我国法律语言中的"仲裁""破产""专利""商标法""公民"。法律英语中外来词语的使用也较为频繁,基于历史原因其主要来源是拉丁语和法语词汇。比如:拉丁词源"ex post facto(追溯)","versus(对抗)","alibi(不在现场证据)","in rem(反对某物)","ad hoc(专门的)",及法语词源"debt(债务)""alien(转让)""jury(陪审团)""voir dire(陪审员资格审查)""proposal(建议)"。

4. 精确用语与模糊用语

法律语言要求表达清晰、精确。一般情况法律语言的使用要尽量避免含糊其辞,但这并不是说法律语言只需要精确用语而不需要模糊用语。相反,在语言的实际应用中,准确意义的表达正是依靠精确用语和模糊用语的共同使用来完成的。在汉英语言系统中,有些词语含义很确切。如:"18 周岁""10 厘米""下午 3 点""40 公斤";"never""all""impossible""without prejudice""and no more"。同样,两个语言系统中也有不少的模糊词汇,比如汉语法律文书中经常用到"情节严重""其他""任何单位和个人""多次""数额巨大"等词义模糊的词语,有很强的不确定性。英语法律语言也是如此,例如,"about(大约)""as soon as possible(尽快)""necessary(必要的)""average(一般的)"。

精确用语在语句中的使用也很常见,如我国《专利法》第 24 条规定:专利的发明创造在申请日以前 6 个月内,有下列情形之一的,不丧失新颖性:

(1) 在中国政府主办或者承认的国际展览会上首次展出的;

(2) 在规定的学术会议或者技术会议上首次发表的;

(3) 他人未经申请人同意而泄露其内容的。

再如在英文传票中表达"你已被本院传唤,请于接到本传票之日起 20 日内在本法院出庭"的意思常采用以下说法:You are summoned to appear and answer in this Court by filing an Answer along with the required fee within twenty (20) consecutive days from the service of this summons, not accounting the day of service.

5. 近义词的并用

法律配对词和三联词是指两个或三个意思相近或者相同的词构成一个短语以表达法律上本来只需要一个词就能表达的概念。近义词在法律语言中的并列使用,体现了法律语言的严肃性和法律文体的准确性和严密性,确保了整体含义的完整、准确。如我国《刑法》中的"寻衅滋事罪是指出于不正当目的的恣意挑衅,无事生非、起哄闹事,进行扰乱破坏,情节恶劣的行为"。仅该罪名定义中近义词并用就多达 4 处。可见,近义词并用在汉语法律语言中的较为普遍。这种情况在法律英语中也较为常见,比如,"sole and exclusive(单一)""each and every(各自)""null and void(无效)"等。此外,实践中还存在强调差别的近义词并用,其使用的目的是为了保证意思表达得完整、准确。例如:"obligation and liability(义务和责任)""sell or transfer(出售或者转让)"。

第二节 法律语言的句法特点

一、陈述句为基本句型

汉英法律语言中的句法最显著特点之一即为基本句型倾向单一化——陈述句型。这一特点的形成是由法律语言正面客观陈明事理的特点决定的,同时陈述句型也与质朴简洁的法律语言特点相符。陈述句型在法律条文中的比例为98%以上。请看以下法律条文:

例1 纳税人销售货物或者应税劳务,应当向索取增值税专用发票的购买方开具增值税专用发票,并在增值税专用发票上分别注明销售额和销项税额。(《增值税暂行条例》第21条)

例2 A contract is an exchange of promises between two or more parties to do or refrain from doing an act which is enforceable in a court of law. (*The Contract Law of the United States of America*)

二、简单短句和复杂长句的结合使用

法律条文依靠法律语言包含性来规范多样的社会行为,因此法律语言必须具有高度的概括性。这一特点体现在句法上即表现为简短句子的使用。例如以下条文:

例3 中华人民共和国的一切权力属于人民。(我国《宪法》总纲第2条)

例4 The Citizens of each State shall be entitled to all Privileges and Immunities of Citizens in the several States. (*The Constitution of the United States of America*, Article IV, Section 2)

在这类简单句中,汉语法律条款常常是无主语的句子,而英文法律条款一定是主谓齐全的,因此在翻译英语被动句时,一般可以将其转换为汉语的无主语句子。

同时,为了确保法律的准确性和严密性,法律语言中多使用结构复杂的长句来避免立法上的漏洞。结构复杂的长句所包含的信息量大,在描述复杂事物时可以达到叙事具体、说理严密、层次分明的效果。如:公司、企业或者其他单位的人员,利用职务上的便利,将本单位的财物非法占为己有,数额较大的,处5年以下有期徒刑或者拘役;数额巨大的,处5年以上有期徒刑,可以并处没收财产。国有公司、企业或者其他国有单位中从事公务的人员和国有公司、企业或者其他委派到非国有公司、企业以及其他单位从事公务的人员有前款行为的,依照本法第382条、第383条的规定定罪处罚。(《刑法》第271条)

这个特点在法律英语中也很突出,如:No person shall be a Senator or Representative in Congress, or elector of President and Vice-President, or hold any office, civil or military, under the United States, or under any State, who, having previously taken an oath, as a member of Congress, or as an officer of the United States, or as a member of any State legislature, or as an executive or judicial officer of any State, to support the Constitution of the United States, shall have engaged in insurrection or rebellion against the same, or given aid or comfort to the enemies thereof. (*The Constitution of the United States of America*, Amendment 14)

三、"的"结构的规范运用

"的"结构是指省略了作为逻辑主语的行为者的语法结构,一般在句子中充当主语成分。常见以下三种表达方式:(1) 由抽象名词组成的"的"结构,如"红的是我的,绿的是你的";(2) 由"动宾词组+的"组成的"的"结构,如"值得高兴的是,他没有受伤";(3) 由"主谓词组+的"组成的"的"结构,如"他指的不是这件事"(俞云根,1986:253)。汉英法律语言中"的"结构的频繁使用是为了达到语言庄重、简洁、严谨的效果,同时体现了法律语言的程式化特点。汉语法律文书中主要使用"动宾+的"的结构。如:对于扣押的物品、文件、邮件、电报,或者冻结的存款、汇款,经查明确实与案件无关的,应当在 3 日以内解除扣押、冻结,退还原主或者原邮电机关。(《刑事诉讼法》第 118 条)

另外,汉语法律语言中"的"结构构成的词组常用来作主语,表示假定的条件,通常前置。如:以营利为目的,制作、贩卖淫书、淫画的,处 3 年以下有期徒刑、拘役或者管制,可以并处罚金。(《刑法》第 170 条)可见,由"的"字结构构成的主语形式具有很强的概括性,可以成为一个具有代表性的概念,从而符合法律语言的需要。

在英语法律文本中"的"含义的表达均使用"of"而非日常用语中的" 's"。例如《美利坚合众国宪法》第 1 条规定:"All legislative Powers herein granted shall be vested in a Congress of the United States, which shall consist of a Senate and House of Representatives."中使用了"a Congress of the United States"而不是日常生活用语"the United States' Congress"。

而法律英语中的条件通常用"if","where","when"句子或短语表示,位置不固定。构成"If /where/when A, then B"逻辑结构。如 The President shall be Commander in Chief of the Army and Navy of the United States, and of the Militia of the several States, when called into the actual Service of the United States. (*The Constitution of the United States of America*, Article II, Section 2)

四、语句形式的模式化

法律语句表达的内容是对人们有普遍约束力的法律规范,因此具有广泛的适用性。这就决定了法律句式需要保持较为固定的形式,以便法律工作的开展及普及。法律句式的模式化在立法和司法领域均有所体现。比如汉语立法语言中常见"……有权……""禁止……""……有……自由"。再如在司法语言中首次对当事人基本情况的表述形式:"被告人王某,男,30岁,汉族,北京丰台区人,住北京丰台区丰台路211号,于2001年3月1日取保候审"。这种句式的模式化规律在法律英语实践中也同样适用,如在合同文本中常用以下句式:"This contract was entered into by and between A (the buyer, holder of America passport <u>123456</u>) and B (the seller) on <u>date month year</u> and shall have the following terms:…"。

五、复合句的使用

为了保持法律语言精确和平实的特点,汉英法律语言常采用简短句式,但为了能够准确地表达复杂的逻辑关系,汉英法律语言均大量使用了复合句式。法律语言复合句式中各句子之间的逻辑关系通过各句之间的逻辑意思关系来体现,根据句子间不同的意思关系可将复合句分为并列、选择、递进、目的、假设、条件、转折、解释等类型。

(一) 并列复合句

并列复合句是由两个或两个以上相互联系的分句组成的复合句,各分句分别表述相关的几件事或同一个事物的几个方面。并列复合句的使用能够使意思表达最大限度地包含某一事物各方面的含义,以确保法律语言表述的周密性。如:判处死刑缓期执行的,在死刑缓期执行期间,如果没有故意犯罪,2年期满以后,减为无期徒刑;如果确有重大立功表现,2年期满以后,减为15年以上20年以下有期徒刑;如果故意犯罪,查证属实的,由最高人民法院核准,执行死刑。(《刑法》第50条)

法律英语中常见"and"连接的复合句。如 The House of Representatives shall be composed of Members chosen every second Year by the People of the several States, **and** the Electors in each State shall have the Qualifications requisite for Electors of the most numerous Branch of the State Legislature. (*The Constitution of the United States of America*, Articles I, Section 2)

(二) 选择复合句

选择复合句各分句之间的关系分为几种情况,要求从中选择一种。几个分句分别说明几种不同的情况,并表示从中有所取舍。汉英法律语言中使用的选择复合句多表示列举性的或者关系,常用"或者","and/or"来表达。请看以下例子:

例5 《企业国有资产法》第34条规定:"重要的国有独资企业、国有独资公司、国有资本控股公司的合并、分立、解散、申请破产以及法律、行政法规和本级人民政府规定应当由履行出资人职责的机构报经本级人民政府批准的重大事项,履行出资人职责的机构在做出决定或者向其委派参加国有资本控股公司股东会会议、股东大会会议的股东代表做出指示前,应当报请本级人民政府批准。"

例 6 **Third Party Information.** The Employee recognizes that the Company has received and in the future will receive from third parties their confidential or proprietary information that has been identified as being proprietary and/or confidential, or that by the nature of the circumstances surrounding the disclosure ought to be treated as proprietary and/or confidential, subject to a duty on the Company's part to maintain the confidentiality of such information and to use it only for certain limited purposes ("Third Party Information").

(三) 递进复合句

递进复合句由两个或两个以上的分句相连所构成,后面分句所表示的意思比前面分句的更进一层。分句之间的顺序固定,不能随意变动。递进复合句主要用来表示行为主体进一步的法律行为,常用"而且""并""并且","not only... but (also)..."等来引导分句表示各句之间意思的递进关系。如:《保险法》第 53 条 投保人申报的被保险人年龄不真实,并且其真实年龄不符合合同约定的年龄限制的,保险人可以解除合同,并在扣除手续费后,向投保人退还保险费,但是自合同成立之日起逾 2 年的除外。

法律英语中常见以"not only... but also..."连接的复合句,例如:Normally, the foreign and Chinese parties enter into a non-binding Letter of Intent with regard to a proposed EJV as a preliminary to a formal contract. It is usually advisable to have as much detail as possible in the Letter of Intent. This is not only to prevent misunderstandings between the parties in the course of negotiating the formal contract, but also to provide allowance for later variation in other project documentation.

(四) 目的复合句

目的复合句表达各分句间行为和目的的关系。由于法律的制定和实施都是为了达到某一或某些目的,因而目的复合句成为引出某种行为的目的逻辑关系的表达方式,多采用"为了","in order to","for the purpose of"等形式。请看下列例子:

例 7 为了保障公民、法人的合法的民事权益,正确调整民事关系,适应社会主义现代化建设事业发展的需要,根据宪法和我国实际情况,总结民事活动的实践经验,制定本法。(《民法通则》第 1 条)

例 8 We the People of the United States, in order to form a more perfect Union, establish Justice, insure domestic Tranquility, provide for the common defence, promote the general Welfare, and secure the Blessings of Liberty to ourselves and our Posterity, do ordain and establish this Constitution for the United States of America. (Preamble of *The Constitution of the United States of America*)

(五) 假设复合句

假设复合句表达分句间假设—后果的逻辑关系。即分句中提出一种假设情况,主句中说明该假设变为现实的后果，常用"如果"，"if"等形式。如：中华人民共和国成立以后本法施行以前的行为，如果当时的法律不认为是犯罪的，适用当时的法律；如果当时的法律认为是犯罪的，依照本法总则第四章第 8 节的规定应当追诉的，按照当时的法律追究刑事责任，但是如果本法不认为是犯罪或者处刑较轻的，适用本法。(《刑法》第 12 条)

法律英语中常见"if"连接的从句结构。如：Every Bill which shall have passed the House of Representatives and the Senate, shall, before it become a Law, be presented to the President of the United States; If he approve he shall sign it, but if not he shall return it, with his Objections to that House in which it shall have originated, who shall enter the Objections at large on their Journal, and proceed to reconsider it. If after such Reconsideration two thirds of that House shall agree to pass the Bill, it shall be sent, together with the Objections, to the other House, by which it shall likewise be reconsidered, and if approved by two thirds of that House, it shall become a Law. (*The Constitution of the United States of America*, Articles I, Section 7)

（六）条件复合句

条件复合句的特点是表达分句间条件—结果的关系，多用于强调某些附加条件时。常使用"……的""只有……才……"，"unless"等形式。如《刑法》第 20 条规定："正当防卫明显超过必要限度造成重大损害的，应当负刑事责任，但是应当减轻或者免除处罚。对正在进行行凶、杀人、抢劫、强奸、绑架以及其他严重危及人身安全的暴力犯罪，采取防卫行为，造成不法侵害人伤亡的，不属于防卫过当，不负刑事责任"。再如：If any Bill shall not be returned by the President within ten Days (Sundays excepted) after it shall have been presented to him, the same shall be a Law, in like Manner as if he had signed it, unless the Congress by their Adjournment prevent its Return, in which Case it shall not be a Law. (*The Constitution of the United States of America*, Articles I, Section 7)

（七）转折复合句

转折复合句的分句间表示相反的意思关系，多用来表示一些例外情况，这些例外情况常用来表示补充条件、减罚免罚等含义。常用"但"或"但是"，"but"，"however"等形式。如下例所示：

例 9 对于犯罪情节轻微不需要判处刑罚的，可以免予刑事处罚，但是可以根据案件的不同情况，予以训诫或者责令具结悔过、赔礼道歉、赔偿损失，或者由主管部门予以行政处罚或者行政处分。(《刑法》第 37 条)

例 10 Section 102(b)(7) of the Delaware General Corporation Law is the other relevant statutory authority relating to the protection of directors from monetary liability. Section 102（b）（7）allows inclusion of a provision in the certificate of incorporation that eliminates or limits (i.e., caps) the personal liability of directors to the corporation or its stockholders for monetary damages for breach of fiduciary duty. The statute, **however**, prohibits limitations on director liability (i) for breach of a director's duty of loyalty, (ii) for acts or omissions not in good faith or involving intentional misconduct or knowing violation of law, (iii) for willful or negligent conduct in paying dividends or repurchasing stock out of other than lawfully available funds, or (iv) for any transaction from which a director derives an improper personal benefit. In essence, Section 102（b）（7）allows a corporation to protect its directors from monetary liability for duty of care violations (*Model Indemnification Agreement by US National Venture Captial Association*)

（八）解释复合句

解释复合句表示分句之间的解释、说明关系。在法律语言中的解释复合句一般是后面的分句对前面分句的解释、说明，且多为总分和并列陈述的形式。请看以下例子：

例 11　被判处管制的犯罪分子，在执行期间，应当遵守下列规定：

（1）遵守法律、行政法规，服从监督；

（2）未经执行机关批准，不得行使言论、出版、集会、结社、游行、示威自由的权利；

（3）按照执行机关规定报告自己的活动情况；

（4）遵守执行机关关于会客的规定；

（5）离开所居住的市、县或者迁居，应当报经执行机关批准。

（《刑法》第 39 条）

例 12　Congress shall have Power：

To lay and collect Taxes, Duties, Imposts and Excises, to pay the Debts and provide for the common Defence and general Welfare of the United States; but all Duties, Imposts and Excises shall be uniform throughout the United States;

To borrow money on the credit of the United States;

To regulate Commerce with foreign Nations, and among the several States, and with the Indian Tribes;

To establish an uniform Rule of Naturalization, and uniform Laws on the subject of Bankruptcies throughout the United States;

To coin Money, regulate the Value thereof, and of foreign Coin, and fix the Standard of Weights and Measures;

To provide for the Punishment of counterfeiting the Securities and current Coin of the United States;

……

六、被动句式的使用

被动句式的使用多见于英语法律文件和汉语法律文件的英译文本中。被动句式主要用于规定行为人的权利义务以及相关法律后果。法律文件中被动句式的使用重点在于表述动作本身,突出了动作的承受者而不是动作的执行者,并客观地对有关事项进行描述和规定。与此同时,被动语态也体现了法律英语庄严、客观、公正的文体特点。请看以下例句:

例 13 民族自治地方的自治机关有管理地方财政的自治权。凡是依照国家财政体制属于民族自治地方的财政收入,都应当由民族自治地方的自治机关自主地安排使用。(《宪法》第 117 条)

参考译文:The organs of self-government of the national autonomous areas have the power of autonomy in administering the finances of their areas. All revenues accruing to the national autonomous areas under the financial system of the state **shall be managed and used** independently by the organs of self-government of those areas.

例 14 Representatives and direct taxes **shall be apportioned** among the several states which **may be included** within this union, according to their respective numbers, which **shall be determined** by adding to the whole number of free persons, including those bound to service for a term of years, and excluding Indians not taxed, three fifths of all other Persons. (*The Constitution of the United States of America*, Article I, Section 2)

七、完整句的使用

法律语言准确性和严密性的特点决定了法律文本中的句子的完整性。完整句即主语、谓语都具备的完全主谓句。法律文本中通常不使用省略句,以确保旨意准确,避免歧义。请看下列例句:

例 15 民族自治地区的人民代表大会有权依照当地民族的政治、经济和文化的特点,制定自治区条例和单行条例。自治区的自治条例和单行条例,报全国人民代表大会常务委员会批准后生效。自治州、自治县的自治条例和单行条例,报省或者自治区的人民代表大会常务委员会批准后生效,并报全国人民代表大会常务委员会备案。

例 16 All States have to contribute to the balanced expansion of the world economy, taking duty into account the close interrelationship between the well-being of the developed countries and the growth and development of the developing countries, and the fact that the prosperity of the international community as a whole depends upon the prosperity of its constituent parts.

八、名词化结构的使用

名词化（nominalization）是指从其他某个词类形成名词的过程或指一个底层小句得出一个名词短语的派生过程，是有关句子和名词短语的一种句法过程，主要指广泛使用能表达动作或状态的抽象名词或其名词功用的非限定动词。不同文体中名词化的应用差异很大，其中法律文体因追求精确和权威而大量使用名词化结构。名词化结构多见于英语法律文本以及汉语法律文本的英译本中。法律文本中名词化结构的使用，可使行文流畅、简洁，表达客观、精确。请看下列例句：

例 17 国家保护社会主义的公共财产。禁止任何组织或者个人用任何手段侵占或者破坏国家和集体的财产。

参考译文：The State protects socialist public property. **Appropriation or damaging of State or collective property by any organization or individual by whatever means** is prohibited

例 18 The obligation under Article 3 and 4 do not apply to **procedures provided in multilateral agreements concluded under the auspices of WIPO relating to the acquisition or maintenance of intellectual property rights.**

第三节 法律语言篇章结构特点

一、程式化的篇章结构

法律语言的第三个主要特点是篇章结构的程式化。法律文书对篇章结构的格式要求很严格，各类法律文本都有一定的格式，这些格式是法律从业者在长期的运用中逐渐积累形成的。对法律文书类型的统一性和差异性的研究对翻译工作的顺利开展至关重要。因为这种研究能够揭示原文本的具体要求、功能以及文本的本质，能够帮助译者超越词汇、句法或文体的等值问题，养成一种文本体裁的系统意识。每一篇法律文本都是一个逻辑严密的整体，而不是相关内容的简单罗列。这种严格的特殊程式便是比较固定的语篇格式，这种格式的固定性有利于保持法律法规的严密性和统一性，能使法律的规范性得到最充分的体现。同时该格式性为法律法规的理解提供了一个较为固定的语境，可以减少对法律法规的曲解和误解。请看以下例子：

例 19 《实用新型专利申请书》，其中部分文字是模式化的，是一种填空式文书。

③ 实用新型名称		①
		（实用新型）
④ 设计人	姓 名 或名称	②
	地址	

⑤ 申请人	姓名或名称	电话
	地址	邮政编码□□□□□□
	国籍或总部所在地国家名称	经常居所或营业所所在地国家名称
	代表姓名	

⑥ 专利代理机构	名称	地址
	专利局给出的代理机构代码□□□□□	代理机构所在地区邮政编码□□□□□□
	代理人姓名	登记号

⑦ □已在中国政府主办或承认的国际展览会上首次展出

　　　　　　　　　　　　　　　　　　　　　　　　□请求费用减缓

□已在规定的学术会议或技术会议上首次发表

⑧ 申请文件清单	⑨ 附加文件清单
1. 请求书　　份　每份　页	□代理人委托书
2. 权利要求书　份　每份　页　项	□不丧失新颖性的证明文件
3. 说明书　　份　每份　页	□要求优先权声明
4. 说明书附图　份　每份　页　幅	□优先权证明材料
5. 说明书摘要　份　每份　页	
6. 摘要附图　份　每份　页　幅	

⑩ 上述以外的设计人	⑪ 上述以外的申请人	⑫ 申请人或代理机构签章
		年　月　日

例 20　英语中的法律篇章通常也遵循一定的格式，如在房屋租赁合同文本中常采用以下格式化条款：

1. RENTAL：Commencing _____ , 20 _____ , TENANT agrees to pay LANDLORD the sum of $ _____ per month in advance on the _____ day of each calendar month. Said rental payment shall be delivered by TENANT to LANDLORD or his designated agent to the following location：_____. Rent must be actually received by LANDLORD, or designated agent, in order to be considered in compliance with the terms of this agreement.

租金：自_____年_____月_____日开始，租客同意在每月第_____日提前向房东支付该月租金_____美元；该租金付款将由租客在下列地址交给房东或者其指定的代理人：_____。租金必须实际支付给房东或者其指定代理人，否则租客被视为违反本租约。

2. SECURITY DEPOSIT: TENANT shall deposit with landlord the sum of $_____ as a security deposit to secure TENANT'S faithful performance of the terms of this lease. The security deposit shall not exceed two times the monthly rent. After all the TENANT's belonging have vacated, leaving the premises vacant, the LANDLORD may use the security deposit for the cleaning of the premises, any unusual wear and tear to the premises or common areas, and any rent or other amounts owed pursuant to the lease agreement or pursuant to Civil Code Section 1950.5.

保证金：租客须向房东提交_____美元保证金，作为租客忠实履行租约条款的保证。保证金不得超过月租金的两倍。在租客搬离其全部物品，腾空住所后，房东可将保证金用于清洁住所，维修因租客不正当使用给住所以及住所的公共场所带来的非正常磨损和损坏，以及支付根据租约和《民法典》第1950.5条所欠付的任何租金或其他金额。

3. OCCUPANTS: The premises shall not be occupied by any person other than those designed above as TENANT with the exception of the following named persons: _____. If LANDLORD, with written consent, allows for additional persons to occupy the premises, the rent shall be increased by $100 for each other person. Any person staying 14 days cumulative or longer, without the LANDLORD'D written consent, shall be considered as occupying the premises in violation of this agreement.

住客：除本租约指定的租客以及以下人士外：_____，其他任何人均不得入住该住所。如果得到房东的书面同意，允许合同约定之外的其他人员入住该住所，则每增加1人，另行收取100美元。如果未获得房东书面同意，任何人入住该住所累计超过14天（含14天），则视为违约入住。

4. SUBLETTING OR ASSIGNING: TENANT agrees not to assign or sublet the premises, or any part thereof, without first obtaining written permission from LANDLORD.

分租或转租：租客同意除非事先获得房东的书面同意，否则租客不得将住所或其中任何部分转租或分租。

5. UTILITIES: TENANT shall pay for all utilities and/or services supplied to the premises with the following exception: _____.

公共事业收费：除以下费用外：_____，租客须为住所向其提供的所有公共事业设施和/或服务付费。

6. PARKING: TENANT _____ is not _____ is (check one) assigned a parking space. If assigned a parking space it shall be designated as space # _____. TENANT may only park a vehicle that is registered in the TENANT'S name. TENANT may not assign, sublet, or allow any other person to use this space. This space is exclusively used for the parking of passenger automobiles by the TENANT. No other type of vehicle or item may be stored in this space without prior written consent of LANDLORD. TENANT may not wash, repair, or paint in this space or at any other common area on the premises.

停车位：租客_____有/_____无（勾选其中一项）指定停车位。如果租客获得了指定停车位，该停车位指定编号为_____。租客只可将登记在本人名下的车辆停放在该停车位。租客不得将该车位转租、分租或者允许他人使用该停车位。该停车位只用作停放租客的私家轿车。未经房东事先书面同意，该停车位不得停放其他类型的车辆或存放其他物品。租客不得在该停车位或住所的任何其他公共场所洗车、修车或者为车辆喷漆。

（李克兴、张新红，2006：353—355）

二、标点符号的使用特点

标点符号是语言表达的重要组成部分，是书面语言表达中不可缺少的要素。标点符号的正确使用可以帮助作者准确地表达自己的思想感情，同时可以帮助读者准确地理解文章所要表达的思想感情。法律语言的严密性和精确性特点要求正确的使用法律书面文本中的标点符号，以达到高度准确地表达法律规范的内容与思想。因此，翻译过程中正确地使用标点符号具有十分重要的意义。

在汉英书面文本中，常见的标点符号主要包括：逗号、句号、分号、冒号、感叹号、问号、引号、括号、省略号、书名号、破折号等。下面我们将对这些常用标点符号的使用做简要地介绍。

逗号使用于两句之间，表示一句话中较长的语音停顿。具体用法有：(1) 用在主语之后，表示对主语的突出和强调；(2) 用在长宾语或者主谓词组充当的宾语的前边；(3) 用在句首状语之后；(4) 用在并列词组之间；(5) 用在独立主语后面；(6) 用在分句之间；(7) 用在关联词语之间，表示需要停顿。

句号多用于陈述句之后，表示平直的语调和叙述的结束。

分号用于较长分句或者词组之间表示停顿，这时的停顿时间长于逗号的停顿。

冒号主要用于提示语之后，表示对事物的解释、罗列或者说明。

感叹号表示强烈的感情，多用于感叹句之后。

问号用于疑问句之后表示疑问。

引号表示文章中引用的部分或者需要引起读者注意的部分。引号使用过程中，需要注意引号与其他标点符号的相对位置。如果是全文引用,那么原文的句号应置于引号内;如果是原文的部分引用,那么原文的标点需置于引号之外。

括号表示文中注释或者补充的部分,如果括号位于句内,括号内不用标点;如果括号位于句外,括号内标点保留。

省略号表示文中的省略部分,省略的部分可能是引文的一部分,也可能是重复的语句,或者是同类人和事。省略号还表示对话中的沉默、语言的中断或者欲言又止。省略号前后不需使用其他标点符号。需要注意的是汉英语言中省略号的不同书写方法:汉语中省略号的形式为"……";而英语中为"..."。

书名号表示书籍、报刊、篇章、剧作、影视或者歌曲的名称。使用时需要注意汉英语言中对书名号的不同表示方式:汉语中一般使用"《 》",而英语中常使用引号、斜体或者下划线来表示书名。

破折号是对后文注释的标示,又表示语意的转换、跃进或语言的中断和延长。

英语法律篇章中主要使用逗号、分号、冒号和句号,汉语中主要使用逗号、顿号、冒号和句号,都很少使用叹号、问号、破折号等。这个特点与法律语言所使用的基本句型是一致的。冒号大多用在列举条目的总提示语之后。冒号后的条目,每条都要另起一行,每条包括的内容之间用逗号或者分号,各条末尾用分号,最后一条末尾用句号。这种形式是同法律语言采用条款形式表述的书面格式相一致的,其目的是为了让人们看起来一目了然,类目分明。

比如,我国《企业破产法》第 14 条规定:人民法院应当自裁定受理破产申请之日起二十五日内通知已知债权人,并予以公告。

通知和公告应当载明下列事项:

(一)申请人、被申请人的名称或者姓名;

(二)人民法院受理破产申请的时间;

(三)申报债权的期限、地点和注意事项;

(四)管理人的名称或者姓名及其处理事务的地址;

(五)债务人或者财产持有人应当向管理人清偿债务或者交付财产的要求;

(六)第一次债权人会议召开的时间和地点;

(七)人民法院认为应当通知和公告的其他事项。

再如,《美利坚合众国宪法》中对国会权利做了具体规定:

The Congress shall have Power To lay and collect Taxes, Duties, Imposts and Excises, to pay the Debts and provide for the common Defence and general Welfare of the United States; But all Duties, Imposts and Excises shall be uniform throughout the United States;

To borrow money on the credit of the United States;

To regulate Commerce with foreign Nations, and among the several States, and with the Indian Tribes;

To establish an uniform Rule of Naturalization, and uniform Laws on the subject of Bankruptcies throughout the United States;

To coin Money, regulate the Value thereof, and of foreign Coin, and fix the Standard of Weights and Measures;

...

To exercise exclusive Legislation in all Cases whatsoever, over such District (not exceeding ten Miles square) as may, by Cession of particular States, and the acceptance of Congress, become the Seat of the Government of the United States, and to exercise like Authority over all Places purchased by the Consent of the Legislature of the State in which the Same shall be, for the Erection of Forts, Magazines, Arsenals, dock-Yards, and other needful Buildings; And

To make all Laws which shall be necessary and proper for carrying into Execution the foregoing Powers, and all other Powers vested by this Constitution in the Government of the United States, or in any Department or Officer thereof.

第四节 口头法律语言的特点

口头法律语言是法律语言中的一种重要形式,与书面法律语言有着同等重要的地位。口头法律语言广泛应用于司法实践中,包含种类颇多。例如搜查、逮捕、拘留用语,法庭中询问当事人、判决等的用语,都采用口头法律语言形式。可见,口头法律语言在司法实践中有着十分重要的作用。

口头法律语言具有很强的专业性,同时具有准确、严密、凝练、庄重、质朴以及程序化的特点。

准确,是口头法律语言的生命,也是其基本特点所在。法律口头语言多应用于较严肃的场合,这就要求语言表达精确、无歧义。严密,是口头法律语言的精髓。口头法律语言的严密性要求语言结构严密、层次分明、逻辑清晰。凝练,是评价口头法律语言精纯的一个重要标准。凝练的口头法律语言要求用最经济的语言材料传递最大量、最高效的信息,力求措辞精确、言简意赅。比如公诉词:"被告人李三持该门市部剔肉刀,朝王六、张五两人头部、胸部、颈部猛扎,乱砍十刀,致使王六、张五两人的心脏被刺破引起大出血而休克死亡。"该公诉词用最凝练的语言简练地说明了被告人李三犯罪事实的主要情节和手段的残忍。质朴是指朴实无华的表现手法。口头法律语言应以具体明确地运用客观事实、相关法律与证据,要求语言平实、准确、严谨,尽量不要使用形象性的描述词语。

一、法庭口语

法庭口译常被看作法律口译的核心部分。法庭口译一般是指在民事或刑事诉讼过程中，当事人或证人由于不通晓当地(国)的通用/官方语言造成理解和表达上的困难时所得到的翻译服务。法庭口译主要分为同声传译(simultaneous interpreting)、交替传译(consecutive interpreting)和视译(sight interpreting)三种。同声传译是指讲话人讲话的同时，拖后几个词开始口译，这种方法对口译人员的要求较高。"同声传译通常只为在庭审过程中只听不说和/或暂时不发言的有关人员而做(如陪审员、陪审团成员、被告等)，多数时候需要同传设备以便口译员在工作时不受干扰。"同声传译在美国、澳大利亚、新加坡等国家和中国香港地区是法庭口译的主要形式。我国急缺同传法庭口译员。"视译可以说是一种口译和笔译的混合体，因此既可以叫作视觉翻译(sight translation)，也可以叫作视觉口译(sight interpreting)"视觉口译的材料往往不会在庭审前给译员，所以需要译员当场口译，材料难度大(如判决书，证词等)，时间紧迫，对译员的语言能力、法律知识和心理素质都是一种考验。法庭口译的特点主要体现在几种口译方式交替进行，对译员的语言素质要求特别高。法庭口译不是单一的某种口译方式。在庭审的时候根据需要，译员一会儿被要求使用同声传译，瞬间又转到交替口译，抑或又转到视觉口译；同时，法庭口译实际也包含了开庭前后的笔译部分。首先，在法庭这样庄重、紧张的气氛中，译员还要在多种口译方式之间来回转换，难度颇大。其次，法庭口译对译员的语言水平要求超过一般的口译。这是因为法庭上的任何一字一词都有可能是法官断案的关键，译员的任何错误都有可能引起误解，造成误判。所以要求法庭口译员必须完整准确、一字不差地(verbatim)翻译源语信息，不得修饰和省略源语信息，不得更改原话语的语体和语域。译员对两种语言都要有较强敏感性，不仅要对语言特征和副语言特征有识别能力，还要有相应的转换能力。说话人的迟疑、重复、口误等都要求被忠实地传译，同时还要注意其说话时的表情、语音、语调。说话人往往还要面对两种语言的地域方言和社会方言。例如，汉语可能是粤语、山东话、四川话等等，而英语有可能是苏格兰英语、南非英语、黑人英语、印度英语等等。从社会方言的角度来讲，"语言会因不同职业、阶层、年龄、性别等因素而形成诸多语言变体。俚语、黑话、行业语等会使口译环境非常复杂，难度亦很大。"

忠实和准确是法庭口译的最基本要求。要达到忠实和准确，译员要完整地、一字不差地(verbatim)传译说话人的话语，不得随意增加、删减、解释、改述，也不能有遗漏、曲解、误传等现象发生。"口译时，在保持语言的自然以及语域、语体、语气不变的基础上，应使语言结构和语义和源语言一致，对模棱两可的话语、错误的开头语以及重复等都应如实翻译。如果没听清或没听懂，口译人员应征得法官的同意后进行澄清；如果在同声传译时没听清或没听懂，通常的做法是由口译人员自己判断插话澄清或继续口译"。中立、保密是法庭口译员的职业道德。回避原则是使法庭口译员保持中立的有效方法。法庭口译人员和控辩双方不应有任何私人关系或其他能够影响译员中立立场的特殊关系，如亲戚、朋友、同学、邻居等。同时，在开庭和休庭前后或期间，法庭口译员都不应和控辩双方人员和其家属等进行交谈和接触；在整个庭审期间，译员也不应观看和收听对本案进行的相关报道，也不应和他人对本案进行讨论，以免受到其他观点的影响，从而最终影响到译员的中立性。这和美国对陪审员的要求相似。由于特殊的身份，译员在庭审前后有可能接触到一些材料，如卷宗、专家证词和法庭判决书等等，这时，译员应严守保密要求，不应向任何人透露任何相关信息。

二、庭审程序语言

程序化是口头法律语言的另一大特点，尤其是法庭中的口头法律语言。各国庭审一般都遵守严格的程序，一般的程序为：(1)宣布开庭(2)法庭调查(3)法庭辩论(4)最后陈述(5)评议和宣判。

(1) 宣布开庭

这个阶段主要包括以下程序：宣布法庭审理过程中的注意事项，宣布案件，查明当事人是否到庭并验证其身份，告知当事人其依法享有的权利，宣布合议庭/陪审团的组成人员、书记员、当事人、诉讼代理人、鉴定人和翻译人员的名单，告知当事人有权对上述人员申请回避，告知被告人享有辩护的权利。这个阶段的内容是程序性的，内容变化不大，翻译人员针对这个特点做充分的准备，才能在翻译实践中得心应手。在美国，通常先由原告方律师做 opening statement(开场陈述)，表明原告的论点。

(2) 法庭调查

法庭调查是开庭审理的中心环节。法庭调查阶段主要处理核实证据、查清犯罪事实是否存在、是否系被告人所为，被告人是否承认起诉书所指控的罪行，实施犯罪的时间、地点、方法、手段、结果、动机和目的，有无法定的从重或从轻处罚的情节等问题。尽管目的、性质、作用有一定差异，但语言的表达方式是类似的。这个阶段的语言既有口头法律语言特点(质证和交叉质证)，又有书面法律的特点(起诉书、专家证词、司法鉴定书等)，其中涉及的专有名词、术语、数字、法律术语和行话较多。译者只有准确地把握了发言人的语言含义才能准确地完成翻译工作。

(3) 法庭辩论

法庭辩论是开庭审理的重要阶段。是在审判人员主持下，当事人根据案件已经查明的事实和根据，用口头辩论方式陈述各自对诉讼争议和事实的看法、理由以及依据，以明确是非和责任。法庭辩论阶段主要包括控辩双方在法庭调查阶段的基础上发表控辩意见。该阶段表现出明显的书面语言的特点，文体正式、篇章较长、句式复杂、语言凝练，其内容具有很强的逻辑性。在美国，双方律师都会以 brief(案件辩论书)作为辩论的基础，也就是说，双方律师的法庭辩论内容不能超出案件辩论书的内容范围。

(4) 最后陈述

最后陈述阶段主要是被告人针对案件事实、庭审过程、诉求等向法庭提出自己的意见、主张和申辩等。被告人通常没有法律专业知识背景，因此他们的发言常缺乏逻辑性和准确性。在美国，通常由原告方律师做 closing statement(最后陈述)，重申原告的论点。

（5）评议和宣判

法庭辩论终结后，当事人不愿调解或调解未能达成协议的，合议庭应当对案件及时进行评议。合议庭应当就案件事实的认定、是非责任的划分、适用的法律及处理结果进行评议。合议庭评议实行少数服从多数的原则，评议结果及不同意见应当如实记入评议笔录，由合议庭成员签字；合议庭评议应当保密。合议庭评议后，无论是公开审理还是不公开审理的案件，都必须公开宣告判决。判决的宣告有当庭宣判和择日定期宣判两种形式：当庭宣判的，应当在10日内向当事人发送判决书；定期宣判的，宣判后立即向当事人发送判决书。人民法院在宣告判决时，应当告知当事人上诉权利、上诉期限和上诉的法院。宣判阶段是对案件的审理做出公开判决，这个阶段的语言主要以书面语言为主。判决书的用词专业、句式复杂、篇章较长、文风严谨正式。

掌握口头法律语言的特点是译者更好理解口头法律语言，进而恰当地进行翻译的前提条件。

第五节　本章小结

本章以从事法律翻译实践的实际需求为出发点，通过分析汉英法律语言的概况和词语、句法、篇章结构以及口头法律语言的特点来体现汉英法律语言的总体特点。法律文本为正式文本，涵盖内容广泛、社会责任重大，这就决定了对法律翻译的准确性要求相当高。法律翻译不能含糊其辞、模棱两可，这就要求译者精确地把握源语言与目标语言的特点及使用方法，从而清晰简练地做好翻译工作。对汉英法律语言的特点及使用方法的掌握是做好汉英法律翻译的基础步骤，需要译者认真对待。

 课后习题

1. 翻译下列法律术语。

active capacity	返还财产
rights of the person	名义当事人
court of arbitration	临终遗嘱
judgment of last resort	养父母
final judgment	避税
citation of authorities	上诉法院
legal fiction	司法审查
doctrine of constitutional supremacy	颁布一部法律
bona fide mortgage	欧洲人权委员会
a case tried *de novo*	立法解释

(续表)

body corporate	具结悔过
in light of the specific conditions of the case	传闻证据
demurrer to the jurisdiction	区域自治
delivery by installments	普遍选举权
notarial will	世界人权宣言
action *in rem*	资产负债表
bailiff	以剥夺财产相胁迫
actionable nuisance	初审法院
forcible felony	公诉人
false imprisonment	司法协助
trespass to chattels	对领土无可争辩的主权
tort liability for negligence	法律冲突
insurance premium	从合同
coercion in fact	共同共有权
general average contribution	原始取得
pecuniary damages	双边条约
extort confessions by torture	不当得利
parol contract	民事责任
consensus *ad idem*	合同的期满
contempt of court	互惠贸易协定

2. 试翻译以下段落,请注意画线部分的翻译。

(1) 请汉译以下段落,尤其注意画线部分的翻译

Every Bill which shall have passed the House of Representatives and the Senate, shall, before it become a Law, be presented to the President of the United States; If he approve he shall sign it, **but if** not he shall return it, with his Objections to that House in which it shall have originated, who shall enter the Objections at large on their Journal, and proceed to reconsider it. **If** after such Reconsideration two thirds of that House shall agree to pass the Bill, it shall be sent, together with the Objections, to the other House, by which it shall likewise be reconsidered, **and if** approved by two thirds of that House, it shall become a Law. But in all such Cases the Votes of both Houses shall be determined by Yeas and Nays, and the Names of the Persons voting for and against the Bill shall be entered on the Journal of each House respectively. **If** any Bill shall not be returned by the President within ten Days (Sundays excepted) after it shall have been presented to him, the same shall be a Law, in like Manner as if he had signed it, unless the Congress by their Adjournment prevent its Return, in which Case it shall not be a Law. (*The Constitution of the United States of America*, Article I,

Section7）

（2）英译下面的段落

中华人民共和国各民族一律平等。国家保障各少数民族的合法的权利和利益,维护和发展各民族的平等、团结、互助关系。禁止对任何民族的歧视和压迫,禁止破坏民族团结和制造民族分裂的行为。

国家根据各少数民族的特点和需要,帮助各少数民族地区加速经济和文化的发展。

各少数民族聚居的地方实行区域自治,设立自治机关,行使自治权。各民族自治地方都是中华人民共和国不可分离的部分。

各民族都有使用和发展自己的语言文字的自由,都有保持或者改革自己的风俗习惯的自由。（《宪法》第4条）

3．翻译下列合同文本节选部分。

Chapter 3 Price and Payment
(For payment on the lump-sum basis)

3.1　In consideration of full and proper performance of its contractual obligations by Licensor，Licensee agrees to pay Licensor the total contract price amounting to _____ (say _____ only) in _____ (currency) by telegraphic transfer（T/T）through Licensee's Bank to Licensor's Bank. The price breakdown is as follows：

　　A. License fee：_____ (Say：_____ only);

　　B. Design fee：_____ (Say：_____ only);

　　C. Technical Documentation fee：_____ (Say：_____ only);

　　D. Technical Service fee：_____ (Say：_____ only);

　　E. Technical Training fee：_____ (Say：_____ only);

3.2　The total contract price shall be firm，fixed and covering all the expenses and charges in relation to the delivery of Technical Documentation，the rendering of Technical Service and Technical Training. Technical Documentation fee is for delivery DDU Destination Airport.

3.3　The contract price specified in Clause 3.1 A，B，C，E shall be paid by Licensee to Licensor in accordance with the following manner and percentage.

3.3.1　_____ Percent（_____%）of the amount, i.e. _____ within _____ (_____) days after Licensee has received the following documents provided by Licensor and found them in order.

　　A. One (1) original and two (2) duplicate copies of a valid export license issued by the competent authorities of Licensor's country, or a written statement of the competent authorities or relevant agency of Licensor's country certifying that no export license is required;

B. One (1) original and one (1) duplicate copy of Irrevocable Letter of Guarantee for advance payment issued by Licensor's Bank in favor of Licensee covering _____ (Say: _____ only), specimen of which is as set forth in Appendix 6;

C. Five (5) copies of profoma invoice covering the total contract price;

D. Five (5) copies of manually signed commercial invoice indicating the amount to be paid;

E. Two (2) copies of sight draft.

3.3.2 _____ Percent (_____%) of the amount, i.e. _____ (Say: _____ only) shall be paid by Licensee to Licensor within _____ days after Licensee has received the following documents provided by Licensor and found them in order.

A. One (1) original and three (3) duplicate copies of airway bill covering the delivery of the technical Documentation, and marked FREIGHT PREPAID or receipt of registered airmail for the delivery of Technical Documentation;

B. Five (5) copies of manually signed commercial invoice indicating the amount to be paid;

C. Two (2) copies of sight draft.

3.4 Technical service fee as specified in Clause 3.1.D shall be paid by Licensee to Licensor according to actual dues once every _____ months after the arrival of the first group of Licensor's technical personnel at Job Site and within _____ days after Licensee has received the following documents submitted by Licensor and found them in order.

A. One (1) copy of time sheets signed by the authorized representatives of both parties;

B. Five (5) copies of manually signed commercial invoice indicating the amount to be paid;

C. Two (2) copies of sight draft.

3.5 Licensee shall have the right to deduct from any payment the withholding taxes, liquidated damages, and/or compensations, if any, which Licensor shall pay under contract.

3.6 All the banking charges incurred in Licensee's Bank shall be borne by Licensee while those incurred outside Licensee's Bank shall be borne by Licensor. (李克兴、张新红, 2006: 253—255)

第三章
法律翻译的基本原则

第一节 概 述

将法律翻译作为一门独立的学科来研究是最近一二十年的事。在此之前，人们或将法律翻译看作科技翻译的一部分，或将法律翻译归类为公文文体翻译的一种。若问"什么是法律翻译？"人们一般会说：法律翻译即法律文件的翻译。法律文件又该如何定义呢？法律文件是一个内涵很广的概念，它包括法律、法规、条约、国际公约、国际惯例、涉外经济合同、司法文书等。法律文件的翻译就其不同目的而言，可分为两种情况。一种是仅供参考用的法律翻译，例如为方便不谙中文的外国人认识中国法律而将部分中文法律条文译成英文，或为方便不谙英文的中国人认识英国或美国法律而将部分英文法律条文译成中文，这类译文是不具有法律效力的。另一种是译文本身为法律文件，具有法律效力，例如外商投资中国内地举办合营企业的合同和章程，一经相关方签署即为有效法律文件，对各方均有法律约束力。前一种翻译属于广义意义上的法律翻译，后一种即为严格意义上的法律翻译。

法学不同于数学、物理学、化学及其他自然科学，法学首先是一门与国家概念紧密相联的科学。法律有国别之分，我们可以说"这是美国法律，那是中国法律"，但自然科学无国别之分。法律一般仅在其相应的司法管辖区内适用，每一个国家或具有独立司法管辖权的地区都有自己独立的法律制度。法律术语和语义系统，都有自己的分类方式、法律来源、研究方法和社会经济原则等。因此，谈到法律翻译，我们首先应对法系和法律体系有所认识。因为法系和法律体系与法律翻译密切相关；离开了法系和法律体系，法律翻译就无从谈起。

谈到翻译，总要讲讲翻译的原则或翻译的标准。其实翻译的原则和标准在本质上是一致的，这两个术语的主要区别在于前者是从译者的角度来考虑翻译活动，而后者是从翻译评论家的角度来评判译文。译者从事翻译活动总要遵循某些翻译原则，而翻译评论家总是要根据某种翻译标准来评判译文。

　　翻译的原则是指翻译活动必须遵循的准绳，它是翻译实践的准绳，是衡量翻译工作效果的标尺。使译文质量符合翻译的标准是翻译工作者不断努力以期达到的目标。切实可行的标准对发挥翻译功效、提高翻译质量具有重要的意义。

　　关于翻译的标准，中外翻译理论家提出了很多观点。严复在总结前人翻译思想的基础上，于1898年提出了著名的"信、达、雅（faithfulness, expressiveness, elegance）"三字标准。该标准已沿用百年。在西方第一个对翻译原则进行探讨的翻译理论家是泰特勒（Alexander Fraser Tytler）。中外翻译理论家在对待翻译标准问题上有很多共同的认识，即在内容上，翻译要忠实于原文；在文字上，要力求通顺流畅；在风格上，要与原作保持一致。所谓"忠实"，首先是指忠实于原作的思想内容。一般情况下，译者应把原作的思想内容完整而准确地传达出来、不得无端加以篡改、歪曲、遗漏或增删。这里所说的思想内容，通常指作品中所叙述的事实、说明的事理、描写的景物，以及作者在叙述、说明、描写过程中所反映的立场观点、所流露的思想情感。但在特殊情况下，因受意识形态等因素的约束，译者在传达原作的思想内容时，可以做出适当的灵活处理。忠实还指保持原作的风格，译者不能对原作的风格任意破坏和改变，不能以自己的风格取代原作的风格。原作是通俗的口语体，译文就不能变成文绉绉的书面体；原文粗俗烦琐，译作就不能变成文雅洗练。所谓"通顺"，是指译文语言必须通俗易懂符合译文语言规范和语言习惯，译文应该没有晦涩难懂、文理不通、逻辑混乱等现象。忠实和通顺是对立统一、相辅相成的。忠实而不通顺，译文的可读性就差，读者不能读懂；通顺而不忠实则无异于改编，失去了翻译的意义。

　　法律翻译是一种法律转换和语言转换同时进行的双重工作。法律翻译与其他文体的翻译有一定的差别，各种文体的翻译也都有各自的侧重点，但所有文体的翻译都始终不能脱离"忠实"和"通顺"的标准。文学作品的翻译重于求"神似"，着力于再现原作的思想内容和艺术品位；科技文体的翻译讲求术语的精当、逻辑的严密和行文的简约规范；新闻文体的翻译在信息的准确传递的基础上要求符合新闻的陈述程式，文字要求雅俗共赏，具有最广泛的可读性；法律要求语气严肃庄重，含义明确，不产生歧义。法律翻译应该采取哪些原则、遵循哪些标准，学术界一直众说纷纭。由于法律文件具有高度的严肃性和严密性，法律翻译必须准确无误地译出原文，遣词造句要仔细斟酌，切忌因一味追求"达"和"雅"而随意解释或删除原意。忠实于原文应该是法律翻译的第一标准。当然，理想的法律翻译应该是"忠实"和"通顺"的完美结合，这也应该是翻译工作者孜孜以求的目标。陈忠诚先生针对我国《宪法》英译文中的某些翻译实例提出了"精益求精"的论断，并撰文列举了若干中英文原文条款的翻译实例，论述法律术语及专业词汇怎样在汉译英时起到译文与原文功能对等的效应。邱贵溪第一次较全面归纳并论述了法律文件翻译的五大原则，这些原则对规范法律文件翻译有一定的指导意义。

根据法律翻译实践,我们将法律翻译的基本原则归纳如下:① 准确严谨性原则;② 清晰简明性原则;③ 前后一致性原则;④ 语言规范化原则。

第二节 法律翻译的原则

一、准确严谨性原则

法律是由国家行使立法权的机关依照立法程序制定,国家政权保证执行的行为规则。语言作为法律的表现形式和法律信息的承载体,必须体现法律的这种社会职能。法律的严肃性决定了法律语言必须准确和严谨。法律文件要求语言准确,法律文件的翻译亦是如此。准确性是法律文本翻译的根本,忠实于原文内容,力求准确无误是法律翻译区别于其他翻译的一个重要的特征。即使是微小的法律文件的翻译失误都可能造成不可挽回的损失。比如有的译者在涉外销售合同的翻译中把 earnest money 即具有担保性质的"定金"译成"订金"。定金,是指合同当事人为了确保合同的履行,依据法律规定或者当事人双方的约定,由当事人一方在合同订立时,或订立后、履行前,按合同标的额的一定比例,预先给付对方当事人的金钱或其他代替物。而订金,是指一方先交付一笔现金给对方,以作为己方履约的担保。这样的误译使得在外商违约时,"订金"被解释为预付款,使外商逃脱了双倍返还定金的责任。可见法律译文的准确严谨是法律翻译的根本,而翻译失真则是法律翻译的大患。法律文本的翻译稍有差错或语义含糊不清,哪怕是微小的失误,都有可能招致严重的后果。

例 1 Contractor shall assume full responsibility for the entire project work until its **acceptance**.

原译:在项目接收之前,承包方应对工程承担全部责任。

改译:在项目验收之前,承包方应对工程承担全部责任。

解析:原译文翻译欠缺准确严谨。原文中的 acceptance 被译为"接收"不准确,该词在句中意思应为"验收",即工程的完工情况必须经过查验,并确定工程的质量等是否符合合同规定的要求。

例 2 **Damages** for breach of contract by one party consist of a sum equal to the loss, including loss of profit, suffered by the other party as a consequence of the breach.

原译:一方违约所导致的损害包括因其违约而使另一方遭受损失的金额,含利润损失。

改译:一方违约的损害赔偿金包括因其违约而使另一方遭受损失的金额,含利润损失。

解析：原译文意思表达不准确，主要是由于没有很好地理解法律术语 damages 一词的准确含义，而是把它当作普通词汇来理解。根据 Merriam-Webster's Dictionary of Law 的解释，damage：loss of harm resulting from injury to person, property, or reputation；而 damages：the money awarded to a party in a civil suit as reparation for the loss or injury for which another is liable. 所以，damages 为普通词汇，其含义是"损害，损失"之意。而原文中的 damages 一词是法律名词，其意思是：损害赔偿金。

例 3　The balance shall be settled **upon the arrival of** the goods at the port of destination.

原译：货到目的港后付清余款。

改译：货到目的港后即行付清余款。

解析：原译文中使用"后"，对时间的限制较为模糊，不够明确。因此，为保证译文的准确严谨性，应加上"即行"两字，明确限定付款期限，使译文的意思更精确。

例 4　……所有董事会成员……须由合营方委派和撤换。

原译：... all the directors shall be appointed and **replaced** by the parties to the venture.

改译：... all the directors shall be appointed and **removed** by the parties to the venture.

解析：中文中的"撤换"，意思是 removed 或 ousted，而 replaced 只有"替换"的含义，这与"撤换"的含义是不同的。

例 5　如果买方对品质有异议，可以在货到目的口岸或收货后 30 天内向卖方提出索赔。

原译：In case the Buyers have disputes over the quality of the goods, the Buyers may, within 30 days after arrival at the destination port or **delivery** of goods, file a claim against the Sellers.

改译：In case the Buyers have disputes over the quality of the goods, the Buyers may, within 30 days after arrival at the destination port or take delivery of goods, file a claim against the Sellers.

解析：原译文同样存在着不准确的问题。该合同条款中"收货"不能简单的译为 delivery。英文中的 delivery 可以指 carrying 或 shipping。所以将"收货"译为 take delivery 才准确严谨。

例 6　In the event of a collision or any other incident of navigation concerning a sea-going ship and involving the penal or disciplinary responsibility of the master or of **any other person in the service of the ship**, criminal or disciplinary proceedings may be instituted only before the judicial or administrative authorities of **the State of which the ship was flying the flag** at the time of the collision or other incident of navigation.

原译:在发生碰撞或任何有关海船的其他航行事故并涉及船长或为船舶服务的任何其他人员的刑事或纪律责任时,刑事或纪律的诉讼,只能向发生碰撞或其他航行事故所悬挂旗帜国家的司法或行政当局提起。

改译:如海船发生了碰撞或任何其他航行事故,需追究船长或船上任何其他船员的刑事或纪律责任时,只能向事发时船旗国的司法或行政当局提出请求。

解析:本例选自《1952年统一船舶碰撞或其他航行事故中刑事管辖权某些规定的国际公约》第1条关于对船舶碰撞有刑事管辖权的法院的描述。原译文中有几处欠精确的地方。其中"any other person in the service of the ship"不可照字面理解为广义的"为船舶服务的人",这里所指的是与前面的"船长"相对应、为船舶服务的"其他船员"。"the State of which the ship was flying the flag"可译为航运界通用术语"船旗国"。"collision or other incident of navigation"在本段落中重复出现,为了简洁,将重复处译为"事发时"。"criminal or disciplinary proceeding may be instituted"中的"instituted"译为"请求"会更好。

例7 In all cases, when it is proved that **the consent** of one of the parties is **vitiated** by fraud or concealment, or when the remuneration is, in proportion to the services rendered, in an excessive degree too large or too small, the agreement may be annulled or modified by the court at the request of **the party affected**.

原译:在任何情况下,如经证明,当事一方同意的事项因欺诈或隐瞒而无效,或报酬与所提供的服务相比,高的过分或低的过分,经受影响的一方请求,法院可以宣告协议无效,或予以变更。

改译:任何情况下,如经证实,一方是在受对方的欺诈或隐瞒的情况下同意协议的;或与所提供的服务相比,救助报酬过高过低,经受害方请求,法院可以宣告协议无效,或予以变更。

解析:本例选自《1910年统一海难援助和救助某些法律规定公约》第7条。原译文将"consent"由名词转换成动词,并译为"同意的事项",语句通顺了,但具体是什么事项,原译文没有指明,容易造成歧义或误解,不符合法律语言要求精确的特点,应改译为"同意协议"。"vitiate"既有"失效"的意思,也有"损害或降低价值"的意思。如果译为"失效",翻译逻辑上有问题。如果"vitiate"取"损害"或"降低"之意,则上句可理解为:在订立救助协议时,由于一方的欺诈或隐瞒行为而使对方同意救助条件,从而使对方的利益受损。这样理解与翻译,语句才通顺,"the party affected"原译文为"经受影响的一方"冗长而含混,改译为"受害方"精炼又达意。

准确和严谨是法律翻译的最根本原则。法律文件所要阐明的就是权利和义务关系,为了维护法律的尊严,不至于因为语义上的分歧而发生纠纷,译文中的每字每句都应做到准确严谨。

二、清晰简明性原则

国家的法律语言通常都是这个国家最正式、最规范的语言。用清晰简明的词语表达法律概念是法律语言最基本的要求。法律翻译亦是如此,如果法律条文翻译的不清晰,这些法律条文不但会无法执行,甚至也可能成为陷阱。法律翻译的清晰和简明体现在使用清晰简明的词语和清晰简明的句式两大方面。

(一) 使用清晰简明的词语

例 8　The remainder of the testator's property should be divided equally between all of our nephews and nieces on my wife's side and my niece.

解析:这是阿肯色州最高法院的一个真实的财产纠纷案,其起因就是该条文表述得不够清晰。立遗嘱人本人只有一位侄女,而太太方面有 22 位侄儿、侄女。在这 23 人中间是平均分配还是先"一分为二"? 根据阿肯色州最高法院的判决,这份遗嘱的一半最后还是被判给了立遗嘱人的侄女。然而,如果把原文写得更清晰一些,改为 The remainder of the testator's property should be divided equally between all of our nephews and nieces on my wife's side as one party and my niece as another. 恐怕这场官司根本就不会发生。

例 9　The servant's liability stems from the duty owed to a third person under the law to conduct HIMSELF so as not to injure others.

解析:这个句子中,代词 HIMSELF,究竟是指 the servant 还是指 a third person? 如果把上文改写成 The servant's liability stems from the duty owed to a third person under the law requiring the SERVANT to act so as not to injure others. 就不会产生歧义。对法律文件的翻译者而言,为求表达准确,要不怕使用重复词,要尽量避免这种含含糊糊的代词。

例 10　The **packing and wrapping** expenses shall be borne by the Buyer.

译文:包装费应由买方负担。

解析:本例中的"packing and wrapping"是同义词并用,更为严谨。但在翻译时,译为一个词就可以了。

例 11　Taxation shall comprise all forms of taxes, including without limitation income tax, capital gain tax, stamp duty, tariffs, import and export duties, impositions, and all fines, fees and rates collected by the taxation authority and other authorities.

译文:税收包括各种形式的税项,包括但不限于税务局和其他主管部门征收的所得税、资本利得税、印花税、关税、进出口税、各种征税及一切罚金、手续费和地方税。

解析:本例中的税名表示性质各不相同的税收,所以得逐一译出,并且用词清晰简明。

例 12　If any person over the age of 16 years who has the custody, charge or care of any child or young person under that age willfully assaults, ill-treats, neglects, abandons or exposes such child or young person... such person shall be guilty of an offence...

译文：16岁以上负责监护、照看和照顾任何年龄在16岁以下的儿童或少年的任何人，如故意袭击、虐待、疏忽、抛弃或遗弃该儿童或少年……也属犯罪。

解析：本例中custody, charge, care三个概念比较难翻译，其含义略有不同：custody指"法律上的抚养权，监护"；charge含有"带领、负责、照看"之意；care是"照顾"。

(二) 使用简明的句式

要使法律文章写得清晰，译得清晰，未必需要使用复杂的语法时态和句型结构，简明的句式往往能达到更好的效果。

例 13　The law holds that the individual is responsible for his acts. The law also indicates what is good and right, and what may and should be done. It also indicate what is evil and wrong, and should not and may not be done. The law further holds that what is evil and wrong is a crime and may not be done, and if done, render the doer liable to punishment. The law also recognize the principle that man has free will and that, with certain exceptions, he exercises free will in commission of any crime that he may commit.

原译：法律认为公民应对自己的行为负责。法律还规定什么是美好和正确的，规范了什么是邪恶和错误的，法律还进一步明确规定哪些邪恶和错误的事是不能做的犯罪行为，如果某人做了这样的事，那么该行为人就要受到惩罚。同样，法律还承认这样一个原则，每个公民除犯罪自由外都具有自由意志，如果某人在各种违法活动中实施其自由意志那么他就可能触犯法律。

改译：法律规定人人应对自己的行为负责，分清善良和正义，并规范人们的行为准则；同时法律还规定，作孽枉法即是犯罪，法不可恕，谁要以身试法，必将受到严惩。法律所主张的原则是人人享有自由意志的权利，但利用意志权利而犯罪者除外。

解析：本例原文共有五句，首句简洁明了，后面的句子长度逐一增加，但并没有增加得过长，并且所有句子的主干保持着相同的"名词＋动词＋直接宾语"的结构，形成了平行结构，而宾语从句所表达的内容随着附加成分的增多愈加具体，体现出推进式的逻辑思维方式。原译文虽然译出了原文的意思，但是语言松散，措辞随意，句法不严谨，呈口语化趋势，无法体现原文句式安排的匠心和威严性特征。改译首先在措辞上表现出相当的文字功底，运用书面语和法律术语，在句式上又根据汉语特点做了适当的调整，将原来的五句变成了两句，而两句中又分别包含了两个并列句，还恰当地运用了汉语的四字结构如"行为准则""作孽枉法""法不可恕""以身试法"等，既缩短了句子的长度,又浓缩了表达的内容,和原文一样体现了法律文本的庄严性和威严性。

例 14 Further, a meeting of the European justice ministers <u>is held</u> every two years.

译文:此外,每两年<u>举行</u>一次欧洲司法部长会议。

例 15 Courts <u>are discouraged</u> from passing sentence of imprisonment on offenders under 21 years of age.

译文:对于未满21岁的罪犯,<u>不鼓励法院判其服刑</u>。

例 16 Unless <u>this account is paid</u> within next ten days, it will be necessary to take appropriate action.

译文:除非在10天内<u>把账还清</u>,否则就有必要采取适当的行动。

解析:例14至16原文都是被动语态,强调的只是行为本身,无需说明行动的主体,因此译文一律采用无主句,行文清楚简明。

英语是一种形合语言,造句注重形式接应,要求结构完整。主语具有显著的作用,除省略句外,每个英语句子都必须有主语。法律英语中没有省略句,所以句句都有主语,这也是造成法律英语中被动语态多的原因之一。而汉语是一种意合语言,造句注重意念连贯,主语的作用不显著,无主句随处可见,所以没有太多的被动语态。无主句不是省略了主语的句子,而是习惯了就这么讲,其主语究竟是什么,往往不容易判断,但是在各种语言环境里它都能表达完整而明确的意思。如果法律英语原句中的被动语态强调的只是行为本身,而无需说明行为主体,则可以译成无主句,达到句式简明的效果。

例 17 No Bill of Lading to be signed for any blockaded port, and if the port of destination be declared blockaded after Bill of Lading has been signed, Owners shall discharge the cargo either at the port of loading, against payment of the expenses of discharge, if the ship has not sailed thence, or, if sailed at any safe port on the way as ordered by Shippers or if no order is given at the nearest safe place against payment of full freight.

译文:不得为发往任何被封锁港口的货物签发提单。如果签发提单后目的港被宣布封锁,船舶尚未起航,船舶所有人可将货物卸载并收取卸载费用。如已起航,则可将货物卸载于托运人指定的途中港口;如无指示,可在附近的安全港口卸载,并收取全部运费。

解析:本例中有三个if引导的条件句,原文句式结构清晰简明,译文很好地保留了"如果"引导的条件句,当然这三个条件句中后两个只用了"如",省略了一个字,但是意思、结构完全相同,语言更加简练。

例 18 Producers of toxic chemicals have the following options:(1) require purchasers to assume responsibility for subsequent spills,(2) deposit money in a damages escrow fund, (3) terminate production, or (4) post a conspicuous disclaimer of liability on every container.

译文:有毒化学品生产商有以下几种选择:(1) 要求买方承担因泄漏造成的责任;(2) 在损害赔偿金托管账户中存放保证金;(3) 停止生产;(4) 在每个集装箱的显著位置张贴免责标签。

解析:本例中原文将四个可供选择的选项用数字表明,各选项都采用了动词词组形式,构成平行结构,内容表达清晰明了,译文同样很好地保留了动词的平行结构。

简明清晰是法律翻译的原则。译者可采用灵活的手段,尽量将译文的意思用简洁、精炼的词语和句式表达出来,以便准确地传递相关信息。

三、前后一致性原则

法律翻译的前后一致性原则是指在法律翻译的过程中用同一法律术语表示同一法律概念的原则。在法律翻译的过程中,我们应自始至终地坚持用同一术语表示同一概念,那些看似同义或近义的词语,都有可能表示不同的概念,因此应严格禁止使用;在法律翻译的过程中如果碰到两个或两个看似同义或近义的法律术语,我们应该清楚地认识到它们并非同义术语,而应尽最大的努力分辨它们之间存在的语义差别,运用确切的词语将它们准确地表达出来。

如 agreement 一词通常有两种译法,即"协定"和"协议"。这种在一套法律文件中不一致的译法在 2000 年出版的《乌拉圭回合多边贸易谈判结果》中得到彻底纠正,"agreement"作为具体法律文本的名称一律译成"协定"。但是动词词组"reach agreement"这一表述根据汉语习惯,译为"达成协议"或"达成一致",而不是"达成协定"。又如,在《民法通则》的英译本中,"法律规定"中的动词"规定"曾被译为 stipulate, specify, prescribe, require 以及 provide 等等;我国《渔业法》中的"禁"字时而被译为 shall be prohibited,时而被译成 shall be forbidden;在同一份合同中,"货物"一会被译成 goods,一会被译成 items。以上法律术语的使用应严格遵守前后一致性的原则。

例 19 保税区的减免税货物、保税货物的监管手续费,应当按照《中华人民共和国海关对进口减税、免税和保税货物征收海关监管手续费的办法》办理。

译文:The Customs supervising fees on the import goods with duty reduction and exemption and that on the *goods in bond* shall be collected in accordance with *the Customs Regulations of the People's Republic of China Governing the Collection of Customs Supervising Fees on Import Goods Granted with Duty Reduction or Exemption and the Bonded Goods*.

解析:仔细研究英译文,我们发现其中的 *goods in bond* 和 *Bonded Goods* 都是指"保税货物"。这就犯了法律翻译前后不一致的错误。

法律文体的行文中,无论是在原文的写作还是在翻译中,所用的词汇及句型的重复率是非常高的。法律文件翻译中如果缺乏一致性无疑会使法律概念混淆,影响法律的精确性。所以,在整个法律文件的翻译中要始终保持关键词在表达上的前后一致性,这样就能避免法律解释上的麻烦,避免因为法律文件翻译不当所引发的官司。

四、语体规范化原则

法律翻译除了要求语言功能的对等之外,还应照顾到法律功能的对等。所谓法律功能对等就是说源语和译入语在法律上所起的作用和效果的对等。唯有如此,才能使译入语精准地表达源语的真正涵义。专业术语是法律英语中最重要的元素,要达到"法律语言规范化"就必须准确地翻译法律专业术语。

例如,几乎任何一份外贸货物进出口合约都涉及如何处理"不可抗力"的条款。根据词义,该短语可译为 force beyond human power, force controlled by God, or irresistible force,然而只有把它译成 force majeure 才是最地道、专业、规范的译法。

再如 motion 一词常被翻译为"动议",虽然 motion 在一般英语中的意思是会议中的动议,但如果作为诉讼程序上的专业术语,则此翻译就不准确了。Black's Law Dictionary 对该词的定义为:"A written or oral application requesting a court to make a specified ruling or order." 所以"申请"比"动议"更适合。attempted crime 译为"试图犯罪"就不如译为"犯罪未遂"更规范。

例 20 The **burden of proof** rests with the defendant.

原译:证明的负担由被告承担。

改译:证明责任由被告承担。

解析:本例中 burden of proof 是法律英语中的专业术语,指"证明责任",原译"证明的负担"显然译得不专业不规范。

例 21 Where, through securities trading at a stock exchange, an investor comes to hold 5 percent of shares issued by a listed company, the investor shall, within three days from the date on which such share holding becomes a fact, submit a written report to the Securities Regulatory Authorities of the State Council, notify the listed company and **make** the fact **known to the public**.

译文:通过证券交易所的证券交易,投资者持有一个上市公司已发行的股份的百分之五时,应当在该事实发生之日起3日内向国务院证券监督管理机构、证券交易所做出书面的报告,通知该上市公司,并予以公告。

解析:本例中涉及的术语和专有名词不少,securities trading(证券交易),a stock exchange(证券交易所),share(股份),the Securities Regulatory Authorities(证券管理机构),the State Council(国务院)等,这些词的翻译一定要符合规范,体现专业性。除了这些术语和专有名词以外,make...known to the public 这个动词短语译为"予以公告"也体现出法律专业特征,如果译成"让公众知晓"或"通知大家"则体现不出法律语言的特点。

例 22　The Vendor shall procure that the Purchaser acquires good title to the Shares free from all charges, lines, encumbrance and claims whatsoever.

译文:卖方应保证买方对该等股份享有有效的所有权,即该等股份之上无任何质押、留置、权利负担和主张。

例 23　Now therefore, in consideration of the premises, and the representations, warranties, covenants, and undertakings of the parties hereinafter set forth, and for other good and valuable consideration, the parties agree among themselves as follows.

译文:鉴于上述事实和各方在下文所做的陈述、保证、约定和承诺,及其他有效和充分的对价,现各方达成协议如下。

例 24　Party A is a company duly organized, validly existing and in good standing as a legal person under the laws of the PRC.

译文:甲方是依据中华人民共和国法律正式成立、有效存续和资格齐备的法人公司。

解析:上述例 22—24 中的原文都含有"good"一词,但肯定不能翻译成普通词汇"好"。"good"一词在法律文件中意思各种各样,我们看看各例句中由"good"构成的词组,以及各自的意思。在例 22 中,"good title"是指法律上有效的所有权,或无可争辩的所有权;例 23 原文中的"good consideration"系"consideration that is valid under the law"意思是法律上有效的约因或者对价;例 24 中的"in good standing"表示符合法律法规要求的,有资格的。上例中"good"一词的翻译必须符合专业化的原则,这样的译文才会更显地道专业。

除了法律专业词汇的翻译,还要注意法律文件中常用句法、句型等的翻译。例如,表示义务性规范的语言,汉语表达式为"有……义务","必须";英语表达式则为"It is the duty of…","have the duty to do sth.","shall"等;

例 25　中华人民共和国公民有依照法律纳税的义务。

参考译文:It is the duty of citizens of the People's Republic of China to pay taxes in accordance with the law.

例 26　Both husband and wife have the duty to practice family planning.

参考译文:夫妻双方均有实行计划生育的义务。

例 27　中华人民共和国公民有受教育的权利和义务。

参考译文:Citizens of the People's Republic of China have the duty as well as the right to receive education.

解析:表示授权性规范的语言,汉语表达式为"(享)有……权利","有权……","可以";英语表达式为"have the right to…","enjoy rights of…","be entitled to...","may"等。

例 28 Citizens and juristic persons shall enjoy the right of honor.

参考译文:公民、法人享有荣誉权。

综上所述,语言规范化原则主要是指在法律翻译中使用官方认可的规范化语言或书面语,以及避免使用方言和俚语。虽然在法律文书的起草和翻译中有许许多多的清规戒律,如慎用被动语态、外来语、重复语、缩略语等等。但译者必须采用专业规范的法律用语,尤其是现行法律中已有界定的词语,真正做到"法言法语"。

第三节 本章小结

以上所讲到的基本原则贯穿在整个法律翻译实践中,不论是合同翻译、立法文本翻译,还是司法文书翻译,都要严格遵循这些原则。译者应在实践中不断学习和体会,以使译文更加准确规范。

 课后习题

1. 根据所学法律英语的翻译原则,改正下列各句画线部分在原译文中的错误或不妥之处。

(1) The Seller shall present the following documents required for negotiation/collection to the banks.

原译:卖方必须将下列单据提交银行谈判或收取。

(2) Under the usance draft, the bearer shall present it to the payer for acceptance before the date of maturity.

原译:如为远期汇票,持票人应在汇票到期前交由付款人接受。

(3) The balance shall be settled upon the arrival of the goods at the port of destination.

原译:余款在货物到达目的港后结算。

(4) Shipment: To be shipped on or before February 28, 2007.

原译:装船:2007年2月28日前装船。

(5) Any claim by the Buyers regarding the goods shipped shall be filed within 15 days after arrival of the goods at the port of destination specified in the relative Bill of Lading and supported by a survey report issued by surveyor approved by the seller.

原译:买方对于装货的任何主张,必须于货到提单规定的目的地15天内提出,并须提供卖方同意的公证机构出具的检验报告。

(6) **Unless** it is legally or physically impossible, the contractor shall execute and complete the works and remedy the defects therein in strict accordance with the contract to the satisfaction of the engineer.

原译:除法律或自然条件不允许的情况之外,承包商应严格遵守合同,依照令工程师满意的标准施工并完工,并改正其中的缺陷。

(7) If such evidence is destroyed or **hidden**, then it would make it very difficult for the **plaintiff** to win the court case.

原译:若该等证据被销毁或收藏,则将大大增加原告人在法院取得案件胜诉的难度。

(8) The Borrower will not do or cause or permit to be done anything which may in any way **depreciate, jeopardize** or otherwise **prejudice the value** of the Agent's security hereunder.

原译:借款人将不会做出或促使或准许他人做出可能在任何方面损耗、妨害或以其他方式妨碍代理人在本契据项下之抵押品的价值的任何事情。

(9) The borrower hereby **irrevocably appoints** the agent and the receiver to be its attorney in accordance with the provision of Clause 13.

原译:借款人特此按照第13条规定作出一项不可撤销的委托,委任代理人及破产管理人作为其律师。

(10) This Agreement may be immediately terminated by one of the Parties, without compensation from either side, in case of bankruptcy, winding up, or legal or factual, direct or indirect, **taking over by a third party of the other party**.

原译:如果另一方破产、结束营业或第三方在法律上或事实上直接或间接接收另一方,任何一方可立即终止本协议,任何一方无需做出赔偿。

2. 根据法律英语的翻译原则,改正或改进下列各句原译文的错误或不妥之处。

(1) 新公司应建立经营管理机构负责企业的日常管理工作。

原译:The new company shall establish a management office which shall be responsible for its daily management.

(2) 本新区内外商投资企业生产的出口产品,除国家另有规定的产品之外,免征关税。

原译:Export products manufactured by foreign invested enterprise in the new Area, except those under other existing regulations by the State, shall be exempted from Customs duty.

(3) 公司职工依法组织工会,开展工会活动,维护职工的合法权益。

原译:The staff and workers of a company organize a trade union in accordance with the law to carry out union activities and protect the lawful rights and interests of the staff and workers.

（4）人民法院有权要求当事人提供或补充证据。

原译：A People's court shall have the authority to request the parties to provide or supplement evidence.

（5）如因违反合同而造成损失的，应由违反合同的一方承担经济责任。

原译：In case of losses caused by a breach of contract, the economic responsibility shall be borne by the party who has breached the contract.

（6）买方自1996年6月1日起分3年偿付卖方全部设备的总金额。

原译：The buyers shall settle the sellers the total value of the entire equipment by installments in three years stating from June 1st, 1996.

第四章

法律语言词汇的翻译

第一节 概 述

我国对外交往日益增多,随之而来的法律活动也日益频繁,因此,对国内外的法律文件的翻译需求空前旺盛。但是受法律翻译人员专业水平的影响,我国法律文件的翻译质量不容乐观。有些法律文件的翻译,并没有体现出法律文体的专业性和规范性,不符合法律词汇特征的翻译随处可见。此外,同一法律概念在同一文本中用多个不同的法律术语表述的情况也很常见。词汇是法律语言的基本组成部分,它包括俚语、术语、行话等。为了提高法律翻译的质量,有必要在了解法律词汇分类的基础上探讨其翻译的原则。

第二节 法律词汇的特点及翻译

一、法律术语

作为一种比较特殊的英语文体,法律英语要求用词准确,表意严谨。而法律英语术语是用来准确表达特有的法律概念的专门用语,具有明确的、特定的法律含义,其他词汇无法替代,是法律英语的精髓。了解这些对于正确理解和应用法律英语起到关键作用。根据法律英语术语的意义结构和语义范围可以把它归纳为常用术语、排他性专门涵义术语、专门法律术语和借用术语四种形式。

(一) 常用术语

法律英语常用术语有两种概念:
1. 不明确表示特定的法律概念,既常用于法律语言中,也是社会日常生活中普遍应用的词语,在两种语域中语义无差别,而且通俗易懂。例如:conduct(行为),write(签字),witness(证人),goods(商品),individual(个人),sum(总额),signing(签署),insurance(保险),gambling(赌博),rule(规则),marriage(婚姻),divorce(离婚)等等。

2. 原来仅表示特定的法律概念,随着法律知识的普及和法制的发展其应用范围不断扩大,结果原来只有法律工作者知晓的术语扩伸到全民词汇领域中。例如:law(法律),lawyer(律师),debt(债务),murder(谋杀),crime(罪行),prison(监狱),court(法庭),contract(合同),police(警察),will(遗嘱),fine(罚款),punishment(惩罚),sentence(判决),robbery(抢劫),theft(偷窃)等等。法律英语常用术语由于是法律工作者和全民通用的,所以其最大特点就是常用性及适用场合广。另外由于这类术语都是常用词,所以其构词能力较强,如 law, lawful 和 lawyer, crime criminal, contract contractual,而且有的具有多义性,应用时要注意词形变化和语境。

(二) 排他性专门涵义术语

这种术语指排斥与法律概念无任何联系的一般涵义而保留特定的法律涵义的法律专门用语。这类术语通常有普通意义方面的涵义和法律方面的涵义。由于两种涵义截然不同,所以必须通过排斥与法律无关的普通涵义才能确定其特定的法律涵义。这类术语的多义现象主要是由于词义范围在历史演变中扩大或缩小而产生的。据此,可将其分为两类形式:

1. 词义外延术语:许多法律专门术语由于其适用范围的扩大而渗透到日常生活中,这时它就不再只具有单一的法律概念了,而是有了普通意义。例如 alibi 是一个法律专门术语,意为"不在犯罪现场",现在词义已扩大为"借口,托辞",甚至还转化为动词"为……辩解"。下列例子中括号内为词汇的法律意义,括号外是其词义扩大到日常用语中的含义:Statute(法令),公司、学校等的章程,条例;jury(陪审团),竞赛时的评奖团;code(法典),电码。

2. 词义缩小产生的术语:与第 1 类术语相反,许多法律专门术语不是专门创造的,而是由于全民词汇的词义外延缩小而从日常生活转用到了法律方面形成的,即在原有一般词义的基础上赋予其新的表示法律概念的意义。例如日常生活用词"box"表示"盒,箱"之义,现在已成为表示法律概念的专门术语,表示"证人席,陪审席"。下列例子中括号内为词汇在日常用语中的含义,括号外是词汇的法律意义。parole(俘房),宣誓假释;complaint(报怨),控告,起诉;exhibit(展览),证据;deed(行为),契约;suit(请求,恳求,一套衣服),起诉。

排他性专门涵义术语由于表示法律概念精确,使用频率高,所以构成法律英语专门术语的主体部分。这类术语虽然都是常用词,但是在语义方面由于它的一般词义和法律专门涵义是截然不同的,所以一般只有精通法律英语的法律工作者才能懂得术语所表示的特定法律概念,而多数人一般只了解其一般涵义。法律英语用词的最大特点就是准确。这类术语有一词多义的特点,所以在实际应用中切不能望文生义,而是一定要借助语境正确理解,以免误用。例如:execution 的一般词义是"实施",但它的法律专门涵义指"(合同等的)执行";limitation 的一般词义是"限制",但它的法律专门涵义是"时效";omission 的一般词义是"省略",但它的法律专门涵义是"不作为";construction 的一般词义是"建筑",但它的法律专门涵义是"解释";determination 的一般词义是"确定",但它的法律专门涵义是"判决、决定";avoidance 的一般词义是"逃避",但它的法律专门涵义是"宣告无效"等等。

(三) 专门法律术语

这类术语因为符合术语的单义性、准确性和所表达的概念严格三个根本特征,所以是严格意义上的标准术语。这三个根本特征是术语和非术语的分界线,具备者为术语,不具备者为非术语。例如:plaintiff(原告)、defendant(被告)、recidivism(累犯)、bigamy(重婚罪)、proximate cause(近因)、negligence(疏忽)、homicide(杀人者)、affray(在公共场所斗殴罪)等就具备这些特征。这些术语名称和指称意义均单一,定义很严格,单义性的实际意义在于它可有效地防止误解,即使在较小的语境中也是如此。反之如果一个词语为多义词,其意义很多时候就难以确定。例如:He delivered a lengthy apology,如果没有具体的语境 apology 的含义就难以确定,因为它除了普通词义"道歉"外还有法律含义"辩护",如果这个词为单义就不会发生意义无法断定的现象。

(四) 借用术语

随着政治、经济和科技的发展,法律调整的内容越来越多,门类的划分也日趋细密,目前已发展成为一个体系庞大、门类众多、结构严密的学科。一些新的法律分支学科和边缘学科应运而生,相关领域内的专门术语大量涌入法律英语专门术语,其中许多术语已站稳脚跟,占有非常固定的一席之地。例如:sadism(性虐待狂)源自心理学,abortion(堕胎)源自医学,artistic work(艺术作品)源自艺术,continental shelf(大陆架)源自地理学,heredity(遗传)源自生物学,ratio(比率)源自数学,incest(乱伦罪)源自社会学,monogamy(一夫一妻制)源自人口学,tariff(关税)源自经济学,average(海损)源自运输,claims(索赔)源自对外贸易,life insurance(人寿保险)源自保险等等。借用术语来源之广,数量之大是很难估计的。随着法律调整内容的扩大,在传统公认的借用术语基础上,更多的借用术语进入法律术语是一种必然趋势。

上述所讲的法律术语的四种分类是相互联系,相互作用,相互协调的。它们之间有特定的语义联系,构成独特的有规律的术语体系,所以,应该既要看到每种术语的鲜明特征也不要忽略法律术语的体系性。

二、法律行话

任何建立在独特知识和技能之上的行业或者职业都会发展出一种独特的话语体

系,即所谓"行话"。一方面,行话确保了行业内部交流的准确,增进行业内部成员的团结;另一方面,它又是外显的符号,对于"外行人"而言,这种符号足以激发他们对于这个行业的好奇、尊重甚至畏惧感觉。法学家、律师、法官为了突出行业的特点,常使用与众不同的表达方式——使用法律术语和行话、套话。比如,burden of proof(举证责任),cause of action(案由),letters patent(专利证书),negotiable instrument(流通票据),reasonable doubt(合理的怀疑),等等。

"行话"与"术语"都是专业性词汇,但两者的规范程度不同。"术语"是规范性的专业用语,比"行话"更适用于书面文件。"术语"可以是对内的,如律师、法官讲话或者法官同律师交流可能使用必要的法律术语;也可以是对外的,如律师对客户——法律所服务的对象,或者普通大众,都可使用法律术语。"行话"完全是对内的,即同行的语言。以下是较为常见的法律行话:

abet	教唆
accessory	帮凶,从犯
accomplice	共犯,同谋
adhesion contract	附意合同
adverse possession	相反占有权
alleged	被指称、被指控的
alter ego	他我,另一个自我
at issue	系争点
case at bar	正在审讯的案件
case law	判例法
cause of action	诉由,案由
circumstantial evidence	环境证据,情况证据
clean hands	清白的
cloud on title	所有权的缺陷
condition precedent	先决条件
consequential damages	间接损害(失)
constructive	推定的
court below	下级法院
damages	赔偿金
day in court	出庭日
due care	应有的谨慎
due process of law	法律正当程序
fixture	(不动产的固定)附属品
foreclosure	取消赎回权的手续

grandfather clause	（新颁法律中的）不追溯条款
hung jury	意见分歧的陪审团
inferior court	初级法院，下级法院
insider trading	秘密交易
interstate commerce	（美）州际商业
issue of fact	事实上的争论点
issue of law	法律上的争论点
last clear chance	最后明显机会
latent defect	隐蔽的缺陷
legal fiction	法律拟制，法律上的假定
liquidated damages	约定违约金，预定违约赔偿金
material	重要的
meeting of the minds	意见一致
misdemeanor	轻罪，行为失检
negotiable instrument	流通票据
on all fours	完全一致的
order to show cause	陈述理由令
pierce the corporate veil	刺破公司面纱
plea bargain	认罪求情协议
preemptive right	优先购买权
prescriptive right	因时效而取得的权利
process	传票
pursuant to stipulation	依照协议
quash	撤销，废止
quiet enjoyment	享有平静权（购地产者不受他人干扰，安定地享有权益）
raise an issue	提出论点
reasonable doubt	合理的怀疑
reasonable man	理性的人
rebuttable presumption	可予驳回的推定
record	诉讼纪录
rescind	废除
retainer	律师聘请费
sequester	扣押（债务人的财产）
service of process	送达传票

sidebar	兼职律师
sharp practice	不择手段的赢利行为,欺诈
specific performance	特定履行令,强制履行令
stale claim	失效的债权(要求)
straw man	(非法交易中)被用作挡箭牌的人
subrogation	代位权
superior court	上级法院
time is of the essence	时间是至关重要的
winding up	结案
work product	(律师)工作成果
without prejudice	不使合法权利受到损害

使用法律行话的主要原因也是其含义的精确性。某些词语在普通英语中有多种意义,但是在法律行话中只有一个明确的含义,如"winding up"指"结案";"work product"指"(律师)工作成果";"record"指"诉讼纪录"等。一般人说"think","start",而在法律语言中则用"hold","commence"。法律行话的使用避免了法律从业人员之间因为不确定某一词的具体含义而造成误解或曲解。所以,翻译人员必须熟悉知晓常用法律行话、套话,才能给出准确的翻译,避免出错。

三、普通词汇表法律含义

在英语语言的发展过程中,词义的演变十分复杂。有些法律英语词汇根据立法和司法工作的实际需要从多义的普通英语词汇中分离出来,这些词语在普通英语中具有某种含义,而在法律英语中则具有另一种含义。下列常用词语是人们所熟知的一些单词或词组,然而在法律语言中他们却具有特定的法律意义。

常用词语	法律含义	汉译
assigns	a person to whom a right or property is assigned	受让人
bill	a draft law	法案
brief	a written statement submitted to a court	案件辩论书
color	apparent legal right	表面权利
consideration	benefit to the promisor or detriment to the promisee	约因,对价
counterpart	a duplicate of a document	副本
covenant	to make a binding solemn agreement	订立合同
cover	to purchase goods to replace those not delivered because of a breach of contract	抵偿
damages	the compensation sought for a loss	赔偿金

常用词语	法律含义	汉译
demise	to lease	转让，遗赠
demur	not to agree	抗辩，反对
depose	to state under oath	宣誓作证
discovery	disclosure of information by the opposing party in a lawsuit	取证
distress	the seizure of goods as security for an obligation	扣押
draft	an order for payment of money	付款通知单
endorsement	the signing of one's name on the back of a document	背书
equitable	relating to equity as opposed to law	平衡法的
finding	determination	判决，裁定
hand	signature	签字
honor	to pay or accept	承兑
instrument	a formal legal document	法律文书
interest	a right or claim to property	权益
issue	living descendants	子女
majority	legal age	法定年龄
master	an employer	雇主
motion	a formal request to a court to seek an order or rule	请求，申请
note	a written promise to pay a debt	票据
paper	an instrument evidencing a financial obligation	票据
party	a litigant in a lawsuit	诉讼当事人
plead	to lift pleadings	申诉
prayer	request for relief addressed to a court	诉讼请求
prejudice	a detriment to legal rights	损害（合法权利）
prescription	the acquisition of a right over a longer period	（取得或消灭）时效
presents	this formal legal document	本文件
provided	upon condition	只要，但是
purchase	to acquire title to land by means other than descent	置得（房屋、地产）
remove	to transfer to another court	移交案件
said	mentioned above	上述的
security	collateral	抵押品
serve	to deliver legal papers	送达（传票）

常用词语	法律含义	汉译
show	to make clear for evidence	证明
specialty	a contract under seal	盖章合同
tender	an offer of money	偿还
tenement	estate in land	地产
utter	to put something counterfeit into circulation	使用（伪币）
virtue	authority or reason	效力
waive	to relinquish	放弃

从以上的列举中我们可以看出普通词汇在法律语言中表达了特殊的法律意义。例如："damage"是造成的"损坏"而"damages"为"损害赔偿金"；"consideration"通常指"考虑""体贴"，而在法律英语中的含义是"对价""约因"。"majority"在法律英语中的含义是"法定年龄"，而不是"大多数"。"virtue"在法律英语中指"效力"；"honor"在法律中的含义是"承兑"；"present"一词在法律中的含义是"这个法律文件"，"by these Presents"的意思是"通过这份法律文件"。词组"without prejudice"的含义也不是"不存偏见"，它的意思是"不使合法权利受到损害"。判断是普通词汇还是法律英语词汇这需要结合一定语境或上下文才能确定。

四、古旧词汇的使用

法律英语词汇的另一个特征是经常使用现在已经很少使用的古旧词汇。古旧词汇包括古代英语和中世纪英语的词语。古英语指的是一直使用到公元1100年的英语，而中世纪英语是指在公元1100年到1500年期间使用的英语。这两个时期从拉丁语、法语和希腊语中借来的外来法律词语70%仍沿用至今。尽管在英美国家要求法律语言"简明大众化"，提倡法律人士在起草法律文件时应尽量避免使用这些词语，但是为了使法律文件句子简练、严谨，更好地反映出法律的文体特征，适当地使用古英语和中世纪英语词汇是有必要的。

一些词语在现代英语中，尤其是在现代英语口语中已不再使用，但在法律文书，或正式的司法场合仍在使用。古词 ye 是 you 的复数"你们"，在普通英语中已经不再使用了，但在法庭开庭时仍沿用 here ye "静听"（宣读、审判）或用古词 oyez "静听"。这里的 here ye 实际相当于现代英语中的 listen up! 使用古英语词语是法律英语词汇的特点之一，因为古英语词语可充分体现法律英语严谨严肃的文体特征。

旧体词均为副词，一般是 here，there 或 where 与 in，on，after，of 等介词结合构成的复合词。在句子中修饰动词时其位置与普通副词类似，修饰名词一般放在后面。here 类和 there 类，多在句中作副词，表示时间、地点、方式和条件等。where 类一般用作连词，也表示时间、地点、方式和条件。使用旧体词不仅可以使合同语言更为简练、规范、严肃,文体更为正式、庄重、严谨,而且避免了用词重复和文句冗长。因此,学会和掌握这类旧体词是十分重要的。

以下主要介绍以"here","there"和"where"为词根的三类旧体词。

(一) 以 here 为词根的旧体词

由于 here 一词的基本含义是"这里""此处",因此以"here"为词根的旧体词大都有"此……""这……""本……"的意思。

1. hereafter,hereinafter,hereunder

这三个词在含义和用法上大体相同,一般可以互相换用,汉译时都有"自此以后""此后下文中"等意思。只是相比之下,hereafter 较为正规、语气较重,hereinafter 和 hereunder 次之。请看例句:

例 1 This contract is made on this 15th day of July, 1986 by ABC Corporation (hereinafter referred to as "Sellers") who agrees to sell and XYZ Corporation (hereinafter referred to as "Buyers"), who agrees to buy the following goods on the terms and conditions as set forth below:

参考译文:本合同由 ABC 公司(以下简称"卖方")与 XYZ 公司(以下简称"买方")于 1986 年 7 月 15 日订立,双方同意按下述条款和条件进行交易:

译文解析:这是一句典型的合同文本的开头语,句中"hereinafter"意为"本合同下文中",用在文本开头,加重语气。

例 2 Each payment to be made hereunder shall be made in American currency.

参考译文:下文提及的每笔交易均应以美元为货币单位。

译文解析:句中 hereunder 也可换成 hereafter,意思不变,意为"本条款以下……"。

2. herein,hereof,herewith

这三个词词义相近,汉译时都可译成"在……中",但 herein 意为"in this..."(在……之中),一般修饰动词;hereof 意为"of this..."(……中的),一般修饰名词;herewith 意为"with this..."(与……一道),一般也修饰动词,试比较以下例句:

例 3 The Sellers reserve the right to cancel this contract at any time if they cannot make the delivery as called for under the terms hereof by reason of circumstances beyond their control.

参考译文:如果由于其自身无法控制的原因,卖方不能按本合同规定的条款交货,卖方保留随时取消合同的权利。

译文解析:"the terms hereof" 意为"the terms of this contract"。

例 4 Excusable Delay where the term is used in this Agreement shall mean those causes of delay specifically identified in Article 7 hereof(Excusable Delay).

参考译文:本协议中使用的"可谅解延迟"一词系指由本协议第七条(可谅解延迟)中特别规定的原因引起的延迟。

译文解析:"in Article 7 hereof"意为"in Article 7 of this agreement"

例 5　Please complete and return the form herein contained.

参考译文:请将文后随附的表格填好寄回。

译文解析:此处的"herein"有"herewith"的含义。

3. hereby,hereto

hereby 意为"by this..."(据此,特此),有时也有"still"、"therefore"(仍然、所以)之意。hereto 通常意为"relate to this..."(与此……有关)。

例 6　As A desires to export to B the goods specified herein and B desires to import the goods from A, A and B hereby agree as follows:

参考译文:鉴于甲方愿意向乙方出口本合同中所规定的物品,且乙方愿从甲方进口上述货物,据此,甲方和乙方特意订立下列条款:

译文解析:此句中的"hereby"意为"据此……"。

例 7　Notwithstanding the foregoing provisions, it is hereby agreed that a Party may transfer all or any part of its interest in the Joint Venture Company to its parent company, any of its subsidiaries or affiliated corporations.

参考译文:尽管有前述规定,各方特此同意任何一方可将其在合营企业中的全部或任何部分权益转让给其母公司、其任何子公司及关联公司。

译文解析:此句中的"hereby"意为"特此"。

(二) 以 there 为词根的旧体词

这类词的构成和用法同以 here 为词根的旧体词完全一样。在含义上,由于 there 的基本意思是"那里""那个方面",因此,以 there 为词根的旧体词在汉译时一般都有"那……""该……""其……"的意思。

例 8　Should either of the parties to the contract be prevented from executing contract by force majeure, such as earthquake, typhoon, flood, fire, war, etc., the prevented party shall notify the other party by cable without any delay, and within 15 days thereafter provide the detailed information of the events.

参考译文:合同任何一方,如因地震、台风、水灾、火灾或战争等不可抗力事件而不能履行本合同时,应立即电报通知对方,并应在之后的 15 天内提供详情。

译文解析:句中 thereafter 强调了"发生不可抗力事件之后的时间点",即"从那以后……"的含义。

例 9　"Statute" means *the Companies Law* (2002 Revised) of the Cayman Islands as amended and every statutory modification or reenactment thereof for the time being in force.

参考译文:"法令"指经修订的、现时有效的开曼群岛《公司法》(2002 年修订),以及对该法令的每一次法定修改或重新制定。

译文解析:句中"every statutory modification or reenactment thereof"意为"every statutory modification or reenactment of the Statute"(该法令协议)。

(三) 以 where 为词根的旧体词

以 where 为词根的旧体词一般使用较少,常用的词有两个:whereas 和 whereby。

1. whereas

在日常用语中 whereas 为连词,意为"而、却、反之"等,表示语气转折。在经济合同中其意通常为"鉴于""有鉴于"。请看以下例句:

例 10　Whereas, A Company is a manufacturer of X and has certain technical information and experiences which may be useful in developing the Product as hereinafter defined, the parties hereto agree as follows:

参考译文:鉴于 A 公司是 X 产品制造商,并拥有可用于开发下列产品的特定技术资料和经验,双方特此达成以下协议:

2. whereby

Whereby 相当于"by which…"结构,在句子中通常具有定语从句引导词的作用,意为"凭……""据……"等。

例 11　This contract is made in a spirit of friendly cooperation by and between Party A and Party B, whereby Party A shall invite Party B for service as a foreign staff on the terms and conditions stipulated as follows:

参考译文:甲方和乙方本着友好合作的精神签订本合同,甲方根据本合同聘请乙方为外籍工作人员,具体的条款和条件如下:

这三类旧体词的含义请参照下表(宋德文,2006:3):

词根	后缀	英文	汉译
here	-after	after this in the contract	在(此)下文
	-before	until this writing(now)	在(此)上文
	-by	in accordance with; by means of; by reason of	根据本…… 因此,特此
	-in	in this writing	在(于)本……
	-inbefore	before/until and including this writing	在(包括)此上文
	-inafter	later and including…in the same contract	在(包括)此下文
	-of	of this writing	对此,于此
	-to/-unto	① about this… ② to this…	关于,至此
	-under	later/under this writing	在下文
	-upon /on	about the point mentioning	就此,因此
	-with	(together) with this point	于此(一起)

(续表)

词根	后缀	英文	汉译
there	-after	after/since that	在(所指)以下
	-by	by that point/means; by that	(所指)因此
	-from	from that point to...	自(所指)
	-in	to the point referred	关于(所指)
	-inafter	after/since that point on	在(包括)所及以下
	-inbefore	before and including that point	在(包括)所及以上
	-of	of that point mentioned	(所指)由此
	-on	on/ about that	关于那一点
	-to	to that writing	(参见)那一点
	-under	later/under that writing	在(所指)以下
	-upon	on the effect of; therefore	因(那)所以
	-with	with that point	(所指)于此
Where-	as	considering/concerning that	根据,鉴于
	by	in accordance with/by what	根据,按照
	in	in (terms and conditions)	在(所指)中
	of	of/about the point noted	关于那(一项)
	on	on/to the point referred	在(所指)上

五、外来词的使用

　　法律英语词汇的第三个特点是经常使用外来词和短语。这主要指拉丁语和法语的大量引入。拉丁语在法律语言中处于权威性的地位。很多拉丁语法律格言和用语反映了法律背后的价值规范,有些涉及实体价值,例如:"Contra bonos mores" 英语解释为:"contrary to good morals",意即"违背善良风俗的"。有些则涉及程序价值,例如:"Accusare nemo se debet" 英语解释为:"nobody is bound to incriminate himself",意即"一个人不应被强迫去做出对其不利的证词"。拉丁词语具有言简意赅、约定俗成、表达更为标准的特点。以下是一些常在法律文件中出现的拉丁语单词、短语以及一些拉丁谚语的举例。

拉丁词语	英文含义	汉译
ab initio	from the beginning	从开始起;自始
ad hoc	for this purpose	特别,临时
ad litem	for the lawsuit	为了诉讼(目的)
alibi	elsewhere (a defense that the accused was elsewhere when the offense was committed)	不在犯罪现场

第四章 法律语言词汇的翻译

拉丁词语	英文含义	汉译
amicus curiae	friend of the court	法庭之友（法院临时顾问）
arguendo	for the sake of argument	为争论起见
bona fide	good faith	真诚的，善意的
casus belli	an act justifying war	宣战原因
casust	a warning	当心
caveat emptor	let the buyer beware	购者当心（购物者自慎，出门不换）
Damnum absque injuria	a loss without injury	不能依法获得补偿的损害
de minimis	negligible, minimal	微量的
de novo	anew	重新
ejusdem generis	of the same class	同类
et al	and others	以及其他等等
ex parte	from one side	片面的，偏袒一方的
expressio unius est exclusio alterius	the express mention of one is the exclusion of another	明示其一即排斥其他
flagrante delicto	in the commission of the offense	犯罪时刻
forum non conveniens	inconvenient forum	不便审理的法院
generalia specialibus non derogant	general words do not derogate from special words	一般不能背离个别 一般法不会损害特别法
habeas corpus	you should have the body	人身保护令状
in pari materia	upon the same subject	有关同一事宜
in propria persona	in his own proper person	亲自
in re	in the matter of	关于，案由
inter alia	among others	在其他事物中
lex loci	the law of the place	属地法
mala fides	bad faith	恶意
nil	nothing	（什么都）没有
non compos mentis	not of sound mood	精神不健全
non obstante veredicto	notwithstanding the verdict	相反的裁决
non sequitur	it dose not follow	不合理的推论
noscitur a sociis	it is know from its associates	文理解释

拉丁词语	英文含义	汉译
nunc pro tunc	now for then	现在代替过去
pari passu	with equal step	公平地,不分先后
per capita	by heads	人均
per curiam	by the court as a whole	依全体法院(同意)
per se	by itself	自身,本身
per stirpes	by roots	按家系(分配无遗嘱的遗产)
pro rata	in proporation	按比例计
pro tem	for the time being	临时,暂时
quid pro quo	something for something	相等的补偿或报酬,对价
quorum	the minimum number of members who must be present for a deliberative assembly to legally transact business	法定人数
reddendo singula singulis	rendering each to each	各对各,各从其文字的本义
scienter	having knowledge	明知,知情
scintilla	little spark	一点点(微弱的证据)
seriatim	one after another	逐条,依次
sine qua non	without which it could not be	绝对必须(的条件或资格)
situs	location	地点,位置
stare decisis	to stand by the decided matters	服从前例
sua sponte	of one's own will	自愿的
sui generis	of its own kind	独特的,自成一类的
ultra vires	beyond the power	越权行为
vel non	or not	或者不
versus	against	诉,对

请看下列常用拉丁谚语:

例 12 Modus et conventio vincunt legem.

英译:Custom and agreement overrule law.

汉译:习惯与合意可以使法律无效。

例 13 Ignorantia facti excusat—Ignorantia juris non excusat.

英译:Ignorance of fact excuses—ignorance of the law does not excuse.

汉译:对事实的不知情可以作为借口,但对法律的无知却不能成为开脱(罪责)的借口。

例 14　Ut poena ad paucos, metus ad omnes perveniat.

英译：That by punishing a few, the fear of punishment may affect all.

汉译：通过惩罚少数人，可以威慑所有人。

例 15　Nullus commodum capere potest de injuria sua propria.

英译：No man should benefit from his own injustice.

汉译：任何人均不得从其不公正立场中获益。

例 16　Res inter alios acta alteri nocere non debet.

英译：A transaction between two parties shouldn't operate to the disadvantage of a third party not in their debt.

汉译：两方当事人之间达成的交易不得损害善意第三方的利益。

拉丁词语很简短，并且这些拉丁词语在法律界沿用了若干个世纪，其含义被界定得十分精确，这些词的运用有助于体现法律文体的严谨和庄重。

法律英语中引入的另一大外来语就是法语了。1066 年诺曼底公爵威廉征服英格兰，法语成为统治语言。法语作为英国法律的通用语言使用至 15 世纪末期。尽管现在法语不再是英国法律的语言，但是很多古法语和法律法语中的词语被保留下来。法律英语词汇中属法语词源的词语数量还是相当大的，而且这些词语已进入基本的法律英语词汇。由于法语词汇形态和发音与英文词汇极其相似，一般人无法辨认法律英语中源自法语的词语。

下面列出法律英语中常见的古法语词语及其英译和汉译。

古法语词	英译	汉译
action	lawsuit	诉讼
alien	to transfer property	转让
assigns	assignees	代理人，受托人，受让人
cestui que trust	beneficiary of a trust	信托受益人
chance-medley	sudden quarrel or fight	非有意伤害或伤人
chose in action	a thing in action	诉讼上的财产，权利上的财产
color	reason, pretext	假托，借口
curtesy	rights of a husband to a wife's property	鳏夫对亡妻的遗产收益权
cy pres	as near as possible	近似原则
delict	wrong; offense	不法行为
demise	grant; lease; death	遗赠，（引起遗赠的）死亡

古法语词	英译	汉译
demur	not to agree	抗辩,反对
easement	a right over use of the property of another person	地役权
en ventre sa mere	in the womb	腹中胎儿,待生胎儿
fee	an inheritable estate in real property	祖传土地,继承的不动产
feme sole	a single women	未婚女子
issue	progeny	子女,后嗣
laches	neglect to assert a right or claim	对行使权利的疏忽、怠慢
lien	an encumbrance on property for the payment of debt	留置权,抵押权
malfeasance	wrongdoing	渎职,滥用职权
mesne	middle,intermediary	(诉讼)中间(程序)的
moiety	the half of anything	(财产等的)一半
ordain	to appoint or order	任命,委任
oyez	hear ye!	肃静
parol	oral	口头的
petty	small,minor	小的,次要的
puisne	junior,inferior	年轻的,资历浅的
purview	principal provisions of a statute or contract	法规文本,条款部分
record	official text of court proceedings	诉讼记录
remise	to give up	让与
residue	all other property	剩余财产
save	except	除……之后
seisin	possession of real property	占用,扣押
specialty	a contract under seal	盖印合同(契约)
style	case name	判例名称
suit	lawsuit	诉讼
suffer	permit	允许
tenant pur auter vie	tenant during the life of another person	(以他人寿命为期的)租户
tort	a wrong or injury	侵权

法律英语中保留的法律法语词语的主要原因是这些法语词语的法律意义比较单一确定,不易产生歧义。有些法律法语词语与普通法律词语是一样的,如"suit"(诉讼),"alien"(转让),"issue"(子女)等,因为在英法两种语言中,这些词的拼写是相同的,含义也大致相同。

六、近义词的并用

英美法规、法律文件(包括契约、遗嘱、信托协议等)中经常有一个句子中出现几个近义词并列的情况,这是我们在翻译上很棘手的一个问题。有时只需要一个词表达,为何要经常连用几个近义词?其实这是法律英语词汇的重要特征之一。近义词的连用有时是为了区别近义词之间的不同涵义,有的则仅是为了表达一个涵义。因此近义词的使用可以分为求异型近义词和求同型近义词两种。

(一)求异型近义词

这种类型的近义词着眼点在各近义词的意义差别部分。请看下面的例子:

例 17 In the course of interpreting or constructing the contract,...

解析:该句中,interpret 与 construct 两词都有解释的意思。但是其意义还是有差别的。interpret 是指意图解释法,即依文件起草背景来确定起草者真实意图的解释。而 construct 是指文意解释法,即严格按字面意义进行的解释。并列使用这一对近义词的目的是区分这对近义词的意义差别之处。翻译时就不能拘泥于其表面涵义,而要使用能体现出其差别的合适的中文词,这才是真正准确的译文。

例 18 Any Crown Servant...solicits or accepts any advantages shall be guilty of an offense

解析:该句中的 solicit 与 accept 两词均有"接受"的意思,其差别点在于 solicit 侧重于招致和勾引(别人的行贿),而 accept 侧重于接受本身,所以二者的中文译文应分别为"招引"(solicit)与"接受"(accept)。

求异型近义词在近义词的使用中占主要地位,其主要目的就是使用这些有细微差别的词来表达法律上的不同意义,翻译时应仔细推敲词与词之间的细微差别,这样的译文才能做到准确严谨。

(二)求同型近义词

除了求异型近义词,在法律语言中还存在着一类很特殊的近义词类型,即"求同型近义词"。与求异型近义词相比,求同型词是少数,但对这一类近义词的理解却比求异型要复杂,对译者的要求也更高。

例 19 ...Any such advantages as is mentioned in this Ordinance is customary in any profession, trade, vocation or calling.

解析:该句中有 profession/trade/vocation/calling 四个近义词,这四个近义词既

有意义重叠的部分,也有意义差异之处。

按照 OED 的解释,"职业"是四个词的共同义项:

Profession: Any calling or occupation by which a person habitually earns his living.

Trade: Anything practiced for a livelihood.

Calling: Ordinary occupation, means by which livelihood is earned.

Vocation: One's ordinary occupation, business or profession.

这四个词虽然都解释为"职业",但是其所强调的重点是不一样的。Profession 可特指神学界、法学界与医学界人士,有时亦指军界人士;Trade 可特指商人与熟练的手艺人;Calling 与 Vocation 都曾有神职、神圣事业的意思。

例 20 The seller shall pay all the customs duties and tariffs for export of the Equipment.

解析:例句中的 custom duties and tariffs 也是求同型近义词,所以两个词表达了同一个意思——关税。

例 21 This Law is formulated and enacted in order to protect the lawful rights and interests of the parties to contracts, safeguarding the socio-economic order and promote the progress of the socialist modernization drive.

解析:例句中的 formulate and enact 就是求同型近义词,法律英语中的"制定本法"常翻译为:"This Law is formulated and enacted"。

请看下面常出现的近义词连用:

acknowledge and confess	act and deed
adjust, compromise, and settle	advice, opinion, and direction
agree and covenant	aid and abet
all and every	all and singular
alter or change	annul and set aside
any and all	assign, transfer
assume and agree	attorney and counselor at law
bind and obligate	build, erect or construct
business, undertaking	by and through
by and with	cancel and set aside
cancel and terminate	cease and desist
cease and come to an end	cease and terminate
chargeable or accountable	changes and modifications
conjecture and surmise	consolidation
convey, transfer	costs, charges and expenses

第四章
法律语言词汇的翻译

deem and consider
documents and writings
due and payable
each and every
entirely and completely
excess and unnecessary
fair and reasonable
final and conclusive
fit and proper
for and during
for and on behalf of
fraud and deceit
free and unfettered
from and after
furnish and supply
give and bequeath
good and sufficient
heed and care
if and when
in and to
in truth and in fact
keep and maintain
legal and binding
levies and assessments
loans or advances
lot, tract or parcel
made and provided
make, declare, and publish
meet and just
mentioned or referred to
modified and changed
nominate, constitute
obligation and liability
observe, perform
ordain and establish

execute and perform
due and owing
each and all
engage, hire and employ
evidencing and relating to
fair and equitable
false and fraudulent
finish and complete
fit and suitable
for and in consideration of
force and effect
free and clear
free and without consideration
full and complete
give and grant
goods and effects
have, hold, and possess
hold and keep
in and for
in my stead and place
indebtedness and liabilities
kind and character
let or hindrance
lien, charge or encumbrance
loss or damages
made and entered into
made, ordained and appointed
maintenance and upkeep
mend, maintain, and repair
mind and memory
nature or description
null, void and of no force
obey, observe and comply with
of and concerning
order and direct

order, adjudge, and decree	over, above
pay, satisfy, and discharge	peace and quiet
perform and discharge	performance or observance
place, install or affix	possession and control
power and authority	release and discharge
relieve and discharge	remise, release and quitclaim
rest and remainder	revoked and annulled
right, title and interest	rights and remedies
rules and regulations	save and except
seized and possessed	sell, transfer, and dispose of
shun and avoid	signed, published
situate, lying, and being in	sole and exclusive
stipulate and agree	suffer or permit
suit, claim or demand	supersede and displace
term or covenant	terminate, cancel or revoke
then and in that event	true and correct
truth and veracity	type and correct
understood and agreed	unless and until
vacate, surrender	void and of no effect
void and of no force	void and of no value

七、模糊词语

法律语言的模糊性，是指某些法律条文或法律表述在语义上不能确指，模糊是表达模糊语义的语言，即内涵无确指，外延不确定的语言。一般用于涉及法律事实的性质、范围、程度、数量无法明确的情况下。如 reasonable time（合理的时间），什么时候才是合理时间呢？还有表示程度的术语：appropriate，take appropriate action（采取适当的行动），怎样才是适当的行动？以及在法律英语中经常出现，如"more than, less than, not more than"等。其实这与法律语言的准确性并不矛盾。之所以使用含义模糊的词汇或表达方式，是为了让意思表达更充分、完整，给执行法律留下足够的空间。法律文献无法把每一种可能都穷尽，不仅不可能也没必要。所以法律英语中含义模糊的词汇或表达方式是为了让意思更充分而使用的，它完全不同于意思含混。

例 22 Whoever conceals, destroys or unlawfully opens another person's letter, thereby infringing upon the citizen's right to freedom of correspondence, if the circumstances are **serious**, shall be sentenced to fixed-term imprisonment of not more than one year or criminal detention.

参考译文:隐匿、销毁或者非法拆开他人信件,侵犯公民通信自由权利,情节严重的,处一年以下有期徒刑或者拘役。

译文解析:本句中的"serious"一词用的就是模糊的表达方式。因为严重到什么程度,没有说明,也无法说明。

在法律英语中是可以使用模糊词语的,但是,不是随意使用的。一般来说在以下条件下可以使用模糊的词语和表达方式。

(1) 在立法上为了更准确地表述法律,最大限度地打击犯罪。

例 23　Whoever commits arson, breaches a dike, causes explosion, spreads poison or uses **other** dangerous means to sabotage any factory, mine, oilfield, harbor, river, water source, warehouse, house, forest, farm, threshing grounds, pasture, key pipeline, public building or any **other** public or private property, thereby endangering public security but causing no serious consequences, shall be sentenced to fixed-term imprisonment of not less than three years but not more than ten years.

参考译文:放火、决水、爆炸、投毒或者以其他危险方法破坏工厂、矿物、油田、港口、河流、水源、仓库、住宅、森林、农场、谷场、重要管道、公共建筑物或者其他公私财产,危害公共安全,尚未造成严重后果的,处3年以上10年以下有期徒刑。

译文解析:本句中的"other"就是一个模糊词语,在列举了主要的犯罪手段和破坏项目之后,再加上"other dangerous means"和"other public of private property"这样的模糊词语,就使这一规定的外延大大扩展了,不仅表述更加严密而且达到了更大限度打击犯罪的目的。如果把模糊词语省略掉或改用确切词语,一方面会使立法失去严谨性,另一方面也很有可能使现实生活中的大量违法犯罪逃脱法律的制裁。

(2) 增强语言表达的灵活性。

在法律事务中,特别是在外交场合,为了避免把话说得过死、太绝,而拴住自己的手脚,说话人往往运用模糊语言来表达自己的观点。

例 24　在《中华人民共和国和美利坚合众国联合公报》中有这么一段:

...and that it intends to **gradually reduce** its sale of arms to Taiwan, leading, over a period of time, to a final resolution.

汉译:……它(美国)准备逐步减少它对台湾的武器出售,并在经过一段时间后,找到最终的解决方案。

解析:本句中对于究竟何时停止向台出售武器,用 gradually reduce(逐步减少),而未说明具体时间。

例 25　The two sides will **maintain contact** and **hold appropriate consultations** on bilateral and international issues of common interest.

汉译:双方将就共同关心的双边问题和国际问题保持接触并进行适当的磋商。

解析:本句中的 maintain contact(保持接触)和 hold appropriate consultations(进

行适当的磋商)都是模糊词语,用来表示一些未定的概念。谁也说不出它们究竟意味着多大程度,但在这里用却是恰如其分,非常贴切,这比用精确的数字表示得更准确,也更有说服力。

(3) 出于礼貌或为了使言语表达更委婉、含蓄。

例 26　Unless this account is paid within next ten days, we will **take further measures**.

参考译文:除非在10天内把账付清,否则我们就将采取进一步措施。

译文解析:本句中的"take further measures"就是模糊词语,它完全可以用"start legal proceedings"或"bring suit"等词语来取代,但是这里为了表达得更委婉含蓄而没有用这样确定的词语来表述。

模糊词语和模糊表达是法律翻译中很棘手的难题,如何翻译模糊词语呢?一般来说,可采取的方法有以下几种:

(1) 对等译法

也就是两种不同语言之间的直译。在有些情况下,尤其是在法律文件起草人可能是有意使用模糊词语时,我们可以采取模糊对等翻译,即用一种语言的模糊词语去翻译另一种语言的模糊词语。

例 27　We the people of the United States, in order to form a more **perfect** union, establish justice, insure domestic tranquility, provide for the **common** defense, promote the **general** welfare, and secure the blessings of liberty to ourselves and our posterity, do ordain and establish this Constitution for the United States of America.

参考译文:我们,合众国的人民,为了建立一个更为完善的联邦、树立公正公平、保障国内安宁、建立共同的国防、提高大众福利,并为确保我们自身和后代能享受自由,特确立并制定本美利坚合众国宪法。

译文解析:本句中的"perfect","common","general"三个模糊词语,对应汉语可译成"完善的""共同的""大众的"。

例 28　If a sentence of imprisonment is imposed, there are limits on the term of imprisonment — **more than** six months and **less than** three years.

参考译文:如判其入狱服刑,则须限制刑期——6个月以上、3年以下。

译文解析:英语中的"more than"和汉语中的"超过、以上","less than"和"少于、以下"可谓模糊对模糊。

例 29　It was reported by the police that murderer was **thin** and **gaunt** with **deep** wrinkles in the back of his neck.

参考译文:据警方报道,该杀人犯又瘦又憔悴,后颈上有很深的皱纹。

译文解析:这个句子中有三个英语模糊词"thin","gaunt"和"deep",可把它们相应译成三个汉语模糊词"瘦","憔悴"和"深"。

（2）变异译法

有时，一种语言中用一个词表达模糊概念，可在翻译时却用另一种语言的非对等词来表达相同的模糊概念，这就是模糊变异译法。

例 30　The state constitution provides that it is lawful for the citizens to carry guns. In recent years <u>hundreds and hundreds of</u> innocent people have died of this and one needs to look for a lesson.

参考译文：该州宪法规定，公民携带枪支是合法的。正因为如此，近年来成千上万无辜百姓惨遭枪击身亡，教训历历在目。

译文解析：本句中 hundreds and hundreds of 的意思是"几百"，这里译作"成千上万"，就是运用了模糊变异译法。

（3）具体情况，灵活处理

翻译就是用一种语言来表达已用另一种语言表达出来的思想，它涉及的两个方面就是对一种语言的正确理解和用另一种语言来准确的表达。由于英汉两种语言的差异所在，有时候可以在不影响理解的基础上，灵活处理。比如，在一种语言中用的是语义精确的表达式，而在翻译时却可根据具体情况，译为模糊词语。反之，原文中用模糊的表达式，翻译时却可化模糊为精确。这种方法在法律英语翻译中同样适用。

例 31　It is <u>two and two makes four</u> that the corporal punishment administered by the defendant was minimal, and not excessive.

参考译文：很显然，被告所施加的体罚属最低限度而并未过当。

译文解析：本句中"two and two makes four"是确切词语，这里译作模糊词语"很显然"。

和文学或其他文体相比，模糊词语的运用要少得多，因为法律英语推崇的是准确严谨。所以，在法律英语的翻译中，遇到模糊词，要根据具体的语境来反复斟酌推敲，这样的译文才能准确得体。

请看下面的模糊词语及其汉译：

adequate	适当的
all reasonable means	非常合理的手段
apparently	显然地
clear and convincing	明确并令人信服的
compelling	强制的
consequential	相应而生的，接着发生的
direct	直接的，直系的
doubt	疑问，疑惑
due care	应有的谨慎
due process	正当程序

duly	正当地,适当地,充分地
excessive	额外的
improper	不适当的
inadequate	不充分的
incidental	非主要的,附带的
in connection with	关于,有关
inconsequential	不重要的,无足轻重的
like	同……一样
malice	蓄意,恶意
manifestly	显然地
meaningfully	具有重要意义或价值地
negligence	过失
obviously	明显地
quite	相当地
reasonable care	应有的照顾,应有的注意
reasonable man	理性的人
reasonable speed	合理的速度
related	相关的
satisfactory	符合要求的
serious misconduct	严重的不当行为
significantly	显著地,意义重大地
similar	类似的,相似的
somewhat	稍微,有点
soon	不久,很快
substantially	大体上地
sufficient	足够的
undue	不当
unreasonable	不合理的
virtually	事实上,实际上

八、准确词语

法律英语有其独特的语言风格特点,而其中最重要、最本质的特点就是语言的准确性。"法无明文规定不为罪",这就要求法律语言要有高度的准确性,只有这样法律规范的内容和领域才能明确界定,法律的效力才能够得以发挥。准确性也是法律语言的权威性和严肃性所要求的。

第四章
法律语言词汇的翻译

例 32 The death penalty may be imposed only for offences of treason, piracy or setting fire to any of Her Majesty's warships or dockyards. It may not in any event be passed on a person **under 18 years of age**, not on a **expectant mother**.

参考译文:死刑仅适用于叛国罪、海盗罪或纵火烧毁女王陛下之任何战舰或造船厂等三种犯罪。无论如何死刑不适用于未满18岁者或孕妇。

译文解析:在此法律条文中,用了三个具体的词语来说明死刑的使用范围,但是又用"under18 years of age"和"expectant mother"这两个具体词语对两种情况予以排除,将死刑的使用范围界定得更加精确。

第三节 本章小结

本章主要介绍了法律词汇的分类及其翻译方法。法律词汇是法律英语的基础,有着明显区别于普通英语的鲜明特征,在了解了其分类的基础上一定要多读多看多积累,在使用中推敲和体会,力求用词精准得当,这样译出来的文章才能算是一篇佳作。

 课后习题

1. 仔细阅读下列句子及其译文,分析各句中画线词语的含义与其在普通英语中含义的差异。

(1) Flexibility provisions, i.e., **swing, carry over and carry forward**, applicable to all restrictions maintained pursuant to this Article, shall be the same as those provided for in MFA bilateral agreements for the 12-month period prior to the entry in to force of the WTO Agreement.

译文:按照本条所保持的一切数量限制的灵活条款(即调用、留用和借用),应与在WTO协议生效前的12个月期间多种纤维协定项下双边协定的灵活条款相同。

(2) A **determination of injury** for purposes of Article VI of GATT1994 shall be based on positive evidence and involve an objective examination of both (a) the volume of the **dumped imports** and the effect of the dumped imports on prices in the domestic market for **like products**, and (b) the consequent impact of these imports on domestic producers of such products.

译文:1994年关贸总协定第6条的损害确定应根据确实的证据做出,并包括对下述两方面的客观审查:(a)倾销的进口产品的数量和倾销的进口产品对国内市场同类产品价格造成的影响;以及(b)这些进口产品对国内同类产品商造成的后续影响。

(3) These rules shall apply to all vessels upon the high seas and in all waters connected **therewith** navigable by seagoing vessels.

译文：本规则各条适用于在公海和连接于公海而可供海船航行的一切水域中的一切船舶。

(4) In the case of a contract which, according to the laws or administrative regulations of the People's Republic of China, is to be formed with the approval of the state, the assignment of the contractual rights and obligations **shall** be subject to the approval of the authority which approved the contract, unless otherwise stipulated in the approved contract.

译文：中华人民共和国法律、行政法规规定应当由国家批准成立的合同，其权利和义务的转让，应当经原批准机关批准，但是已批准的合同中另有约定的除外。

(5) If any other Party shall come under the control of any third Party or parties other than by which it is controlled at the date hereof or other than by an Affiliate of it for the purposes of a **bona fide** reorganizing...

译文：如果另一方为任何第三方所控制（在本合同之日受其控制或为善意重组之目的受一家关联公司控制的除外）……

(6) The formation of this contract, its validity, interpretation, execution and settlement of disputes in connection herewith shall be governed by the laws of the People's Republic of China, but in the event that there is no published and **publicly available** law in the PRC governing a particular matter relating to this Contract, reference shall be made to general international commercial practices.

译文：本合同的订立、效力、解释、执行及合同争议的解决，均受中华人民共和国法律管辖。中国颁布的法律对合同相关的某一事项未做规定的，参照国际商业惯例。

(7) A warranty, representation, undertaking, indemnity, covenant or agreement on the part of two or more persons binds them **jointly and severally**.

译文：两人或两人以上的保证、陈述、承诺、赔偿、约定或协定，各人共同和分别受其约束。

(8) The date of the receipt issued by transportation **department concerned** shall be regarded as the date of delivery of the goods.

译文：由承运的运输机构所开具的收据的日期即被视为交货日期。

(9) If the Non-Disposing Party **elects** to purchase the interest to be transferred at fair market value, the Non-Disposing Party shall include in the Acceptance Notice that it **so elects**, and shall include in the Acceptance Notice a list of at least two international recognized accounting firms with experience in conducting valuations in China.

译文:如果非转让方决定以公共视为市价购买拟转让的股权,应在接受通知中表明其此等意向,并在其中列出至少两家在中国进行评估方面具有经验的国际知名会计事务所的名单。

(10) The information contained in this announcement is accurate and complete in all **material** aspects.

译文:本公告所载信息在各主要方面概属准确完备。

2. 仔细阅读下列句子及其译文,找出译句中能体现相关法律英语词汇特点之处并加以分析。

(1) 合同生效后,当事人就质量、价款或者报酬、履行地点等条款没有约定或者约定不明确的,可以协定补充。

译文:If, after the contract made by and between the parties becomes effective, there is no agreement therein on the terms and provisions regarding quality, price or remuneration and place of performance, etc., or such agreement is unclear, the parties may, through consultation, agree upon supplementary terms and provisions.

(2) 保管期届满或者寄存人提前领取保管物的,保管人应当将原物及其孳息归还寄存人。

译文:If the safekeeping duration expires or the depositor claims and retrieves the article before the expiry date, the safekeeping party shall return to the depositor the original article and the interest generated therefrom.

(3) 合营企业的一切活动应遵守中华人民共和国的法律、法令和有关条例规定。

译文:All the activities of a joint venture shall comply with the provision of the laws, decrees and pertinent regulations of the People's Republic of China.

(4) 第一次董事会会议应在公司营业执照签发后一个月内召开。

译文:The first board meeting shall be convened within one month after the issuance of the Company's business license.

3. 请写出表格中拉丁语的英文和中文含义,并将用法举例中的英文译成中文。

拉丁词语	英文含义	中文含义	用法举例
ab initio			trespass ab initio
ad interim			an ad interim report
ad litem			agent ad litem
alibi			lodge a special defense of alibi

（续表）

拉丁词语	英文含义	中文含义	用法举例
bona fide			bona fide holder
			bona fide error
mala fide			mala fide business purpose
bona fides（用作单数）			a party whose bona fides is unshakable
mala fides（用作单数）			the mala fides of the company
de novo			a case tried de novo
ex parte			an ex parte testimony
flagrante delicto			be caught flagrante delicto
habeas corpus			Habeas Corpus Act 1679
in personam			in personam action (action in personam)
in rem			in rem action (action in rem)
inter alia			The contract stipulates, inter alia, that the parties shall submit any dispute to arbitration.
lex loci			lex loci actus
non obstante verdicto			judgment non obstante verdicto
nunc pro tunc			nunc pro tunc judgment
per capita			per capita consumption
per curiam			per curiam opinion/decision

（续表）

拉丁词语	英文含义	中文含义	用法举例
per se			negligence per se, per se negligence nuisance per se, per se nuisance
pro rata			pro rata contribution
pro tem/tempore			pro tempore judge
seriatim			deliver their opinions seriatim
sui generis			sui generis qualities
ultra vires			ultra vires act
versus			the plaintiff versus the defendant

第五章

典型法律句式翻译

由于法律文本意思艰深晦涩、用词古板守旧、句型复杂冗长等特点,使得法律翻译的难度大大高于其他类型的翻译实践。法律文本用词用语有僵化的倾向,某些句型重复使用的频率非常高;而且,法律翻译的一个重要原则就是保持术语和句型结构在译文中的同一性。因此,如果能掌握此类典型句型的翻译,可以大大提高法律翻译工作的效率。本章撷取法律文本中的高频句型并就其典型译法进行讲授。

第一节 典型法律英语句式的翻译及解析

一、Otherwise 的翻译

Otherwise 在法律英语中的用法主要有三种:(1) 跟 unless 引导的句子连用,引导让步状语从句;(2) 放置在连词 or 之后使用;(3) 与 than 连用,通常用来否定句子的主语。

例 1 In this Article, unless the context otherwise requires: "Afternoon" means the period of a day between noon and midnight;

译文:除上下文另有规定外,本条中,"下午"指一天中正午到午夜之间的时间段。

分析:Unless the context otherwise requires...意思是"除……另有……外";有时这个结构也以被动形式出现,如 unless in any enactment it is otherwise provided,...(除成文法另有规定外)。

例 2 Unless otherwise instructed and except as provided in Article 5, a bank presenting a documentary draft shall:

译文:除非另有指示,且除第 5 条中另有规定外,提示跟单汇票的银行必须做到下列各项:

分析:原句中用的是 unless otherwise 引导被动从句的省略结构。

例 3 "Settle" means to pay in cash, by clearing-house settlement, in a charge or credit or by remittance, or otherwise as agreed.

译文:"结算"指以现金支付,通过票证清算行结算,通过借记或贷记方式结算,通过汇付结算,或以当事人约定的其他方式结算。

分析:如果 otherwise 与 or 连用,其意思与起连接作用的连词 or 之前的短语相同。

例 4 All certificates for shares shall be consecutively numbered or otherwise identified and shall specify the shares to which they relate.

译文:所有的股权凭证应连续编号或者以其他方式识别,且其应标明该等股权证书代表的股份。

例 5 No Contract or any part hereof shall be revoked otherwise than—by another Contract executed in accordance with section 5.

译文:合同或其任何部分均不得撤销,除非根据第 5 条签订的另一份合同而撤销。

分析:otherwise than 在法律句式中一般只用在否定句中,作用相当于 unless 或 by other means than...,otherwise 只起一个方式状语的作用。译为"除了……之外,除非"。

例 6 No will or any part hereof, which is in any manner revoked, shall not be revived otherwise than by the re-execution hereof in accordance with section 5.

译文:遗嘱的全部或任何部分,无论以任何方式撤销后,其全部或任何部分效力均不能恢复,除非按照第 5 条之规定重新签订。

二、Where 引导的从句

在普通英文中,用 where 引导的状语从句,一般为地点状语从句。但在法律英文中,where 引导的是条件状语从句,相当于"in the case where"。其最典型的译法是"凡……" or "如……"。

例 7 All disputes arising in connection with or during the performance of this Contract shall be settled through friendly negotiations. Where settlement cannot be reached, the disputes shall be submitted for arbitration.

译文:所有与本合同有关的或在履约过程中发生的争议,均应通过友好协商的方式解决。如果协商无法解决,应将争议提交仲裁。

例 8 Where the Borrower has full power and authority to enter into this Agreement, to make the borrowings, to execute and deliver the Note and to incur the obligations arising therefrom, all the actions in question shall, properly and necessarily, be authorized by legal persons.

译文:借款人拥有充分的权力订立本协议、借贷资金、签署并交付票据并承担由此产生的义务,上述全部相关行为均应经法人适当和必需的授权。

分析：where 引导条件状语从句，有时在翻译中可以省略不译。

例 9　This provision is intended to ensure that where an amendment to the Certificate of Incorporation affects only a series of Preferred Stock, such amendment may be approved by only the holders of the affected series of Preferred Stock, without the necessity of approval by the holders of Common Stock.

译文：本规定意在确保当对开业证明的修订仅影响某一轮优先股时，该等修订仅需由该等受影响系列的优先股持有人批准，而无需普通股持有人批准。

例 10　Where the sum payable is expressed in words and also in figures, and there is a discrepancy between the two, the sum denoted by the words is the amount payable.

译文：应付金额同时用大小写表示而两者有差异的，应以大写所表示的金额为准。

但有些时候，where 在法律语境中引导的仍有可能是一个地点状语从句或者定语从句。译者在进行具体翻译时要谨慎辨认。

例 11　The Delaware Court of Chancery is considered by many to be the nation's leading business court, where judges expert in business law matters deal with business issues in an impartial setting; and...

译文：很多人都认为特拉华州衡平法院是全国领先的商业法院。在该法院中，作为商业法律事务专家的法官们置身于一个可以公正处理商业问题的环境；并且……

分析：原句中 where 引导的就是一个定语从句，修饰先行词 court。

三、Subject to 句式的翻译

该短语在法律英文中一般都与"agreement"、"section"、"contract"等法律文件名或文件中特定条款名配合使用。通常可翻译成"受制于……的规定""在遵守……规定的前提下""根据……规定"以及"在符合……的情况下"等。

例 12　Subject to any additional vote required by the Certificate of Incorporation, the number of directors of the Corporation shall be determined in the manner set forth in the Bylaws of the Corporation.

译文：受制于公司章程中有关新增投票的规定，公司董事会的人数应以公司内部章程细则中规定的方式确定。

例 13　The rights of the holders of the Series A Preferred Stock and the rights of the holders of the Common Stock under the first sentence of this Subsection 3.2 shall terminate on the first date following the Series A Original Issue Date (as defined below) on which there are issued and outstanding less than [_____] shares of Series A Preferred Stock (subject to appropriate adjustment in the event of any stock dividend, stock split, combination, or other similar recapitalization with respect to the Series A Preferred Stock).

译文:A系列优先股持有人和普通股持有人在本第3.2款第一句项下的权利应在A系列初始发行日(定义见下文)之后,发行在外的A系列优先股首次少于[_____]股(须受制于以下对A系列优先股进行适当调整的情况:任何分红、拆股、股份合并或类似的资本结构调整)之日终止。

例 14 The consequence of this broad definition is that dividends, stock repurchases, and stock redemptions are all subject to the same tests and restrictions.

译文:这一广泛定义的后果是,分红、股份回购和股份赎回都须遵守同样的测试和限制规定。

例 15 *California Corporations Code* Section 166 defines "distributions to shareholders" to include all transfers of cash or property to shareholders without consideration, including dividends paid to shareholders (except stock dividends), and the redemptions or repurchases of stock by a corporation or its subsidiary (subject to certain exclusions, such as the repurchase of stock held by employees).

译文:《加利福尼亚州公司法》第166条将"向股东进行分配"定义为包含对股东做出的所有无对价的现金或财产转让,包括向股东支付分红(股份分红除外),以及公司或其子公司进行股份赎回或回购(须遵守某些例外规定,例如对员工所持股份的回购)。

四、Without prejudice to 句式的翻译

Without prejudice to 这个英文法律短语相当于普通英文中的"without affecting"。跟在其后的通常是一个指代某项法律条款的名词。但 without prejudice to 对有关事物或条款的规限程度,没有 subject to 那么强硬。Subject to 规限的程度是必须"符合"或"依照"有关条款或规定,而 without prejudice to 强调不要影响或损害其规限的事物。在汉语中,可以翻译为"在不损害……的原则下""在不影响……的前提下"等。

例 16 The Directors may from time to time provide for the management of the affairs of the Company in such manner as they shall think fit and the provisions contained in the three next following paragraphs shall be without prejudice to the general powers conferred by this paragraph.

译文:董事可以随时以其认为合适的方式做出有关公司事务管理方面的规定,并且在之后的三段中所包含的规定不应影响本段中已经授予的一般权力。

例 17 Without prejudice to this clause, the following contract shall be treated as duly executed.

译文:在不影响本条规定的原则下,以下合同应视为已正式签署。

例 18 Without prejudice to Article 11 hereof and subject to the provisions of the Statute, the Company may by Special Resolution reduce its share capital and any capital redemption reserve fund.

译文：在不损害第11条的前提下，并且在遵守法令规定的前提下，公司可以通过特别决议减少其股本以及任何资本赎回预留资金。

五、For the purpose(s) of 句式的翻译

在大部分情况下，普通辞典里"为……目的"这一解释并不适合法律英语中的"for the purpose(s) of..."。如果紧跟这个短语的是某个法律条款的指代编号（如章、条、款、节等），首选译文是"就（有关）章、条、款、节而言"，其次才是"为了实施该（条法例）"。倘若原英文中的"for the purpose(s) of..."与"章、条、款、节等"无关，而该短语又可以用"for"或"in order to"去取代（这种用法在法律英文中属于少数），则可译成"为了"。在法律英文写作中，更多专家建议用 for 代替短语"for the purpose of..."，并相信有关法律句子的意义不会有任何改变；倘若需要明确表达"为了……（目的）"的这个概念，不定式短语 in order to... 则是更好的、更不容易产生歧义的选择。

例 19　"Goods" means all things that are treated as movable for the purposes of a contract for storage or transportation.

译文："货物"指为储存或运输合同的目的而可转移的所有物品。

分析：原句中的 for the purposes of 与条款无关，翻译为"为了……之目的"。

例 20　For the purposes of subsection (4)(b), the "net value" of an asset is the value of the asset less (i) the amount of any proceeds of the sale of an asset, to the extent the proceeds are applied in partial or total satisfaction of a debt secured by the asset and...

译文：就第(4)(b)条而言，资产的"净价值"是指该资产的价值减去(i)买卖资产的任何收益中用于清偿部分或全部该资产担保的债务数额，及……

分析：原句中的 for the purposes of 后面跟的是条款，因此不能翻译成"为了……之目的"，而应该理解为"就……而言"，译文中意译为"就第(4)(b)条而言"。

六、Provided that 句式

"Provided that..."是一个普通英文中很少使用的古旧词，但在法律文书中广泛使用。其用法与"if"或"but"非常类似，汉语中的意思相当于"倘若/如果"或"但"。该短语放在句首，引导出的是法律英语中的一个条件分句，与"if"、"when"或"where"引导的法律条件句没有本质上的差异；但如果该短语之前存在一个主句，则它表示的是一个与之前的陈述相反的"例外"，相当于"with the exception of..."，译成"但"或"但是"。

例 21　However, permanent residents of the Region who are not of Chinese nationality or who have the right of abode in foreign countries may also be elected members of the Legislative Council of the Region, provided that the proportion of such members does not exceed 20 percent of the total membership of the Council.

译文：但是，非中国籍的香港特别行政区永久性居民和在外国有居留权的香港特别行政区永久性居民也可以当选为香港特别行政区立法会议员，但其所占比例不得超过立法会全体议员的20%。

例22 A Director and his appointed alternate Director shall be considered only one person for the purpose of quorum, provided always that if there shall at any time be only a sole Director, the quorum shall be one.

译文：就法定人数而言，董事及其指定的替补董事应当仅视为一人，但如果在任何时候仅有一名董事，则一名董事的出席即构成法定人数。

七、Notwithstanding 句式的翻译

介词 notwithstanding 在普通英文中的使用极为罕见，但其在法律英文中被频繁使用。它的译法跟 although/though/even if 引导的状语从句没有太大分别，基本上都可以译成"尽管……""即使……"，表示一种让步。但该词所引导的并非是一个让步状语从句，因为在习惯用法上该词之后不跟句子，只跟一个名词性短语。虽然该词也可作连词使用，跟一个完整的让步状语从句，但这种用法并非是法律英语中的典型用法。

例23 Notwithstanding the foregoing, in the event of a redemption pursuant to the preceding sentence, if the Available Proceeds are not sufficient to redeem all outstanding shares of Series A Preferred Stock, the Corporation shall ratably redeem each holder's shares of Series A Preferred Stock to the fullest extent of such Available Proceeds, and shall redeem the remaining shares as soon as it may lawfully do so under Delaware law governing distributions to stockholders.

译文：尽管有上述规定，若根据上一句发生赎回时，可用资产不足以赎回所有发行在外的A系列优先股，则公司应按比例在最大范围内用该等可用资产赎回每一位持有人的A系列优先股，并应在其根据特拉华州适用于股东分配的法律可合法赎回剩余股份时，尽快赎回该等剩余股份。

例24 The obligation of an accommodation party may be enforced notwithstanding any statute of frauds and whether or not the accommodation party receives consideration for the accommodation.

译文：尽管存在关于欺诈票据的成文法，融通当事人的义务仍可得到强制执行，无论融通当事人是否收到了作为融通的对价。

例25 Notwithstanding any other contrary provision in these Articles, so long as any Series A Preferred Shares are outstanding, any action that effects or approves any of the following transactions involving the Company or any of its Subsidiaries shall require the written approval of not less than seventy-five percent (75%) of all issued and outstanding Common Shares and Series A Preferred Shares, voting together as a single class.

译文：尽管本章程可能有任何其他相反规定，只要任何 A 系列优先股目前是流通在外的，任何实现或批准下列涉及公司或其附属子公司交易的行为需要至少 75% 所有已发行在外的普通股和 A 系列优先股持有人书面批准。

八、Save/Except for 句式的翻译

Save 词源上是一个法文词，在法律英文中，它是一个与 except(for)意思相同的介词，汉语的译文为"除……外"。不管是 save 还是 except（for）之后都可以跟一个名词性短语，也可以跟一个从句或另一个介词短语。如：save in accordance with the provisions of this implementing rules。需要注意的是，save/except as（is）provided / stipulated 可以用 unless otherwise provided/stipulated 替代。

例 26 "Selling Expenses" means all underwriting discounts, selling commissions, and stock transfer taxes applicable to the sale of Registrable Securities, and fees and disbursements of counsel for any Holder, except for the fees and disbursements of the Selling Holder Counsel borne and paid by the Company as provided in Subsection 2.6.

译文："销售费用"指对出售可登记证券适用的所有承销折扣、销售佣金和股份转让税，及任何持有人的律师费用和支出，但第 2.6 款中约定的、应由公司承担的出售股东律师的费用和支出除外。

例 27 When a general meeting is adjourned for thirty days or more, notice of the adjourned meeting shall be given as in the case of an original meeting; save as aforesaid it shall not be necessary to give any notice of an adjournment or of the business to be transacted at an adjourned general meeting.

译文：当某一次股东大会被推迟 30 天以上（含），有关被推迟会议的通知应依照原始会议相同的方式发出；除上述情况外，没有必要发出任何有关推迟会议或在推迟的大会上拟议业务交易的通知。

第二节　典型法律汉语句式的翻译与解析

我们把法律条文中表达法律规范的特殊句式分为三类：（1）禁令句；（2）允许句；（3）要求句。在描述与分析这三类表达法律规范的立法文句时，有几点说明：

（1）禁令句表达禁止性规范；允许句表达授权性规范；要求句表达义务性规范。

（2）这种立法文句类型描写，属句式范畴，不属句型范畴。句型是按句子结构划分的，如主谓句、兼语句、连动句、双宾语句等。而句式是按表达特点划分的，如"把"字句突出处置的语义，"被"字句强调被动。

（3）对法律条文中表达法律规范的特殊句式，是根据法律语体特征命名和描写的。

一、法律条文中的禁令句

(一)"不得"字句

用"不得"字句表达禁止性规范,庄重、严肃、简洁、明快。"不得"一般译为 shall not,然而,"不能"常译为 may not。这和英文中一些否定表达方法对应一致,故不再重复。主要注意,根据实际情况,选择程度不同的否定表达方式。

例 28 没收财产是没收犯罪分子个人所有财产的一部或者全部……在判处没收财产的时候,<u>不得</u>没收属于犯罪分子家属所有或者应有的财产。(《刑法》第 59 条)

参考译文:Confiscation of property refers to the confiscation of part or all of the property personally owned by a criminal... When a sentence of confiscation of property is imposed, property that the criminal's family members own or should own shall not be subject to confiscation.

与"不得"语义相近的,还有"不许、不准、不能"等。

例 29 判决宣告以前一人犯数罪的,除判处死刑和无期徒刑的以外,应当在总和刑期以下、数刑中最高刑期以上,酌情决定执行的刑期;但是管制最高<u>不能</u>超过 3 年,拘役最高<u>不能</u>超过 1 年,有期徒刑最高<u>不能</u>超过 20 年。

参考译文:For a criminal who commits several crimes before a judgment is pronounced, unless he is sentenced to death or life imprisonment, his term of punishment shall be decided in such a way that it may not exceed the total of the terms for all the crimes and must be longer than the maximum term for any one of the crimes, depending on the circumstances of each case. However, the term of public surveillance **may not** exceed three years, the term of criminal detention **may not** exceed one year, and fixed-term imprisonment **may not** exceed twenty years.

(二)"禁止"字句

"禁止"字句在汉译英的过程中,通常翻译为 be prohibited 句式。

例 30 <u>禁止</u>任何人利用任何手段扰乱社会秩序。扰乱社会秩序情节严重,致使工作、生产、营业和教学、科研无法进行,国家和社会遭受严重损失的,对首要分子处五年以下有期徒刑、拘役、管制或者剥夺政治权利。

参考译文:It shall **be prohibited** for anyone to disturb public order by any means. If the circumstances of the public disturbance are so serious that work, production, business, education or scientific research cannot be conducted and the state and society suffer serious losses, the ringleaders shall be sentenced to fixed-term imprisonment of not more than five years, criminal detention, public surveillance or deprivation of political rights.

例 31　国家保护社会主义的公共财产。禁止任何社会组织或者个人用任何手段侵占或者破坏国家或集体的财产。

参考译文：The State protects socialist public property. Appropriation or damaging of State or collective property by any organization or individual by whatever means **is prohibited**.

（三）"处"字句

用"处"字句表示禁止性规范有以下几个特点：（1）在语义上，与"不得"字句不同的是，用具体的制裁来表示禁令。（2）在结构上，主语往往为"的"字结构，突出犯罪主体或犯罪行为，简洁、庄重；谓语部分的"处"字突出对犯罪主体或犯罪行为的处置。

"处"字句一般为被动句，为使行文简洁，执法机关一般不出现。有时为了使语义明确，执法机关也可以出现。通常翻译为 be sentenced to 句式。

例 32　阴谋颠覆政府、分裂国家的，处无期徒刑或者 10 年以上有期徒刑。

参考译文：Whoever plots to subvert the government or dismember the state **shall be sentenced to** life imprisonment or fixed-term imprisonment of not less than ten years.

例 33　策动、勾引、收买国家工作人员、武装部队、人民警察、民兵投敌叛变或者叛乱的，处无期徒刑或者十年以上有期徒刑。（《中华人民共和国刑法》第 93 条）

参考译文：Whoever instigates lures or bribes a state functionary or a member of the armed forces, the people's police or the people's militia to defect to the enemy and turn traitor or to rise in rebellion **shall be sentenced to** life imprisonment or fixed-term imprisonment of not less than ten years.

（四）"是"字句

"是"字句规定什么行为是犯罪，语气坚决，表达禁止性规范，庄重、简练。与"处"字句不同的是，它不表述具体的处罚。常翻译成 refer to，用来解释说明。

例 34　明知自己的行为会发生危害社会的结果，并且希望或者放任这种结果发生，因而构成犯罪的，是故意犯罪。

参考译文：An intentional crime **refers to** a crime committed by a person who clearly knows that his act will produce socially dangerous consequences but who wishes or allows such consequences to occur.

例 35　组织、领导犯罪集团进行犯罪活动的或者在共同犯罪中起主要作用的，是主犯。对于主犯，除本法分则已有规定的以外，应当从重处罚。

参考译文：A principal criminal **refers to** any person who organizes and leads a criminal group in carrying out criminal activities or plays a principal role in a joint crime. A principal criminal shall be given a heavier punishment unless otherwise stipulated in the Specific Provisions of this Law.

例 36　剥夺政治权利<u>是</u>剥夺下列权利：

（一）选举权和被选举权；

（二）宪法第 45 条规定的各种权利；

（三）担任国家机关职务的权利；

（四）担任企业、事业单位和人民团体领导职务的权利。

参考译文：Deprivation of political rights **refers to** deprivation of the following rights：

（1）the right to vote and to stand for election；

（2）the right provided for in Article 45 of the Constitution；

（3）the right to hold a position in a state organ；and

（4）the right to hold a leading position in any enterprise, institution or people's organization.

二、法律条文中的允许句

"可"字句

"可"字句是汉语中表达授权性规范比较典型的句式，常用"可""可以"，语气比较缓和，没有强制性。通常译为 may 句式。

例 37　国家为了公共利益的需要，<u>可以</u>依照法律对土地进行征用。

参考译文：The State **may**, in the public interest, requisition land for its use in accordance with the law.

例 38　国家在必要时<u>得</u>设立特别行政区。在特别行政区实行的制度按照具体情况由全国人民代表大会以法律规定。

参考译文：The State **may** establish special administrative regions when necessary. The systems to be instituted in special administrative regions shall be prescribed by law enacted by the National People's Congress in the light of specific conditions.

例 39　凡在中华人民共和国领域外犯罪，依照本法应当负刑事责任的，虽然经过外国审判，仍然可以依照本法处理；但是在外国已经受过刑罚处罚的，<u>可以</u>免除或者减轻处罚。

参考译文：If any person commits a crime outside the territory of the People's Republic of China for which according to this Law he would bear criminal responsibility, he may still be dealt with according to this Law, even if he has already been tried in a foreign country. However, if he has already received criminal punishment in the foreign country, he **may** be exempted from punishment or given a mitigated punishment.

其他表示允许的句式还有:"行使"字句,"有"字句等,但较"可"字句并不常见。

三、法律条文中的要求句

(一)"应"字句

"应"字句表达义务性规范,语气比较缓和,常用"应当、应"字。通常与英语法律文本中的 shall 句式相对应。

例 40　代理人不履行职责而给被代理人造成损害的,应当承担民事责任。

参考译文:An agent **shall** bear civil liability if he fails to perform his duties and thus cause damage to the principal.

注意:在民事案件中,"有罪"称 liable;而在刑事案件中,"有罪"称 guilty。

例 41　人民法院和人民检察院对于不通晓当地通用的语言文字的诉讼参与人,应当为他们翻译。

参考译文:The people's courts and the people's procuratorates **shall** provide translation for any party to the court proceedings who is not familiar with the spoken or written languages commonly used in the locality.

(二)"须"字句

通常指 must 与"必须"对应。

例 42　一切国家机关和国家工作人员必须依靠人民的支持,经常保持同人民的密切联系,倾听人民的意见和建议,接受人民的监督,努力为人民服务。

参考译文:All States organs and functionaries **must** rely on the support of the people, keep in close touch with them, heed their opinions and suggestions, accept their supervision and do their best to serve them.

(三)"的"字句

"的"字句是指,由"的"构成以"的"字结构为标志的句子。"的"字结构事实上是中文省略了作为逻辑主语的行为者,而"的"字结构是在句子中充当主语的一种语法结构。它们主要有以下几种形式:由抽象词组成,如"红的是我的,绿的是你的";由"动宾词组+的"组成,例如,"值得高兴的是,他没有受伤";由"主谓词组+的",例如:"他指的不是这件事"。"的"字结构在法律文书中尤为常见。"的"字结构的多种形式中,用于法律文书的主要有"动宾词组+的",如:"构成犯罪的""获得证书的"等等。

汉英法律语言中"的"字结构的频繁使用是为了达到语言庄重、简洁、严谨的效果,同时体现了法律语言的程式化特点。如:对于扣押的物品、文件、邮件、电报,或者冻结的存款、汇款,经查明确实与案件无关的,应当在3日以内解除扣押、冻结,退还原主或者原邮电机关。

另外,汉语法律语言中"的"字结构构成的词组常用来作主语,表示假定的条件,通常前置。如：以营利为目的，制作、贩卖淫书、淫画的，处3年以下有期徒刑、拘役或者管制，可以并处罚金。可见，由"的"字结构构成的主语形式具有很强的概括性，可以成为一个具有代表性的概念，从而符合法律语言的需要。总之，需要用一个名词性的成分表达这一概念。

例43　阴谋颠覆政府、分裂国家的，处无期徒刑或者10年以上有期徒刑。

参考译文：**Whoever** plots to subvert the government or dismember the state shall be sentenced to life imprisonment or fixed-term imprisonment of not less than ten years.

最后，法律英语中的条件通常用if，where，when句子或短语表示，位置不固定。构成"If/where/when P1, then Q"逻辑结构。因此，当汉译英时，"的"字句通常翻译为if句式或where句式。

例44　监护人不履行监护职责或者侵害被监护人的合法权益的，应当承担责任；给被监护人造成财产损失的，应当赔偿损失。人民法院可以根据有关人员或者有关单位的申请，撤销监护人的资格。

参考译文：If a guardian does not fulfill his duties as guardian or infringes upon the lawful rights and interests of his ward, he shall be held responsibility; if a guardian causes any property loss for his ward, he shall compensate for such loss. The people's court may disqualify a guardian based on the application of a concerned party or unit.

例45　企业之间或者企业、事业单位之间联营，组成新的经济实体，独立承担民事责任、具备法人条件的，经主管机关核准登记，取得法人资格。

参考译文：If a new economic entity is formed by enterprises or an enterprise and an institution that engages in economic association and it independently bears civil liability and has the qualifications of a legal person, the new entity shall be qualified as a legal person after being approved and registered by the competent authority.

需注意的是，有时在立法表述时，在一个法律条文中往往连用或并列使用几个"的"字结构。

例46　有下列情形之一，进行信用诈骗活动的，处5年以下有期徒刑或者拘役，并处2万元以上20万元以下罚金；数额巨大或者有其他严重情节的，处5年以上10以下有期徒刑，并处5万元以上50万元以下罚金；数额特别巨大或者有其他特别严重情节的，处10年以上有期徒刑或者无期徒刑，并处5万元以上50万元以下罚金或者没收财产：

　　a. 使用伪造、变造的信用证或者附随的单据、文件的；
　　b. 使用作废的信用证的；
　　c. 骗取信用证的；
　　d. 以其他方法进行信用证诈骗活动的。

四、常用短语词组

以上提到的典型英语法律句式中,有些与中文的典型法律句式相对应,例如:情态动词 must 句式,与"……必须……"对应,shall 与"……应当……""……应……"对应等等。除此之外,中文法律文本中还有一些很有特点的短语词组应用其中。

(一)"对"字词组的使用

"对"字词组是指,由介词"对"或"对于"组成的,充当句子成分的介词结构。它们在立法语言中是用来表达"假定"的含义,其所表述的对象具有特殊性,使得人们注意到其需要特别处理的法律特征。

例 47　对于被判处死刑、无期徒刑的犯罪分子,应当剥夺政治权利终身。

参考译文:Criminals who are sentenced to death or to life imprisonment shall be deprived of political rights for life.

例 48　对于预备犯,可以比照既遂犯从轻、减轻处罚或者免除处罚。

参考译文:An offender who prepares for a crime may, in comparison with one who completed the crime, be given a lighter or mitigated punishment or be exempted from punishment.

例 49　对于未遂犯,可以比照既遂犯从轻或者减轻处罚。

参考译文:An offender who attempts to commit a crime may, in comparison with one who completed the crime, be given a lighter or mitigated punishment.

例 50　对于中止犯,应当免除或者减轻处罚。

参考译文:An offender who discontinues a crime shall be exempted from punishment or be given a mitigated punishment.

(二)"为"字词组

"为"字词组是指,以"为""为了"作标记,法律文本开头第一章第一条,常用"为"字句说明制定该法之目的。通常翻译为 in order to 词组。

例 51　为了保护劳动者的合法权益,调整劳动关系,建立和维护适应社会主义市场经济的劳动制度,促进经济发展和社会进步,根据宪法,制定本法。

参考译文:This Law is formulated in accordance with the Constitution **in order to** protect the legitimate rights and interests of laborers, readjust labor relationships, establish and safeguard a labor system suited to the socialist market economy, and promote economic development and social progress.

例 52　为了强化预算的分配和监督职能,健全国家对预算的管理,加强国家宏观调控,保障经济和社会的健康发展,根据宪法,制定本法。

参考译文:This Law is formulated and enacted in accordance with the Constitution

in order to strengthen the distribution and supervision functions of budget, improve the budget management of the State, intensify the macro-regulation and control of the State, and ensure the sound development of economy and society.

译文解析:原文中"制定本法"前,连续有 4 个目的状语,这是中文法律文件句子结构。我们在译成英语时,应按照译入语的习惯做结构调整,把"制定本法"放在句首,译成"This Law is formulated and enacted"。原文"预算的管理"为专业管理,应译成 the budget management,不能译成 the budget administration。Administration 是行政管理。

(三)"由"字词组

"由"字词组是指那些以"由"字为标记的词组,在句子中充当状语成分。通常表示动作的执行者,常译为 by 句式.

例 53　对于犯罪情节轻微不需要判处刑罚的,可以免予刑事处分,但可以根据案件的不同情况,予以训诫或者责令具结悔过、赔礼道歉、赔偿损失,或者<u>由</u>主管部门予以行政处分。

参考译文:If the circumstances of a person's crime are minor and do not require punishment, he may be exempted from criminal sanctions; however, he may, according to the different circumstances of each case, be reprimanded or ordered to make a statement of repentance, offer an apology, pay compensation for the losses or be subject to administrative sanctions **by** the competent department。

(四)"下列"词组

"下列"词组是指,以"下列"为标记的词组;通常译为 the following。

例 54　中华人民共和国公民在中华人民共和国领域外犯<u>下列</u>各罪的,适用本法:
(1) 反革命罪;
(2) 伪造国家货币罪,伪造有价证券罪;
(3) 贪污罪,受贿罪,泄露国家机密罪;
(4) 冒充国家工作人员招摇撞骗罪,伪造公文、证件、印章罪。

参考译文:This Law is applicable to the citizens of the People's Republic of China who commit any of **the following** crimes outside the territory of the People's Republic of China:
(1) counterrevolution;
(2) counterfeiting national currency and counterfeiting valuable securities;
(3) embezzlement, accepting bribes and divulging state secrets; and
(4) posing as a state functionary to practice fraud and forging official documents, certificates and seals.

例 55　被判处管制的犯罪分子,在执行期间,必须遵守下列规定：

(1) 遵守法律、法令,服从群众监督,积极参加集体劳动生产或者工作；

(2) 向执行机关定期报告自己的活动情况；

(3) 迁居或者外出必须报经执行机关批准。

对于被判处管制的犯罪分子,在劳动中应当同工同酬。

参考译文：A criminal who is sentenced to public surveillance must observe **the following** rules during the term in which his sentence is being executed：

(1) observe laws and decrees, submit to supervision by the masses and actively participate in collective productive labor or work；

(2) report regularly on his own activities to the organ executing the public surveillance; and

(3) report and obtain approval from the organ executing the public surveillance for any change in residence or departure from the area.

Criminals sentenced to public surveillance shall, while engaged in labor, receive equal pay for equal work.

类似的还有"如下",常翻译为 as follows.

例 56　附加刑的种类如下：

(1) 罚金；

(2) 剥夺政治权利；

(3) 没收财产。

参考译文：The supplementary punishments are **as follows**：

(1) Fines；

(2) Deprivation of political rights; and

(3) Confiscation of property.

第三节　本 章 小 结

法律文件中的英语具有用词准确、规范,结构严谨,句子冗长等特点。法律翻译的英译中,除了要研究原语的语言特点外,关键还应理解原文,读懂原文。要读懂、理解原文,笔者认为主要需要掌握两点：(1) 理解法律英语中的专门用语；(2) 理解法律英语的句子结构,尤其是对长句的理解,在这个基础上进行两种语言的转换。

做好法律翻译的英译中的另一个重要方面,是要研究目的语(即汉语公文体用语)的特点。同法律英语一样,中文的法律用语也有其用词特点及行文句子结构特点,即用词准确、简练,行文以短句为主,有时还使用一些文言连词等特点。在翻译过程中,我们可按照原语中的不同用词,相应地使用中文中的这些法律用词。同时我们翻译工作者应经常阅读我国全国人民代表大会制定的各种法律,及国务院制定的行政法规,学习研究上述法规的用词、用语,不断丰富中文法律用词,进而掌握现代中文公文用语。

做好法律文本汉译英的工作,同样要求译者同时熟悉两种语言的法律文本的特点。能够对应的地方对应起来;不能对应的地方,要恰当进行处理。

另外,法律翻译涉及政治、经济、司法、军事、商贸等多个领域,因此,翻译工作者还应学习、熟悉上述领域的专业术语。

 课后习题

1. 汉译英,并分析其句法特征和涉及的典型句式。

(1) 最高人民法院设立巡回法庭,探索设立跨行政区划的人民法院和人民检察院,探索建立检察机关提起公益诉讼制度。

(2) 中国共产党第十八届四中全会提出的总目标是建立中国特色社会主义法治体系,建设社会主义法治国家。

(3) 中国共产党第十八届四中全会提出的重大任务是:完善以宪法为核心的中国特色社会主义法律体系,加强宪法实施;深入推进依法行政,加快建设法治政府;保证公正司法,提高司法公信力;增强全民法治观念,推进法治社会建设。

(4) 债权人为2人以上的,按照确定的份额分享权利。债务人为2人以上的,按照确定的份额分担义务。

2. 英译汉。

(1) Without prejudice to the rights of the Attorney General every complainant or informant shall be at liberty to conduct the complaint or information respectively and to have the witnesses examined and cross-examined by him or by counsel on his behalf.

(2) If, upon the hearing of a claim, the claimant does not appear, the Board may strike out the claim, without prejudice, however, to the restoration of such claim by the Board, on the application of the claimant, on such terms as it may think just.

(3) The Licensee shall not be entitled to take any proceedings in any of the aforesaid matters; provided, however, that the Licensor may, at its own discretion and cost, prosecute or otherwise stop or prevent such actual or threatened infringement in the name of both the Licensor and the Licensee or either of them, and in each case the Licensee shall render all reasonable assistance required by the Licensor.

(4) Notwithstanding subsection (4)(a) but otherwise subject to subsections (4) and (5), the interest of a lessor of fixtures, including the lessor's residual interest,

is subordinate to the conflicting interest of an encumbrancer of the real estate under a construction mortgage recorded before the goods become fixtures if the goods become fixtures before the completion of the construction. To the extent given to refinance a construction mortgage, the conflicting interest of an encumbrancer of the real estate under a mortgage has this priority to the same extent as the encumbrancer of the real estate under the construction mortgage.

(5) Save under and in accordance with the provisions of this section no action shall lie in any civil court against a magistrate for any act done in a matter over which by law he has no jurisdiction or in which he has exceeded his jurisdiction.

(6) Save as is provided in this Ordinance, no claim within the jurisdiction of the Board shall be actionable in any court.

(7) Unless in any enactment it is otherwise provided, the period of imprisonment, which may be imposed by a magistrate exercising summary jurisdiction, in respect of the non-payment of any sum of money adjudged to be paid by a conviction, whether it be a fine or in respect of the property the subject of the offence, or in respect of the injury done by the offender, or in respect of the default of a sufficient distress to satisfy any such sum, shall be such period as, in the opinion of the magistrate, will satisfy the justice of the case, but shall not exceed in any case the maximum fixed by the following scale....

(8) Except for an indorsement covered by subsection (c), if an instrument bears an indorsement using words to the effect that payment is to be made to the indorsee as agent, trustee, or other fiduciary for the benefit of the indorser or another person, the following rules apply:...

(9) For the purpose of the Landlord and the Tenant Ordinance and for the purpose of these presents the rent in respect of the said premises shall be deemed to be in arrear if not paid in advance as stipulated by Clause 1 hereof.

(10) Where an employee is granted any period of annual leave, the employer shall pay him annual leave pay in respect of that period not later than the day on which he is next paid his wages after that period.

第六章

立法文本翻译

第一节 概 述

一、立法文本的类型

立法文本(规范性法律文书)是由国家立法机关正式颁布的各项法律法规,对公民具有普遍约束力。立法文本主要包括各类法律、法规、规章、条例、国际公约、国际条约以及国际惯例等。其主要目的是规范公民的行为标准、公民的权利与义务等。这类文本为人们设定了社会行为标准,同时也规定了判定违法行为的依据。我国的立法文本有宪法、法律、行政法规、国际条约、特别行政区法、地方性法规、经济特区法规、司法解释等八个类别。

作为众多法律文本中的规范性文本,立法文本中的法律语言具有很强的专业性、正式性、规范性、逻辑性和严谨性。尽管法律语言"简明化和大众化"的呼声很高,但立法文本仍保持庄重、严谨、正式的文体风格,以体现立法文本的严肃性。

二、立法文本的结构

立法文本具有高度程式化的篇章结构,每部法律都是一个整体而非各法条的简单罗列。一部法律内部具有很强的逻辑关联性,从而实现表述清晰明确。为了更加准确的传达法律法规的具体内容,立法者通常采用比较固定的篇章模式来承载立法内容。经过对比研究,我们发现汉英立法语篇的结构模式大致相同,两类语篇都是由描写性成分过渡到规定性成分、由颁布命令和/或前言过渡到具体条文;其结构层次分明,都是采用从宏观到微观、从总论/总则到条文、从重要条文到次要条文的语篇结构(张新红,2000)。

尽管世界各国法律制度和立法规范不尽相同,但立法文件的篇章结构模式却很相似,一般分为 preliminary provisions(总则), principal provisions(分则)和 final provisions

(附则)三部分组成(Sarcevic,1997:127)。"总则"一般位于一部法律的第一部分,概括地介绍该法律的立法目的、立法原则、立法依据、法的原则、法的制定与颁布、法的效力、法的适用以及法的解释。一般具体包括标题、序言、简称、适用条款等内容。"分则"是整部法律的主体部分,是总则内容的具体化讲述。分则一般包括两部分内容:substantive provisions(实质性条款)和 administrative provisions(管理性条款)(Sarcevic,1997)。实质性条款一般对有关法律主体的权利、义务、行为、事件及后果做出规定。管理性条款则适用于对法律机关的规范。"附则"涵盖对总则和分则的补充性内容,主要包括:违反与惩罚、制定实施细则的授权、保留、废止、修订、暂时使用条例、施行条款、附录等。

(一) 立法文本总则

总则一般位于每部法律的第一部分,概括地介绍该法律的立法目的、立法原则、立法依据、法的原则、法的制定与颁布、法的效力、法的适用以及法的解释。一般具体包括标题、序言、简称、适用条款等内容。根据各国法律制度和立法规范的不同原则,以上三部分的主要内容和结构安排也有所差异。各国法律实践中对于不同的法律文件采用的具体格式也会有所差异。如中国的立法文本内容一般安排格式如下:

标题、制定、公布、实施信息和序言

总则

分则

适用与备案

附则

以《中华人民共和国刑法》的总则内容安排格式为例:

标题、制定、目录

第一编　总则

第一章　刑法的任务、基本原则和适用范围

第二章　犯罪

第三章　刑罚

第四章　刑罚的具体运用

第五章　其他规定

而美国宪法的总则部分只包含了标题和序言两部分内容:

The Constitution of the United States of America

Preamble

We the People of the United States, in Order to form a more perfect Union, establish Justice, insure domestic Tranquility, provide for the common defence, promote the general Welfare, and secure the Blessings of Liberty to ourselves and our Posterity, do ordain and establish this Constitution for the United States of America.

下面我们将对总则部分的核心内容：标题和序言，以及在英语法律文件总则中常出现的关键术语解释部分的特点及翻译方法进行详细分析。

1. 标题

当人们阅读一篇文章或一本书时，首先映入眼帘的就是标题。一般来说，标题是对整篇文章或整部书内容的高度概括，其主要特征是简洁、醒目、鲜明，译好标题对于了解全文或全书的内容和主旨以及激发读者的阅读兴趣都极其重要。

随着中国与世界经济文化交流的进一步加深，我们不断吸收国外的先进成果，同时把我们所取得的成就传播到国外，翻译就成为中外交流与合作过程中的桥梁。标题的翻译是译者在翻译作品时需要仔细推敲的部分。译者在翻译文章标题时，不可望文生义，一挥而就，必须慎之又慎。既不能将自己的思路拘泥于原文的结构形式，又不可肆意发挥。好的文章标题翻译不仅应做到忠实、通顺且尽可能简洁地再现原文，而且应具备标题的三大功能：即信息功能（提供文章的主题和内容）、美感功能（简洁明快，新颖醒目）和祈使功能（诱发读者的阅读欲）。这就要求译者在理解原文的基础上，确定表达以求简洁地道。

总的来说，作品可大致分为文学作品和非文学作品两大类，而这两类作品分别有自己的特点。因此在翻译其标题时应采取不同的方法进行处理，下面将重点讨论法律文本标题的特点及其翻译方法。

世界各国立法文本都有标题。标题是对整部法律内容和目的的高度概括，其主要特征是简洁、醒目、鲜明。标题的翻译对于了解整部法律的内容和主旨都极其重要。立法文本的标题有长短之分，这个特点在英语立法文本中尤其突出。为了使立法文本能够更方便的被引用，各国立法者多采用短标题作为立法文本的标题。如《中华人民共和国行政法》只是简单的由国名（中华人民共和国）和法律名称（行政法）两部分组成。再如加拿大某法案标题 Youth Criminal Justice Act，2002，仅由法案名称（Youth Criminal Justice Act）和颁布年份（2002）组成。

长标题多见于英语立法文件中，通常是法律正文内容的组成部分。长标题通常会对相关法律的立法范围和立法意图做详细的描述，使读者能够迅速地把握立法者的立法目的和该法律的适用范围。因此，在英语立法文件中长标题常被立法者用来作为解释立法目的的工具。在这种情况下，长标题成为某些法律不可或缺的内容之一。为了明确表述，长标题一般都采用长句的形式，多以 An act... 开头，后面用 to amend...，to make... 和 for the purpose... 等动词或者词组来表示该法律的立法意图和立法范围。长标题也有长短之分，相对较短的如：An Act respecting Procedure in Criminal Cases, and other matters relating to Criminal Law. 较复杂的如：An Act to prevent the unlawful training of persons to the use of arms, and the practice of military evolutions and to authorize Justices of the Peace to seize and detain arms collected or kept for purposes dangerous to the public peace. (An Act further to amend the "Act to make further provision for the government of the North West Territories",Canada)

掌握了汉英立法文本的标题形式特点,下面我们将对立法文本中的标题翻译方法进行阐述。

英国学者 Newmark 认为,在语篇标题的翻译过程中,译者应该充分发挥能动性对目标标题进行分类。通常可分为描述性(descriptive)标题和暗示性(allusive)标题。描述性标题适用于在非文学语篇中简明地说明语篇的主题和目的,而暗示性标题则适用于文学作品与通俗的新闻写作,在这类语篇标题的翻译过程中,译者能够充分地发挥自己的想象力来更好地表达原文的意境。这便是语言运用要求的结果,译者根据读者的需要来变通与之相适应的翻译形式。我们研究语篇标题翻译的目的便是归纳翻译过程中的变通方式,以总结出一定的规律来帮助译者更好地完成翻译工作。按以上分类原则,立法文本标题属于描述性标题,通常对法律文本的主题和主旨做出简明的交代。接下来将对立法文本标题翻译中常采用的方法和原则进行介绍。

(1) 直译法

对等法是法律文本标题翻译过程中使用最多的一种技巧,它基本上是直译原文标题的表达形式,可变通性很小。这种翻译方法体现了奈达提出的两类对等翻译(Nida,1964:159)之一的形式对等和严复翻译标准中的"信"。同时反映了随着各国交流的加强,相同或者相似信息的法律语言载体的互相融合。适合采用直译法翻译的标题通常具有这样的特点:标题本身十分具体,基本表述了文章要说的内容。就整部法律内容来看,标题本身的交际信息是十分具体、足够明确的,对它进行直接翻译足以反映语篇的内容。这种标题翻译方法是原语篇标题最理想的对等转换方式。在法律翻译实践中,译者大多采用直译法,原因就在于这种方法在语言形式上与原语篇标题的措辞最为贴近。可见,该方法主要适用于短标题和较短长标题的翻译,如:

《中华人民共和国民法通则》采用直译法译为英文便是 General Principles of the Civil Law of People's Republic of China;而 The Constitution of United States of America 可直接译为《美利坚合众国宪法》。

这种翻译方法在其他非文学作品标题的翻译中也比较常用,如:

《中国的教育》Education in China

《抓住时机,推进改革》Seize the Opportune Moment to Advance the Reform

Food and Health《食品与健康》

London Fire Leaves 1700 Homeless《伦敦火灾,1700 人失去家园》

(2) 增减法——保留和突出原标题中的核心词

增减法是对直译法的一种补充与调整。有时译者可能认为原文标题过泛、过长,用直译法翻译后的标题不符合目标读者的阅读习惯。这时就要求译者采用必要的技术手段,增强译文标题的可读性。这种方法主要适用于长标题的翻译。在翻译长标题的过程中,原语篇标题本身可能会在交际过程中提供过量的信息,如将所有信息都直译为中文的标题，不符合中国读者的阅读理解习惯。因此，在翻译此类标题时，译者应保留和突出原标题的中心词句、力求简洁醒目。

例如：

《毛泽东早期著作中关于中国革命的思想》译为 Mao Zedong's Thoughts on China's Revolution in His Early works。《20世纪初叶反抗日本占领台湾的斗争》译为 The Struggle Against Japanese Occupation of Taiwan in the Early 20th Century。

上面两例中汉语标题的中心词分别是"思想"和"斗争"，作者用了较长的定语来修饰这两个词，在这种情况下可以首先把中心词提取出来放在句首，然后将原标题中的定语成分转换成英语标题中的介词短语，放在句子的后半部分，使之成为后置的状语成分。

《中华人民共和国促进科技成果转化法》，其主标题词中的关键词应当是"科技成果"与"转化"，译为 Scientific and Technological Achievement Transformation Law of PRC 准确地表达出该法的法律效力和管辖范围。

以上两种翻译原则广泛应用于非文学作品标题翻译，尤其是法律文本标题的翻译。下面我们将对汉语法律文本标题英译的具体翻译方法做具体地介绍：

首先，在立法文本标题的翻译方面，我们应该直接移植英美法系国家、地区制定法的命名模式。我们翻译法律文本的目的就是满足英语国家、地区的读者的阅读需求，直接依照他们的模式去翻译、命名是迎合目标读者的阅读与理解习惯的最好方式。其次是要认真对比英语立法文件名称"格式词"的不同涵义，如：Law，Act，Code，Ordinance，Regulation，Rule，Interpretation，Decision 等。需要特别注意的是，在进行具体研究时，应当主要参考英语原文的法律专业词典、法律著作、文献，而不只依赖普通的英汉词典、英汉法律词典等间接的书籍、文献。此外，还需将英语的表达方式与中国的法律文化特点相结合，为中国法律法规找到相对应的英语名称。

中英语言的表达顺序和方式一般是相反的，但在法律法规名称表达顺序方面，却有惊人的相似。英国法律中高频率地使用"主标题词"（比如：Vagrancy）+"格式词"（比如：Act，Regulations，Rules，Order）+"制定法被通过的年限"的命名方式。该命题模式与中国汉语的表达顺序完全相同。有了典型的命名模式，接下来就是如何恰当使用"格式词"的问题了。

常见的名称"格式词"有：Law，Act，Code，Ordinance，Regulation，Rule，Interpretation，Decision，Resolution 等，它们有着各自不同的涵义。为了更准确地了解这些格式词的含义，下面列出《布莱克法律词典》的有关释义摘要：

law 是一个大概念，泛指一切具有法律约束力的国家规范性文件；也指英美法系中的判例法（包括普通法和衡平法）、习惯法等。但在英美法律实践中，几乎不用 Law 为具体的法律命名，英美国会制定的成文法，通常都以 Act 命名。Law 通常是一个描述性用语。而中国属于大陆法系国家，一切法律法规均属制定法的范畴，因此在翻译我们法律时，通常是由 law。这体现了中国与英美法系国家法律文化之间的差异。

decision 是指对事实、法律（于法律文书）考虑后做出的决定（a determination arrived at after consideration of facts, and, in legal context, law）；一个普通的非技术或法律的词（a popular rather than technical or legal word）；司法或准司法性质的决定（a determination of a judicial or quasi judicial nature）；法院宣布的判决或命令（a judgment or decree pronounced by a court in settlement of a controversy submitted to it and by way of authoritative answer to the questions raised before it）。在我国，全国人大"决定"常译作 Decision。

resolution 是指官方机构或会议以投票表决方式通过的正式意见或意志。Resolution 与 Law 主要的区别在于，前者仅用于表示立法机关对某一特定事件或事务的意见，并且只有临时的效力；而后者则意指对人或事在广泛意义上具有永久性的指引和控制效力。所以，根据我国"决定""规定"和"办法"等文件所特有的临时性特点，它们可译为 NPC（Legislative）Resolution。

interpretation 意为发现和查明制定法、遗嘱、合同或其他文书之意图的方法或程序（the art or process of discovering and ascertaining the meaning of a statute, will, contract, or other written document）；"解释"可以是"法定性"的，这种法定性的基础是解释具有像法律本身一样的权威性，也可以是"原则性"的，这种原则性则建立于解释所拥有的内在合理性。由此可见，最高法院的各种司法解释可以译作 Judicial Interpretation。全国人大的立法解释则可译为 NPC Legal（或 Legislative）Interpretation。

ordinance 指由权力机关制定的规则（a rule established by authority）；法律或者制定法（law or statute）；该术语最通常的语义是指市镇自治机关的立法机构所制定的立法文件。

regulation 是关于管理或行政管理的规则（rule）、命令（order）；调整原则（a regulating principle）；命令书（percept）；由政府行政当局颁发的具有法律效力的规则或命令。复数的 Regulations，其语义基本相同，指由不同的政府部门颁发的，旨在实现法律宗旨的文件。比如，Treasury Regulations 表明了（美国）国内税务局在如何解释国内税收法典方面的立场，其宗旨是为纳税人和国内税务局的工作人员在适用税法的各种规定方面提供一般和具体的规则。可见，Regulation 是一种具有法律效力的文件。Regulation 通常被译为"规则""规章"和"法规"，因此政府部门具有法律效力的各种规范性文件或者地方性法规常译为 Regulation。

rule 是指确定的标准（an established standard）；指引（guide）；条例（regulation）；由权力机构制定，指引行为规范的原则或条例，如立法机关、公司、法院、公共机构等的规则；法律规则；道德规范；对确定、详细的事实状态赋予了具体、详细法律后果的令状、命令书（percept）。国务院各部委、地方政府的规章也可以译为 rules。

order 意为命令（mandate）；令状（percept）；权力机关的命令或指示（command or

direction authoritatively given);规则或规例(rule or regulation)。

从以上定义可知,Ordinance,Regulation(s),Rules,和 Order 在很多情况下可以用于相互解释,说明它们具有共同的含义,即由权力机关制定,具有法律效力的行为规则。但各自的含义还是存在一定的差别,比如 Ordinance 的第二种语义("法律或者制定法")是 Regulation(s),Rules 和 Order 所没有的。

准确地掌握以上"格式词"的含义对做好法律文本标题翻译至关重要,有助于实现原标题与译文在标题意义的体现形式上的基本对应。

2. 序言

序言是立法文本的重要组成部分,并非所有的法律都有序言部分。英美法系的立法序言通常以程式化的一个或者几个从句来标示,常见的形式有:"whereas...","given that...","in view of..."。如世界上第一部关于版权的法律——英国的 *Statute of Anne*(1710) 的序言中采用了 whereas 引导的句式:**Whereas** Printers, Booksellers, and other persons, have of late frequently taken the Liberty of Printing, Reprinting, and Publishing, or causing to be Printed, Reprinted, and Published Books, and other Writings, without the Consent of the Authors or Proprietors of such Books and Writings, to their very great Detriment, and too often to the Ruin of them and their families: For Preventing therefore such practices for the future, and for the Encouragement of Learned Men to Compose and Write useful Books; May it please Your Majesty, that it may be Enacted, and be it Enacted by the Queens most Excellent Majesty, by and with the Advice and Consent of the Lords Spiritual and Temporal, and Commons in this present Parliament Assembled, and by the Authority of the same, That from and after the Tenth Day of April, One thousand seven hundred and ten, the Author of any Book or Books already Printed, who hath not Transferred to any other the Copy or Copies of such Book or Books, Share or Shares thereof, or the Bookseller or booksellers, Printer or Printers, or other Person or Persons who hath or have Purchased or Acquired the Copy or Copies of any Book or Books, in order to Print or Reprint the same, shall have the sole Right and Liberty of Printing such Book and Books for the Term of One and twenty Years, to Commence from the said Tenth Day of April, and no longer; and that the Author of any Book or Books already Composed and not Printed and Published, or that shall hereafter be Composed, and his Assignee, or Assigns, shall have the sole Liberty of Printing and Reprinting such Book and Books for the Term of fourteen.

Whereas 引导的句式在司法文本中也很常见,如某专利转让合同书第一部分规定:

WHEREAS, the Licensor possesses and continually develops advanced Production

Technology (as defined below) and Technical Know-how (as defined below) needed for designing, developing, manufacturing, testing, marketing, selling and maintaining the Products (as defined below);

WHEREAS, the Licensor has the right and desire to license the Production Technology and Technical Know-how to the Licensee and to provide Technical Assistance, Technical Documents and Technical Training (each as defined below) to the Licensee;

WHEREAS, the Licensee desires to obtain from the Licensor through licensing the right to use the Production Technology and Technical Know-how needed to manufacture, modify, design, develop, test, market, sell and maintain the Products; and

WHEREAS, the Licensor desires to provide and the Licensee desires to obtain the right to use such Production Technology and Technical Know-how on terms and conditions set forth in this Agreement (as defined below).

而现代的立法文本较少采用以上形式,如美国宪法的序言就直接采用了常用的句式表明了美国宪法的立法目标:We the People of the United States, in Order to form a more perfect Union, establish Justice, insure domestic Tranquility, provide for the common defence, promote the general Welfare, and secure the Blessings of Liberty to ourselves and our Posterity, do ordain and establish this Constitution for the United States of America.

3. 术语解释

定义核心术语的部分多见于英美法系立法文本。该部分用来解释本部法律中出现的特定术语,一般按字母顺序排列。如果某术语在某章节中有特定的含义,则在相关章节的开始加以定义。术语解释在司法文本中也较为常见,例如某合同文本中第一部分对该合同中所出现的术语做了解释:

Definitions

As used in this Agreement, the following words shall have the meanings set forth below.

"Agreement" shall mean this technology license agreement with the date set forth above between A Ltd. and B Ltd. (together with all schedules hereto), as the same may be supplemented and amended from time to time in accordance with its terms.

"Affiliate" shall mean, as to any entity or person (legal or natural) directly or indirectly controlling, directly or indirectly controlled by or under direct or indirect common control with such entity or person, except that for purposes of this Agreement the Licensee shall not be deemed to be an Affiliate of the Licensor. For purposes of this definition, the term "control" shall mean (i) owning fifty percent [(50%)] or more of registered capital or assets of a party, (ii) is entitled to appoint fifty percent [(50%)] or more of the management personnel, or (iii) is entitled to appoint or nominate a majority number of the directors.

"China" shall mean the geographical areas currently under the jurisdiction of the People's Republic of China, excluding for the purpose of this Agreement, the Hong Kong and Macao Special Administrative Regions, and Taiwan, and "Chinese" shall have a corresponding meaning.

"Existing Technology" shall mean Production Technology and Technical Know-how owned and commercially used by the Licensor and its relevant Affiliates as of the Effective Date.

"Equity Joint Venture Contract" shall mean the Equity Joint Venture Contract between A Ltd. and B Ltd., for the establishment of the Licensee, (together with all schedules thereto), as the same may be supplemented and amended from time to time in accordance with its terms.

"Production Technology" shall consist of processes, technical drawings, industrial designs, production instructions, technical specifications and documentation, and methods of working related to or for the manufacture of the Products. A list describing the Production Technology is set out in Schedule 3.

"Products" shall mean the products identified in Schedule 5 produced by the Licensee from time to time during the term of this Agreement.

"Project Documents" shall mean, collectively, the articles of association of the Licensee, the Equity Joint Venture Contract.

"Technical Documents" shall mean written information possessed by the Licensor (or its relevant Affiliates) and needed for assembling, manufacturing, testing and maintaining the Products [and, subject to the relevant provisions of Clause 2 hereof, shall include all revisions of such written information developed by the Licensor (or its relevant Affiliates) after the Effective Date]. All Technical Documents shall be in English.

"Technical Know-how" shall consist of technical information, know-how, manufacturing techniques, engineering data, specifications of materials and other information relating to, in respect of, or for use with the Production Technology and which is necessary to enable the Licensee to use the Production Technology properly and efficiently for the manufacture of the Products to a standard and quality similar to the standard and quality of similar products manufactured by the Licensor and its relevant Affiliates. A list describing the Technical Know-how is set out in Schedule 3.

"United States Dollars" shall mean the lawful currency of the United States of America.

再如美国 *The Investment Company Act of 1940* 在定义部分对"Investment company"的含义做了详尽的解释。

Definitions

When used in this title, "investment company" means any issuer which—

1. a. is or holds itself out as being engaged primarily, or proposes to engage primarily, in the business of investing, reinvesting, or trading in securities;

b. is engaged or proposes to engage in the business of issuing face-amount certificates of the installment type, or has been engaged in such business and has any such certificate outstanding; or

c. is engaged or proposes to engage in the business of investing, reinvesting, owning, holding, or trading in securities, and owns or proposes to acquire investment securities having a value exceeding 40 per centum of the value of such issuer's total assets (exclusive of Government securities and cash items) on an unconsolidated basis.

2. As used in this section, "investment securities" includes all securities except (A) Government securities, (B) securities issued by employees' securities companies, and (C) securities issued by majority-owned subsidiaries of the owner which (i) are not investment companies, and (ii) are not relying on the exception from the definition of investment company in paragraph (1) or (7) of subsection (c).

（二）立法文本主体

中国和英美法系国家的立法文本的主体部分通常按照各部法律所涉及的内容以及其内在的法律关系以条款的方式列举出来的。中国的法律根据内容需要，可以分编、章、节、条、款、项、目。"编、章、节、条"的序号用中文数字依次表述，"款"不编序号；"项"的序号用中文数字加括号依次表述；"目"的序号用阿拉伯数字依次表述。编、章、节、条的表述方法，条理清晰，显示出法律的严谨性。

如《中华人民共和国刑法》中的章、节、条、款设置：

第二章　犯罪

第二十一条　为了使国家、公共利益、本人或者他人的人身、财产和其他权利免受正在发生的危险，不得已采取的紧急避险行为，造成损害的，不负刑事责任。

紧急避险超过必要限度造成不应有的损害的，应当负刑事责任，但是应当减轻或者免除处罚。

第一款中关于避免本人危险的规定，不适用于职务上、业务上负有特定责任的人。……

在翻译实践中,"编"一般译为"part";"章"一般对应"chapter";"节"常译作"section";"条"译为"article";"款"译作"paragraph";"项"译作"subparagraph";"目"译作"item"。

例如,"《中华人民共和国宪法》第 34 条第 1 款"应译为:The first paragraph of Article 34 of the Constitution of the People's Republic of China.

目前有些人民法院引用法律、法令等条文时,对于条、款、项、目的顺序尚不明确。对引用条文的写法,译者应注意以下几个方面:

(1) 引用法律、法令等的条文时,应按条、款、项、目顺序来写,即条下为款,款下为项,项下为目。

(2) 如果某一条下面没有分款而直接分列几项的,就不要加"第一款",例如《××法》第 10 条只有(一)、(二)、(三)三项,就不要写"第 10 条第 1 款第×项"。

(3) 过去颁布的规范性的文件中,如对条、款、项、目的使用另有顺序,或另用其他字样标明条款时,仍可按照该文件的用法引用。

英美法系通常采用 article,section,subsection,paragraph 和 subparagraph。

"article"通常会用英语明确表达出来,其中的数字用罗马大写数字表示,如"Article I","Article II",并且单独占一行空间。美国 *Black's Law Dictionary* 中对"article"做了以下解释:Article:A separate and distinct part (as a clause or stipulation) of writing, esp. in a contract, statute, or constitution. 可见"article"是宪法、制定法或者合同文本中独立的、显著的部分。一般可译为"条"。要提醒读者注意的是"article"与"articles"的区别,后者应译为"条例"。

"Section"中的数字也用罗马大写数字表示,如"Section I","Section II"等。"Section"在法律语境中的翻译尚无固定译法,译者需要在充分理解法律语篇的基础上发挥能动性,灵活翻译。"Section"通常可译为"条""节"或者"款"。

"Section"译为"条"时,"subsection"则译为"款"。*A Dictionary of the Law* 中对"section"和"subsection"做了以下解释:Section:a subdivision of a statute or document, represented by the symbol § (or § for "sections"). Most statues and codes are divided into sections. Subsection:A part within a section of an act. Each section is denoted as a number with brackets. For example, s.78 (1) of the Trade Practices Act would read as section 78 subsection 1.(陈忠诚,2000:605)

"Section"译为"节"时,其概念大于"article"。例如在 *Agreement on Trade-Related Aspects of Intellectual Property Rights*(《与贸易有关的知识产权协定》)中第二部分包括 8 个 section,每个 section 下又包含若干 article,此时的"Section"便译为"节"。

在美国宪法中"Section"频繁出现,所表述的概念小于"article"。译者将其统一译为"款",这已经成为一种约定俗成的译法。

"Paragraph"与"subparagraph"常译作"条""款"。它们的数字常用括号内小写的罗马数字标示。如 sub-paragraph(iii) of paragraph (b) of subsection (4) of section 18,一般译为第 18 条第 4 款第 2 段第 3 节。在引用时常简写作"s 18(4)(b)(iii)",其中"s"表示"section"(Varo and Hughes,2002)。

(三)立法文本附则

附则部分一般包含各类杂项信息,包括用于申请、登记、信息传递等目的的规定表格;详细再现正文所论及的主要事件和行为的表格等;与某法律或法规的实施相关的一系列废止文件;临时性或过渡性条款,等等(Varo and Hughes,2002)。如《中华人民共和国担保法》中的附则部分内容包括:

第七章　附则

第九十二条　本法所称不动产是指土地以及房屋、林木等地上定着物。本法所称动产是指不动产以外的物。

第九十三条　本法所称保证合同、抵押合同、质押合同、定金合同可以是单独订立的书面合同,包括当事人之间的具有担保性质的信函、传真等,也可以是主合同中的担保条款。

第九十四条　抵押物、质物、留置物折价或者变卖,应当参照市场价格。

第九十五条　海商法等法律对担保有特别规定的,依照其规定。

第九十六条　本法自 1995 年 10 月 1 日起施行。

第二节　语言特点

立法语言指的是由国家立法机关制定并颁布的宪法、各种法律、法规、法令、决定、命令以及立法解释和司法解释等规范性法律文本中所使用的语言。在本书第二章中,我们对法律语言的特点做了概括的分析。作为法律语言的一个分支,立法语言具有法律语言的一般特点。同时相比于其他领域的法律语言而言,立法语言具有更强的权威性。

一、立法语言的权威性

法律规范是由国家权利机关制定的,体现了统治阶级的意志。法律规范是各国社会最高的行为准则,规定了公民的权利和义务准则。这种内容上的逻辑性决定了立法语言必须显示充分的权威性。请看下列例子:

例 1　我国《宪法》第 5 条中规定:"中华人民共和国实行依法治国,建设社会主义法治国家。国家维护社会主义法制的统一和尊严。一切法律、行政法规和地方性法规都<u>不得</u>同宪法相抵触。一切国家机关和武装力量、各政党和各社会团体、各企业事业组织都必须遵守宪法和法律。一切违反宪法和法律的行为,必须予以追究。任何组织或者个人都不得有超越宪法和法律的特权。"

例 2 我国《刑法》第 13 条中规定:"一切危害国家主权、领土完整和安全,分裂国家、颠覆人民民主专政的政权和推翻社会主义制度,破坏社会秩序和经济秩序,侵犯国有财产或者劳动群众集体所有的财产,侵犯公民私人所有的财产,侵犯公民的人身权利、民主权利和其他权利,以及其他危害社会的行为,依照法律应当受刑罚处罚的,都是犯罪,但是情节显著轻微危害不大的,不认为是犯罪。"

例 3 我国《刑法》第 22 条中规定:"为了犯罪,准备工具、制造条件的,是犯罪预备。对于预备犯,可以比照既遂犯从轻、减轻处罚或者免除处罚。"

例 4 我国《美利坚合众国宪法》第一章第 3 节中规定"Immediately after they shall be assembled in Consequence of the first Election, they shall be divided as equally as may be into three Classes. The Seats of the Senators of the first Class shall be vacated at the Expiration of the second Year, of the second Class at the Expiration of the fourth Year, and of the third Class at the Expiration of the sixth Year, so that one third may be chosen every second Year;(*and if Vacancies happen by Resignation, or otherwise, during the Recess of the Legislature of any State, the Executive thereof* may *make temporary Appointments until the next Meeting of the Legislature, which* shall *then fill such Vacancies.*)(The preceding words in parentheses were superseded by the 17th Amendment, section 2.)"

上述例子中"必须""不得""应当""可以","shall","may"等词语的使用充分地显示出法律规范文本中所使用语言的权威性特点。

概括而言,立法语言的权威性通过法律规范的义务性、禁止性、授权性规范来具体体现。

(一) 义务性规范

义务性规范是规定法律行为主体必须做出一定行为的法律规定。义务性规范常通过"应当……""有……义务""必须……","shall","must"等表达方式体现内容的义务性含义,进而体现出立法语言的权威性。

请看以下例子:

例 5 我国《刑法》第 48 条中规定:"死刑只适用于罪行极其严重的犯罪分子。对于应当判处死刑的犯罪分子,如果不是必须立即执行的,可以判处死刑同时宣告缓期 2 年执行。死刑除依法由最高人民法院判决的以外,都应当报请最高人民法院核准。死刑缓期执行的,可以由高级人民法院判决或者核准。"

例 6 我国《老年人权益保障法》第 14 条规定:"赡养人应当履行对老年人经济上供养、生活上照顾和精神上慰藉的义务,照顾老年人的特殊需要。赡养人是指老年人的子女以及其他依法负有赡养义务的人。赡养人的配偶应当协助赡养人履行赡养义务。"

例 7 我国《宪法》第 53 条规定:"中华人民共和国公民**必须**遵守宪法和法律,保守国家秘密,爱护公共财产,遵守劳动纪律,遵守公共秩序,尊重社会公德。"

例 8 《美利坚合众国宪法》第一章第五节中规定:"Each House <u>shall</u> keep a Journal of its Proceedings, and from time to time publish the same, excepting such Parts as may in their Judgment require Secrecy; and the Yeas and Nays of the Members of either House on any question <u>shall</u>, at the Desire of one fifth of those Present, be entered on the Journal."

例 9 《美利坚合众国宪法》第一章第七节中规定:"Every Bill which <u>shall</u> have passed the House of Representatives and the Senate, <u>shall</u>, before it become a Law, be presented to the President of the United States; If he approve he <u>shall</u> sign it, but if not he <u>shall</u> return it, with his Objections to that House in which it <u>shall</u> have originated, who shall enter the Objections at large on their Journal, and proceed to reconsider it. If after such Reconsideration two thirds of that House <u>shall</u> agree to pass the Bill, it shall be sent, together with the Objections, to the other House, by which it shall likewise be reconsidered, and if approved by two thirds of that House, it <u>shall</u> become a Law. But in all such Cases the Votes of both Houses <u>shall</u> be determined by Yeas and Nays, and the Names of the Persons voting for and against the Bill <u>shall</u> be entered on the Journal of each House respectively. If any Bill <u>shall</u> not be returned by the President within ten Days (Sundays excepted) after it shall have been presented to him, the Same <u>shall</u> be a Law, in like Manner as if he had signed it, unless the Congress by their Adjournment prevent its Return, in which Case it shall not be a Law."

(二)禁止性规范

禁止性规范是规定法律关系主体不得做出某些行为的规定。禁止性规范一般通过"禁止……""不得……","shall not","may not"等形式表达立法文本的禁止性内容。

请看下面例子:

例 10 我国《宪法》第 37 条规定:"中华人民共和国公民的人身自由不受侵犯。任何公民,非经人民检察院批准或者决定或者人民法院决定,并由公安机关执行,不受逮捕。<u>禁止</u>非法拘禁和以其他方法非法剥夺或者限制公民的人身自由,<u>禁止</u>非法搜查公民的身体。"

例 11 我国《妇女权益保障法》第 23 条规定:"各单位在录用职工时,除不适合妇女的工种或者岗位外,<u>不得</u>以性别为由拒绝录用妇女或者提高对妇女的录用标准。各单位在录用女职工时,应当依法与其签订劳动(聘用)合同或者服务协议,劳动(聘用)合同或者服务协议中<u>不得</u>规定限制女职工结婚、生育的内容。<u>禁止</u>录用未满 16 周岁的女性未成年人,国家另有规定的除外。"

例 12 《美利坚合众国宪法》第一章第 2 节中规定:"**No** Person **shall** be a Representative who **shall not** have attained to the Age of twenty five Years, and been seven Years a Citizen of the United States, and who **shall not**, when elected, be an Inhabitant of that State in which he shall be chosen."

例 13 《美利坚合众国宪法》第一章第 9 节中规定:"The Migration or Importation of such Persons as any of the States now existing shall think proper to admit, shall not be prohibited by the Congress prior to the Year one thousand eight hundred and eight, but a tax or duty **may** be imposed on such Importation, **not** exceeding ten dollars for each Person."

(三) 授权性规范

授权性规范是指法律关系行为主体可以做出或要求别人做出一定行为的规定。授权性规范一般通过"可以……""有权……""有……权利","may"等形式表达授权性规范内容。

请看下列例子:

例 14 《民法通则》中第 63 条第 1 款规定:"公民、法人<u>可以</u>通过代理人实施民事法律责任。"

例 15 我国《未成年人保护法》第 3 条规定:"未成年人<u>享</u>有生存权、发展权、受保护权、参与权等<u>权</u>利,国家根据未成年人身心发展特点给予特殊、优先保护,保障未成年人的合法权益不受侵犯。未成年人享有受教育权,国家、社会、学校和家庭尊重和保障未成年人的受教育权。未成年人不分性别、民族、种族、家庭财产状况、宗教信仰等,依法平等地<u>享</u>有权利。"

例 16 《美利坚合众国宪法》第一章第 7 节中规定"Every Order, Resolution, or Vote to which the Concurrence of the Senate and House of Representatives **may** be necessary(except on a question of Adjournment)shall be presented to the President of the United States; and before the Same shall take Effect, shall be approved by him, or being disapproved by him, shall be repassed by two thirds of the Senate and House of Representatives, according to the Rules and Limitations prescribed in the Case of a Bill."

(四) 情态动词的翻译

从以上例句中可以看出,立法语言中情态动词的使用频率很高,因此我们有必要对法律英语中的情态动词的翻译做简要地介绍。立法文本中常见的情态动词主要有"must","may","shall"。具体翻译方法参见第五章,这里不再赘述。

二、语句结构特点

立法语句是立法文本的基本组成部分,对立法语句结构的正确理解是准确翻译整个立法文本的先决条件。立法语句常见以下两种分析方法:一种是按语法分析;一种是操作分析。前者是按语法规则来分析立法语句,如语态、主从句等。后者更多地关注立法语句的功能成分,如法律主体、法律主观要件、情况以及条件(Fung & Watson-Brown,1994:4)。通过分析立法语句的结构,译者可以迅速找出语句的主题及宗旨。

通常法律主体就是立法句中第一个主动语态的主句的主语,它指代的是行为者,也包括主语补足语。法律主体并不限于立法句的主句中的名词。如果把立法句分为主语和谓语,当动词是主动语态时,法律主体属于动作的行为者,正如被动句的真正主语(Fung & Watson-Brown,1994:5)。

法律的主观要件在揭示主题的立法句的谓语部分。谓语部分一般包括动词以及修饰短语和其他修饰成分。第一个主句的主动语态谓语就是寻找法律主观要件的关键。有时,含有主题的句子的动词是被动语态。这暗示着翻译时应使用主动语态代替被动语态来突出法律主观要件。当然,法律主观要件不仅仅是动词,还包括一些描述法律主观要件的修饰成分(Fung & Watson-Brown,1994:6)。Coode把谓语的修饰成分分为情况和条件。法律英语中常使用"if"、"where"和"when"来引出情况和条件,"if"强调"如果","where"强调"在……情况下",而"when"更强调时间。但有些时候这三者很难区分,在某些场合下可以互相代替。

请看下面例句:

例17 中华人民共和国公民的通信自由和通信秘密受法律的保护。除因国家安全或者追查刑事犯罪的需要,由公安机关或者检察机关依照法律规定的程序对通信进行检查外,任何组织或者个人不得以任何理由侵犯公民的通信自由和通信秘密。

参考译文:The freedom and privacy of correspondence of citizens of the People's Republic of China are protected by law. No organization or individual may, on any ground, infringe upon the freedom and privacy of citizens' correspondence except in cases **where**, to meet the needs of state security or of investigation into criminal offences, public security or procuratorial organs are permitted to censor correspondence in accordance with procedures prescribed by law.

译文分析:原文规定了公民通信自由和通信秘密受到保护,但在"因国家安全或者追查刑事犯罪的需要",和"由公安机关或者检察机关依照法律规定的程序对通信进行检查"的情况下可以对公民的通信自由和通信秘密进行干涉,这时译文采用了"where"来排除文中列出的两种情况。

例 18 修改经批准的技术引进合同的技术标的内容、价格、期限及保密期限条款,应当经签约各方协商一致并征得原审批机关书面同意。

参考译文:If amendments are to be made to provisions of an approved technology import contract on such matters as content, price, duration of the contract term or term of confidentiality, the matter shall first receive the written approval of the original examing and approving organ after it has been discussed and unanimously supported by the various aignatories to the contract.

译文分析:原文假设了"修改经批准的技术引进合同的技术标的内容、价格、期限及保密期限条款"成立的条件"应当经签约各方协商一致并征得原审批机关书面同意",译文中选用"if"转换为条件状语。

例 19 The Senate shall have the sole power to try all impeachments. **When** sitting for that purpose, they shall be on oath or affirmation. **When** the President of the United States is tried, the Chief Justice shall preside; And no person shall be convicted without the concurrence of two thirds of the members present.

参考译文:所有弹劾案,只有参议院有权审理。在开庭审理弹劾案时,参议员们均应宣誓或誓愿。如受审者为合众国总统,则应由最高法院首席大法官担任主席;在未得出席的参议员的三分之二的同意时,任何人不得被判有罪。

译文分析:"when"在引出情况和条件时更多地强调事件发生的时间,在第一个"when"引导的句子中,译为"在……时候";而在第二个"when"引导的句子中则译为"如果……"。

例 20 Every bill which shall have passed the House of Representatives and the Senate, shall, before it become a law, be presented to the President of the United States; **if** he approve he shall sign it, but **if** not he shall return it, with his objections to that House in which it shall have originated, who shall enter the objections at large on their journal, and proceed to reconsider it. **If** after such reconsideration two thirds of that House shall agree to pass the bill, it shall be sent, together with the objections, to the other House, by which it shall likewise be reconsidered, and **if** approved by two thirds of that House, it shall become a law. But in all such cases the votes of both Houses shall be determined by yeas and nays, and the names of the persons voting for and against the bill shall be entered on the journal of each House respectively. **If** any bill shall not be returned by the President within ten days (Sundays excepted) after it shall have been presented to him, the same shall be a law, in like manner as **if** he had signed it, unless the Congress by their adjournment prevent its return, in which case it shall not be a law.

参考译文:经众议院和参议院通过的法案,在正式成为法律之前,须呈送合众国总统;总统如批准,便须签署,如不批准,即应连同他的异议把它退还给原来提出该案的议院,该议院应将异议详细记入议事记录,然后进行复议。倘若在复议之后,该议院议员的 2/3 仍然同意通过该法案,该院即应将该法案连同异议书送交另一院,由其同样予以复议,若另一院亦以 2/3 的多数通过,该法案即成为法律。但遇有这样的情形时,两院的表决均应以赞同或反对来定,而赞同和反对该法案的议员的姓名,均应由两院分别记载于各院的议事记录之内。如总统接到法案后 10 日之内(星期日除外),不将之退还,该法案即等于曾由总统签署一样,成为法律。只有当国会休会因而无法将该法案退还时,该法案才不得成为法律。

译文分析:原文中出现了六个以"if"引出的表示情况的句子,均强调了假设出现的情况。因此译文中都选择了"如果……"的含义,为了避免单调变换为"若……"。

译者在把握法律英语中表示情况和条件的引导词"if","where"和"when"的使用方法和特点(即:"if"强调"如果","where"强调"在……情况下",而"when"更强调时间)的基础上,要通过对语境的整体性分析判断,从而正确地从中做出选择。

第三节　立法文本的翻译分析

立法文本的翻译要求译者再现原文的法律概念、法律规范、法律传统、法律效力和法律效果等法律要素,以准确传达原文的法律内容和立法目的。因此对等原则是立法文本翻译过程中需要遵守的最基本的原则。而法律词语和语句的对等则是实现立法文本对等翻译的前提。

一、立法文本中词语的翻译

(一)词语的选用

立法文体的庄重性和严肃性通过词语的选用来体现。立法语言具有很强的专业性和正式性,用词强调词义精确、逻辑严密、正式严谨。在立法文本的翻译过程中,译者应充分考虑到立法词语的以上特点,注意选词的正式性、专业性、严谨性和规范性。请看下面例句:

例 21　当事人应当遵循公平原则确定各方的权利和义务。

参考译文:The parties shall abide by the principles of fairness in defining the rights and obligations of each party.

译文解析:

(1)根据原文语境可以看出例句中的"当事人"是一个复数概念,因此应译为"parties"。

(2)立法文本中的"应当"多译为"shall"。在立法文本中表示强制性承担法律义务,如表示"应该或必须"做某事时,应用 shall,而不能用 must 或 should。

(3)"遵循"在其他文体中常译作"obey",但译文中的"abide by"是更为正式的法律用语。

(4)"权利和义务"在立法文本中的出现频率很高,通常译为"rights and obligations"。译文中的"of each party"对权利和义务做了限定,体现了立法文本语言的准确性和严密性。

例 22 建设用地使用权期间届满前,因公共利益需要提前收回该土地的,应当依照本法第 42 条的规定对该土地上的房屋及其他不动产给予补偿,并退还相应的出让金。

参考译文:Prior to the term of the right to use construction land expires, where it is necessary to take back the land in advance by virtue of public interests, compensations shall, in accordance with Article 42 of this Law, be given to the houses and other realties on such land, and corresponding land transfer fees shall be returned back.

译文解析:

(1)在立法文本中"……前"一般译为"prior to",而不使用"before"。"prior to"为正式法律用语。

(2)"因公共利益需要提前收回该土地的"表示一种假设的情况,译文选用"where"作为引导词。

(3)译文中的"in accordance with"为正式用词,意为"根据、依照"。法律英语中表示"根据"的,通常有三个词汇,即"in accordance with","under","pursuant to"。"according to"为非正式用语,多用于口语。

(4)原文中的"本法"译为"this Law",在文中特指《中华人民共和国物权法》,因此要大写。

例 23 集体所有的土地作为建设用地的,应当依照土地管理法等法律规定办理。

参考译文:Where a piece of collectively-owned land is used as construction land, it shall be handled in accordance with the terms, conditions and provisions on land administration and other related laws.

译文解析:

(1)原文中"集体所有的土地作为建设用地的",概括了属于这种条件的所有情况,用"where"来引导比较恰当。"if"强调如果,"when"强调时间,而"where"强调在……情况下。

(2)原文中的"土地管理法等法律规定",应理解为"土地管理法等法律条款的规定",因为每部法律文件都是由各条款组成的,因此,应译成"the terms, conditions and provisions on land administration and other related laws"。

例 24　The disposal of material from demolitions and excavations and of other surplus material (whether natural or man-made), except to the extent that disposal areas within the Site are specified in the Contract.

参考译文：弃置拆除、开挖的材料和其他剩余材料（无论是天然的还是人造的），但弃置在合同约定的现场内弃置区域的除外。

译文解析：

（1）"except"在原文中引导表示解除条件的状语。在立法文本中，一般通过使用实质性条款用语来设置解除条件的结构。"except"引导的句式常出现在句尾，相当于我们法律文本中的限制性但书。一般译为"……，但……"。

（2）原文中的"The disposal of..."是英语法律文本中的名词化结构作主语行文特点的显示，但为了确保译文的间接性并顾及汉语法律文本的行文特点，应译为动宾结构"弃置……"。

（3）原文句中使用了被动句式"...are specified..."，在理解过程中，我们可以对句子的结构进行调整，将主宾调换，理解为"the Contract specifies..."，译为"合同约定了……"。这样可以把原文的语言重点突出地表达出来，并且更加符合法律英语的行文特点。

例 25　The times, places and manner of holding elections for Senators and Representatives, shall be prescribed in each state by the legislature thereof; but the Congress may at any time by law make or alter such regulations, except as to the places of choosing Senators.

参考译文：各州州议会应规定本州参议员及众议员之选举时间、地点及程序；但国会得随时以法律制定或变更此种规定，唯有选举议员的地点不在此例。

译文解析：

（1）原文中的"thereof"是法律英语用词，意为"of each state"，因此"the legislature thereof"应译为"各州州议会"。"thereof"中"there"指代上文中提及的内容，"of"则限定了前后内容的介词关系。

（2）"by law"是"依法""按照法律"之意。

（3）"such...as..."是英语法律文本中的常见说法。文中使用"such...as..."引导定语从句对"regulations"进行了限定性修饰。

（二）名词与动词的转换

名词结构是英语法律文本的行文特征之一。英语法律语言中多使用名词结构，而汉语立法文本多使用动词结构。将汉语法律条文中的动宾结构与英语法律文本中以名词为中心的短语互译，是使译文简练清晰的有效方式之一。因此，在汉英立法文本互译的过程中，译者应该根据两者的特点灵活地对汉英法律语言中的动词和名词结构进行转化，使译文更好地适应目标读者的需求。将原文中的动词转化为名词的过程称

为动词的名词化,多见于汉英法律文本翻译;而名词转化为动词的过程则为名词的动词化,常见于英汉法律文本翻译。请看以下例句:

例 26　设立外资企业,必须有利于中国国民经济的发展,并且采用先进的技术和设备,或者产品全部出口或者大部分出口。

参考译文:The establishment of enterprises with foreign capital shall be beneficial to the development of China's national economy; they shall use advanced technology and equipment or market all or most of their products outside China.

译文解析:

(1) 例句中文文本中"设立……"为动宾结构,表意清晰简洁。翻译时将动词结构转化为名词化结构:"The establishment of enterprises with foreign capital",有效地保持原文的基本语序及句法特征,迎合了读者的习惯。

(2) "并且采用先进的技术和设备"的逻辑主语为"外资企业",翻译时应该补充,但为了避免重复,可用"they"代替。

例 27　当事人一方延迟履行义务。

参考译文:Either party to contract delays in performance of the obligations.

译文解析:

(1) 原文中的"履行义务"为动词结构,在译文中恰当地名词化译为"performance of the obligations"。

(2) 原文中的"一方"在汉语合同立法文本中经常出现,指"当事人一方""当事人的任何一方"之意。在中译英时,不能按字面翻译为"one party"或"one of the Parties",从英文的含义来说"one party"是指"a particular party"之意,是指当事人中确定的一方。"either",按牛津高级词典解释,是指两者之一。根据原文含义,"当事人一方",是指未履行义务的当事人中的任何一方,而不是确定的某一方。因此这里的"一方"应当译成"either party"或"either of the parties"。

例 28　依法成立的合同,受法律保护。

参考译文:The contract established in accordance with law shall be under the protection of law.

译文解析:

(1) "依法"即"根据法律",是立法文本中常见的法律用语。法律英语中表示"根据"的,通常有三个词汇,即"in accordance with","under","pursuant to"。

(2) "受法律保护"含有"应当"的意思,因此译为"shall"。

(3) "保护"是汉语法律语言中的动词结构,英译时采用了"under the protection of law"的名词性结构。

例 29　订立借款合同,借款人应当按照贷款人的要求提供与借款有关的业务活动和财务状况的真实情况。

参考译文：In concluding and entering a loan contract, the borrower shall provide the truthful information about the business activities and financial conditions relating to the loan in accordance with the requirements of the lender.

例 30　In case of conclusion of the contract, it shall be legally binding upon both parties.

参考译文：合同一旦订立，对双方当事人均具有法律约束力。

译文解析：

上例中的名词化结构"conclusion"在汉译时转化为动词"订立"更符合中文法律语言的习惯。

例 31　Partial delivery of the goods is allowed.

参考译文：允许分批交货。

译文解析：

（1）译文将原文中的名词性结构"partial delivery"转化为中文的动词化结构"分批交货"。

（2）这个例子体现了汉英法律语言中主动语态与被动语态的转换。汉语立法文本中较少使用被动语态，而英语法律文本中的被动语态使用较为频繁。被动语态与主动语态的恰当转换可以突出立法文本的严肃性和权威性特点。

（三）近义词与形近词的翻译

近义词与形近词是在立法文本的翻译过程中需要处理的难点之一。这些词语中有些词形相近，可词义相异。有些词语意思相近但用法迥异，使用时不可相互替代。如果译者错误地使用法律专业术语就可能导致立法文书适用法律不当，甚至造成严重后果。请看以下常见易混淆的词语：

1. "犯罪嫌疑人"和"被告人"

这两个词语均表示刑事案件中的审查对象，表面上看含义相同。但在法律语言中却表示不同的法律概念。"犯罪嫌疑人"是指立案侦查的对象，"被告人"则是指起诉阶段的审查对象。被告人可以是受害人在法院直接起诉的对象，所以犯罪嫌疑人可以变为被告人，但被告人不会转换为嫌疑人。两个称呼表示不同的性质和诉讼阶段。在法律文本翻译过程中，"犯罪嫌疑人"常译作"criminal suspects"而"被告人"多译作"defendant"。

2. "二审"和"再审"

"二审"和"再审"的核心词相同，都是审理的意思。而且"再"也有第二次的意思，因此在翻译实践中常常成为译者不易区分的难点。在法律语言中，"二审"和"再审"是完全不同的法律概念。"二审"又称"上诉审"，是按第二审程序审理的案件，是上一级人民法院依照上诉程序对一审法院的判决、裁定进行第二次审理的诉讼活动。而"再审"则是按照申办监督程序，对已经发生效力但确有错误的判决或者裁定所进行的重新审理,此类案件,可由上级法院进行审理,也可由上级法院指定原法院审理。在法律文本翻译中,"二审"常译为"second instance";"再审"则译为"retrial"。

3. "惯犯"和"累犯"

"惯犯"和"累犯"都侧重于行为人的人身危险性,注重行为人的研究,二者都具有较大的人身危害性,具有反社会性。它们在犯罪次数上都有多发性、反复性。"惯犯"是指犯罪已成习性,在较长时间内反复多次实施同种犯罪行为的人。"累犯"是指犯罪分子被判处了有期徒刑以上的刑罚,在服刑完毕或者免除刑罚后的一定期限内又犯应当判处有期徒刑以上刑罚之罪的罪犯。累犯与惯犯还是有较大的区别,这种区别主要表现在法律规定上:(1) 行为人有前科是成立累犯的必要条件,而惯犯则不存在这种限制,有前科的可以成立惯犯,无前科的而屡次实施犯罪的,同样可以成立惯犯;(2) 惯犯反复实施的必须是同种犯罪,而累犯则没有同种犯罪和异种犯罪的限制;(3) 累犯要求前后罪须为被判处一定刑罚之罪,而惯犯则无此要求;(4) 在主观方面,累犯实施犯罪行为所持的心理态度,既可以是直接故意,又可以是间接故意。惯犯实施犯罪行为所持的心理态度则只能是直接故意,间接故意实施犯罪,不能成立惯犯;(5) 构成累犯的犯罪种类多,而构成惯犯的犯罪种类仅限于盗窃、赌博等罪。成立惯犯,客观上必须具有犯罪行为的惯常性,即行为人在客观方面表现为犯罪行为的同一性、多次性和时间上的长期性;成立惯犯,行为人必须在主观上具有基于惯常犯罪的心理倾向而多次产生实施同一犯罪的故意,存在继续犯罪的倾向。在法律文本翻译中,"惯犯"常译作"habitual offender";而"累犯"多译为"recidivist"。

4. "拘役"和"拘留"

"拘役"和"拘留"均含有扣留,限制人身自由的含义。但"拘役"和"拘留"是两个完全不同的概念,二者既不能相互代替,也不能混淆使用。"拘役"是对犯罪分子短时间内剥夺人身自由,就近强制实行劳动改造的刑罚方法。拘役由公安机关就近执行,在执行期间,被判处拘役的犯罪分子每月可以回家一天至两天,参加劳动的,可以酌量发给报酬。"拘留"分刑事拘留、行政拘留和司法拘留三种。刑事拘留是刑事诉讼中的一种强制措施,是公安机关、人民检察院在侦察过程中,遇有紧急情况时,对现行犯或者重大嫌疑分子暂时性剥夺其人身自由的一种强制措施。行政拘留是指公安机关对于违反了行政法律规范的公民,所做出的在短期内限制其人身自由的一种处罚措施。司法拘留是指在民事诉讼过程中,对严重妨害民事诉讼活动的当事人及其他诉讼参与人或第三人所采取的、在一定期间限制其人身自由的一种强制措施。在法律文本翻译中,"拘役"常译作"criminal detention";而"拘留"多译为"detention"。

5. "罚金"和"罚款"

"罚金"和"罚款"也是一组典型的近义词。二者都含有处罚的含义,又都表示以现金的形式处罚。但在法律语言中,"罚金"和"罚款"的含义有着本质的区别。"罚金"是刑法附加刑之一,是刑罚处罚的一种方式,属财产刑,其适用对象是触犯刑法的犯罪分子和犯罪法人。并且只能由人民法院依刑法的规定判决，除此之外，其他任何单位和个人都无权行使罚金权。"罚款"是行政处罚手段之一，是行政执法单位对违反行政法规的个人和单位给予的行政处罚。不需要经人民法院判决，只要行政执法单位依据行政法规的规定，做出处罚决定即可执行。比如，违反治安管理处罚条例，由公安局依治安管理处罚条例规定的程序即可执行。违反工商管理，由工商行政管理机关依据工商行政管理的具体规定程序做出决定即可执行。在法律文本翻译中，"罚金"常译作"penalty"，而"罚款"多译为"fine"。

6. "可以""应该"和"必须"

"可以""应该"和"必须"在立法文本中出现的频率很高，三个词均表示法律规定内容的可行性，三者的主要区别在于语义的轻重差别。"可以"表示许可的含义，指法律赋予公民、法人或者国家机关、社会团体的某种权利，实施与否由法律行为主体决定。"可以"所在的条款表示授权性法律规范，赋予某种行为的被容许性。"应该"是对公民需履行的义务做了原则性规定或提出一般性要求，为公民的行为设立的框架。"应该"所在的法律条款表示义务性规范。"必须"条款对公民的行为做了义务性规范，具有强制执行力。在法律文本翻译中，"可以"常译作"may"，"应该"一般译为"shall"，而"必须"多译为"must"或"shall"。

7. "judgment"、"decree"、"decision"和"sentence"

"judgment"、"decree"、"decision"和"sentence"均指法庭对案件各方当事人的权利和义务或是否承担责任问题做出的最后裁定。以上四词在中文中都译为"判决"，但在用法上有着很大的区别。"judgment"主要是指对于民事案件的判决，有时可与"decision"互换，但其正式程度要高于后者。"decree"主要用于衡平法院的判决以及离婚案件的判决。而"sentence"则主要在刑事案件判决中使用。

8. "negligence"和"fault"

"negligence"是指"过失""疏忽"。"fault"意为"过错""过失"。可见二者的含义有重叠之处，但在法律语境里，"negligence"和"fault"的使用有着严格的区分。"negligence"在法律上是指未达到一个正常情理的人在当时情况下根据法律所应达到的注意标准，即应当注意时却没有注意从而对他人的人身或者财产造成损害的行为。而"fault"是一种心理状态，通常作为侵权或不法行为责任的构成要件，本质上是一个道德概念，表示被告是有责任的，因为他本来应该和能够避免或者阻止该致损行为的发生。在法律文本翻译中，"negligence"常译作"过失"，而"fault"多译为"过错"。

9. "must"、"shall"、"should"和"may"

"must"、"shall"、"should"和"may"在立法文本中使用频率很高，但译者对它们的理解和使用不甚准确，存在误译的现象。在日常英语中，"must"、"shall"均有"必须""应当"的含义，且较"shall"而言，"must"的语气和程度都要重些。但立法文本较少使用"must"，而更多地使用"shall"来表示必须""应当"的含义。带有"shall"的法律条款多表示义务性的法律规范,在立法文本中可以理解为强制性的法律规范。"should"主要标明一种道义上的责任或者义务,没有法律上的强制性,一般译为"应该"。"may"则表示许可性的法律规范,一般译为"可以""有权"。

10. "assault"和"battery"

"assault"和"battery"是《中华人民共和国刑法》和《中华人民共和国侵权法》中与殴打伤害有关的概念,这两个词比较容易混淆。"assault"意为企图伤害罪,指威胁或者使用暴力使得他人合理地认为伤害或者侵犯性的身体接触即将发生,或者通过威胁实施殴打使得他人合理地认为殴打即将发生。而"battery"意为殴击罪,是指对他人非法使用暴力的行为。构成此罪有三个基本要件:(1) 被告实施了犯罪行为,包括作为和不作为;(2) 被告的心理状态可能是故意也可能是轻率;(3) 对被害人的伤害结果可能是身体伤害或者侵犯接触。简言之,"assault"是指企图实施武力伤害他人,"battery"是指对这种威胁的实施。

11. "compensation"和"damages"

"compensation"和"damages"在法律语境中均指对受损害方提供的金钱救济。但二者有着本质的区别。"compensation"是指一方当事人的行为致使另一方当事人的人身、财产或者权益受损害,从而由前者向后者支付的用以作为补偿的金钱;还指因公共目的而致使土地被征用或者受到破坏性影响,从而给土地所有人或占有人价值相当的金钱补偿。而"damages"是指一方当事人的行为致使另一方当事人的人身、财产或者权益受损害,从而由前者向后者支付的用以作为赔偿的金钱。因此在法律文本翻译实践中,"compensation"常译作"补偿",而"damages"则译为"损害赔偿"。

12. "tax avoidance"和"tax evasion"

"tax avoidance"和"tax evasion"的目的和后果都是避免缴纳税款,减轻纳税负担,但二者的法律概念有着本质的区别。"tax avoidance"是指纳税人利用一切合法手段来尽量减少和避免纳税。"tax evasion"是指采取各种非法手段来避免应尽的纳税义务,如少报应税收益或者多报营业费用。因此在法律文本翻译实践中,"tax avoidance"常译作"避税",而"tax evasion"多译为"逃税、偷税漏税"。

诸如此类的近义词和形近词在汉英立法文本中大量存在,这就要求译者注意积累归纳,从而更准确地理解、区分和应用翻译过程中遇到的近义词与形近词,从而确保立法文本译文的高质量。

二、立法文本中语句的翻译

(一) 立法文本语句结构分析

语句是构成立法文本的基本单位。法律语句常使用复杂句和完整句,这个特点在立法文本中尤其突出。对句子结构的分析,主要是要求译者准确地把握复杂语句的主语和谓语结构,然后明确各从句或短语结构中的主要成分,这样译者才能对整个语句和篇章有一个准确的把握。对复杂的立法语句结构的分析有助于译者更好地理解原文,进而提高译文的准确性。

请看下列例句:

例 32　如买方所定船只到达装港后,卖方不能按买方所通知的时间如期装船时,则空舱费及滞期费等一切费用和后果均由卖方承担。如船只因临时撤换、延期或退关等情况而未能及时通知卖方停止发货者,在装港发生的栈租及保险费等损失的计算,应以代理通知的装船日期(如货物晚于船代理通知的装船日期抵达装港,应以货物抵港日期)为准,在港口免费堆存期满后第 16 天起应由买方负担,除人力不可抗拒的情况外。但卖方仍负有载货船只到达装港后立即将货物装船的义务并负担费用及风险。前述各有关费用均凭原始单据核实支付。

语句结构分析:

原文条款包含四部分内容,下面我们来对每个部分进行结构分析:

(1) 第一部分为"如买方所定船只到达装港后,卖方不能按买方所通知的时间如期装船时,则空舱费及滞期费等一切费用和后果均由卖方承担。"① 这部分的主语是:"费用和后果",谓语是"由……承担","卖方"则是动作的发出者。② "如买方所定船只到达装港后,卖方不能按买方所通知的时间如期装船时",是一个条件从句,交代了在该假设情况下,主语发生谓语动作。从句中"买方所定船只到达装港后"是一个时间状语,"卖方不能按买方所通知的时间如期装船"则是核心的假设情况。③ 主句中的"空舱费及滞期费等"是主语"费用"所包含的内容,在译文中可用同位语或者举例的方式表达。

(2) 第二部分为"如船只因临时撤换、延期或退关等情况而未能及时通知卖方停止发货者,在装港发生的栈租及保险费等损失的计算,应以代理通知的装船日期(如货物晚于船代理通知的装船日期抵达装港,应以货物抵港日期)为准,在港口免费堆存期满后第 16 天起应由买方负担,除人力不可抗拒的情况外。"① 这部分的主语是:"计算",谓语是"由……承担","卖方"则是动作的发出者。② "如船只因临时撤换、延期或退关等情况而未能及时通知卖方停止发货者"、"如货物晚于船代理通知的装船日期抵达装港"和"除人力不可抗拒的情况外"是表示假设条件的从句;"在港口免费堆存期满后第 16 天起"是表示时间的假设情况,以上从句交代了在这些假设情况下,主语发生谓语动作。

(3) 第三部分为"但卖方仍负有载货船只到达装港后立即将货物装船的义务并负担费用及风险。"① 这部分的主语是:"卖方",谓语是"负有将货物装船的义务"、"负担费用及风险"。② "载货船只到达装港后"是表示时间的假设情况,交代主语发出谓语动作的条件。

(4) 第四部分即为原文的最后一句话。① 主语为"费用",谓语为"支付"。主语和谓语之间是被动的语态关系,译文中应予以体现。② "前述各有关"是主语的限定语,在译文中应采用定语的形式。"凭原始单据核实"是支付发生的副词条件。

参考译文:Should the sellers fail to load the goods within the time as notified by the buyers, on board the vessel booked by the buyers after its arrival at the port of shipment, all expenses such as dead freight, demurrage, etc., and consequences thereof shall be borne by the sellers. Should the vessel be withdrawn or replaced or delayed eventually or the cargo be shut out, ect., and the sellers are not informed in good time to stop delivery, the calculation of loss for storage expenses and insurance premium thus sustained at the loading port shall be based on the loading date notified by the agent to the sellers (or based on the date of arrival of the cargo at the loading port in case the cargo should arrive there later than the notified loading date). The above-mentioned loss to be calculated from the 16th day after expiry of the free storage time at port shall be borne by the buyers with the exception of force majeure. However, the sellers shall undertake to load the cargo immediately upon the carrying vessel's arrival at the loading port at their own risks and expenses. The payment of the aforesaid expenses shall be effected against presentation of the original vouchers after being checked.(李克兴、张新红,2006)

例33 当事人在订立合同过程中知悉的商业秘密,无论合同是否成立,不得泄露或者不正当使用。泄露或者不正当地使用该商业秘密给对方造成损失的应当承担损害赔偿责任。

语句结构分析:

例句中条款包含两部分内容,下面我们来对每部分结构进行分析:

(1) 第一部分内容为"当事人在订立合同过程中知悉的商业秘密,无论合同是否成立,不得泄露或者不正当使用"。① 这部分的主语是:"当事人",谓语是"不得泄露或者不正当使用",其宾语为"商业秘密"。② "在订立合同过程中知悉的"是对"商业秘密"的修饰成分。我们在翻译时,"商业秘密"可选择定语从句来表达。法律英语中的定语从句中经常使用"such...as"作为关系代词,很少用 which, that 作关系代词,把所修饰的词或词组放在 such 和 as 之间,这样使表达的意思明确,避免发生误解或争议。"无论合同是否成立"交代了主语执行动作的假设情况。

(2) 第二部分内容为"泄露或者不正当地使用该商业秘密给对方造成损失的应当承担损害赔偿责任。"这部分的主语是"……的(当事人)",谓语是"承担……责任"。"应当……"显示了立法文本的规范性以及其对当事人的约束力,应译为"shall"。

参考译文:Either of the parties shall not disclose or unfairly use such business secrets as the parties learn in concluding and entering into a contract, no matter whether the contract is established or not. Provided that if, due to disclosure or unfair use of the business secrets in question, either party causes the other party to suffer losses, the party in question shall be liable for the damages.

例 34　中华人民共和国年满18周岁的公民,不分民族、种族、性别、职业、家庭出身、宗教信仰、教育程度、财产状况、居住期限,都有选举权和被选举权;但是依照法律被剥夺政治权利的人除外。

语句结构分析:

例句中条款包含两部分内容,下面我们来对每部分结构进行分析:

(1) 第一部分内容为"中华人民共和国年满18周岁的公民,不分民族、种族、性别、职业、家庭出身、宗教信仰、教育程度、财产状况、居住期限,都有选举权和被选举权"。① 这部分的主语是:"公民",谓语是"都有选举权和被选举权"。② "中华人民共和国年满18周岁的"是对主语的限制成分。③ "不分……"引导的句子成分采用一系列并列的名词结构对主语实施谓语动作的条件做了进一步的规范,明确规定了公民实施选举权和被选举权的绝对性。我们在翻译时,可以选用插入语方式来表达该部分的内容,译为"regardless of nationality, race, sex, occupation, family background, religious belief, education, property status, or length of residence"。

(2) 第二部分内容为"但是依照法律被剥夺政治权利的人除外"。这部分的主语是"……的人",谓语是"(被)除外"。"but"引导的句子补充限制了第一部分内容,规定了选举权和被选举权被剥夺的条件限制。该部分内容可译为"except..."来体现除外的情况。

参考译文:All citizens of the People's Republic of China who have reached the age of 18 have the right to vote and stand for election, regardless of nationality, race, sex, occupation, family background, religious belief, education, property status, or length of residence, except persons deprived of political rights in accordance with law.

例 35　If the seller, in accordance with the contract or this Convention, hands the goods over to a carrier and if the goods are not clearly identified to the contract by markings on the goods, by shipping documents or otherwise, the seller must give the buyer notice of the consignment specifying the goods.

语句结构分析:

例句中条款包含三部分内容,下面我们来对每部分结构进行分析:

(1) 第一部分内容为"If the seller, in accordance with the contract or this Convention, hands the goods over to a carrier",这部分的主语是"the seller",谓语是"hands...over..."。"If"从句引出一种假设的条件,中间采用插入语成分进一步说明了主语发出动作的条件规范。翻译时应注意插入语的顺序。

(2) 第二部分内容为"and if the goods are not clearly identified to the contract by markings on the goods, by shipping documents or otherwise",第二个"if"引导的从句进一步限制了主语发生动作的假设条件。这部分的主语是"the goods",谓语使用了被

动语态。"or otherwise"意为"或相反""或其他"。"and/or"在立法文本中经常使用，尽量涵盖所有的情况，显示了法律条文的严密性。在翻译时，应把法律的这种严密性体现在译文中，"and/or"多译为"及/或"。

（3）第三部分为"the seller must give the buyer notice of the consignment specifying the goods"，该句子是整个句子的主干内容，在前面两部分的假设条件下，主语应做出谓语的动作，即卖方必须向买方发出列明货物的发货通知。

参考译文：如果卖方按照合同或本公约的规定将货物交付给承运人，但货物没有以货物上加标记、或以装运单据或其他方式清楚地注明有关合同，卖方必须向买方发出列明货物的发货通知。

例 36　Instructions for the issuance of letters of credits, the letters of credit themselves, instructions for any amendments thereto and the amendments themselves shall be complete and precise. In order to guard against confusion and misunderstanding, banks shall discourage any attempt to include excessive detail in the letters of credits or in any amendment thereto.

语句结构分析：

例句用句号隔开两部分内容，下面我们来对每部分结构进行分析：

（1）第一部分句式采用"主语＋系动词＋表语"的简单结构。主语包含四个并列成分："instructions for the issuance of letters of credits, the letters of credit themselves, instructions for any amendments thereto and the amendments themselves"，翻译时应注意译文的简洁清晰。

（2）第二部分主语是"banks"，谓语为"shall discourage..."。句子使用"in order to..."引导的状语结构，来说明主语动作的目的。"in the letters of credits or in any amendment thereto"作为"excessive detail"的修饰成分出现。可译为"在……中"。

（3）需要重点提示的是"thereto"的译法。"thereto"在原文中两次出现。"thereto"为法律用词，在"any amendments thereto"中是指"to the letter of credit"。这是因为在上文已提及"the letter of credit"，下文中不想重复使用。在法律英语中常常使用这类词，此类用词还有 thereof, therein, herein, hereof, hereto, whereas 等等。使用此类词是为了避免重复，使行文准确，简练。在翻译时，应注意此类词后的确切含意，即搞清 to, in, of, in 等后的含义。

参考译文：开立信用证的指示、信用证本身、有关对信用证修改的指示以及其修改书本身，必须完整、明确。为防止混乱和误解，银行应劝阻在信用证或其修改书中加入过多细节的企图。

例 37　(1) Now the Condition of the above-written Guarantee is such that (2) if the Contractor shall duly perform and observe all the terms provisions conditions and stipulations of the said Contract on the Contractor's part to be performed and observed in accordance with the true purport intent and meaning thereof (3) or if on default by the Contractor the Guarantor shall satisfy and discharge the damages sustained by the Employer thereby up to the amount of the above-written Guarantee then this obligation shall be null and void but otherwise shall be and remain in full force and effect (4) but no alteration in terms of the said Contractor or in the extent or nature of the Works to be executed, completed and defects in the Works remedied thereunder and no allowance of time by the Employer of the Engineer under the said Contract nor any forbearance or forgiveness in or in respect of any matter or thing concerning the said Contract of the part of the Employer or the said Engineer shall in any way release the Guarantor from any liability under the above-written Guarantee.

语句结构分析：

这是一个复杂的长句，为了便于分析，原文已经按照意群标明了序号。全句包含四部分内容，中间只用了一个逗号隔开。整个句子的几部分含义由if, or, but等连词区分开。

(1) ① 第一部分内容是整个句子的主干部分，句子成分比较简单，采用了"主语＋系动词＋表语"的基本句型结构。除above-written及such that为法律英语用词外，其他部分用语与普通英语表达别无两样。② "the above-written"是对"Guarantee"的限定词，法律语言为了更明确限定Guarantee，又以"such"作强调限定，同时进一步限定that引导的表语从句。在翻译时，应把上述限定的语气译出来，可译成："上述保证书，规定如下"。

(2) ① 第二部分内容句中主语为"the Contractor"，谓语为"perform and observe"。② 句子的后半部分用"of the said Contract"来修饰"terms provisions conditions and stipulations"。又补以"on the Contractor's part to be performed and observed"，把责任限定到合同中规定的承包人一方所要履行和遵守的所有条款、条件及规定。继而又以"in accordance with the true purport intent and meaning thereof"明确提出承包人履行这些条款、条件及规定的根据。这样就以三个介词短语和一个不定式短语把前后两部分严密组织在一起，把承包人对于合同应承担的责任作为此保证书有效的一个条件讲得清清楚楚，翻译时，应注意保证对原文文体的适应性原则，译好上述三个短语的严密结构，不必苛求短句。③ 句中的"thereof"为法律英语用词，意为"of the Contract"。

(3) ① 第三部分内容以"or if"引出如果承包人不执行所规定的条款后果的可能性——保证人应负有赔偿业主损失的责任。原文在阐述这一层意思时，既简明又严密。② 接着指明赔偿金额以"up to the amount of the above-written Guarantee"为准。③ 随后又以"then"引出赔偿后，保证书将"shall be null and void"。④ 最后以"but otherwise"引出另一种假设的相反的情况。翻译此段时应注意译文语言的逻辑关系，以通顺地再现原文含义。这部分内容可译成："或者如果承包人违约，则保证人应赔偿业主因此而蒙受的损失,直至到达上述保证金额,届时,本保证书所承担的义务即告终止,否则保证书仍保持完全效力。"

(4) 第四部分的内容较长。主语为三个并列结构:"no alteration","no allowance"和"any forbearance or forgiveness",确定了主语,我们可以发现三个主句的限制成分都很多,这就大大增加了阅读理解的难度。句子的谓语为"shall release"。原句的主干即为"no alteration and no allowance nor any forbearance or forgiveness shall release..."。这样将复杂的句子分解之后,我们就可以清晰地把握句子的主干和主旨了。

参考译文:兹将履行上述书面保证书的条件规定如下:如果承包人应切实履行并遵守所签署的上述合同中规定的承包人一方按合同的真实旨意、意向和含义所应履行和遵守的所有条款、条件及规定或者,如果承包人违约,则保证人应赔偿业主因此而蒙受的损失,直至到达上述保证金额,届时,本保证书所承担的义务即告终止,否则保证书仍保持完全效力,但所签合同条款的改变或对工程的施工、完成及根据合同修补其缺陷的性质和范围的任何变更,以及业主或工程师根据上述合同给予的时间宽限,或上述工程师方面对上述合同有关事宜所做的任何容忍或宽恕,均不能解除保证人所承担的上述保证书规定的义务。(傅伟良,2013)

要掌握立法文本中的句子结构,就要理清各句子之间的结构。首先要找出主句的主语谓语部分,确定句子的主干内容。先去掉与之相关的各种限制短语或从句,再找出并列句或主从句之间的连接词,把并列部分或从属部分进行适当切割,再对每一切割部分进行上述过程的分解,就可明确各部分之间的关系。在此基础上进行翻译,才能保证译文的质量。

(二) 主语的翻译

要准确地把握原文的整体含义,译者需要把握构成原文各语句的主干,而主干是由句子中的主语和谓语成分确定。因此,正确地翻译语句中的主语和谓语成分是做好翻译的起点。

语言学家对主语有三种不同的理解:(1)认为主语是针对谓语动词而言的;(2)认为主语指陈述的对象,即主语是被陈述的,谓语则是对主语加以陈述的;(3)认为主语是主题。汉语中的主语和谓语,主要采用第二种观点,即认为它们是陈述和被陈述关系。而英语主语则交代了主题,指明该句讲的是什么。汉语常见名词性主语、动词性主语、表示时间处所和条件的词语作主语、介词引出动作者作主语、别的介词短语和主谓短语作主语。(赵元任,《汉语口语语法》)而英语中常见名词、代词、形容词、动词、介词短语、少量表示数量概念的名词词组充当句子的主语成分。总体而言,汉语和英语的主语在句子中的位置以及语法功能基本能保持一致。但在某些情况下也存在着差异,例如:汉英主语的词的构成不同,在句子中汉英主语所构成的结构也有一定的差别。

主语的确定是汉英法律文本翻译中首要解决的问题之一。主语选择的正确和恰当与否，将会直接影响原文信息的对等性。在汉英立法文本互译过程中，译者对两种语言的主语结构和位置的差异性的处理将决定译文的翻译质量。下面我们将具体介绍汉英法律文本中主语成分的译法。

1. 对等译法

汉英立法文本中名词性主语的翻译是较为简单的一种，一般原文中的名词性主语在译文中也对应译为名词性主语。

例38　The House of Representatives shall be composed of members chosen every second year by the people of the several states, and the electors in each state shall have the qualifications requisite for electors of the most numerous branch of the state legislature.

参考译文：众议院应由各州人民每两年选举一次之议员组成，各州选举人应具有该州州议会中人数最多之一院的选举人所需之资格。

译文解析：

原文句中包含两个分句，第一个分句为名词性主语"The House of Representatives"译为"众议院"，第二个分句同样使用名词性主语"the electors"译为"各州选举人"。

2. 主动态与被动态的转换

汉英法律文本行文具有不同的特点：汉语的法律条文中主语多使用主动语态，而英语法律条文中的主句常使用被动语态表达，在汉英立法文本互译的过程中，要求译者根据汉英法律语言表达的不同特点，灵活转换主动态与被动态，以使译文更好地满足目标读者的需求。

例39　为了维护国家基本经济制度，维护社会主义市场经济秩序，明确物的归属，发挥物的效用，保护权利人的物权，根据宪法，制定本法。

参考译文：In accordance with the Constitution Law, this Law is enacted with a view to maintaining the basic economic system of the state, protecting the socialist market economic order, clearly defining the attribution of the res, bringing into play the utilities of the res and safeguarding the real right of the right holder.

译文解析：在例文"制定本法"前，有五个并列的目的状语，这是中文法律文件句子结构。我们在译成英文时，应按法律英语的表达习惯做结构调整，把"制定本法"放在句首，译为"This Law is enacted..."。五个并列的目的状语置于后面，将目的状语"为了"译为"with a view to"，后接五个并列的成分"maintaining the basic economic system of the state"，"protecting the socialist market economic order"，"clearly defining the attribution of the res"，"bringing into play the utilities of the res"，"safeguarding the real right of the right holder"。

例 40   This Constitution, and the laws of the United States which shall be made in pursuance thereof; and all treaties made, or which shall be made, under the authority of the United States, shall be the supreme law of the land; and the judges in every state shall be bound thereby, anything in the Constitution or laws of any State to the contrary notwithstanding.

参考译文：本宪法及依本宪法所制定之合众国法律；以及合众国已经缔结及将要缔结的一切条约，皆为全国之最高法律；每个州的法官都应受其约束，任何一州宪法或法律中的任何内容与之抵触时，均不得有违这一规定。

译文解析：原文中包含四个并列的主语结构："this Constitution"，"the laws of the United States which shall be made in pursuance thereof"，"and all treaties made"，"or which shall be made"，其中后三个主语结构均采用被动语态表达方式，符合英语立法文书的行文特点。但在中译的过程中，译者应该结合中文法律文书的特点，将其转化为主动语态，译为"本宪法及依本宪法所制定之合众国法律；以及合众国已经缔结及将要缔结的一切条约"。

3. "零主语"的翻译

立法文本为了实现客观、公正、严密、精确，从而达到权威的目的，一般避免使用主语，通过拉开与读者的距离，获得庄重、凝重的修辞效果。我国的立法文本中的语句常采用"零主语"（没有主语）的主语形式，从而保证法律语言中的主语概念的准确性和范围的概括性。常见的"零主语"句式为"……的……"。中文立法文本中的"零主语"形式在英译时可以考虑以下几种方法：

（1）补充主语

补充法是指在翻译过程中根据对原文的准确理解，将中文立法文本中省去的主语部分补充出来，以保证译文的完整性。请看例句：

例 41   凡在中华人民共和国领域外犯罪，依照本法应当负刑事责任的，虽然经过外国审判，仍然可以依照本法追究，但是在外国已经受过刑罚处罚的，可以免除或者减轻处罚。

参考译文：Any person who commits a crime outside PRC territory and according to this law bear criminal responsibility may still be dealt with according to this law even if he has been tried in a foreign country; however, a person who has already received criminal punishment in a foreign country may be exempted from punishment or given a mitigated punishment.

译文解析：

原文"依照本法应当负刑事责任的"中省略了动作的执行者，我们在翻译时可以将主语补出，以适应英文法律文本行文重主语的特点。译文中补出"Any person"作主语是恰当的，体现了英语重主题，汉语重主语的特点。

（2）宾语变主语

立法文本英译过程中时，处理"……的"句式的翻译时，除了补充省略的主语以外，还可以选取句子中重点阐述对象即宾语成分作为译文的主语。请看例句：

例42 犯罪的行为或者结果有一项发生在中华人民共和国领域内的，就认为是在中华人民共和国领域内犯罪。

参考译文：Either the act or consequence of a crime which takes place within PRC territory is deemed to have been committed within PRC territory.

译文解析：

原文可以理解为：在中华人民共和国领域内，犯罪的行为或者结果有一项发生，就认为是在中华人民共和国领域内犯罪。可见，原句宾语为"犯罪的行为或者结果有一项发生"，因此我们可以选其作为句子的主语。故上文的主语可译为"either the act or consequence of a crime"。

（三）谓语的翻译

法律语言中经常使用两个或三个意思相近或者相同的动词构成一个短语以准确表达概念。这种近义词并列使用的方式，体现了法律语言的严肃性和法律文体的准确性和严密性，确保了整体含义的完整、准确。请看以下例子：

例43 为保证人民法院正确、及时审理行政案件，保护公民、法人和其他组织的合法权益，维护和监督行政机关依法行使行政职权，根据宪法制定本法。

参考译文：For the purposes of safeguarding correct and timely trial of administrative cases, protecting the lawful rights and interests of citizens, legal persons and other organizations and ensuring and supervising the exercise of administrative power by administrative organs according to law, this Law is formulated and enacted in accordance with the Constitution.

译文解析：例文中的"制定本法"意为制定并颁布本法。翻译时常采用同义词连用来表达这两层含义。英语法律文本中经常同时使用"formulated and enacted"来表示"制定"，这种说法确保了译文的准确性。

例44 当事人之间订立有关设立、变更、转让和消灭不动产物权的合同，除法律另有规定或者合同另有约定外，自合同成立时生效；未办理物权登记的，不影响合同效力。

参考译文：As regards a contract concluded and entered into by the related parties concerned on the creation, alteration, alienation or termination of the real right of a realty, it shall go into effect upon the conclusion of the contract, unless it is otherwise prescribed by any law; and the validity of the contract is not affected, whether the real right has been registered or not.

译文解析：原文中"订立合同"一般理解为制定并实施合同。为了保证原文两层含义的准确表达,我们应将其译作"conclude and enter into a contract"连用的方法。

例 45 This agreement is made and entered into by and between Party A and Party B.

参考译文:本协议由甲方和乙方签订。

译文解析:原文中同时使用同义动词"make"和"enter into"来表达"签订"之意,这种动词连用的表达方法可保证原文的含义的准确性和严密性。

例 46 The Corporation acknowledges and agrees that the Technology it receives from Party A during the term of the Contract shall be kept secret and confidential.

参考译文:公司承认并同意在合同期内由甲方提供的技术系属秘密。

译文解析:原文同时使用同义动词"acknowledge"和"agree"来表达"签订"之意,准确无歧义。如不采用同义词连用,无论是"acknowledge"还是"agree"的单独使用,都会因各自的多义而引发争议。

(四) 定语的翻译

法律文本中使用大量的修饰限定成分来明确对主体或核心词的规范,以达到结构严密、规范精确的目的。这个特点决定了法律文本中定语从句的频繁使用。在处理定语的翻译时,我们通常选用"such...as"或 which 作为关系引导词。法律文本中"such...as"引导的定语从句较"which/that"而言更加准确、严密,被修饰限定的成分通常位于 such 和 as 之间。在被限定词的内容不易产生歧义时,我们也可以选用"which/that"作为引导词。请看下面例子:

例 47 中华人民共和国副主席协助主席工作。中华人民共和国副主席受主席的委托,可以代行主席的职权。

参考译文:The Vice-President of the People's Republic of China assists the President in his work. The Vice-President of the People's Republic of China may exercise such parts of the functions and powers of the President as the President may entrust to him.

译文解析:原文的第二部分"受主席的委托代行主席的部分职权",选用关系代词"such...as"来引导限制性的定语从句。原文译为"exercise such parts of the functions and powers of the President as the President may entrust to him"意思明确,不会引起误解。如选用"which"或"that"把句子译成"exercise parts of the functions and powers of the President which/that the President may entrust to him"会使译文产生歧义。后一种译法可能会有两种理解:一个认为定语从句只修饰"powers of the President";而另一个则认为该定语从句是修饰"powers of the President"和"functions of the President"。

例 48 业主对建筑物内的住宅、经营性用房等专有部分享有所有权,对专有部分以外的共有部分享有共有和共同管理的权利。

参考译文：As regards such exclusive parts within the buildings as the residential houses or the houses used for business purposes, an owner shall enjoy the ownership thereof, while as regards the common parts other than the exclusive parts, the owner shall have common ownership and the common management right thereof.

译文解析：(1) 原文"建筑物内的住宅、经营性用房等专有部分"可以理解为"建筑物内的住宅和经营性用房的专有部分"，因此选用"such...as"来引导定语从句对"专有部分"进行限制性修饰。原文译作"such exclusive parts within the buildings as the residential houses or the houses used for business purposes"。

(2) 原文中"业主对……享受所有权"和"对……享有共有和共同管理的权利"中宾语部分内容与前文重复，因此使用"thereof"代替，否则译文将变成"an owner shall enjoy the ownership of such exclusive parts within the buildings as the residential houses or the houses used for business purposes"和"the owner shall have common ownership and the common management right of the common parts other than the exclusive parts"。可见，"thereof"的使用可使译文行文更加简洁、正式。

例 49 建筑物及其附属设施的费用分摊、收益分配等事项，有约定的，按照约定；没有约定或者约定不明确的，按照业主专有部分占建筑物总面积的比例确定。

参考译文：As regards such matters as the expenses allocation and the proceeds distribution of a building or any of its affiliated facilities, in case there exists any stipulation for these, such stipulation shall apply; in the case of no stipulation or unclear stipulation, these matters shall be determined in accordance with the proportion of each owner's exclusive parts to the total area of the building.

译文解析：(1) 原文"建筑物及其附属设施的费用分摊、收益分配等"可理解为"事项"的限制性规范，故选用"such...as"。将所修饰的内容"事项"置于 such 和 as 之间，原文译为"such matters as the expenses allocation and the proceeds distribution of a building or any of its affiliated facilities"。

(2) 原文对"……事项"的处理分两种情况做了规定，我们可以理解为"关于……的事项"，因此译文中应补出"as regards"。

(3) 原文列举了针对建筑物及其附属设施的费用分摊、收益分配等事项的两种处理情况："有约定的……；没有约定或者约定不明确的……"，这种表达方式的英译通常选用"in case..."。

例 50 Each House shall be the judge of the elections, returns and qualifications of its own members, and a majority of each shall constitute a quorum to do business; but a smaller number may adjourn from day to day, and may be authorized to compel the attendance of absent members, in such manner, and under such penalties as each House may provide.

参考译文：参众两院应各自审查本院的选举、选举结果报告和本院议员的资格，每院议员过半数即构成可以议事的法定人数；不足法定人数时，可以一天推一天地延期开会，并有权依照各该议院所规定的程序和罚则，强迫缺席的议员出席。

译文解析：

（1）原文"in such manner, and under such penalties as each House may provide"句中将被限定词"manner"和"penalties"置于 such 和 as 之间，各自和不同的介词搭配。该定语从句应译为"依照各该议院所规定的程序和罚则"。

（2）原文中的"business"是一个正式词汇，表示"工作、职责、任务"。根据《COBUILD 英汉双解词典》对"business"做了以下定义：生意、商业、企业、职责、要务、眼前所关心之事、活动、行为、难事。因此我们应该在正确理解原文的基础上对"business"的译法做慎重考虑，以免误译。

例 51 In all cases affecting ambassadors, other public ministers and consuls, and those in which a state shall be party, the Supreme Court shall have original jurisdiction. In all the other cases before mentioned, the Supreme Court shall have appellate jurisdiction, both as to law and fact, with such exceptions, and under such regulations as the Congress shall make.

参考译文：在一切有关大使、公使、领事以及州为当事一方的案件中，最高法院有最初审理权。在上述所有其他案件中，最高法院有关于法律和事实的受理上诉权，但由国会规定为例外及另有处理条例者，不在此限。

译文解析：

（1）例句法条中规定"In all cases affecting ambassadors, other public ministers and consuls, and those in which a state shall be party, the Supreme Court shall have original jurisdiction."该句中存在一个"in which"引导的定语从句来修饰限定先行词"those"。句中的"those"指意明确，表达不易产生歧义。因而可以选用"which"作引导词。再者，在"that"、"this"、"those"、"these"等指示代词作先行词的定语从句中，多用"which"引导定语从句，一般不选用"such...as"作为引导词。

（2）原文中"with such exceptions, and under such regulations as the Congress shall make"是"such...as"引导的限定性定语从句，被限定词"exceptions"和"regulations"位于 such 和 as 之间，确保了表述的准确严密。译者应注意被限定词的不同介词搭配。这部分应译为"但由国会规定为例外及另有处理条例者，不在此限。"

例 52 To exercise exclusive legislation in all cases whatsoever, over such District（not exceeding ten miles square）as may, by cession of particular states, and the acceptance of Congress, become the seat of the government of the United States, and to exercise like authority over all places purchased by the consent of the legislature of the state in which the same shall be, for the erection of forts, magazines, arsenals, dockyards, and other needful buildings;

参考译文：对于由某州让与而由国会承受，用以充当合众国政府所在地的地区（不逾十里见方），握有对其一切事务的全部立法权；对于经州议会同意，向州政府购得，用以建筑要塞、弹药库、兵工厂、船坞和其他必要建筑物的地方，也握有同样的权力。

译文解析：

（1）原文"To exercise exclusive legislation in all cases whatsoever, over such District (not exceeding ten miles square) as may, by cession of particular states, and the acceptance of Congress, become the seat of the government of the United States"的结构比较复杂，在"such...as"引导的定语从句中有两个插入语："by cession of particular states"和"the acceptance of Congress"。掌握句子的结构，是做好翻译工作的重要步骤。在翻译过程中，应在理解全文的基础上按逻辑顺序合理排列插入语和定语从句的汉语顺序。原文中的两个插入语所表示的含义当是"exercise exclusive legislation"实现的条件。该句应译为"对于由某州让与而由国会承受，用以充当合众国政府所在地的地区（不逾十里见方），握有对其一切事务的全部立法权"

（2）原文"and to exercise like authority over all places purchased by the consent of the legislature of the state in which the same shall be, for the erection of forts, magazines, arsenals, dockyards, and other needful buildings"部分含有一个"in which"引导的定语从句，修饰限定"the state"。该定语从句中的先行词指意明确，表达不易产生歧义。因而可以选用"which"作引导词。

为了使译文表意清晰准确，避免产生歧义，我们在翻译法律文本过程中通常选用"such...as"作为定语从句的引导词，但在有特殊语法要求且不易产生歧义的情况下，可以选用其他引导词。定语从句的翻译应强调对原文的深层理解，从而增强译文的选词的准确性。

（五）状语的翻译

状语主要用来修饰动词和整个句子，状语主要分为以下九类：时间状语、地点状语、方式状语、让步状语、目的状语、原因状语、结果状语、条件状语和伴随状语。在法律语言中常见时间状语、条件状语、方式状语和目的状语来说明对规定规范的时间、条件、方式和目的的限制。

1. 时间状语

立法文本中常使用时间状语来说明条文规范的时间性限定。请看下列例句：

例53　不动产物权的设立、变更、转让和消灭，依照法律规定应当登记的，自记载于不动产登记簿时发生效力。

参考译文：As regards the creation, alteration, alienation or termination of the real right of realty, it shall go into effect since the date when it is recorded in the realty register in case the registration thereof is required by law.

译文解析：原文规定应登记的不动产的设立、变更、转让和消灭在登记时起发生效力，通过时间状语从句"自记载于不动产登记簿时"对效力发生的时间做了限定。这个时间状语从句可译为"since the date when it is recorded in the realty register"。

例 54　The Congress, whenever two thirds of both houses shall deem it necessary, shall propose amendments to this Constitution.

参考译文：举凡两院议员各以 2/3 的多数认为必要时，国会应提出对本宪法的修正案。

译文解析：原文中使用"whenever"引导的时间状语从句："whenever two thirds of both houses shall deem it necessary"来对主句中主语发出谓语动作的时机做出限定，即"举凡两院议员各以 2/3 的多数认为必要时，国会应提出对本宪法的修正案。"

2. 条件状语

立法文本中常使用假设条件状语和例外条件状语来假设列举和例外排除所规范内容的条件。在假设条件状语从句中，经常使用引导词"if"、"where"、"when"和"in case"。在例外条件状语从句中常使用引导词"provided"、"except"和"unless"。请看以下例句：

例 55　不动产物权的设立、变更、转让和消灭，经依法登记，发生效力；未经登记，不发生效力，但法律另有规定的除外。

参考译文：Until it is registered in accordance with law, the creation, alteration, alienation or termination of the real right of a realty shall come into effect; Unless it is otherwise prescribed by any law, it shall have no effect *if* it is not registered in accordance with law.

译文解析：原本包含两部分内容。第二部分内容可理解为"如果不动产物权的设立、变更、转让和消灭未经登记，那么不发生效力"。可见，原文的假设条件强调"如果……"，因此我们应选择"if"作为译文条件状语从句的引导词，该部分可译为"it shall have no effect if it is not registered in accordance with law"。

例 56　**Where** a contract has been validly concluded but dose not expressly or implicitly fix or make provisions for determining the price, the parties are considered, in the absence of any indication to the contrary, to have impliedly made reference to the price generally charged at the time of the conclusion of the contract for such goods sold under comparable circumstances in the trade concerned.

参考译文：如果合同已有效地订立，但没有明示地规定价格，在没有任何相反表示的情况下，双方当事人应视为已默示地引用订立合同时此种货物在有关贸易的类似情况下销售的通常价格。

译文解析：原文中"where"引导假设条件状语从句，来对主句发生动作的假设性条件做了限定。"where"引导条件状语从句时,更强调"在……情况下"的含义,因此原文可译为"如果合同已有效地订立,但没有明示地规定价格,在没有任何相反表示的情况下……"。

例 57 物权的取得和行使,应当遵守法律,尊重社会公德,不得损害公共利益和他人合法权益。

参考译文:One shall, **when** acquiring or exercising a real right, comply with the law, respect social morals and may not infringe upon the public interests or the lawful rights and interests of any other person.

译文解析:原文可以理解为"取得和行使物权的时候,应当……",这个条件状语从句强调假设发生的时间,因此可选"when"作为译文条件状语从句的引导词。该部分内容可译为"when acquiring or exercising a real right"。

例 58 **In case of** the removal of the President from office, or of his death, resignation, or inability to discharge the powers and duties of the said office, the same shall devolve on the Vice President, and the Congress may by law provide **for the case of** removal, death, resignation or inability, both of the President and Vice President, declaring what officer shall then act as President, and such officer shall act accordingly, until the disability be removed, or a President shall be elected.

参考译文:如遇总统被免职,或因死亡、辞职或丧失能力而不能执行其权力及职务时,总统职权应由副总统执行之。国会得以法律规定,在总统及副总统均被免职,或死亡、辞职或丧失能力时,由何人代理总统职务,该人应即遵此视事,至总统能力恢复,或新总统被选出时为止。

译文解析:原文使用了"in case"及其变形"for the case of"来对总统职权交替的情况做了假设。译者应根据上文的语境对其具体含义做出判断,以使译文表意恰当准确。在本文中,我们可将其译为"如遇总统被免职,或因死亡、辞职或丧失能力而不能执行其权力及职务时……"和"在总统及副总统均被免职,或死亡、辞职或丧失能力时……"。

例 59 (全国人大常委会)在全国人民代表大会闭会期间,对全国人民代表大会制定的法律进行部分补充和修改,但是不得同该法律的基本原则相抵触。

参考译文:To enact, when the National People's Congress is not in session, partial supplements and amendments to statutes enacted by the National People's Congress **provided that** they do not contravene the basic principles of these statutes.

译文解析:原文可理解为"全国人大常委会可对除了与宪法基本原则相抵触的部分外的法律进行修改和补充"。我们可选用"provided"作为"除了……"例外状语从句的引导词,该部分可译为"provided that they do not contravene the basic principles of these statutes"。

例 60　The trial of all crimes, **except** in cases of impeachment, shall be by jury; and such trial shall be held in the state where the said crimes shall have been committed; but when not committed within any state, the trial shall be at such place or places as the Congress may by law have directed.

参考译文：对一切罪行的审判,除了弹劾案以外,均应由陪审团裁定,并且该审判应在罪案发生的州内举行;但如罪案发生地点并不在任何一州之内,该项审判应在国会按法律指定之地点或几个地点进行。

译文解析:"except"是一个较明显的例外条件状语的标识,多与短语连用,一般译为"除了……"。而"except that"引导的例外条件从句一般并不明确特定行为模式的例外情形,而是为了设置专门的限制。因而一般不宜译成"除……外",多译为"……,但……"。

例 61　当事人之间订立有关设立、变更、转让和消灭不动产物权的合同,<u>除</u>法律另有规定或者合同另有约定<u>外</u>,自合同成立时生效;未办理物权登记的,不影响合同效力。

参考译文：As regards a contract entered into by the related parties concerned on the creation, alteration, alienation or termination of the real right of a realty, it shall go into effect upon the conclusion of the contract, **unless** it is otherwise prescribed by any law; and the validity of the contract is not affected, whether the real right has been registered or not.

译文解析:原文"除法律另有规定或者合同另有约定外",是中文法律文本中常见的排除条件状语从句。翻译时,我们可以选择"unless"作为译文中排除条件状语从句的引导词。"unless"一般明确特定行为模式的例外情形,常引导句子。该部分内容可译为"unless it is otherwise prescribed by any law"。

3. 方式状语

立法文本内容通常会涉及法律行为主体履行或者不履行法律行为的方式,比如交货方式等。因此方式状语对明确法律规范的内容起着重要的作用。请看下列例句:

例 62　物权的种类和内容,由法律规定。

参考译文：The varieties and contents of real rights shall be prescribed by law.

译文解析:原文可以理解为"物权的种类和内容,由法律规定的方式确定",因此我们可以采用以下译法"The varieties and contents of real rights shall be prescribed by law"。

例 63　Representatives and direct taxes shall be apportioned among the several states which may be included within this union, according to their respective numbers, which shall be determined **by** adding to the whole number of free persons, including those bound to service for a term of years, and excluding Indians not taxed, three fifths of all other Persons.

参考译文：众议员人数及直接税税额，应按联邦所辖各州的人口数目比例分配，此项人口数目的计算法，应在全体自由人民——包括订有契约的短期仆役，但不包括未被课税的印第安人——数目之外，再加上所有其他人口之3/5。

译文解析：原文中使用"by"引导的方式状语来说明各州人口数目计算的方法。由于原文交代的计算方式较为复杂，翻译时我们可以不把"by"明确译出，请参考以下译法"此项人口数目的计算法，应在全体自由人民——包括订有契约的短期仆役，但不包括未被课税的印第安人——数目之外，再加上所有其他人口之3/5。"

4．目的状语

目的状语用来明确法律规范的目的。常见的目的状语引导词有"in order to"，"to"，"so as to"等，目的状语的引导词通常可以相互替代使用。请看以下例句：

例64　当事人签订买卖房屋或者其他不动产物权的协议，为保障将来实现物权，按照约定可以向登记机构申请预告登记。预告登记后，未经预告登记的权利人同意，处分该不动产的，不发生物权效力。

参考译文：In case the related parties entered into a purchase agreement on a premise or the real right of any other realty, they may apply for advance notice registration to the registration organ **so as to** ensure the realization of the real right in the future.

译文解析：当事人签订协议的目的就是为了保障将来实现物权，这一目的性状语在译文中可选用"so as to/to/in order to"来引导。

例65　We the people of the United States, **in order to** form a more perfect union, establish justice, insure domestic tranquility, provide for the common defense, promote the general welfare, and secure the blessings of liberty to ourselves and our posterity, do ordain and establish this Constitution for the United States of America.

参考译文：我们美利坚合众国的人民，为了组织一个更完善的联邦，树立正义，保障国内的安宁，建立共同的国防，增进全民福利和确保我们自己及我们后代能安享自由带来的幸福，乃为美利坚合众国制定和确立这一部宪法

译文解析：原文使用"in order to"作为引导词来说明美国宪法制定的目标。"in order to"一般译为"为了……"。

第四节　本章小结

立法文本的翻译是一项艰巨的工作，分析并掌握立法文本的类型、结构、语言特点是译者开展翻译工作的基础，对以上特点的准确把握和应用有助于译者高质量地完成

立法文本的翻译工作。在此基础上译者还需准确理解复杂语句的结构,能够精确把握立法文本中词语和语句的翻译方法,以实现对原法律文本内容的准确传达和再现。

课后习题

1. 请翻译下列文章标题。
(1) 试论依法行政
(2) 谈建设创新型国家
(3) 深化改革　扩大开放　促进经济结构调整
(4) 以权谋公而不能谋私
(5) 精神损害行为的认定及赔偿探讨
(6) 精神文明发展规律论
(7) 社会主义核心价值体系深入人心
(8) 中国共产党十八届四中全会公报
(9) 确立以人为本的发展观是"十五期间"经济社会发展的必然要求
(10) 利用国债为落后地区经济增长筹集启动资金

2. 请翻译中美两国宪法序言。
(1)《中华人民共和国宪法》序言

序　　言

社会主义的建设事业必须依靠工人、农民和知识分子,团结一切可以团结的力量。在长期的革命和建设过程中,已经结成由中国共产党领导的,有各民主党派和各人民团体参加的,包括全体社会主义劳动者、社会主义事业的建设者、拥护社会主义的爱国者和拥护祖国统一的爱国者的广泛的爱国统一战线,这个统一战线将继续巩固和发展。中国人民政治协商会议是有广泛代表性的统一战线组织,过去发挥了重要的历史作用,今后在国家政治生活、社会生活和对外友好活动中,在进行社会主义现代化建设、维护国家的统一和团结的斗争中,将进一步发挥它的重要作用。中国共产党领导的多党合作和政治协商制度将长期存在和发展。

中华人民共和国是全国各族人民共同缔造的统一的多民族国家。平等、团结、互助的社会主义民族关系已经确立,并将继续加强。在维护民族团结的斗争中,要反对大民族主义,主要是大汉族主义,也要反对地方民族主义。国家尽一切努力,促进全国各民族的共同繁荣。

中国革命和建设的成就是同世界人民的支持分不开的。中国的前途是同世界的前途紧密地联系在一起的。中国坚持独立自主的对外政策,坚持互相尊重主权和领土完整、互不侵犯、互不干涉内政、平等互利、和平共处的五项原则,发展同各国的外交关系和经济、文化的交流;坚持反对帝国主义、霸权主义、殖民主义,加强同世界各国人民的团结,支持被压迫民族和发展中国家争取和维护民族独立、发展民族经济的正义斗争,为维护世界和平和促进人类进步事业而努力。

本宪法以法律的形式确认了中国各族人民奋斗的成果,规定了国家的根本制度和根本任务,是国家的根本法,具有最高的法律效力。全国各族人民、一切国家机关和武装力量、各政党和各社会团体、各企业事业组织,都必须以宪法为根本的活动准则,并且负有维护宪法尊严、保证宪法实施的职责。

(2)《美利坚合众国宪法》序言

Preamble

We the People of the United States, in order to form a more perfect Union, establish Justice, insure domestic tranquility, provide for the common defense, promote the general Welfare, and secure the Blessings of Liberty to ourselves and our Posterity, do ordain and establish this Constitution for the United States of America.

3. 请翻译下列法条,尤其注意各条文之间的结构安排。

Liability arising in contract

(1) This section applies as between contracting parties where one of them deals as consumer or on the other's written standard terms of business.

(2) As against that party, the other cannot by reference to any contract term——

(a) When himself in breach of contract, exclude or restrict any liability of his in respect of the breach; or

(b) claim to be entitled——

(i) to render a contractual performance substantially different from that which was reasonably expected of him; or

(ii) in respect of the whole or any part of his contractual obligation, to render no performance at all, except in so far as (in any of the cases mentioned above in this subsection) the contract term satisfies the requirement of reasonableness. [cf. 1977 c. 50 s. 3 U.K.]

4. 请翻译下列法律条文。

全国人民代表大会任期届满的两个月以前,全国人民代表大会常务委员会必须完成下届全国人民代表大会代表的选举。如果遇到不能进行选举的非常情况,由全国人民代表大会常务委员会以全体组成人员的三分之二以上的多数通过,可以推迟选举,延长本届全国人民代表大会的任期。在非常情况结束后一年内,必须完成下届全国人民代表大会代表的选举。(《中华人民共和国宪法》第60条)

5. 请翻译下列法条,尤其注意各句子结构的分析。

精神病人在不能辨认或者不能控制自己行为的时候造成危害结果的,不负刑事责任;但是应当责令其家属或者监护人严加看管和医疗。

间歇性的精神病人在精神正常的时候犯罪,应当负刑事责任。

醉酒的人犯罪,应当负刑事责任。(《中华人民共和国刑法》第 15 条)

6. 请将下列文本译成汉语

(1)

The Organization and its Members, in pursuit of the Purposes stated in Article 1, shall act in accordance with the following Principles.

a. The Organization is based on the principle of the sovereign equality of all its Members.

b. All Members, in order to ensure to all of them the rights and benefits resulting from membership, shall fulfill in good faith the obligations assumed by them in accordance with the present Charter.

c. All Members shall settle their international disputes by peaceful means in such a manner that international peace and security, and justice, are not endangered.

d. All Members shall refrain in their international relations from the threat or use of force against the territorial integrity or political independence of any state, or in any other manner inconsistent with the Purposes of the United Nations.

e. All Members shall give the United Nations every assistance in any action it takes in accordance with the present Charter, and shall refrain from giving assistance to any state against which the United Nations is taking preventive or enforcement action.

f. The Organization shall ensure that states which are not Members of the United Nations act in accordance with these Principles so far as may be necessary for the maintenance of international peace and security.

g. Nothing contained in the present Charter shall authorize the United Nations to intervene in matters which are essentially within the domestic jurisdiction of any state or shall require the Members to submit such matters to settlement under the present Charter; but this principle shall not prejudice the application of enforcement measures under Chapter Ⅶ.

(摘自《联合国宪章》)

(2)

§ 2-201. Formal Requirements; Statute of Frauds.

a. Except as otherwise provided in this section a contract for the sale of goods for the price of $500 or more is not enforceable by way of action or defense unless there is some writing sufficient to indicate that a contract for sale has been made between the parties and signed by the party against whom enforcement is sought or by his authorized agent or broker. A writing is not insufficient because it omits or incorrectly states a term agreed upon but the contract is not enforceable under this paragraph beyond the quantity of goods shown in such writing.

b. Between merchants if within a reasonable time a writing in confirmation of the contract and sufficient against the sender is received and the party receiving it has reason to know its contents, it satisfies the requirements of subsection (1) against such party unless written notice of objection to its contents is given within 10 days after it is received.

c. A contract which does not satisfy the requirements of subsection (1) but which is valid in other respects is enforceable

ⓐ if the goods are to be specially manufactured for the buyer and are not suitable for sale to others in the ordinary course of the seller's business and the seller, before notice of repudiation is received and under circumstances which reasonably indicate that the goods are for the buyer, has made either a substantial beginning of their manufacture or commitments for their procurement; or

ⓑ if the party against whom enforcement is sought admits in his pleading, testimony or otherwise in court that a contract for sale was made, but the contract is not enforceable under this provision beyond the quantity of goods admitted; or

ⓒ with respect to goods for which payment has been made and accepted or which have been received and accepted.

7. 请将下列文本译成英语。

全会强调,党的领导是中国特色社会主义最本质的特征,是社会主义法治最根本的保证。把党的领导贯彻到依法治国全过程和各方面,是我国社会主义法治建设的一条基本经验。我国宪法确立了中国共产党的领导地位。坚持党的领导,是社会主义法治的根本要求,是党和国家的根本所在、命脉所在,是全国各族人民的利益所系、幸福所系,是全面推进依法治国的题中应有之义。党的领导和社会主义法治是一致的,社会主义法治必须坚持党的领导,党的领导必须依靠社会主义法治。只有在党的领导下依法治国、厉行法治,人民当家做主才能充分实现,国家和社会生活法治化才能有序推进。依法执政,既要求党依据宪法法律治国理政,也要求党依据党内法规管党治党。

全会明确了全面推进依法治国的重大任务,这就是:完善以宪法为核心的中国特色社会主义法律体系,加强宪法实施;深入推进依法行政,加快建设法治政府;保证公正司法,提高司法公信力;增强全民法治观念,推进法治社会建设;加强法治工作队伍建设;加强和改进党对全面推进依法治国的领导。

第七章
国际商务合同的翻译

国际商务合同是国际商务中当事人确立商务关系、履行权利和义务以及解决纠纷的基本法律文件。此类合同具有涉外交易性质,因此通常采用中英文书面形式。无论采用何种书面形式,由于合同具有法律效力,合同双方必须严格按照合同的约定,全面履行合同义务,这就需要对合同的文字斟词酌句,力求准确无误。由于各类合同标的不同,所以性质各异,内容相差巨大,因而掌握通用合同条款的翻译,就成为合同翻译的基本技巧。本章将以国际商务合同为研究范本,对国际商务合同的语言特点进行分析,在此基础上讲授商务合同中通用条款的翻译方法,探索不同合同中相同条款的用词、句式、语篇特点,总结典型条款的翻译规律。

第一节 国际商务合同翻译原则和方法

我国翻译界,对于翻译标准的争论由来已久。最常见的翻译标准就是严复提出的"信、达、雅"。此外,还有不少翻译界同仁从各种侧面论述过翻译的标准,各种主张、观点虽然不太一致,但没有根本不同。历史证明,严复提出的著名的"信、达、雅"的翻译标准,一直对我国的翻译工作起着良好的指导作用,至今仍为我国译界许多人士用来开展译事活动和总结翻译经验的指导思想。在进行国际商务合同文书的翻译时,应坚持四个大的具体原则:准确性原则、精炼化原则、一致性原则、规范化原则。

一、准确性原则

由于国际商务合同的专业性和兼容性越来越强,因此,合同的内容也就日趋精确和完备。合同的翻译不同于文艺作品的翻译,一般不讲求文采和修辞。这就要求译者在翻译合同文件时,把"准确严谨"作为首要标准提出,尤其是合同中的法律术语、关键词语的翻译更应予以特别重视。有时为了避免产生歧义,有些词语的翻译必须保持同一种译法,特别是合同中的专业术语和关键词语都有着严格的法律涵义,在翻译专业术语和关键词语时,一定要透彻地理解原文的精神实质,对原文的内容既不歪曲,也不随意增减。

例1 女职工违反国家有关计划生育规定的,其劳动保护应当按照国家有关计划生育规定办理,不适用本规定。

译文:Labour protection of those women staff and workers that run counter to state stipulations concerning family planning should be treated according to State stipulations concerning family planning. The Regulations are thus inapplicable.

改译:These Regulations do not apply to any violation of state family planning measures by a woman employee whose labor protection is regulated by the said measures.

例2 外国合营者如果有意以落后的技术和设备进行欺骗,造成损失的,应赔偿损失。

译文:If the foreign joint-venturer causes losses by deception through the intentional use of backward technology and equipment, he shall pay compensation for the losses.

改译:If the foreign joint-venturer causes any loss or losses by deception through the intentional use of backward technology and equipment, he shall pay compensation therefore.

二、精炼化原则

翻译商务合同文件还应遵循精练的原则,即用少量的词语传达大量的信息。简单、扼要的语言是立合同最好的语言。翻译合同文件也应如此,应尽量做到舍繁求简,避免逐词翻译、行文拖沓。

例3 More than 80 percent of the 35,000 commercial enterprises in Guangdong involve Hong Kong businessmen, with ICAC intelligence indicating many bribe with impunity, through lavish gifts, entertainment and kick-backs.

译文:在广东省35 000家商业机构中,超过百分之八十与香港有生意上的往来。廉署情报人员指出这些生意上的往来涉及许多贿赂罪行,然而这些罪行并没有受到法律的制裁。贿赂专案包括赠送贵重的礼物、提供高档的娱乐招待以及给予巨额的现金回扣。

改译:在35 000家广东商业机构中,八成以上有港商参与,据廉署情报显示,许多港商以大量馈赠、殷勤款待和丰厚回扣行贿,却能逍遥法外。

例4 Incidental damages to an aggrieved seller include any commercially reasonable charges, expenses or commissions incurred in stopping delivery, in the transportation, care and custody of goods after the buyer's breach, in connection with return or resale of the goods or otherwise resulting from the breach.

译文:给受损害的卖方造成的附带损失包括:卖方因为停止交付货物、停止运输货物、不再照管和存放货物、将货物退回或者转售而支出的任何商业上合理的费用或佣金,或者因为买方违约而另外支出的其他费用。

改译:受损卖方的附带损失包括:买方违约后卖方因停止交付货物、运输货物、照管和存放货物、退还或转售货物而支出的任何商业上合理的费用或佣金,或者因买方违约而另外支出的其他费用。

三、规范化原则

语言规范化原则,主要是指在合同翻译中使用官方认可的规范化语言或书面语,以及避免使用方言和俚语。在合同文书的起草和翻译中必须强调采用官方用语,尤其是现行合同中已有界定的词语。

例 5 Unless the contrary intention clearly appears, expressions of "cancellation" or "rescission" of the contractor the like shall not be construed as a renunciation or discharge of any claim in damages for an antecedent breach.

译文:除非明显存在相反的意思表示,否则"取消"或"解除"合同或类似表示不应被解释为放弃就前存违约所提出的索赔请求。

分析:原文中的"shall"在此不是表示"将来时",而是法律用语的一种语言形式,一般译为"应该"或"应";如果译为"将"则失去原文的风格和特征。

例 6 The Company generally would find the director approval approach preferable, as the director representative on the Board has a fiduciary duty to the corporation when acting in the capacity of a director.

译文:公司一般会更偏向于采纳董事批准的方法,因为董事会中的董事代表在执行其董事职务时对公司负有信托义务。

分析:义务性规范是"规定法律关系主体必须依法做出一定行为的法律规范",其汉语的表达方式是"有……的义务""必须"等;英语的表达方式是"It is the duty of...","has the duty of...","shall","must"等。

例 7 For all employees, annual leave entitlements accrue during the probationary period but annual leave generally may not be taken during that period.

译文:对所有员工而言,带薪年假试用期即开始累计,但试用期内一般不得休息年假。

分析:禁止性规范是指禁止法律关系主体为某种行为的法律规范。汉语的表达方式通常是"严禁""禁止""不得""不能"等,而英语的表达方式除"prohibit"外,还可以使用"shall not","may not","must not","not allowed","can not","no one may/is..."等方式表示。这一例句中用的是被动语态。

例 8　An employee who has not completed 12 months of continuous service in any one calendar year shall be entitled to paid leave in proportion to the number of completed months of service in that year rounded to the nearest whole day.

译文：若一名员工在任一日历年度内的连续服务期不满 12 个月，则其带薪年假应根据其当年度实际工作的月份数按比例计算，四舍五入之最接近的一整天。

例 9　No stockholder, however, shall be entitled to so cumulate such stockholder's votes unless（i）the names of such candidate or candidates have been placed in nomination prior to the voting, and（ii）the stockholder has given notice at the meeting, prior to the voting, of such stockholder's intention to cumulate such stockholder's votes.

译文：但是，除非（i）该等候选人已在表决前被提名，并且（ii）在表决前的会议中股东已发出通知告知其意图行使累积投票权，否则任何股东均无权行使累积投票权。

分析：授权性规范指的是"规定法律关系主体依法有权自己为某种行为以及要求他人为或不为某种行为的法律规范"。其汉语的表达方式为"享有……的权利""有权……"等等，而英语的表达方式是"have the right to…"，"enjoy the rights of…"，"be entitled to…"，"may"等。

第二节　国际商务合同的词汇特点及翻译

合同文件是合同双方签订并必须遵守的法律文件，因此合同中的语言应体现其权威性。英文合同用语的特点之一就表现在用词上，力求使合同表达的意思准确无误，达到双方对合同用词无可争议的程度。本节将对国际商务合同的词汇特点进行梳理，并介绍其翻译方法。

一、商务合同中特殊词汇的首字母大写

英文合同中，除句首词的第一个字母需要大写外，有些特殊词的首字母也需大写，而且这些词语的首字母大写已经形成了固定的用法。在翻译这类词汇时应该了解其使用的常见类别，以免译错。涉外合同中大写字母的运用主要有以下几方面：

合同当事人：包括 the Sellers, the Buyers, the Licensee, the Licensor, the Supplier, the Purchaser, the Borrower 等等。

例 10　The undersigned Sellers and Buyers have agreed to close the following transaction according to the terms and conditions stipulated below.

译文：在本合同文末签字的买方和卖方同意按下述条款达成本项交易。

合同关键词：在国际商务合同中，凡是用定义条款加以说明的关键词语的首字母

会以大写形式出现。例如 Agreement,Technical Information,the Exclusive Right,the Licensed Products,Licensed Patents,the Licensor's Know-how,Interest Period,RMB,USD,Iraq Dinar 等。

机构组织和法律:例如:the Stockholm Chamber of Commerce,Technical Service Team,the Joint Venture Company,and the Bank of China,Beijing Branch 等等。

此外,当合同中提及"合同"、合同的"具体条款""附件"或者相关文件时,首字母会大写。

例 11　Either **Party** may transfer all or part of its registered capital contribution to the **Company** to any third party, provided that it first obtains the unanimous approval of the **Board** and the approval of the **Approval Authority** and complies with the provisions of this **Article**.

译文:任何一方均可将其在公司注册资本中的全部和部分出资转让给任何第三方,但该转让首先须经董事会一致通过并经审批机构的批准,并符合本条的规定。

二、商务合同中 thereof, herein 等古语词语的翻译

英语中的一些旧体词语,如 hereto,thereafter,whereby,在现代英语中已很少使用。但在合同和其他法律文件中仍屡见不鲜。这些旧体词多数为副词,由 here,there 和 where 作前缀加上介词组成,在句中一般作定语或状语。其作用主要是为了避免重复,同时也起着承接合同条款的作用。常见古体词如下:

here 代表 this。例如:hereafter = following this; hereby = by this means or by reason of this; herein = in this; hereof = of this; hereto = to this; herewith = with this; hereunder = under this; hereinafter = later in this Contract; hereinbefore = in a preceding part of this Contract 等。

there 代表 that。例如:thereafter = after that; thereby = by that means; therein = in that; thereinafter = in that part of a Contract; thereof = of that; thereto = to that; thereunder = under that part of a contract; thereupon = as a result of that 等。

where 代表 which,与介词组合,一般为关系副词,引出定语从句,如:whereof = of which。

对这些古体词语的翻译,应根据上下文采用灵活的方法处理。

例 12　The titles to the Articles in this Agreement and in the said Exhibits are for convenience of reference only, not part of this Agreement, and shall not in any way affect the interpretation **hereof**.

译文:本协议各条款和协议附录中使用的标题,仅为了查阅方便而设,并非本协议的构成部分,任何情况下均不得影响对<u>本协议内容</u>的解释。

分析:原文中 thereof 中的 there 代表 that,因此 thereof 可以替换成 of that

Agreement.

例 13 "Licensed Products" means the devices and products described in Schedule 1 annexed **hereto** together with all improvement and modification thereof or development with respect **thereto**.

译文:"许可产品"系指本协议附表 1 中所述的设备和产品,以及对其进行的全部改进和修改或与其相关的开发。

分析:原文中 hereto 中的 here 代表 this,thereto 中的 there 代表 those;因此 hereto 可以替换成 to this Agreement/Contract,thereto 可以替换成 to those Products。

例 14 The Company **hereby** acknowledges that Indemnitee has certain rights to indemnification, advancement of expenses and/or insurance provided by [Name of Fund/Sponsor] and certain of [its][their] affiliates (collectively, the "Fund Indemnitors").

译文:公司特此承认,受偿方有权享受某些由[基金/资助人名称]及其某些关联公司(统称"基金赔偿方")提供的补偿、费用垫付款和/或保险。

分析:hereby 常用于法律文件、合同、协议书等正式文件的开头语;在条款中需要强调时也常用到。相当于 by means of, by reason of this,可以翻译为"特此、因此、兹"。

例 15 **Whereas** Party B has the right and agrees to grant Party A the rights to use, manufacture and sell the Contract Products of Patented Technology;

Whereas Party A desires to use the Patented Technology of Party B to manufacture and sell the Contract Products;

The Representatives authorized by the Parties to this Contract have, through friendly negotiation, agreed to enter into this Contract under the terms, conditions and provisions specified as follows:...

译文:鉴于乙方有权并同意将含有专利技术的合同产品的使用权、制造权和销售权授予甲方;

鉴于甲方希望利用乙方的专利技术制造并销售合同产品;

双方授权代表经友好协商,同意根据以下条款、条件和规定签订本合同:……

分析:whereas 意思是 considering that,可以翻译为"鉴于,就……而论"。常用于合同协议书的开头段落中,以引出合同双方要订立合同的理由或依据。

例 16 A certificate in writing under the hand of one Director or the Secretary of the Company that a share in the Company has been duly forfeited on a date stated in the declaration shall be conclusive evidence of the fact **therein** stated as against all persons claiming to be entitled to the share.

译文:由公司的一名董事或秘书签发的表明公司某一股份已经于公告中所述日期

被正式没收的书面证明即是结论性的证据,证明其上所述事实,该书面证明可用于对抗所有主张对该股份享有权利之人。

分析:therein 的意思是 in that, in that particular, in that respect, 可以翻译为"在那里、在那点上、在那方面"。在表示上文已提及的"合同中的……,工程中的……"等时使用。例如,表示"修补工程中的缺陷":the remedy of any defects therein, 此处 therein 表示 in the Works;表示"用于工程中的材料或机械设备":materials or plant for incorporation therein, 这里的 therein 表示 in the Works。therein 一般置于所修饰词后,紧邻修饰词。

三、商务合同中情态动词的用法和翻译

在法律英语中,主要情态动词或使用频率最高的情态动词依次是"shall","may","must"和"should"。就翻译而言最困难的是"shall"。shall 主要表示应当履行的义务、债务和应承担的法律责任。如果未履行 shall 表明的合同上的义务,则视为违约。在没有法律和合同的强制情况下或与表示权利、义务无关的情况下,不宜使用 shall。shall 一词不受主语的人称影响。至于 shall 一词的译法,应根据合同的具体内容采用灵活的译法,一般可译为"应""应当"或"必须",也可处理为"将""可以"或不译出来。在商务合同文体中,通过 may 提出的要求通常不带强制性,有时为实现要求还准许附加条件;也可在一定条件下表示允许或许可。may not 可表示根据特定规定或要求而"不得"或"不可以",语气不及 shall not 强烈,使用也不及 shall not 普遍。

例 17 双方首先应通过友好协商,解决因本合同发生的或与合同有关的争议。如果协商未果,合同中又无仲裁条款约定或争议发生后未就仲裁达成协议的,可将争议提交有管辖权的人民法院解决。

译文:The parties hereto **shall**, first of all, settle any dispute arising from or in connection with the contract by friendly negotiations. Should such negotiations fail, such dispute **may** be referred to the People's Court having jurisdiction on such dispute for settlement in the absence of any arbitration clause in the disputed contract or in default of agreement reached after such dispute occurs.

分析:上句中的 shall 和 may 表达准确。出现争议后应当先行协商,所以采用了义务性"约定"(shall),如果协商解决不了,作为当事人的权利,则用选择性"约定"(may)。

例 18 The formation of this contract, its validity, interpretation, execution and settlement of the disputes shall be governed by related laws of the People's Republic of China.

译文:本合同的订立、效力、解释、履行和争议的解决均受中华人民共和国法律的管辖。

分析：shall 没有译出。

例 19　The Buyers may, within 20 days after arrival of the goods at he destination, lodge a claim against the sellers for shortweight being supported by Inspection Certificate issued by a reputable public surveyor.

译文：货物抵达目的港 20 天内，买方可以凭有信誉的公共检验员出示的检验证明向卖方提出短重索赔。

分析：原文中 may 提出的要求不附加强制性。

例 20　Any amendments to this Contract, or to any of the appendices annexed hereto, shall come into force only after a written agreement providing for such amendments has been duly signed by Party A, Party B, Party C and Party D, and approved by the original examination and approval authority.

译文：对合同及合同所有附件的修正，应在修正案的书面协议由合同四方签署并经原审批机关批准后方可生效。

分析：该条是表示合同修正与改动程序和效力方面的规定。有些国际商务合同生效不是以双方签字作为成立条件，而是以国家批准为成立条件的。因此，其变更和修正也必须经审批机关批准。这一点在我国的一些涉外法律和法规中均有明确的规定，如果一份合同的生效条件是须经国家批准，若当事人双方就该合同的修正达成一致意见，而没有就其达成协议报原审批机关批准，那么，其修改合同的行为是无效的。因此，shall come into force only after 译成"只有经……后方可生效"。

should 在合同中通常只用来表示语气较弱的假设，多翻译成"万一"或"如果"，极少译成"应该"。

例 21　The board meeting shall be convened and presided over by the Chairman. Should the chairman be absent, the vice-Chairman shall, in principle, convene and preside over the board meeting.

译文：董事会会议应由董事长召集、主持；若董事长缺席，原则上应由副董事长召集、主持。

分析：原文中的 should 表示的是一种假设。

例 22　任何单位和个人实施他人专利的，除本法第十四条规定的以外，都**必须**与专利权人订立书面实施许可合同，向专利权人支付专利使用费。……专利权的所有权单位或者持有单位**应**当对职务发明创造的发明人或者设计人给予奖励。

译文：Except as provided for in Article 14, any entity or individual exploiting the patent of another **must** conclude a written licensing contract with the patentee and pay the patentee a fee for the exploitation of its or his patent.... The entity owning or holding the patent right on a job-related invention-creation **shall** reward the inventor or designer.

分析:任何人利用他人发明的专利,必须与专利权人订合同,并有所付出。否则,这就是侵权。但专利权持有单位是否一定要给予专利的职务发明人任何个人奖励,则不必用必须去强制。倘若该发明人领的是单位的工资,住的是单位的房子,用的是单位的设备,而且又是利用正常上班时间搞的创造发明,有关单位未必一定要给予奖励。但作为国家鼓励创造发明的政策,单位应当给予有关个人适当奖励,只有这样,才能进一步提高个人从事创造发明的积极性。所以,原文用"必须"和"应当",合情合理。译文则用 must 对"必须","shall"对"应当",更无可非议。翻译中选词如此具有区别性,体现了法律翻译的严肃和准确性。

四、并列同义词语的翻译

国际商务合同力求正式准确,为避免可能出现的误解或分歧,同义词(近义词)并列的现象十分普遍。合同中的词语并列现象有时是出于严谨的考虑,有时也属于合同用语的固定模式。在普通英语里,有些同义词有时可以互换,但在英文合同中这些同义词就不能随便互换,因为它们表达的权利和义务是有一定的区别的。英文合同中有两类同义词,第一类同义词就是有同义的词,另一类是词义有明显差异的同义词。例如,terms 在合同中一般指付款或费用(手续费、佣金等有关金钱的)条件,而 conditions 则指其他条件,但是"terms and conditions"常常作为固定模式在合同中出现,就不宜分译成"条件和条款",而直接合译成"条款"。又如,alter and change 两个的意思都是变更、改变,作为同义词组使用。对于合同中的并列现象,翻译时应仔细考虑单词的内涵、合同文体以及句法要求等相关因素。译者可以利用动态对等理论,就是译文与原文在效果(或功能)上达到对等。

例 23 The heading and marginal notes in these conditions shall not be deemed part thereof be taken into consideration in the interpretation or construction thereof or of the contract.

译文:本合同条件中的标题和旁注不应视为合同本文的一部分,在合同条件或合同本身的理解中也不应考虑这些标题和旁注。

分析:此句中的"interpretation"和"construction"意思均为"理解,解释"。

例 24 Both Parties hereto hereby agree willingly to bind and obligate themselves to act and perform as follows.

译文:本合同双方据此同意受本协议约束,执行以下条款……

分析:bind and obligate 应该说是近义词,前者指约束,后者指具体负有什么样的义务,二者经常同时出现,表示"使……有义务做"。

当然,并非所有看似配对词和三联词都只有一个意义。配对的近义词其法律上的含义在某种程度上还是有一定差异的。例如,房地产合约中常会碰到 sell, transfer or dispose 这一短语。sell 一定是指以金钱进行的房地产交易,与后两个单词在概念上有实质差别。遇到这种情形时,译者需要确定其中哪个词属于更常用的现代英语中的普通词,译者需要译的就是这个普通词。

例 25　For the damage or loss due to natural causes within the responsibilities of the ship-owner or the underwrite, the Seller shall not consider any claim for compensation

译文:由于自然原因引起的、属于船东或保险人责任范围内的损害或损失,卖方不考虑对索赔做出补偿。

分析:通常情况下,"damage"表明实值受到损坏,而"loss"表示全损。根据国际货物运输保险惯例,有些保险承保货物的全损,而有些只承保部分损失。关于合同中当事人的利益,此句用了"damage or loss"两个同义词来表述。这一连用同样表明合同的正式性,突出其明确性。

五、商务合同中多义词的翻译

在商务合同英语中,一词多义或一义多词的现象较为普遍。要透彻理解这些词义,必须结合上下文,仔细推敲。合同文体具有很强的逻辑性,翻译时绝对不能孤立片面地和静止地去理解条款中的词义,应全面客观地去理解和选择词义。例如,action是法律英语中最常用的单词之一,它有两个意思:"诉讼",相当于 lawsuit,如:file an action(提起诉讼),cause of action(诉因);"作为",与不作为(forbearance)对应。

例 26　Party A shall defend Party B in any action resulting from the infringement of the licensed intellectual property.

译文:因侵犯经许可的知识产权而导致的任何诉讼,甲方应当为乙方进行抗辩。

例 27　Any negligent conduct of Party A, whether it is action or forbearance, that resulted in loss of Party B shall be deemed to be breach of this Contract.

译文:甲方的任何疏忽行为,无论是作为还是不作为,只要引起乙方损失,即可视为甲方违反本合同。

在处理合同中多义词语的翻译时,有时需要根据词性确定词义。英语中有许多书写形式相同却有着不同词性的词,而词性不同,意义也有所差异。在翻译时首先要判定这个词在原文中的词性,根据词性进一步确定其词义。

例 28　The Contractor's Representative shall be present at the site throughout normal working hours except when on sick leave, or absent for reasons connected with the proper performance of the Contract.

例 29　The Contractor shall at all time keep the premises free from accumulation of waste materials or rubbish caused by the Works and at the completion of the Works shall remove all remaining materials from and about the premises and shall leave the Site and Plant safe, clean and ready for Use.

分析:上述两个条款中均含有 leave 一词,其中第 1 款中的 leave 是名词,意思是

"假期";第2款中的 leave 是动词,意思是"保持"。

有时,译者需要根据上下语境确定合同中多义词的词义。

例 30　Upon the arrival of the goods at the place of delivery, the Buyers claim an allowance of USD 500 on account of inferior quality.

译文:货物运抵交付地点后,由于货物质量不佳,买方要求索赔 500 美元。

分析:句中的 allowance 与动词 claim 搭配,意思为"赔偿费"。

例 31　Both Party A and Party B shall make a liberal allowance for such unforeseen circumstances arising during transit.

译文:甲、乙双方应充分考虑到运输中所发生的意外情况。

分析:句中的 allowance 在 make allowance for 结构中应该理解为,在做某种决定时,"考虑到某事物或事件"。

合同英语中会涉及各类不同的专业。专业不同,某些词语的词义也就相应地需要调整。当根据词性和语境确定词义无法实现时,译者需要判断待定词语所属的专业,根据专业类型确定词义。

例 32　A contract may be formed if an offer is accepted within the specified time and in the required manner.

译文:如果在规定时间内并以规定的方式接受要约,合同即可成立。

例 33　The draft is accepted by the negotiating bank.

译文:议付行对汇票进行了承兑。

分析:在法律英语中 accept 有一个最常用的意思:在合同法中,accept 与要约 offer 相对应,如 revoke an acceptance(撤回承诺);accept 也经常出现在票据法中。

六、商务合同中其他特定词语的翻译

合同英语中有些词语的运用与其他文体的英语相比,也是有区别的。这些词语在国际商务合同中已形成一种固定的用法,体现出合同文本的独特风格。

(一) subject to 的翻译

该短语在法律英语中一般跟"agreement","section","contract"等法律文件名或文件中特定条款名配合使用。通常可翻译成"受制于……的规定""(须)遵守……的规定""根据……规定""在符合……的情况下"以及"在不抵触……下"等。翻译 subject to 时,应根据其后宾语的具体内容,参照其基本含义,采用符合合同语言规范的翻译方法。

例 34　The provisions of this section are subject to any third party rights provided by the law relating to realty records, and the contract for sale may be executed and recorded as a document transferring an interest in land and shall then constitute notice to third parties of the buyer's rights under the contract for sale.

译文：第三方根据有关不动产登记的法律所取得的权利，优于本条各款的效力；但上述买卖合同可作为转让土地权益的凭证，经签订和登记后，即构成对第三方有关买方依买卖合同所取得权利的通知。

例 35 Subject to the provisions of the next section on modification and waiver, such course of performance shall be relevant to show a waiver or modification of any term inconsistent with such course of performance.

译文：受制于下一条有关修订和弃权的规定，此种履约习惯可用于表明对与履约习惯相矛盾的任何条款的放弃或修改。

例 36 Even though all or part of the price is payable in an interest in realty the transfer of the goods and the seller's obligations with reference to them are subject to this Article, but not the transfer of the interest in realty or the transferor's obligations in connection therewith.

译文：即使全部或部分价款以不动产权益支付，货物的转让以及卖方对货物的义务也应遵守本条规定，但不动产权益的转让和其转让人的相应义务不受制于本条规定。

（二）in consideration of 的翻译

在合同英文中，in consideration of 主要体现了权利与义务的一致性。即：一方履行某种义务完全是以另一方履行某种义务为条件或前提的，经常译为"考虑到""鉴于""由于"等。

例 37 In consideration of the Licenses and technical assistance provided herein, the Joint Venture Company shall pay Party A technical assistance fees in USD.

译文：考虑到本协议规定的许可以及提供的技术援助，合资公司将以美元的方式支付甲方技术援助费。

in consideration of 还可以表示合同一方或双方由于某种利益而履行某种义务。

例 38 Although their prices seem higher than those of other makers at first sight, experienced buyers prefer to purchase their products in consideration of long-term benefit.

译文：乍看起来，他们的价格似乎比其他厂家的商品高一些，可是有经验的买主考虑到长远的利益，宁愿购买他们的产品。

（三）be entitled to 的翻译

be entitled to 在法律英语中表示"给某人权利做某件事情"，尤其在表示权利的场合中，体现出该权利在法律上的强制性。翻译时可译为"有权""有资格"等，但在具体的译文处理上，应根据上下文确定。

例 39　Unless otherwise agreed and subject to the provisions of this Article on C. I. F. contracts, the buyer is not entitled to inspect the goods before payment of the price when the contract provides...

译文：除非另有约定且本条有关成本加运费加保费合同之条款另有规定，否则在合同做下列规定时买方无权在付款前验货：……

例 40　When the buyer sells goods under subsection (1), he is entitled to reimbursement from the selleror out of the proceeds for reasonable expenses of caring for and selling them.

译文：买方依据第(1)款出售货物时，其有权就照管及出售货物所支出的合理费用从卖方处或者从出售所得中获偿。

例 41　After the buyer has wrongfully rejected or revoked acceptance of the goods or has failed to make a payment due or has repudiated, a seller who is held not entitled to the price under this section shall nevertheless be awarded damages for non-acceptance under the preceding section.

译文：若买方不当拒收或撤销接受货物、未能支付到期价款，或毁弃合同，则法院即使认定卖方无权依据本条之规定请求赔偿价款，仍可判定卖方取得前述条款规定的拒收货物的损害赔偿。

（四）Whereas 的翻译

whereas 属连词，是合同文件中经常使用的句式，意思相当于 taking into consideration the fact that...。由其引出的从句，在合同文体中常称为"鉴于句"。"鉴于句"属叙述性条款，一般写在合同的开头，用以说明合同当事人订约的目的、意图、缘由等，而在其他场合不宜使用。例如：

例 42　WHEREAS Party A has been a leading trading company in the field of the said products and is willing to arrange the manufacture, assembly and marketing of the said products, and

WHEREAS both parties are desirous to establish a joint venture company to manufacture, assemble and market the said products.

NOW, THEREFORE, in consideration of the premises and mutual covenants herein contained, the parties hereto agree as follows:...

（五）商务合同中 this 的用法及翻译

this 在合同中主要修饰 Contract or Agreement，可译成"本合同或本协议"；但在修饰日期时，表示签合同的日期。例如：

this Contract/agreement "本合同"

This Contract is made this 29th day of March, 2003 by and between...（正式用

法）

This Contract is made on the 29ᵗʰ, March, 2003 by and between...（非正式用法）

例 43 THIS CONTRACT, made and entered into this 17th day of May, 2013 by and between AAA, a corporation duly organized and existing under the laws of (name of country) with its domicile at _____ (hereinafter referred to as Party A), and BBB, a company incorporated and existing under the laws of _____ with its domicile at _____ (hereinafter referred to as Party B),

（六）商务合同中结尾部分"in witness whereof /thereof / in Testimony Whereof"的翻译

在合同结尾，有时大写 IN WITNESS WHEREOF / THEREOF，表示所签合同事项的证据。一般翻译为"以兹证明""特此立（证）据""以此立（证）据"。

例 44 IN WITNESS WHEREOF, the parties hereto have executed this Contract in duplicate by their authorized representatives.

WITNESS：_____   WITNESS：_____

Party A：_____   Party B：_____

译文：兹证明：本合同由双方授权代表签订，一式两份。

见证人：_____   见证人：_____

甲方：_____   乙方：_____

例 45 IN TESTIMONY WHEROF we have hereto signed this Document on _____ and accepted on _____.

译文：我方于_____签署本文件，并于_____已接受此文件，特此为证。

第三节　国际商务合同的句式特点及翻译

商务合同规定各方当事人的权利和义务。商务合同一经依法订立，就成为一种法律文件而对缔约各方具有法律约束力，成为商务活动中解决争议的法律依据。合同的这一性质影响着其文字载体的风格。如果说商务合同的用词具有专业、准确、正式的特点，那么商务合同的句法则有结构严谨、句式较长的特点。本节结合翻译难点，重点探讨长句，尤其是状语从句、定语从句和被动句的特点和翻译方法。

一、状语从句的翻译

国际商务合同是合同各方就相互权利义务关系达成一致意见而订立的书面文件。

这种书面文件主要约定双方应享有的权利和应履行的义务,但这种权利的行使和义务的履行,均附有各种条件。当这些条件满足时,当事人的权利才能实现,或义务方可履行。因此,国际商务合同中大量使用条件句式,而含有条件句式的主语中往往含有 shall 构成表示义务的复合谓语,这是国际商务合同中的一大特点。当然,根据实际情景的需要,主句中也可以使用 may 或者 must 等情态动词。下面介绍一些国际商务合同中经常使用的状语从句及其翻译方法。

(一) if 引导的状语从句

"if"在状语从句中通常翻译为"如""如果"或"若"。另外,合同中含有条件句的主句中的谓语部分,大多含有 shall 表示义务或责任。

例 46　If a warehouse in good faith believes that goods are about to deteriorate or decline in value to less than the amount of its lien within the time provided in subsection (a) and Section 7-210, the warehouse may specify in the notice given under subsection (a) any reasonable shorter time for removal of the goods and, if the goods are not removed, may sell them at public sale held not less than one week after a single advertisement or posting.

译文:若仓储人善意地相信,在(a)款和第 7-210 规定的时间内,货物即将变质或减损到低于其留置权的数额,仓储人可以在(a)款规定的通知中指定任何合理的更短的时间要求转移货物,若货物未被转移,在不少于一周的单独广告或公告之后,可以拍卖这些货物。

例 47　If a lien is on goods stored by a merchant in the course of its business, the lien may be enforced in accordance with subsection (a) or (b).

译文:若留置权存在于商人在其交易过程中储存的货物之上,留置权可以依(a)或(b)款执行。

例 48　Also, if the consent rights are contained in the charter, the investor can argue that an act by the Corporation in contravention of those provisions would be void or voidable rather than simply a breach of contract.

译文:同时,若章程中包含此同意权,投资人可争辩公司违反该等规定采取的行动是无效的或可撤销的,而非仅仅属于违约。

另外,if 有时被用来引导省略句,构成 if any, if required, if possible, if necessary, if agreeable 等结构。

例 49　The Company's lien (if any) on a share shall extend to all dividends or other monies payable in respect thereof.

译文:公司的股份留置权(如有)适用于所有红利或其他与之相关的应付项目。

(二) unless 引导的状语从句

在合同英语中，unless 常与 otherwise 连用，表示"除非另有……者外"。另外，在 unless 引出的条件句中，有时常用 unless 的省略结构。

例 50 Unless the bill of lading otherwise provides, a carrier may deliver the goods to a person or destination other than that stated in the bill or may otherwise dispose of the goods, without liability for misdelivery, on instructions from:...

译文：除非提单另有规定，承运人根据下列人的指示可以向提单之外的人或目的地交付，而不承担交付错误的责任：……

例 51 Working through the lunch hour will not accrue overtime compensation, unless agreed in advance by the employee's manager.

译文：除非该员工事先得到经理的同意，否则午餐时间加班没有加班费。

例 52 The Board of Directors shall meet at least [monthly][quarterly], unless otherwise agreed by a vote of the majority of Directors.

译文：除非另行经过半数以上董事表决同意，否则董事会应至少每[月][季度]举行一次会议。

分析：原句中用了 if 和 unless 两个条件句，其中 unless 条件句用的是省略形式。

(三) in case/in case(s) of 引导的状语从句

"in case"或"in case of"通常翻译为"如""如果""若""倘若"等。in case 在表示条件时，其可能性要弱于 if 引导的条件从句。

例 53 In case of an equality of votes, the Chairman shall not have a second or casting vote.

译文：如果出现票数相同的情况，董事长不得第二次投票或者投决定票。

例 54 Pursuant to the resolutions passed by the Joint Shareholders' Meeting of June 8, 2005, any Option must be exercised prior to the day before the seventh **anniversary** of the Grant Date, after which date it shall automatically become void and therefore non-exercisable, except in case of death of the Beneficiary as defined in Article 6.2.3.

译文：根据 2005 年 6 月 8 日股东联席会议通过的决议，任何期权的行权必须在授予日七周年届满之日前，此后将自动失效，且不可行权，第 6.2.3 条所述的受益人死亡的情形除外。

例 55 In case the buyer fails to carry out any of the terms and conditions to this Contract with the Seller, the Seller shall have the right to terminate all or any part of this Contract with the buyer or postpone shipment or stop any goods in transit and the Buyer shall in every such case be liable to the Seller for all losses, damages and expenses thereby incurred.

译文:若买方未能履行与卖方所订合同之任何条款,卖方有权终止与买方的全部或部分合同,或延期交货,或截留运输中的货物。在任何一种情况下,买方应负责赔偿卖方由此产生的损失、损坏和相应的费用。

例 56　In case the Buyer finds any document incorrect, the buyer is obliged to cable the Seller indicating the incorrect items. The cable shall be sent within 15 (fifteen) days after the Bank of China, Shanghai Branch has received the Seller's documents.

译文:买方如发现文件有误,应在中国银行上海市分行收到卖方文件之日起 15 天内电告卖方,并指出错误项目。

(四) in the event of/that 引导的状语从句

商务合同中也常常使用 in the event of/that 引导的状语从句来表示条件。

例 57　In the event of any liquidation, dissolution or winding up of the Company, either voluntary or involuntary, merger or acquisition of the Company in which the Members of the Company do not own a majority of the outstanding shares of the surviving corporation, or a sale of substantially all of the assets of the Company, distributions to the Members of the Company shall be made in the following manner:

译文:在任何清算、公司解散或终止(无论自愿或非自愿)、公司合并或收购的情形下,公司股东未能拥有其后存续公司发行在外的绝大多数股份,或公司所有实质性资产一次性出售,则公司股东应以如下方式进行分配:

例 58　In the event of conflict between the provisions on arbitration formulated and prepared prior to the effective date of this Law and the provisions of this Law, the provisions hereof shall prevail.

译文:本法施行前制定的有关仲裁的规定与本法的规定相抵触的,以本法为准。

例 59　In addition, in the event provision is to be made for blank check preferred, appropriate consideration should also be given to building in references to such other potential series of Preferred Stock in the contractual agreements providing for additional rights and obligations of the holders of Series A Preferred Stock (such as the Investors' Rights Agreement, Right of First Refusal and Co-Sale Agreement, and Voting Agreement).

译文:此外,若加入空白支票优先股的条款,应适当地考虑在约定 A 系列优先股持有人的额外权利和义务的合同性协议(例如《投资者权利协议》《优先购买权和共售权协议》及《表决权协议》)中对其他潜在优先股系列做出规定。

（五）should 引导的状语从句

"should"引导状语从句，一般翻译为"如果""由于"或"若"。

例 60 Furthermore, California law will require a fairness opinion in connection with certain interested party transactions, so the parties should take particular care if a merger, reorganization or asset sale involves a potentially interested party.

译文：此外，加利福尼亚州法律将要求就某些关联交易出具公平意见，所以若一项合并、重组或资产出售涉及潜在的利益相关方，则各方应特别注意。

例 61 甲方根据经营盈利情况、乙方的绩效考核分数、乙方的行为和工作表现及乙方在甲方工作的工龄调整薪酬；乙方未达到甲方规定的工作量、质量指标及相关规定的将不予加薪。

译文：Party A will adjust Party B's remuneration as per its operation and profits and Party B's performance appraisal, behavior, performance and working years in Party A. Should Party B fail to meet the requirements of Party A regarding the workload, the quality and the other similar aspects, Party A will not increase Party B's salary.

例 62 甲方根据公司经营利润情况及乙方的行为和工作表现每年进行工资调整。乙方如未能按照甲方规定的标准完成绩效目标时，甲方有权调整乙方工资级别的标准。

译文：Party A will adjust Party B's salary in each year as per its operation and profits and Party B's behavior and performance. Should Party B fail to meet the performance goal as specified by Party A, Party A shall have the right to adjust Party B's salary standards.

例 63 Should the effect of Force Majeure continue more than one hundred and fifty (150) consecutive days, both parties shall settle the further execution of the Contract through friendly negotiations as soon as possible.

译文：如不可抗力事件延续到 150 天以上时，双方应通过友好协商方式尽快解决继续履约的问题。

（六）providing/provided 引导的状语从句

在商务合同中，"provided (that)"常用于在合同的某一条款中需要做进一步规定时，或在做规定时语气上表示转折时。在中译英时，要注意该词组的使用。有时从中文上看，尽管没有"但规定""进一步规定"的表述，但翻译时，应加上"provided that"。需要注意的是，使用 provided (that) 引出从句表示条件时，常表示当事人所希望的条件，这一点与 if 引出的从句是不同的。

例 64　We can sell a lot of said trousers provided that your price is highly competitive.

译文：如果你方价格很有竞争性,我方就可大量出售。

例 65　If the technical documentation supplied by Party B is not in conformity with Clause 7.2 to the Contract. Party B shall, within 20 days after the receipt of Party A's notification, airmail free of charge to Party A the correct, complete and legible version.

译文：如果乙方提供的技术资料不符合第 7 条第 2 款之规定,则乙方应在收到甲方的通知之日起 20 天内,免费将正确完整、清晰易读的技术资料通过航空邮寄方式发给甲方。

分析：在上述两句中,第一句中的条件是当事人所希望发生的情形,用 provided that 引出;第二句中的条件显然不是合同当事人希望出现的,所以不能用 provided that 引出,应用 if 引出。

例 66　Either side may replace the representative it has appointed provided that it submits a written notice to the other side.

译文：任何一方都可更换自己指派的代表,但需书面通知对方。

二、定语从句的翻译

从句法角度上讲,定语从句是次要成分,但在语言作用上,却占有重要地位。在商务合同中,为了使条款明确清晰,排除被误解的可能性,经常使用大量结构复杂的定语从句来精确说明一些名词。定语从句与中心词分离的现象十分普遍,一个名词带有多个并列的定语从句,或者一个定语从句修饰多个中心词的情况也很常见。英语的定语从句可分为限定性定语从句和非限定性定语从句两大类,两者之间的区别在于限制意义是强还是弱,前者的限制意义很强,后者的限制意义很弱。定语从句在商务合同中一般有三种翻译方法:合并法、分译法和混合法。

(一) 限定性定语从句

限制性定语从句与先行词的关系十分密切。在翻译商务合同中这类从句时,往往采用合译的手法,常把限制性定语从句译成汉语的"……的"结构,并置于被修饰词之前。

例 67　The total number of shares of all classes of stock which the Corporation shall have authority to issue is (ⅰ) [＿＿＿＿] shares of Common Stock, $[＿＿＿＿] par value per share ("Common Stock") and (ⅱ) [＿＿＿＿] shares of Preferred Stock, $[＿＿＿＿] par value per share ("Preferred Stock").

公司有权发行的、所有类别股份的总数为:(ⅰ) [＿＿＿＿]股普通股,每股票面价值[＿＿＿＿]美元("普通股")及(ⅱ) [＿＿＿＿]股优先股,每股票面价值[＿＿＿＿]

美元("优先股")。

例 68 "Termination" occurs when either party pursuant to a power created by agreement or law puts an end to the contract otherwise than for its breach. On "termination" all obligations which are still executory on both sides are discharged.

译文:如果任何一方非因违约,而是根据协议所创设的或法律所赋予的权力结束合同,该合同即告"终止"。合同一旦"终止",当事人尚待履行的所有义务即被解除。

例 69 A contract which does not satisfy the requirements of subsection(1) but which is valid in other respects is enforceable...

译文:不符合本条第1款要求但在其他方面有效的合同,在下列情况下仍可强制执行:……

例 70 A contract for sale of goods may be made in any manner sufficient to show agreement, including conduct by both parties which recognizes the existence of such a contract.

译文:货物买卖合同可以通过任何足以表明当事人已达成协议的方式订立,包括通过承认合同存在的当事人的行为而订立。

限制性定语从句的翻译方法,除以上最基本的合译法外,有时还可采用分译的方法处理。

例 71 A contract for the sale of minerals or the like (including oil and gas) or a structure or its materials to be removed from realty is a contract for the sale of goods within this Article if they are to be severed by the seller but until severance a purported present sale thereof which is not effective as a transfer of an interest in land is effective only as a contract to sell.

译文:出售将与不动产分离的矿物或类似物质(包括石油和天然气)的合同,以及出售将与不动产分离的建筑结构或其材料的合同,属于本条调整范围内的货物买卖合同,只要此种物品与不动产的分离系由卖方进行;但在分离之前,如果卖方的现售不构成土地权益的有效转让,则该现售在效力上只相当于一项销售合同。

例 72 An offer by a merchant to buy or sell goods in a signed writing which by its terms gives assurance that it will be held open is not revocable, for lack of consideration, during the time stated or if no time is stated for a reasonable time, but in no event may such period of irrevocability exceed three months; but any such term of assurance on a form supplied by the offeree must be separately signed by the offeror.

译文:如果商人在签名的书面函件中提出出售或买进货物的要约,且要约条款保证该要约将保持有效,则即使无对价,在要约规定的有效期限内,或如果未规定期限,在合理期限内,要约不可撤销。但在任何情况下,此种要约不可撤销的期限都不超过

3个月。而且,如果此种保证条款载于受要约人所提供的表格上,则该条款必须由要约人另加签名。

例 73 A definite and seasonable expression of acceptance or a written confirmation which is sent within a reasonable time operates as an acceptance even though it states terms additional to or different from those offered or agreed upon, unless acceptance is expressly made conditional on assent to the additional or different terms.

译文:只要在合理时间内做出了明确及时的承诺表示,或寄送了书面确认书,那么即使此种表示或确认书对原要约中的或原先达成的条款进行了补充或与其有所不同,该表示或确认书仍具有承诺的效力,除非明确规定,以要约人同意这些补充的或不同的条款为承诺的生效条件。

(二)非限定性定语从句

非限制性定语从句是先行词的附加说明,去掉了也不会影响主句的意思,它与主句之间通常用逗号分开。非限制性定语从句的翻译基本上采用分译的方法处理。分译时可重复先行词或省译先行词。

例 74 The Seller shall not be responsible for the delay of shipment or non-delivery of the goods due to Force Majeure, which might occur during the process of manufacturing or in the course of loading or transit.

译文:凡在制造或装船运输过程中,因不可抗力致使卖方不能或推迟交货时,卖方不负责任。

分析:原文把信息的重心放在句首,先表明卖方的免责事项,接着再规定由于什么原因引起的不能交货或延迟交货才会免责,而对不可抗力又做了限定。翻译时译者应采用逆序的方法将原文表示免责条件的移到句首。

例 75 Delaware offers a well-developed body of case law interpreting the DGCL, which facilitates certainty in business planning.

译文:特拉华州提供了可用以解释特拉华州公司法的发达的判例法体系,这增强了商业规划中的确定性。

三、被动语态的翻译

合同英语中被动语态的使用比较广泛。有时是因为没有必要说出合同所涉及的当事人,有时是为了突出和强调行为动作的承受者,或者是为了便于行文上的连贯等原因。在具体翻译的处理上,应采用较灵活的翻译技巧,做到在内容上忠实于原文,在语言形式上规范通顺。

例 76 This Project Fee Agreement ("Agreement") effective this 24th day of December 2012, by and between John Smith ("Consultant"), and Energy Efficiency Project Investment Company, Limited ("EEPIC") is hereby entered.

译文:John Smith 和节能投资公司于 2012 年 12 月 24 日签订本项目佣金协议。

分析:在商务合同的一些被动语态句子中,往往出现由 by 或 between 引起的短语,在句中作状语。为了突出动作的施动者,翻译时可将它转换为主语。

例 77　The production design, technology of manufacturing, means of testing, materials prescription, standard of quality and training of personnel shall be stipulated in Chapter 3 herein.

译文:本合同第三章规定了生产设计、制造工艺、测试方法、材料配方、质量标准以及人员培训等内容。

分析:当被动语态的状语与主语之间有包容关系时,可将状语部分译成汉语的主语。在原句中,stipulate 的状语部分包含了原句的主语内容,翻译时可以把状语译为主语。

例 78　Payment shall be made by net cash against sight draft with Bill of Lading attached showing the shipment of the goods. Such payment shall be made through the Bank of China, Beijing Branch.

译文:凭即期汇票和所附表明货物发运的提单通过中国银行北京分行以现金支付。

分析:如果原句中没有涉及合同的当事人,翻译时可以处理为无主句。原句中的 payment 作主语,可译为汉语的一个动词。

第四节　经贸合同基本格式和条款的翻译

一、经贸合同基本格式(中英文对照版)

合同 CONTRACT

日期:合同号码:
Date: Contract No.:
买方:(The Buyers)　　　卖方:(The Sellers)
兹经买卖双方同意按照以下条款由买方购进,卖方售出以下商品:
This contract is made by and between the Buyers and the Sellers; whereby the Buyers agree to buy and the Sellers agree to sell the under-mentioned goods subject to the terms and conditions as stipulated hereinafter:

（1）商品名称：

Name of Commodity：

（2）数量：

Quantity：

（3）单价：

Unit price：

（4）总值：

Total Value：

（5）包装：

Packing：

（6）生产国别：

Country of Origin：

（7）支付条款：

Terms of Payment：

（8）保险：

insurance：

（9）装运期限：

Time of Shipment：

（10）起运港：

Port of Lading：

（11）目的港：

Port of Destination：

（12）索赔：在货到目的口岸 45 天内如发现货物品质，规格和数量与合同不附，除属保险公司或船方责任外，买方有权凭中国商检出具的检验证书或有关文件向卖方索赔换货或赔款。

Claims：

Within 45 days after the arrival of the goods at the destination，should the quality，Specifications or quantity be found not in conformity with the stipulations of the contract except those claims for which the insurance company or the owners of the vessel are liable，the Buyers shall，have the right on the strength of the inspection certificate issued by the C.C.I.C and the relative documents to claim for compensation to the Sellers.

（13）不可抗力：由于人力不可抗力的缘由发生在制造，装载或运输的过程中导致卖方延期交货或不能交货者，卖方可免除责任，在不可抗力发生后，卖方须立即电告买方及在 14 天内以空邮方式向买方提供事故发生的证明文件，在上述情况下，卖方仍须负责采取措施尽快发货。

Force Majeure：

The sellers shall not be held responsible for the delay in shipment or non-delivery of the goods due to Force Majeure, which might occur during the process of manufacturing or in the course of loading or transit. The sellers shall advise the Buyers immediately of the occurrence mentioned above the within fourteen days there after. The Sellers shall send by airmail to the Buyers for their acceptance certificate of the accident. Under such circumstances the Sellers, however, are still under the obligation to take all necessary measures to hasten the delivery of the goods.

（14）仲裁：凡有关执行合同所发生的一切争议应通过友好协商解决，如协商不能解决，则将分歧提交中国国际贸易促进委员会按有关仲裁程序进行仲裁，仲裁将是终局的，双方均受其约束，仲裁费用由败诉方承担。

Arbitration：

All disputes in connection with the execution of this Contract shall be settled friendly through negotiation. In case no settlement can be reached, the case then may be submitted for arbitration to the Arbitration Commission of the China Council for the Promotion of International Trade in accordance with the Provisional Rules of Procedure promulgated by the said Arbitration Commission. The Arbitration committee shall be final and binding upon both parties, and the Arbitration fee shall be borne by the losing parties.

二、经贸合同条款翻译

（一）合同中的货物名称、品质和数量条款

1. 货物的名称

货物的名称必须准确、科学、规范，通常要包括品牌、属性和用途三个要素。

2. 品质条款

货物的品质通常不容易向对方表达，但是我们也可以从下面几个方面来展示：

（1）凭样品（by sample）

（2）凭标准（by standard）

（3）凭品牌（by brand）

（4）凭产地（by origin）

（5）凭规格（by specification）

（6）凭文字说明（by description）

我们来看一个例子：Chinese Groundnut, F. A. Q. Moisture（max 13%），Admixture （max 5%），Oil Content（min 44%）。其中 F. A. Q. 是一个专业术语，是 Fair Average Quality 的缩写，意思就是"良好平均品质"。

3. 数量条款

数量条款包括计量单位、计量方法和具体数量三部分。下面我们来介绍一些国际常用的计量单位：

（1）重量：用于一般的天然产品（羊毛、棉花、谷物、矿产品及部分工业制品）。常用单位：克(g)；公斤(kg)；盎司(ounce—oz)；磅(pound—Lb)；公吨(metric ton—M/T)；长吨(long ton)；短吨(short ton)等。

（2）个数：杂货及工业成品，如：成衣、文具、纸张、玩具等。常用单位：件(piece—pc)；套(set)；打(dozen)；罗(gross—gr)；令(ream—rm)；卷(roll coil)等。

（3）面积：木板、玻璃、地毯、铁丝网等。常用单位：平方米(sq. m.)；平方英尺(sq. ft.)；平方码(sq. yd.)。

（4）长度：布匹，塑料布，电线电缆，绳索等。常用单位：米(m)；英尺(ft)；码(yd)。

（5）容积：部分谷物，小麦，玉米等，及流体物质和气体物品。常用单位：升(liter—L)；加仑(gallon—gal)；蒲式耳(bushel—bul)。

（6）体积：木材，钢材等，要用立方 Cubic 来表示。常用单位：立方米(cu. m.)；立方英尺(cu. ft.)；立方码(cu. yd.)。

（二）合同中的价格、装运时间和保险条款

1. Price 价格条款

价格条款中要包括计价单位，货币名称，单位价格金额和价格术语。比如：￡100. CIF. London each dozen 这段描述的意思是到伦敦港的到岸价是每打100英镑。其中，CIF 是贸易术语，是指"到岸价格"，是 Cost Insurance and Freight 的缩写。（贸易术语通常用来解释贸易运输风险转移或者卖方费用问题，共有13种，一般都要加上装运港或者目的港等的名称。）

2. Time of Shipment 装运时间

装运时间通常要注明(1)限定装船时间；(2)限定最后日期；(3)限定日（在收到信用证一段时间内，买方在银行为卖方开具证明，当买方付不到钱时由银行付款，但开证费用大。）

3. Insurance 保险条款

保险条款＝由谁办理（the insured）＋向谁办理（the insurer）＋投保险别（coverage）＋投保金额（insurance amount）＋（责任条款）

保险包括基本险(general risk)和附加险(additional risks)。基本险用来保证船只安全，是必选的，附加险是用来保证货物安全，是双方协商选的。

必选的基本险按重要性排列为 F. P. A.（平安险 With Free from Particular Average），W. P. A.（水渍险 With Free from Water Average）和 A. R.（一切险 All

Risks)。

常见的附加险也分为一般附加险(general additional risk)和特殊附加险(Special additional risk)。

一般附加险包括以下几种：

(1) Theft, Pilferage and Non-Delivering Risk (T.P.N.D.) 偷窃提货不着险

(2) Fresh Water and Rain Damage Risk 淡水雨淋险

(3) Shortage Risk 短量险

(4) Intermixture and Contamination Risk 混杂玷污险

(5) Leakage Risk 渗漏险

(6) Clash and Breakage Risk 碰损破碎险

(7) Taint of Odor Risk 串味险

(8) Sweat and Heating Risk 受潮受热险

(9) Hook Damage Risk 钩损险

(10) Breakage of Packing Risk 包装破损险

(11) Rust Risk 锈损险

特殊附加险包括以下几种：

(1) War Risk 战争险

(2) Strike Risk 罢工险

(3) On Deck Risk 舱面险

(4) Import Duty Risk 进口关税险

(5) Failure to Deliver Risk 交货不到险

(6) Rejection Risk 拒收险

通常保险条款要写成：Sb. insure the goods with 承保人 against 险种 for / on % of the invoice value.

比如：买方委托卖方按发票全额的120%投保水渍险和偷窃提货不到险，保险费由买方承担。The Buyer hereby / will entrust the Seller to insure the goods against W.P.A. and T.P.N.D. for 120% of the invoice value. The insurance premium should be borne by the Buyer.

(三) 合同中的包装、运输标志和保险条款

1. Packing 包装条款

包装条款要包括包装材料，具体要求以及其他要求。一般采用笼统表示和具体规定两种方式。通常只有在双方达到共识时才使用笼统表示方法。比如以下描述：customary packing; seaworthy packing; packing suitable for long distance; 等等。

具体规定的描述如：

(1) 木箱装,每箱装30匹,每匹40码。

To be packed in wooden cases, 30pieces per case of 40 yd each.

(2) 铁桶装,每桶净重25公斤。

In iron drum of 25kg net each.

(3) 用聚丙烯编制包装袋,每包重50公斤,以毛重作净重,包装袋质量良好,适于海运,包装袋上用英语写上品名、重量、原产国别和包装日期。

To be packed in polypropylene woven bags, 50kg each, gross for net. The bags, should be fairy good in quality and suitable for ocean transportation, on which the name of the goods, weight, country of origin and package date should be written / marked in English.

2. Shipping Mark (运输标志/唛头)

运输标志通常要包括以下内容:

(1) 一些指示性(indicative marks)和警告性(warning marks)的图画和语言。

比如:上指的双箭头表示This side up;雨伞表示Keep dry;玻璃杯表示Breakable或者Handle with care;等等。还有一些语言,比如:poisons 有毒;explosives 易爆;inflammable 易燃;等等

(2) 运输标志:a.目的港名称 b.件号 c.买卖双方代号

(3) 出口地:比如Made in China.

3. Guarantee of Quality 保证条款

保证条款需要注明保证内容和保证时间,即保证的起至日期。

比如:承包商同意对不符合图纸规格的工程部分进行返工,并保证工程进行,同意完工一年后对有证据证明因瑕疵材料或工艺造成的缺陷进行补救。

The contractor agrees to redo the part of the project which are not conformed to the drawings' specification with the other projects performed / done meanwhile, remedy defects caused by / result from / arise from faulty materials and workmanship which are proved by evidence in one year after the completion of the project.

(四) 合同中的检验索赔、支付和运输条款

1. Inspection and Claims (检验索赔条款)

(1) 检验条款=检验权的规定(检验机构)+检验的内容(检验证书)+检验时间

通常检验证书有以下写法:

Inspection Certificate of Quality / Quantity / Weight / Value / Health /...

Disinfection Inspection Certificate 消毒检验证书

Sanitary Inspection Certificate 卫生检验证书

来看以下两句合同内容和其翻译:

双方同意以装运港中国进出口商品检验局签发的品质及数量检验证书为最后依

据对双方具有约束力。

It is mutually agreed that the goods are subject to the Inspection Certificate of Quality and Inspection Certificate of Quantity issued by China Import and Export at the port of shipment. The Certificate shall be binding on both parties.

在交货前制造商应就订货的质量、规格、数量、性能做出准确全面的检验，并出具货物与本合同相符的检验证书。该证书为议付货款时向银行提交单据的一部分，但不得作为货物质量、规格、数量、性能的最后依据，制造商应将记载检验细节的书面报告附在品质检验书内。

Before delivery the manufacturer should make a precise and overall inspection of the goods regarding quality, quantity, specification and performance and issue the certificate indicating the goods in conformity with the stipulation of the contract. The certificates are one part of the documents presented to the bank for negotiation of the payment and should not be considered as final regarding quality, quantity, specification and performance. The manufacturer should include the inspection written report in the Inspection Certificate of Quality, stating the inspection particulars.

（2）索赔条款＝索赔权的规定＋索赔时间＋索赔依据＋赔付方法

买方对于装运货物的任何异议必须于装运货物的船只到达目的港后30天内提出，并须提供经卖方同意的公正机关出具的检验报告，如果货物已经加工，买方即丧失索赔权利。属于保险公司或轮船公司责任范围的索赔，卖方不予受理。

Any discrepancy on the shipped goods should be put forward within 30 days after the arrival of the vessel carrying the goods at the port of destination and the Buyer should present the Survey Report issued by the Surveyor agreed by the Seller. If the goods have been processed the Buyer will loss the right to claim. The Seller shall not settle the claim within the responsibility of the Insurance Company or Ship Company.

品质异议须于货物到达目的港30天内提出，数量异议须于货物到达目的港15天提出，但均须提供相关检验机构的证明，如属卖方责任，卖方应予以收到异议20天内答复，并提出处理意见。

Any discrepancy about quality should be presented within 30 days after the arrival of the goods at the port of destination; any discrepancy about quantity should be presented within 15 days after the arrival of the goods at the port of destination, both of which cases should be on the strength of the certificates issued by the related surveyor. If the Seller is liable he should send the reply together with the proposal for settlement within 20 days after receiving the said discrepancy.

2. Terms of Payment 支付条款

支付条款＝支付方式＋支付时间。支付方法有很多，来看一些常见的：信用证

letter of credit (L/C);现金 in cash;支票 by check;信用卡 credit card;汇票 draft/bill of exchange;…

其他相关词汇:信汇 mail transfer;电汇 telegraphic transfer;开证行 opening bank;通知行 negotiating bank;托收银行 collecting bank;代收银行 remitting bank

买方应不迟于 12 月 15 日,将 100%的货款用电汇预付至卖方。

The Buyer should pay 100% of the sale amount to the Seller in advance by telegraphic transfer not later than Dec. 15th.

买方应凭卖方开具的即期汇票于见票时立即付款。

The Buyer should make immediate payment against the presentation of the draft issued by the Seller.

买方对卖方开具的见票后 20 天付款的跟单汇票于提示时应予以承兑,并应于汇票到期日付款。

The Buyer should accept the documentary draft at 20 days' sight upon the presentation and make payment on the maturity.

买方通过卖方可接受的银行在装运前一个月开立以卖方为抬头的保兑的不可撤销的信用证,有效期至装运后 15 天。

The Buyer shall open a confirmation irrevocable L/C in favor of the Seller with/through the bank acceptable to the Seller, one month before the shipment.

3. Terms of shipment 运输条款

运输条款中要说明运输方式和价格条件,比如:In case of FOB Terms. 其中有一些贸易术语需要大家注意,例如:FOB(Free on Board)装运港船上交货,指货物在指定的装运港越过船舷,卖方即完成交货。这意味着买方必须从该点起承担货物灭失或损坏的一切风险。FOB 术语要求卖方办理货物出口清关手续。CIF(Cost, Insurance and Freight)成本加保险费、运费,按此术语成交,货价包括从装运港至约定目的地港的通常运费和约定的保险费,故卖方除具有与 CFR 术语的相同义务外,还应为买方办理货运保险,支付保险费。

(五) 合同中的不可抗力、延期和仲裁条款

1. Force Majeure 不可抗力条款

不可抗力条款=不可抗力时间+(当事方)采取的行动

在运输中,或许会遇到一些非人为因素的影响或者破坏,这个时候我们需要事先协商好如何解决以免发生不必要的争执。

如果遭遇无法控制的时间或情况应视为不可抗力,但不限于火灾、风灾、水灾、地震、爆炸、叛乱、传染、检疫、隔离。如要是不可抗力一方不能履行合同规定下义务,另一方应将履行合同的时间延长,所延长的时间应与不可抗力事件的时间相等。

Any event or circumstance beyond control shall be regarded as Force Majeure but not restricted to fire, wind, flood, earthquake, explosion, rebellion, epidemic, quarantine and segregation. In case either party that encounters Force Majeure fails to fulfill the obligation under the contract, the other party should extend the performance time by period equal to the time that Fore Majeure will last.

如果不可抗力持续6个月以上,合同双方应尽快通过友好协商的方式调整继续履行合同事宜。如果双方不能达成协议,则根据合同中第12条款通过仲裁决定。

If the Force Majeure last over 6 months, the two parties of the contract should settle the case of continuing the contract by friendly negotiation as soon as possible. Should the two parties fail to reach an agreement will be settled by arbitration according to Clause 12 of the contract thereof.

2. Late Delivery and Penalty 延期交货和惩罚条款

合同中,如果有一方未能完全履行合同,或者按照合同规定交货,应该受到惩罚。

如果乙方因自身原因而未准时完工,乙方应付违约罚款,每天按总价的千分之一计算,即一千二百六十美元整。

If party B fails to finish the work on schedule due to its own reason, he shall pay to the other party the penalty at 1‰ of the total value of the work per day, that is USD one thousand two hundred and sixty dollars.

如果合资一方未能按本合同第5条规定按期付款,违约方应在逾期后一个月付给另一方10%的利息。如果违约方逾期3个月仍未如资,合同另一方根据本合同第53条规定有权终止合同并向违约方索赔损失。

Should either joint-venturer fails to pay the contribution on schedule according to Clause 5, the default party should pay the other 10% of the interest one month after the dead line. The other party shall hold right to terminate the contract or to claim the damage against / to him according to Clause 53 thereof, if the default party has not done so three months after the deadline.

3. Arbitration 仲裁条款

如果合同双方产生争议,往往有以下几种解决方法:

(1) Negotiation 协商,这也是最好的解决方式。

(2) Consultation / Mediation 调解,这个时候会有第三方的介入。

(3) Arbitration 仲裁,这是组织或者机构的介入。

(4) Litigation 起诉

凡因本合同引起的或与本合同有关的任何争议应协商解决。若协商不成,应提交中国国际经济贸易仲裁委员会深圳分会,按照申请时该会当时施行的仲裁规则进行仲裁。仲裁裁决是终局的,对双方均有约束力。

Any dispute arising from or in connection with the Contract shall be settled through friendly negotiation. In case no settlement is reached, the dispute shall be submitted to China International Economic and Trade Arbitration Commission (CIETAC), Shenzhen Commission, for arbitration in accordance with its rules in effect at the time of applying for arbitration. The arbitral award is final and binding upon both parties.

第五节 本章小结

本章从涉外商务合同的翻译原则入手,重点介绍了商务合同的词汇特点及翻译策略、句式特点及翻译策略等知识。学生通过本章学习应系统了解商务合同的定义、分类及主要构成要素、国际商务合同的语言特点、国际商务合同的翻译技巧,重点是国际商务合同长句和难句的翻译技巧。课程结束后,学生应具备熟练翻译或起草国际商务基础合同的能力。

 课后习题

1. 将下列段落译成汉语。

(1) The formation of this Contract, its validity, interpretation, execution and settlement of disputes in connection herewith shall be governed by the laws of the People's Republic of China.

(2) When a Party wishes to transfer all or part of its registered capital contribution to a third party, it shall provide a written notice to the other Party.

(3) If Party A materially breaches this Contract, Party B or its successor in interest is entitled to terminate this Contract or claim damages for the breach of contract. If Party B materially breaches this Contract, Party A is entitled to request Party B, by issuing a written notice, to redress the breach within fifteen (15) days upon receiving such notice. If Party B fails to redress the breach within the fifteen (15)-day period, party A is entitled to rescind the Contract and claim damages for the breach of contract.

(4) In the event of the seller's failure to effect loading when the vessel arrives duly at the loading port, all expenses including dead freight and/ or demurrage charges thus incurred shall be for the Seller's account.

(5) After arrival of the goods at the port of destination, the Buyer shall apply to China commodity Inspection Bureau (hereinafter referred to as CCIB) for a further

inspection as to the specifications and quantity/weight of the goods.

(6) By irrevocable Letter of Credit to be available by sight draft remain valid for negotiation in China until the 15th day after the aforesaid time of shipment.

(7) Upon receipt the Defaulting Party shall, as its own expense, promptly take all action necessary to remedy such failure. If the Defaulting Party therewith shall fail to correct such default or if immediate correction is not possible, shall fail to commence and diligently continue effective action to correct such default within 10 days following notification thereof from the Aggrieved Party, the Aggrieved Party may terminate this Agreement.

(8) The Contract, made out, in Chinese and English, both version being equally authentic, by and between the Seller and the Buyer whereby the Seller agrees to sell and the Buyer agree to buy the under mentioned goods subject to terms and conditions set forth hereinafter as follows:

(9) All the information provided by the Company relating to the manufacture and sale of its products is provided secret and confidential, and the Consultant agrees not to disclose such information without the Company's authorization.

(10) All expenses (including inspection fees) and losses arising from the return of the goods or claims should be borne by the Sellers. In such case, the Buyers may, if so requested, send a sample of the goods in question to the Sellers, provided that sampling is feasible.

2. 将下列段落译成英语。

（1）双方本着平等互利的原则，经友好协商，依照有关法律，同意按照本合同的条款，建立经销关系。

（2）为保护由供应商向经销商传授的专有知识，本合同终止后一年内，经销商不得在其营业场所内生产、购买、销售或转售与经销产品竞争的货物。

（3）责任方应尽快将发生不可抗力事故的情况以电传或电子邮件的方式通知对方，并于14天内以航空挂号信将有关当局出具的证明文件提交另一方确认。

（4）甲、乙方合作经营的目的是：本着加强经济合作和技术交流的愿望，采用先进而适用的技术和科学的经营管理方法、提高产品质量，发展新产品，并在质量、价格等方面具有国际市场的竞争能力，提高经济效益，使合作各方获得满意的经济效益。

（5）当合同终止和/或合资公司即将清算时，董事会应制定清算的程序和原则并确定清算委员会成员。

（6）从4月1日起到10月20日止这一期间内交货，但以买方信用证在3月20日前到达卖方为限。

（7）如不可抗力事故延续至120天以上，双方将（经过协商）,（根据事故对履约的影响程度),确定是否终止合同或履行合同的部分责任。

(8) 如果发生不可抗力事件,一方在合同项下受不可抗力影响的义务在不可抗力造成的延误期间自动终止,并且其履行期限应自动延长,延长期间为终止的期间,该方无须为此承担违约责任。

(9) 在合作期间,由于地震、台风、水灾、火灾、战争或其他不能遇见并且对其发生和后果不能防止和避免的不可抗力事故,致使直接影响合同的履行或者不能按约定的条件履行时,遇有上述不可抗力事故的一方,应立即将事故情况电报通知对方,应在15天内提供事故的详细情况及合同不能履行、或者部分不能履行,或者需要延期履行的理由的由相关公证部门开具的有效证明文件。

(10) 合同期满时,如引进技术所涉及的专利尚未期满,应当按照有关规定办理。

(11) 若双方在执行本合同或与本合同有关的事情时发生争议,应首先友好协商;协商不成,可向有管辖权的人民法院提起诉讼。

3. 请将下列文本译成英语。

(1)

第一章 一 般 规 定

第 1 条 为了保护合同当事人的合法权益,维护社会经济秩序,促进社会主义现代化建设,制定本法。

第 2 条 本法所称合同是平等主体的自然人、法人、其他组织之间设立、变更、终止民事权利义务关系的协议。

婚姻、收养、监护等有关身份关系的协议,适用其他法律的规定。

第 3 条 合同当事人的法律地位平等,一方不得将自己的意志强加给另一方。

第 4 条 当事人依法享有自愿订立合同的权利,任何单位和个人不得非法干预。

第 5 条 当事人应当遵循公平原则确定各方的权利和义务。

第 6 条 当事人行使权利、履行义务应当遵循诚实信用原则。

第 7 条 当事人订立、履行合同,应当遵守法律、行政法规,尊重社会公德,不得扰乱社会经济秩序,损害社会公共利益。

第 8 条 依法成立的合同,对当事人具有法律约束力。当事人应当按照约定履行自己的义务,不得擅自变更或者解除合同。

依法成立的合同,受法律保护。

(2)

居 间 合 同

第 424 条 居间合同是居间人向委托人报告订立合同的机会或者提供订立合同的媒介服务,委托人支付报酬的合同。

第 425 条　居间人应当就有关订立合同的事项向委托人如实报告。

居间人故意隐瞒与订立合同有关的重要事实或者提供虚假情况,损害委托人利益的,不得要求支付报酬并应当承担损害赔偿责任。

第 426 条　居间人促成合同成立的,委托人应当按照约定支付报酬。对居间人的报酬没有约定或者约定不明确,依照本法第 61 条的规定仍不能确定的,根据居间人的劳务合理确定。因居间人提供订立合同的媒介服务而促成合同成立的,由该合同的当事人平均负担居间人的报酬。

居间人促成合同成立的,居间活动的费用,由居间人负担。

第 427 条　居间人未促成合同成立的,不得要求支付报酬,但可以要求委托人支付从事居间活动支出的必要费用。

第八章

涉外诉讼文书的翻译

诉讼文书,主要是指各级公安机关,检察院及法院在处理刑事、民事、行政诉讼等法律事务中,依法定权限和诉讼程序制定的,具有法律效力的一种重要的司法文书。就其法律意义而言,诉讼文书为实施法律的有效工具,是进行法律活动,明确当事人权利义务的有效凭据,同时也是实现公正司法,维护社会公平、正义的有效载体(陈建平,2007)。

中国自改革开放以来,特别是加入世贸组织后,国际交往空前频繁,涉及政治经济文化等各个领域,在这个过程中不可避免地出现各种各样的摩擦和冲突。中国司法机关在处理众多的涉外案件的同时也需要处理各类英语法律文件。对于不懂英语的律师而言,在处理涉外案件时,如果有关诉讼文书的译本不准确,就会影响律师对案情的了解及进行客观而准确的分析。事实上,对一份诉讼文书的准确翻译是很困难的,由于各国法律体系和法律制度的不同,同一法律术语在不同语言或不同国度里的意义相差很大,有时甚至完全不同。因此为了避免因不同法律体系及法律制度而引起的争议,在翻译之前我们应当先对诉讼文书有一定的了解。提交给法庭的诉讼文书涉及很多的术语及专有名词,这就需要诉讼文书的翻译者对对方国家的法律有较深的了解并学习过专业的法律英语。

在我国,诉讼分为民事诉讼、行政诉讼和刑事诉讼,因此诉讼文书也分为民事诉讼文书、行政诉讼文书和刑事诉讼文书三类。每类诉讼文书按照法定程序又分为若干种。例如,民事诉讼文书主要分为民事起诉状、民事答辩状、传票、上诉状及民事判决书等。英美法系国家的诉讼文书种类与我国大致相同但又有所差别。例如:英美国家的诉讼文书也包括:Civil complaint(民事起诉状),Answer to Complaint(民事答辩书),Civil judgment(民事判决书),Indictment(刑事控诉书),Answer to Indictment(刑事答辩状),Criminal sentence(刑事判决书),Information(公诉书),Writ of Summons(传票)等等,但是也有些诉讼文书是英美国家所特有的,如诉讼中间裁决书(the Interlocutory Judgment),诉讼中间禁令(the Interlocutory Injunction)等。如果译者不熟悉中英文各类诉讼文书及相关知识,那么他的译文很有可能谬误百出,外行话连篇。下一节是对诉讼文书语言特点及文体风格的研究,希望能为读者提供一些参考。

第一节 诉讼文书的语言特点及文体风格

一、语言特点

(一) 用词准确恰当

诉讼文书是一种十分严肃的特殊种类文书,直接关系到当事人的生命、财产等基本权利。文书的制定者们也试图以最精确的语言和形式来表达法律概念和法律事实。因此,诉讼文书的首要特点就是用词准确恰当。

准确使用法律术语。例如"故意"和"过失","既遂"与"未遂","正当防卫"与"防卫过当"等等都有概念上的区别。法律诉讼文书的术语多而繁琐,不同类型的案件有不同的诉讼程序和特定术语,不能混淆。在翻译诉讼文书之前,译者必须对这些诉讼程序和特定术语有着正确而深刻的理解。

例 1 董事责任保险(D & O),是"董事和高级职员责任保险"的简称,是指以公司董事和高级职员向公司或第三者承担的民事赔偿责任为标的的一种保险。

原译:D & O is the abbreviation for directors' and officers' liability insurance. The **standard** of insurance is the civil compensate liability by the company's directors and the senior officers for the company or a third party.

分析:很显然,这里把"标的"译成"standard"是错误的,"标的"是法律术语,指的是当事人之间的权利义务关系,应译为对应概念的法律英语词汇 subject。

改译:D & O is the abbreviation for directors' and officers' liability insurance. The insurance **subject** is the civil compensate liability by the company's directors and the senior officers for the company or a third party.

准确使用近义词。在诉讼文书中,用错近义词就会影响法律文书的严肃性,造成不良的后果。例如,在汉语里面"服法"与"伏法"都含有因犯罪受到法律制裁的意思,但实质上有很大的区别。"服法"指有罪而接受刑罚的处罚,范围较广,包括"伏法"在内,除死刑外还包括其他刑罚在内,指服从刑事制裁。"伏法"指因犯了重罪而被判处死刑,并已经执行死刑。又如"强制"和"强迫"都含有用力压服的意思。"强制"是通过硬性规定的手段强迫执行,有不可抗拒的力量,程度上要比"强迫"重。"强迫"则多指强加在精神上的压力而使对方屈服,适用范围较广。像这些汉语中容易用错的近义词不胜枚举,诉讼文书的文体十分严肃正式,稍不注意就会因一字之差而谬以千里。法律英语的语言特点之一就是大量使用同义词和近义词。多数在英美法系受过专业培训的文书撰稿人常常会把意义相同或类似的词组都用在一个地方,这类词形式多样,细分包括配对词、三联词、同义词、近义词、重言词等,这些都被笼统地称为同义词和近义词。英汉两种不同的诉讼文书关于近义词的处理与英汉各自的语言特点有关,值得我们特别关注。

正确使用简称和缩语。简称,是指对复杂名称的简化形式。缩语,是由词组紧缩而成的合成词。在诉讼文书中使用汉语简称和英文缩语时,应当注意以下几点:

① 在首次出现名称时必须用全称,并说明后文使用的是什么简称或缩语,以免因所指不明确而引起不必要的麻烦。

例 2 The U. S. Supreme Court held that the defendant's rights had been violated.

改写:The United States Supreme Court held that the defendant's rights had been violated.

例 3 The Court announced its decision in the case on Sept. 5, 2008.

改写:The Court announced its decision in the case on September 5, 2008.

② 在涉外诉讼文书中应尽量不用简称和缩语,但是如果一个简称或缩写的应用已经非常普遍,在一般用法中已经取代了全称,则可以使用,但在英语中使用此缩语时不应该使用表示缩写的英文句点(.)。如"亚洲太平洋地区经济合作组织"汉语简称"亚太经合组织",英语则缩写为"APEC",而不是"A. P. E. C."。

例 4 The N. A. A. C. P. was the subject of a profile on C. B. S. last week.

改译:The NAACP was the subject of a profile on CBS last week.

分析:NAACP 是 National Association for the Advancement of Colored People(美国)全国有色人种协进会的缩写,CBS 是(美国)哥伦比亚广播公司(Columbia Broadcasting System)的缩写。

例 5 The defendant in the case is R.J. Reynolds Industries, Inc..

分析:在本例中,字母 R 和 J 后面的句点(.)应当保留,因为这个缩写所代表的含义并非广为人知。一般来说,这样的缩写应当使用全称,但是在上面的例子中不能用全称,因为缩写 R.J.是公司注册名称中使用的。当行文中涉及的公司在其注册名称中含有一个或多个缩写时,如 R.J. Reynolds Industries, Inc.,应当保留缩写,而且不要把缩写所代表的全称全部拼出,除非公司的注册名称中已经全部拼出,如 Exxon Shipping Company。这条规则适用于所有的公司名称中,包括 Co., Corp., Inc. 和 Ltd.。

③ 不要滥用简称。在汉语诉讼文书中正确使用简称的确能够使文书言简意赅,简练得体,但是若滥用起来就会使人莫名其妙,不知所云,尤其在涉外文书和涉外活动中更叫人一头雾水。例如:"某职业技术学校"简称为"某技校","人造皮革厂"简称为"人革厂"等等,都使人啼笑皆非。

(二) 语言正式规范

诉讼文书不同于一般的写作文体,要求语言精准规范。使用规范语言指的是忌用口语和方言及力求使用中性词。

诉讼文书的语言表达不要口语化。英语口语中我们经常用生动的短语,但这在法律文书的写作和翻译中是不合时宜的。

例 6 警察到达犯罪现场后即上楼对犯罪团伙的首要分子进行搜捕。

原译:On arriving at the scene of the crime, the cops ran up the stairs in search of the big enchilada.

分析:在原译中有两处分别出现了口语中的"cops 警察"和"big enchilada 大人物",这种用语在诉讼文书中是很不规范的,应当改译为:On arriving at the scene of the crime, the policemen ran up the stairs in search of the leader of the crime syndicate.

同样地,在诉讼文书中也不得使用方言和俚语。在司法实践中,在笔录中可以适当的使用,但必须加注予以说明。

例 7 本有效遗嘱的订立者于2003年10月12号去世。

原译一:On Octorber 12, 2003, the testator of this valid testament kicked the bucket.

原译二:On Octorber 12, 2003, the testator of this valid testament passed on to her heavenly reward.

译文解析:前述例子中,第一个译句不恰当之处在于句子含俚语,这在法律文书或其他正式文书中都是不规范的。第二个译句虽然避免了俚语,但走到另一个极端,读起来文绉绉的,又有失简洁。

改译:The testator of this valid testament died on October 12, 2003.

例 8 The parties shall distribute profits and share losses in proportion to their respective percentage of investment. The Parties shall only be liable for the indebtedness of the Company up to the amount of their investment in the registered capital of the Company.

原译:双方按各自的出资比例来进行利润的分配和亏损的分担。但是双方对公司的责任只须负责至其各自对公司注册资本的出资额。

分析:这个例子的译文后半部分虽然在意思表达上没有错误,但似乎过于口语化,不太符合法律的行文规范。

改译:双方按各自的出资比例分配利润、分担亏损。但各方承担的责任以其在公司注册资本中的出资额为限。

力求使用中性词。英汉两种语言按感情色彩都可分为褒义词、贬义词和中性词三类。所谓中性词是感情色彩不明显的词语,既不褒也不贬。研究在诉讼文书中为何使用中性词,不仅具有重要的实践意义,而且具有重大的理论意义。

各国法律和司法的价值观和理念同过去相比有很大的不同。现代司法讲求的是公平与正义,法律面前人人平等,司法中立,司法独立。现代诉讼文书的用词要求反映了现代司法的价值观,即不使用带有强烈感情色彩的词语,而是使用客观中性的词语。那种主张诉讼文书要"爱憎分明、言辞激烈、贬斥罪犯"的观点有悖于司法中立原则,不利于保护当事人的基本权利。

二、文体风格

(一) 格式规范

诉讼文书属于应用文体,一般有固定的行文格式,有些虽然没有特别规定,但是在实践中逐渐形成了被普遍采用的格式。不同类型的诉讼有不同的诉讼文书与之对应,如民事诉讼起诉书格式就不同于刑事起诉书格式;上诉书的格式也不同于起诉状。

(二) 叙事明晰,论据充分合法

诉讼文书中叙述具体要素时不能含糊不清,因为这些要素是构成案件事实的重要组成部分,从一定程度上讲,它们是案件事实在法律关系上的体现,特别是与犯罪构成或者法律关系有着密切关系的要素,更应该详细叙述。叙述事实时必须把因果关系交代清楚,存在于民事和刑事纠纷中的因果关系往往比较复杂,要善于透过现象找出行为和结果之间的联系。叙述事实的过程也是说理的过程,就是所提的论点要符合法律规定,不能与法律相悖,说理上承事实,下启结论。翻译诉讼文书难于普通翻译就在于它必须把语言特点,法律知识及逻辑思维三者紧密结合。

(三) 朴实庄重,忌夸张渲染

诉讼文书的文风是朴实无华,是非分明,实事求是,开门见山,一针见血。其首要目的就是清楚地表明当事人观点和立场,提供合理合法的论据支持。在一些议论性的诉讼文书中,偶尔运用修辞性的华丽辞藻可以起到强调观点的作用,但是千万不要因用了华丽的表达而丢掉或混淆了重要的法律观点。观点重要性远大于表达形式。

汉语中的四字词语随处可见,如:丧尽天良、迫不得已、万般无奈等等,这些词语如果频繁出现在民事诉讼状中,让人读起来觉得好像在抒发个人的情感而非说明及叙述事实。在刑事案件中也有类似的情况出现,比如一个罪犯被宣判为终身监禁或者死刑(life imprisonment or death)时,该判决书往往被译为:性质极其恶劣,情节后果极为严重,民愤极大;惨无人道,社会影响极大;罪大恶极,处以死刑,立即执行。

诉讼文书应当避免使用描述性的语言,因为文书所要表达的是客观事实而不是主观思想,此外,对文书内容的大肆渲染也不符合诉讼文书朴实无华和庄重严谨的文体风格。

例 9　合资企业的各方应按照各自在企业注册资本中的份额分享利润。

原译：The parties to the venture shall share the profits in proportion to their respective contribution to the registered capital.

改译：A venture shall share the profits in proportion to its share in the venture's registered capital.

例 10　A joint venture is encouraged to market its products outside China. Export products may be distributed to foreign markets through the joint venture directly or through associated agencies, and they may also be distributed through China's foreign trade agencies.

改译：A joint venture is encouraged to market its products outside China, either directly or indirectly—through its related agencies or (through) China's foreign trade agencies.

分析：原译句拖沓累赘，其实想要表达的意思很简单，如果在表达准确完整的前提下，化繁为简，反而能收到极好的效果，进而提高翻译质量。

第二节　涉外诉讼文书翻译要点

一、首尾两部分的翻译

诉讼文书种类较多，按照文书体裁主要分为：诉状，答辩状，裁决文书，上诉状，执行文书，证票，笔录等。诉讼文书的结构都相对稳定，有些是以固定的表格形式出现，比如传唤书（summons），有些虽没有固定表格格式，但基本上是由首部，正文，结尾三部分构成。此类文书的首部一般包括文书标题、当事人身份事项，尾部则包括送达单位及具状人、具状时间等。其中，文书标题和称谓需要特别注意。

（一）文书标题

通过文书标题，即可了解该诉讼文书的主要类型及法律性质，因此标题的翻译极其重要。陈建平先生指出，翻译标题时可采用套译法，这一主张现已为司法实践所普遍接受。例如：民事判决书可译为 Civil judgment；刑事判决书译为 Criminal sentence；授权委托书 Power of Attorney；宣誓书 Affidavit；民事裁定书 Civil order，等等。但是，对于有些标题的翻译也没有完全统一的标准，例如，民事起诉书就有好几种译法，Complaint，Statement of Claim，Bill of Complaint 或 Petition，这主要是因为英美国家对起诉书名称有不同的规定，如美国《民事诉讼法》就被称为 Complaint，而在英国又被称为 Statement of Claim。

笔者认为可以把使用范围最广、在英美国家属于标准名称的译法作为标准译法，如民事起诉状可译为 Complaint 或 Statement of Claim，不宜再译为其他名称。在翻译实践中，可根据当事人的国籍和送达法院所在国进行取舍，把普遍性和特殊性结合起来，注意各国法律的差异，灵活变通（李克兴，2004）。例如：在美国，法院在正式审理刑事案件之前，会根据行政执法部门调查的结果决定是否起诉所指称的被告人，如果理由充分，大陪审团会制作并向法院提交起诉被告人的正式书面文件 Indictment。这里值得一提的是，并不是所有的刑事起诉书都翻译成 Indictment，实际上 Indictment 的准确翻译应当是控诉书（a formal written document showing criminal charges brought by a grand jury），美国《联邦诉讼规则》规定所有涉及重罪 felony（假定量刑在一年以上）的刑事案件都必须有大陪审团出具的控诉书。Indictment 不同于由检察官制作并提交给法院的指控刑事犯罪的公诉书 Information（a formal criminal charge brought by the U.S. attorney alone, that is, without any participation by the grand jury in the charging decision. Misdemeanor cases are ordinarily prosecuted by the filing of an Information）。在大多数的州，Information 适用于轻罪 misdemeanor（假定量刑在一年以下）的案件。可见在翻译汉语诉讼文书标题的时候，首先要找到英语中与之相对应的同类型的诉讼文书标题的准确翻译。

（二）称谓

当事人的称谓在文书的开头部分需要列明。诉讼文书中使用的称谓一定要符合法律规定，不能想当然的随意乱用。在我国，民事诉讼法和行政诉讼法称当事人为"原告""被告""第三人"，而刑事诉讼法称"自诉人""被告人"。多一个字少一个字，在法律上的身份就不同了。法人或其他组织的主要负责人在诉讼中的称谓也是不一样的，依照有关规定，法人的主要负责人称为"法定代表人"，其他组织的主要负责人称为"代表人"。同样的，根据英美国家法律规定，在不同类型的案件中当事人的称谓也是有区别，因此对于当事人称谓的翻译必须准确。

例 11 陪审团宣告被告人误杀罪名成立。

原译：The jury declared the defendant the charge of manslaughter.

例 12 现在见证的委托书是本人委托住在中华人民共和国武汉市×路×号的××为我正式合法代理人。

原译：Now THIS DEED WITNESSTH that I (the principal) appoint ×× of No. ×, × Lu, Wuhan, and the People's Republic of China, (the agent) to be my true and lawful agent.

译文解析：例 1 中"被告人"正确的译法应该是 the accused。例 2 中代理人译为 agent 多用在商务领域，在语义上是不对应的，事实上为授权人利益而从事某类行为或某一特定行为的是 attorney，所以较为对应的译文应该是 attorney。

除了以上所列举的特定称谓外，某些及物动词加后缀-ee，表示一类人，这类人是动作的承受者。以"ee"结尾的词在法律英语中使用的频率是很高的。例如：assignee

受让人,受托人;appointee 被指定人;bargainee 买主;blackmailee 被勒索者;detainee 被拘留者,判决的囚犯;devisee 受遗赠者;employee 雇员;licensee 领有执照者;murderee 被谋杀者;offeree 受盘人;testee 测试对象;trustee 受托人。

在法律英语中的有些称谓也可以通过加上名词后缀-ant 来表示,例如:appellant 上诉人;applicant 申请人;defendant 被告;litigant 诉讼人;inhabitant 居民。

总之,不管法律英语中称谓如何构成,在翻译汉语诉讼文书中的称谓时一定要符合英美法的表达习惯,力求精准,任何模糊的或意义有偏差的称呼都是不符合要求的。

(三) 中英文诉讼文书比较

英美国家所制作的诉讼文书在首尾格式上与我国有较大的不同,在翻译的时候一定要特别留意。我们可以从对比中找到一些翻译技巧。

我国民事起诉状的基本格式及内容:

民事起诉状

原告:姓名、性别、出生年月、民族、文化程度、工作单位、职业、住址。
(原告如为单位,应写明单位名称、法定代表人姓名及职务、单位地址)
被告:姓名、性别、出生年月、民族、文化程度、工作单位、职业、住址。
(被告如为单位,应写明单位名称、法定代表人姓名及职务、单位地址)
诉讼请求:(写明向法院起诉所要达到的目的)
事实和理由:(写明起诉或提出主张的事实依据和法律依据,包括证据情况和证人姓名及联系地址)
证据来源,证人姓名和住址:

　　此致
_____人民法院

　　　　　　　　　　　　　　　　　　　　　　　具状人:(签名或盖章)
　　　　　　　　　　　　　　　　　　　　　　　委托代理人:
　　　　　　　　　　　　　　　　　　　　　　　_____年_____月_____日

英美国家民事起诉状的基本格式及内容:

　　　　　　　　　　　　　　　　　　　　　　U. S. DISTRICT COURT
　　　　　　　　　　　　　　　　　　　　　　RECEIVED AND FILED
　　　　　　　　　　　　　　　　　　　(DATE):_____ BY DEPUTY
　　　　　　　　　　　　　　　　　　　　　　CLERK _____

UNITED STATES DISTRICT COURT
SOUNTHERN DISTRICT OF OCEANA
Plaintiff(s):
VS.
Defendant(s):

　　　　　　　　　　　　　　　　　　　　　　COMPLAINT
　　　　　　　　　　　　　　　　　　　　　　CIVIL ACTOIN Case No.:

(续)

```
                              COMPLAINT
Ⅰ  Nature of the Action
Ⅱ  Parties
Ⅲ  Jurisdiction and Venue
Ⅳ  Factual Allegations
Court 1：First Cause of Action
Court 2：Second Cause of Action
…
Ⅴ  Prayer for Relief
Ⅵ  Jury Demand
Dated _____
RESPECIFULLY SUBMITTED,
_____ (Signature of Plaintiff)
Attorney of Plaintiff(s) _____
```

  通过以上两份民事起诉书可以看到,中文的民事起诉状中原被告的身份是放在文书最开始的部分,正文结束后的结尾部分是提交的法院的名称,并在文书末尾的右下方填写具状人和委托代理人的签名及该诉状呈交的日期。而在英文起诉状中,诉状提交的日期和法院受理人的签名位于文书首部的左上角,紧接着受理该诉状的法院名称及原被告的身份,与之相对应处于并列位置上的是该文书的性质和案件编号,正文内容叙述详尽后便是结尾部分的原告和原告律师的签名。可见,中英文诉讼文书在格式上有很多的差异,那么在翻译诉讼文书首尾部分的时候应该遵循什么样的原则呢?

  关于格式上的问题,有人提出"客随主便"的原则,主张译文应当适应原文,不打乱原文的格式及总体安排。这种主张秉承了普通翻译所倡导的基本原则,即所谓的"信"。但是,涉外诉讼文书的翻译毕竟不同于普通翻译,因为它涉及翻译后的文本是否与原来的文本具有同等法律效力的问题。所以针对中英文诉讼文书格式上的具体差异,可以做一些适当的调整。比如把一份中文的起诉状翻译成英文时,可以将送达法院移至首部,紧接在标题之后,这样的调整符合英美国家法律工作者行文规范和阅读习惯,相关的外籍当事人看起来一目了然,自然会以严谨的态度来看待翻译过来的英文文本。

  例如,以下是一份从中文翻译成英文的起诉书基本格式:

> Complaint
> To:_____ People's Court
> Plaintiff:
> Domicile:
> Legal Representative:
> Defendant:
> Domicile:
> Legal Representative:
> Claims:
> Facts and Reasons:
> Plaintiff:_____
> Date:_____

二、诉讼文书中有关时间的翻译

与表述时间联系最密切的词便是介词,如 on,after,before,by 等等。在普通英语里面运用介词来表示时间也许不是很困难的事,但在法律文书中使用这些介词却复杂得多,因为法律文书中的时间表述要求很准确,翻译的时候要注意所提到的日期是否包括在内,以避免产生歧义。

例 13 你已被本法院传唤,请于接到本传票之日起 20 日内到本院出庭。

原译:You are summoned to appear in the Court within 20 days from the service of this summons.

改译:You are summoned to appear and answer this action in the Court named above by filing an Answer along with the required answer fee with twenty (20) consecutive days from the service of this summons, not accounting the days of the service. If the twentieth day is a Saturday, Sunday or legal holiday, the time will run until the end of the next day which is NOT a Saturday, Sunday or legal holiday.

译文解析:改译后的句子显然优于原译,因为改译的句子中的 20 日不仅用 twenty days 而且同时用数字 20 表述,以避免这一关键性的日期被轻易涂改,更值得一提的是译者对一些可能产生的争议做了明确界定,如 20 日这一期限是否包括本日,如果第 20 日是节假日怎么办。一般说来,如果要完成一项行动的时段的最后一天正好是星期六或星期日,那一天就不计算在内,那项行动可以在下一个工作日或营业日完成。

诉讼翻译中,关于时间概念的介词比较分析:

(1) after 不包括所提到的日子。

(2) before 不包括所提到的日子。

(3) on 一词被解释为包括所指的日期。短语 on and after 和 on and from 经常连用。在某一天有时也用 on or about 这个短语。

例 14　Authorities suspect the victim was slain on or about Sept. 15.

参考译文：警察怀疑被害人大约是在 9 月 15 日遇害的。

例 15　Party A shall be unauthorized to accept any orders or to collect any account on and after September 20.

参考译文：自 9 月 20 日起，甲方已无权接受任何订单或收取任何款项。

（4）by 这个词表示到某一日期履行的行为可在该日之前或者甚至在当日履行。

例 16　A clause in the agreement provides that the tenant shall leave this building by June 30, 2008 (the expiration date of the lease).

参考译文：合同中有一款规定，承租人须在 2008 年 6 月 30 号（租约到期日）前离开租用的房屋。例句中用的 by 表示承租人可在 6 月 30 号之前离开也可在 6 月 30 号当天离开。

（5）between 一般用来表示以两个指明的日子或日期为界限的时段，是不包括提出作为界限或终端的日子或日期的。然而这条规定不是绝对的，有的场合也表达包括两个终端，或者表示第一个日期要包括在内，最后一个日期不要包括在内，为了避免产生歧义，我们可以这样处理。

例 17　The appointee may exercise his right between July 1, 2008 and July 30, 2008.

分析：上句中用了 between 是否包括 July 1 和 July 30 不清楚。

改译：① The appointee may exercise his right after July 1, 2008 and before July 30, 2008. ② The appointee's right begins on July 1, 2008 and ends on July 30, 2008.

（6）from...to...也是常用来表示时间的介词短语，从某一天或指定的日期（例如某一特定行动的日子）开始计算一段时间，开始计算的那个日子或日期要排除在外，而这一时段的最后一天要包括在内。

例 18　The fifth clause of the contract specifies that the extension of term of validness on this contract is from June 1, 2003 to June 30, 2003, inclusive of the day of June 30, 2003.

参考译文：合同第五款规定该合同从 2003 年 6 月 1 号到 2003 年 6 月 30 号这段时间继续有效，包括 6 月 30 号。

（7）within 这个词排除第一天而包括最后一天，它后面也可接 of, after 或 from 等介词，在每种表述里，所述日期都不计算在内。

例 19　This letter of guarantee is valid within 30 days from the date when Contractor receives the advance money of the contract till the goods have been endorsed, opened and checked, and got their passing reports.

参考译文：本保函从承包商收到合同预付款之日起直至所有货物均签署开箱验货

合格报告后 30 天内有效。

（8）as of 意为"截至"，是一个注明日期的行话，as of 用来把一件事情定在一个时间而另一个时间承认这件事情，用在对当前到以后某个日期的趋势做预测。

例 20　本公司自 5 月 1 日起将用新地址。

参考译文：Our company shall have a new address as of May 1.

例 21　Termination of this Agreement shall cancel, as of the date the termination shall become effective, all orders that may not have been shipped.

参考译文：本协议终止时，于终止生效之日起，停止一切尚未装运的订货。

译文解析：第二个例子把 as of 译为"于……之日起"是不对的，原文的意思不是"从那个日期"，as of the date 的意思是在终止之日，即 on the date of termination。

例 22　The new contract takes effect as of October 1.

参考译文：新合同 10 月 1 日起生效。

译文解析：译句中用"起"这个字也是不正确的，原文的意思是"在十月一日生效"，从法律效力上来说，"在 10 月 1 日生效"和"从 10 月 1 日"是一样的，中文译文基本上把意思表达出来了，但是没有注意到细节问题。在正常情况下，如果说 This contract is effective as of a certain date，应当译为"本合同于某年某月某日生效"。

法律文书中对时间翻译的准确性要求很高，有些与时间有关的词语意思比较清楚，如 on，before，after，through，starting，ending，terminating，expiring 等，译者在工作中应尽量使用这些词而不是那些容易引起歧义的词，或者在可能引起歧义的地方特别加以说明。

三、选用正式的书面体，避免日常生活用语

诉讼文书的语言特点之一就是措辞严谨，因此翻译的时候应选用正式的书面语，避免口语和日常生活用语，请看下表：

正式用语	日常用语	中文意思
accord	give	给予
adequate	enough	足够的
aggregate	total	总共的
as to	about	大约
attain	reach	达到
commence	begin	开始
cease	stop	停止
constitute	make up	组成
deem	consider	认为
effectuate	carry out	实施

(续表)

正式用语	日常用语	中文意思
exclusive	only	仅有的,独有的
expiration	end	过期
for the duration of	during	在……期间
furnish	give, provide	提供
initiate	begin	开始
in the excess of	more than...	多于
in the event that	if	假如
on or about	on	在某天
on or before	by	到……为止
originate	start	起源于
prior to	before	在……之前
provided that	if	如果
retain	keep	保持
render	make, give	给予
subsequent to	after	在……之后
said, same such	the, this, that	这,该
terminate	end, finish	终止
utilize	use	利用

例 23 该公司的成立不符合国家有关规定。

参考译文：The foundation of this company is not **in conformity with** the **provisions** of the relevant laws and regulations issued by the state.

译文解析：原句中的"符合"不用 accord,而是用介词短语 in conformity with,更正式一些。原文中的"规定"应译成 provisions,而不能译成 stipulations,provisions 为法律正式用词,而 stipulations 是一般词汇,在英语法律文件中,很少用,或不用。

例 24 当事人达成仲裁协议,一方向人民法院起诉的,人民法院不予受理,但仲裁协议无效的除外。

参考译文：A people's court shall not accept an action **initiated** by either of the parties **in the event that** the Parties have **concluded and entered into** an arbitration agreement, unless the arbitration agreement is invalid.

译文解析：原句中"向法院起诉"意思是"首先向法院提起诉讼",这里的动词用的是 initiate,而没有用 begin,begin 为一般常用词汇,更好的选择应为 initiate。原句"当事人达成仲裁协议"这里应理解为一个条件状语从句,省略了"如果",因此翻译成 in the event that,而不用 if 这个非正式词汇。原句中"达成仲裁协议"并不是简单地译为 reach an arbitration agreement。在法律文件中,表示签订协议和签订合同时,英语有四种正式表达法,即：sign, make, conclude and entered into an agreement（a contract),使用时可选四种的任何两组,属于法律英语中的同义词连用。译文中concluded and entered into 即签订之意,用语规范且避免了所选的词被曲解。

四、诉讼专业词汇的翻译

诉讼文书中涉及大量的专业词汇,熟悉并掌握这些专业词汇是翻译涉外诉讼文书的前提和基础。诉讼文书中的专业词汇大体上可以分为两大类,第一类是诉讼文书中特有的词汇,第二类是法律活动中经常出现的法律术语。

(一) 诉讼文书中特有的词汇

诉讼文书中特有的词汇有很多,例如:送达 service,起诉 file a case,诉讼 litigation,诉讼代理人 agent and litem,提起公诉 institute a public prosecution,刑事拘留 criminal detention,刑事自诉状 self-incriminating criminal complaint,诉讼时效 statute of limitation,上诉 appeal,等等。

例 25 A defendant who waives service must within the time specified on the waiver form serve on the plaintiff's attorney (or unrepresented plaintiff) a response to the complaint and must also file a signed of the response with the court. If the answer or motion is not served within this time, a default judgment may be taken against the defendant. By waiving service, a defendant is allowed more time to answer than if the summons had been actually served when the request for waiver of service was received.

参考译文:放弃送达的被告必须在格式放弃书所确定的时间内,向原告律师(或无代理人的原告)送达对起诉状的回应书,并须将签字的回应书提交于法院。如果在该时间内没有送达答辩状或者动议书,法院将会下达对被告不利的不应诉判决。与传票已实际送达相比,当放弃送达的请求收到时,放弃送达允许被告有更多的时间做出答辩。

译文解析:上述例子原文中出现很多诉讼词汇,如 waive service 放弃送达,complaint 起诉状,answer 答辩状,motion 动议书,a default judgment 不应诉判决,summon 传票,等等,如果不懂这些词汇特有的法律意义,诉讼文书的翻译便无从谈起。

例 26 外国当事人向中国法院提交的离婚起诉状、离婚答辩状、委托书、意见书和上诉书等诉讼文书,必须经过其本国公证机关公证,并由中国驻该国使领馆认证。中国法院依据中国法律予以判决,如果在中国境外的外国当事人对一审判决不服,可以在收到判决书次日起 30 日内提出上诉;上诉期经申请可以延期,但延期最长不超过 30 日。

参考译文:Litigation documents submitted by the foreigner to a Chinese court, such as complaint for divorce, the bill of defense, the power of attorney, the legal opinion and the instrument of appeal must be notarized by the notary office of his or her country and confirmed by the Chinese Embassy or Consulate to the said foreign country. The Chinese courts make a judgment in accordance with Chinese law. If the foreigner residing outside the People's Republic of China disagrees with the judgment of first instance, he or she may file and appeal within thirty (30) days from the date of receipt of the judgment. The specified time limit can be extended upon application of the foreign party, but the maximum time for an extension is no longer than thirty (30) days.

译文解析：原文含有很多的诉讼词汇，例如，"提交诉状""予以判决""一审"，等等，都是中文诉讼文书中经常出现的字眼，熟练掌握它们相应的法律英语表达方式是很有必要的。

（二）法律活动中常用到的法律术语

法律术语的翻译是法律翻译里面最难的部分之一，因为这些术语与普通法系国家的法律渊源和法律制度密不可分。如在英美国家的诉讼文书中经常提及 breach of contract 违约，tort of negligence 过失侵权，strict liability 严格责任，damages 损害赔偿，joint and several liability 连带责任，probable cause 合理依据，等等。

例 27　Since contributory negligence is an affirmative defense, the complaint need contain no allegation of due care of plaintiff.

参考译文：因共同过失为积极抗辩，故起诉书无需包含关于原告应有注意的声明。

例 28　一审法院在审理案件的过程中，严重违反了民事诉讼法的程序规定，错误地认定与案件有关的事实，裁决我公司承担根本不存在的损害赔偿责任，侵犯了我公司的合法权益。

参考译文：In the trial course of this case, the first-instant court committed grave violation of the Civil Procedure Law of the People's Republic of China; its finding of relevant facts is erroneous and its decision ordering this company to pay certain non-existent damages is quite a violation of this company's legal rights.

第三节　常见涉外诉讼类文书样例及翻译

一、涉外民事诉讼法律文书翻译

涉外民事法律关系是一种广义的具有涉外因素的民事法律关系，有别于一国国内的民事法律关系，它包括在国际交往中产生的各种涉外财产关系及婚姻家庭关系。涉外民事法律关系的主体、客体、内容三个要素中，总有一个或几个要素涉及国外。例如,涉外民事法律关系的主体一方或各方为外国人,外国法人或外国国家;构成涉外民事法律关系的客体的物位于外国;产生,变更,消灭某项民事权利义务关系的法律事实发生在国外。

(一) 涉外民事授权委托书的翻译

授权委托书是当事人把自己的民事权利授予委托代理人的证明文书,即指一个人授权他人作为代理人为授权人利益从事某类行为或某一特定行为的一种书面文件。授权委托书可分为一般授权委托书(general power of attorney)和特别授权委托书(special power of attorney)两种。前者的授权是总括性的或全权的,而后者所授权力是特定的,即这种委托书将代理的权力仅仅局限在一项交易的范围之内或某一特定事项上。中外授权委托书的基本格式类似,主要分为如下三部分:

第一部分,首部:
① 标题。写明"民事授权委托书"或"委托书"。
② 民事委托人和代理人基本情况。

第二部分,正文。写明代理事项的内容、权限和范围,委托权限、有无转委托和委托期限等。注意一定要列明代理权限范围,并写上"全权代理""特别代理""诉讼代理"。

第三部分,尾部。委托人签字盖章,写明具书时间。

范例1:

State of California City of Los Angles 　　　POWER OF ATTORNEY PRINCIPAL PARTY: USA FURNITURE TRADING CORP. REPRESENTATIVE: Stuart D. Sherell. I, Stuart D. Sherell, President of USA Furniture Trading Corp. hereby appoint Tom King from Louis & King Law Firm to act on behalf of USA Furniture Trading Corp., in regard to bringing a file against Greenhouse Trade Co., Ltd., Zhejiang Province, China for the latter's breach of the contract entered by the said two parties. Now this deed witnesseth that I appoint Tom King of No. 17, Xihu Road, Hangzhou City, People's Republic of China, (the "Attorney") to be my corporation's true and lawful attorney and in the name of my corporation to do and execute all or any of the following acts, deeds and things in the People's Republic of China: (1) To negotiate with the legal representative of Greenhouse Trade Co., Ltd. in respect of penalty and damages; (2) To submit and execute all necessary legal documents as may be required by the court in respect of the said Complaint;	加利福尼亚州 洛杉矶市 　　授权委托书 授权方:美国家具贸易公司 法定代表人:斯图亚特·D.舍瑞尔 本人,斯图亚特·D.舍瑞尔,美国家具贸易公司总裁,特此委托路金律师事务所唐金瑞律师代理美国家具贸易公司就中国浙江省绿家贸易公司违约一案提起的诉讼。 现在所见证的委托书是我委托住在中华人民共和国杭州市西湖路17号的唐金瑞(以下称为"代理人")为我公司的正式和合法代理人,代理人得以我公司的名义行使和执行下列行为、文书和事务: (1)与中国浙江省绿家贸易公司法定代表人就违约金及损害赔偿金进行商谈; (2)提交并签署法院所要求的有关诉讼的一切必需的法律文件;

(续)

(3) To promptly appear at the court at the times appointed by the court; (4) To accept any reasonable and acceptable compensation that may be payable by Greenhouse Trade Co., Ltd. in the respect of damage pursuant to the judgment; (5) In the event of the judgment ruled in favor of the defendant, Greenhouse Trade Co., Ltd., Tom King will continue to act for the USA Furniture Trading Corp. to appeal. And I hereby agree to ratify and confirm all that the Attorney may do or cause to be done in pursuance of this Deed which I declare shall continue in force until notice of the revocation hereof shall be actually received by the Attorney for the time being acting in exercise of the powers hereby conferred. President (signature) USA Furniture Corp. Date: [signature of notary] [seal of notary]	(3) 根据法院指定的时间按时出庭; (4) 依法院判决,接受绿家贸易有限公司可能支付的有关损害的任何合理和可接受的补偿; (5) 如果法院做出有利于被告绿家贸易有限公司的判决,唐金瑞将继续代理美国家具贸易公司提出上诉。 我特此同意批准和确认代理人按照此委托书所做的或将做的行为,我宣布此委托书将继续生效直到代理人在履行本委托书授予的权利过程中收到撤销此委托书的通知为止。 美国家具贸易公司总裁 签名: 日期: 公证员签字: 公证员盖章:

范例 2:

民事授权委托书	Power of Attorney
本民事授权委托书委托方华森服装公司是依据《中华人民共和国公司法》成立的有限责任公司,办事处设在北京市朝阳区。该公司授权委托志成律师事务所的夏明芳先生就华融贸易公司诉华森服装公司一案作为该方一审、二审或再审的诉讼代理人。 委托事项为:代为答辩,出庭,提出反诉,调查取证,并向有关法庭递送有关证据,进行和解,接受法庭调解,接受或放弃或变更诉讼请求,准备上诉状和提出上诉,申请再审,申请在审理中或审理前的证据保全及财产保全措施,申请强制执行法庭有效文件,接收送达的法庭文件,签收裁决、判决、传票及任何其他的法庭文件,处理与所有与上述事务有关的相应问题。	We, Huasen Garments Company, a corporation duly organized and existing pursuant to the Company Law of People's Republic of China with its office at Chaoyang District, Beijing, hereby appoint and empower Xia Mingfang from Zhicheng Law Firm to be our agent ad litem in the first and second instances and/or retrial respectively, as well as in the enforcement procedures, with respect to the case of Huarong Trade Company vs. Huasen Garments Company. We further appoint and empower the above-mentioned attorney to prepare the answer and appear before the competent court hearing; to counter-claim, to investigate, collect, and deliver to the relevant court any related evidence; to make compromise; to accept any mediation presided over by court; to admit, waive or modify the claims; to prepare the statement of appeal and file an appeal; to apply for retrial; to apply for measures of evidence preservation and measures of property preservation during or before the proceedings; to apply for enforcement of the valid court documents; to accept service of court documents; to sign and receive verdicts, judgments, summons, decisions and any other court documents, and to handle all other issues in connection with the said matter.

(续)

夏明芳先生有权提议和委托律师事务所的其他律师参与、履行并解决与此案相关的各事项。我们认可上述指定的委托人在授权范围内所做的行为及签署的文件。	In particular, we appoint and empower Mr. Xia Mingfang to nominate and authorize any other lawyer of the law firm to engage in, fulfill and implement any of the matters and issues as contemplated herein. We further grant our recognition to the acts made and the documents signed by the attorney mentioned above within the limits of the powers granted herein.
我公司特此确认该授权委托书自签署之日起及执行期间有效。	We hereby confirm that this Power of Attorney shall remain in full force from the date of signature and/or seal through the completion of the matters as set forth in this Power of Attorney.
我公司于证人面前在这份授权委托书上签字盖章。 委托人：华森服装公司 受托人：夏明芳 日期：	In witness whereof we cause this Power of Attorney to be duly signed and/or sealed. Appointer: **Huasen Garments Company** Appointee: **Xia Mingfang** Date：

授权委托书的翻译要点：

（1）注意授权委托书中频繁出现的正式程度较高的词或短语的翻译。范例1是一份英文授权委托书及中译本，英文委托书措辞很正规严谨，例如使用 appoint, act on behalf of, bring a file against, breach of the contract, in regard to, pursuant to the judgment, in the event of 等，译文的措辞也体现了法律文件的严谨，appoint 被译为"委派"，act on behalf of 被译为"代理"，bring a file against 翻译为"提起诉讼"，breach of the contract 译为"违约"，in regard to 译为"就"，pursuant to the judgment 译为"依法院判决"，in the event of 译为"如果"。范例2是中文的授权委托书及英文译文，中文委托书中有很多法律专业术语，如"诉讼代理人""答辩""出庭""反诉""调查取证""递送""和解""法院调解""放弃或变更诉讼请求""上诉""再审""证据保全"等等，翻译的时候必须用词准确，找到法律英语中对应的术语，不能妄自造词，该委托书的英文译文就处理的非常好，"诉讼代理人"翻译为 agent ad litem，"答辩"翻译为 answer，"出庭"翻译为 appear before the competent court hearing，"反诉"译为 counter-claim，"调查取证"译为 investigate and collect，"递送"译为 deliver，"和解"译为 make compromise，"法院调解"译为 mediation presided over by court，"放弃或变更诉讼请求"译为 waive or modify the claims，"上诉"译为 appeal，"再审"译为 retrial，"证据保全"译为 evidence preservation。

（2）注意授权委托书中常用套句的翻译。中英文授权委托书中都有一些常用的套句，翻译的时候不妨对号入座，既可以节省时间，又能使译文更加专业，例如：

① I, ..., hereby appoint...to act on behalf of...in regard to... 我××特此委托××就……一事代表××。

② We... hereby appoint and empower... to be our agent ad litem with respect to... 我们××特此授权委托××关于……一事为我们的代理人。

③ Now this deed witnesseth that I appoint... to be my corporation's true and lawful attorney and in the name of my corporation to do and execute all or any of the following acts, deeds and things... 现在所见证的委托书是我委托××为我公司的正式和合法代理人，代理人得以我公司的名义行使和执行下列行为、文书和事务：……

④ And I hereby agree to ratify and confirm all that the Attorney may do or cause to be done in pursuance of this Deed which I declare shall continue in force until notice of the revocation hereof shall be actually received by the Attorney for the time being acting in exercise of the powers hereby conferred. 我特此同意批准和确认代理人按照此委托书所做的或将做的行为，我宣布此委托书将继续生效直到代理人在履行本委托书授予的权利过程中收到撤销此委托书的通知为止。

⑤ We further grant our recognition to the acts made and the documents signed by the attorney mentioned above within the limits of the powers granted herein. 我们认可上述指定的委托人在授权范围内所做的行为及签署的文件。

⑥ We hereby confirm that this Power of Attorney shall remain in full force from the date of signature and/or seal through the completion of the matters as set forth in this Power of Attorney. 我公司特此确认该授权委托书自签署之日起及执行期间有效。

⑦ In witness whereof we cause this Power of Attorney to be duly signed and/or sealed. 我们于证人面前在这份授权委托书上签字盖章。

（二）涉外民事起诉书的翻译

涉外民事起诉书是指涉外民事案件的原告人或其法定代理人，为维护自己的民事权益就有关民事权利和义务的争议向有管辖权的法院陈述纠纷事实，阐明起诉理由，提出诉讼请求的法律文书。中英文起诉书的基本格式及内容在前面已经简单介绍过，虽然中英文起诉书首尾部分格式存在较大差异，但正文及其主要内容都包括事实陈述及理由，诉讼请求等重要内容：

① 事实陈述和理由。这部分是起诉状的核心。事实陈述和理由是原告提出诉讼请求的材料来源，也是有管辖权的法院裁决权益纠纷的重要依据。第一，事实部分。首先要写明涉外民事案件的案情，如时间、地点、人物、原因、事件经过、结果等，特别是双方争议的焦点及提起诉讼时的状况。第二，理由部分。在叙述事实的基础上，分析认定被告行为或案件事实的性质。要列举证据，分析证据的价值、对证据的真实性和可靠性提供相应的说明，准确援引相关的法律法规，得出被告应承担法律责任或纠纷应如何解决的结论。

②诉讼请求。要简明扼要地写出具体的请求法院予以解决的民事权益争议。例如,侵权赔偿案件,原告要求被告赔偿经济损失。应当具体写明医疗费、住院费、营养费、误工费,以及精神损害赔偿费(注意,如果原告提出精神损害赔偿的话,在涉外法律文书的翻译过程中一定要将精神损害部分翻译清楚,否则如果当事人在一审中没提精神损害赔偿,一审裁判生效后又以精神损害赔偿为诉讼请求向法院起诉的,法院不予受理)、诉讼费各多少元,共计多少元。

范例3:

起诉书	Complaints
江苏省南京市中级人民法院 原告:陶氏化学公司 地址:美国加州旧金山 Brandon 大道200号 法定代表人:霍华德·约翰逊 职位:陶氏化学公司中国地区主管 被告:江苏省ACD石油产品公司 地址:江苏省南京市东湖区石头街50号 法定代表人:李明善 职位:江苏ACD石油产品公司经理 诉讼请求: 1. 请求法院判决被告支付原告货款526 000元及利息14 000元,共计540 000元。 2. 判决被告承担诉讼费用。 事实与理由: 被告系原告在中国江苏省多种产品的经销商之一。自2003年9月至2004年10月,原告将总价值526 000元的多种产品发往被告。上述的多批交易均由被告签订并予以接收。尽管原告反复要求被告付款,被告却未能按时付清货款。 原告认为,原被告之间的这一货款纠纷应适用中国法律。被告收到原告交付的润滑油之后未能按时付清货款,由此给原告造成了巨大的经济损失。因此,按照中国的相关法律法规,被告必须承担因不付款所致的民事责任。基于以上理由,依据《中华人民共和国民法通则》第106条及第112条,和《中华人民共和国民事诉讼法》第108条及其他相关可适用法律法规,原告特此向南京市中院提起诉讼。 原告:陶氏化学公司 日期:2007年11月1日	To: Jiangsu, Nanjing, Intermediate People's Court Plaintiff: Dow Chemical Company Domicile: NO. 200, Brandon Avenue, Los Angles, California, America Legal Representative: Howard Johnson Position: Executive of China Branch of Dow Chemical Company Defendant: Jiangsu ACD Company for Petroleum Products Domicile: 50 Stone Street, East Lake, Nanjing, Jiangsu, China Legal Representative: Li Mingshan Position: Manager of Jiangsu ACD Company for Petroleum Products Claims: 1. To order the Defendant to pay to the Plaintiff the due amount of RMB 526,000 for the dispatched products, plus the interests of 14,000 Yuan thereon, in the aggregate of RMB 540,000 Yuan; 2. To order the court fees to be borne by the defendant. Facts and Reasons: The defendant was one of the distributors of the Plaintiff for various kinds of products in the territory of Jiangsu Province, China. From September, 2003 to October, 2004, the Plaintiff dispatched various kinds of products in the aggregate values of RMB 526,000 Yuan. (see Exhibit I) Each of the said transactions was duly signed and received by the Defendant (see Exhibit II). Though the Plaintiff has repeatedly demanded payment, the Defendant fails to liquidate the outstanding debts in due time. It is the Plaintiff's position that the indebtedness arising out of the transactions between the Plaintiff and the Defendant shall be under the jurisdiction of the China's laws. The Defendant's refusal to satisfy the agreed amounts after receipt of the above-mentioned lubricants resulted in tremendous economic losses on the side of the Plaintiff (see Exhibit III). Therefore, pursuant to the relevant PRC laws and regulations, the Defendant shall assume the civil liabilities accordingly for such nonpayment. By reason of the forgoing, in accordance with Articles 106 and 112 as set forth in *the PRC General Civil Law*, Article 108 as set forth in *the PRC Civil Procedural Law* and other applicable laws and regulations, the Plaintiff hereby files this case with the Court for your adjudication. Plaintiff: Dow Chemical Company Date: Nov. 1st, 2007

(续)

| 附件:
1. 原告营业执照复印件;
2. 法定代表人资格复印件;
3. 授权委托书复印件;
4. 证据一:历次交易发货单;
5. 证据二:历次交易收据;
6. 证据三:损失明细。 | Attachments
1. One copy of the Plaintiff's business license;
2. One copy of the original Certificate of the Legal Representative;
3. One copy of the original Power of Attorney;
4. Exhibit I: Invoices for each transaction;
5. Exhibit II: Receipts for each transaction;
6. Exhibit III: Lists of losses. |

范例 4:

FIRST JUDICIAL DISTRICT COURT
THE STATE OF VIRGINIA, RICHMOND,
CIVIL DIVISION
CIVIL COMPLAINT

弗吉尼亚州里士满第一司法区法院
民事审判庭
民事起诉书

Wilson Lee,
Plaintiff,   Case No. Dr. 64.879
Vs.   Dept. No. 6
Nan Chen
Defendant,

原告   威尔逊·李   案件编号:Dr. 64.879
诉   部门编号:6
被告   陈楠

Comes now, Plaintiff above named and hereby complaints of Defendant and cause of action alleges:	上述原告向法庭呈递诉状起诉被告,提出如下诉讼理由:
I That Plaintiff is a resident of the State of Virginia, and is now, and for period of more than six weeks last past, and preceding the commencement of this action has been a bona fide resident of the State of Virginia, and has continuously resided, and been actually physically and corporeally present and domiciled during all of said period in the State of Virginia, and now resides and is domiciled herein and has had, and still has the intent to make the State of Virginia his home, residence and domicile for an indefinite of time.	一 原告系弗吉尼亚州居民,他现在以及在过去超过六周时间内均居住在该州。在本诉讼开始之前,原告一直是一位真正的弗吉尼亚州居民,他在上述时间内连续实际居住于弗吉尼亚州,并设有住所于此地。原告已经并将仍然有意将弗吉尼亚州作为其今后的家、居所和永久住所。
II That Plaintiff and Defendant were lawfully joined in marriage on September 22, 2004, in Shanghai, China, and that ever since said time have been and now are husband and wife.	二 原告和被告于2004年9月22日在中国上海市依法定程序结婚,夫妻关系持续至今。
III That there are no minor children born as the issue of said marriage.	三 原、被告结婚以来未生育任何孩子。

(续)

IV	四
That Plaintiff should be awarded as his sole and separate property all that property he had prior to the marriage to include the residence located at 4200 Victoria Avenue, Nassau County, the State of Florida, and his personal jewelry, car and effects; that Defendant shall be awarded as her sole and separate property all that property she had prior to the marriage to include the residence located at 242 Xujiahui Road, Shanghai, China, and her personal jewelry, belongings, and effects.	请求法院判定属于原告个人的单独财产包括:他婚前所拥有的全部财产,这些财产包括位于佛罗里达州拿骚县维多利亚大道4200号的住宅,以及他的个人珠宝、私人小轿车和财物。请求法院判定属于被告个人的单独财产包括:她婚前所有的全部财产,包括她位于中国上海市徐家汇路242号的住所以及她的个人珠宝、所有物和财物。
V	五
That any and all property and/or debts and obligations incurred or acquired by either of the parties from and after the date hereof shall be the sole and separate property or responsibility and obligation of the one so acquiring the same.	从本诉讼提起之日起及其之后,任何一方当事人所获得或发生的任何财产和(或)债务,应属于其个人专有的单独财产或债务。
VI	六
That Plaintiff and Defendant are incompatible. Wherefore, Plaintiff prays judgment as follows: 1. That Plaintiff be granted an absolute decree of divorce from the Defendant, that the bonds of matrimony now and heretofore existing between the parties be dissolved; and that the parties hereto be released from all the obligations therefore. 2. That Plaintiff be awarded as his sole and separate property all that property he had prior to the marriage to include the residence located at 4200 Victoria Avenue, Nassau County, the State of Florida and his personal jewelry, car and effects; that Defendant shall be awarded as her sole and separate property all that property she had prior to the marriage and her personal jewelry, belongings, and effects. 3. For such other and further relief as to the court may seem just and proper in the premises.	原被告夫妻关系不和。 为此,原告请求法院做出如下判决: 1. 准许原告与被告离婚,当事人现存的婚姻关系宣告解除,由此解除双方当事人之间的所有义务。 2. 请求法院判定属于原告个人的单独财产包括:他婚前所拥有的全部财产,这些财产包括位于佛罗里达州拿骚县维多利亚大道4200号的住宅,以及他的个人珠宝、私人小轿车和财物。请求法院判定属于被告个人的单独财产包括:她婚前所有的全部财产,包括她位于中国上海市徐家汇路242号的住所以及她的个人珠宝、所有物和财物。 3. 法院认为的合理及适当的其他和进一步补偿。
Dated: This third day of June, 2007. Kingdom Legal Firm, (Signature) Franz Zwolensky Attorney at Law Virginia Bar NO. 000296 643 Mount Avenue, Richmond, Virginia 23463 (703)423-6576	日期:2007年6月3日 金盾律师事务所 (律师签字) 弗朗斯·斯洛文斯基 弗吉尼亚州律师证号:000296 弗吉尼亚州,里士满,蒙特大道,643号 邮编:23463 电话:(703)423-6576

民事起诉书的翻译要点：

(1) 我国的民事起诉状送达法院应放在起诉书的末尾，翻译成英文的时候却将送达法院放置到最前面，这样做比较符合英美律师和法律工作者的行文习惯，便于他们阅读。我国的民事起诉书翻译成英文时并没有完全改头换面，虽然对送达法院的位置做了调整，但是其他部分都尽可能地遵循中文起诉书的格式要求。如第一部分介绍原被告的身份事项，第二部分原告则向中华人民共和国相关法院提出了具体的诉讼请求，第三部分对事实和理由进行陈述，最后提交与诉讼有关的材料，这些都是符合中文起诉书的规范，与英美的民事起诉书的要求是不一样的。此外，中文涉外起诉书中有一些经常用到的句子，如：

① "原告认为，原被告之间的纠纷应适用中国法律"可译为 It is the Plaintiff's position that the dispute arising between the Plaintiff and the Defendant shall be under the jurisdiction of the China's laws.

② "被告的某些行为或被告未尽到应尽的义务给原告带来了巨大的经济损失"可译为 The Defendant's deed to... or The Defendant's failure to... resulted in tremendous economic losses on the side of the Plaintiff.

③ "按照中国的相关法律法规，被告必须承担因……所致的民事责任"可译为 Pursuant to the relevant PRC laws and regulations, the Defendant shall assume the civil liabilities accordingly for....

④ "基于以上理由，依据《中华人民共和国民法通则》第……条，和《中华人民共和国民事诉讼法》第……条及其他相关可适用法律法规，原告特此向贵法院提起诉讼，请予以公断"可译为 By reason of the forgoing, in accordance with Article...as set forth in the PRC General Civil Law, Article...as set forth in the PRC Civil Procedural Law and other applicable laws and regulations, the Plaintiff hereby files this case with the Court for your fair adjudication.

(2) 将英文的民事起诉书翻译成中文时几乎可以完全保留原文的格式和具体要求(见范例2)。英文的起诉书在正文的很多部分也会经常用到一些惯用语和套句，译者应熟悉并好好运用这些惯用语和套句，例如：

① Now comes the Plaintiff,..., by and through his or her attorney,..., and as for his or her complaint, states as follows：兹有原告××经由他的/她的律师××代理，就其起诉状，作如下陈述：……

② Comes now, plaintiff above named and hereby complaints of Defendant and for cause of action alleges：上述原告向法庭呈递诉状起诉被告，提出如下诉讼理由：……

③ This is an action for damages based on...in violation of...这是一起因违反……基于某种行为所引起的损害赔偿诉讼。

④ Jurisdiction of this court is based upon... 本法院的管辖权是依据……

⑤ Jurisdiction over state law claims herein is based on... 本案对于州法律上的请求的管辖权乃是依据……

⑥ Venue lies in this District pursuant to... 依据……审判地处在本地区。

⑦ Therefore, Plaintiff prays for the relief he or she is entitled to pursuant to... and the regulations propounded pursuant thereto, including... 因此原告请求根据……及相关规则有权获得的救济，包括……

⑧ Wherefore, Plaintiff prays for judgments as follows: or Wherefore, Plaintiff respectfully requests that this court grant the following relief: 为此，原告请求法院做出如下判决：……

（三）涉外民事答辩书的翻译

涉外民事答辩书是指涉外案件中的被告或被上诉方，针对原告或上诉人的指控，进行有理有据的答辩的法律文书。答辩是被告的一种权利，它对于法庭查明事实真相、辨明是非曲直，进而做出公正裁决有决定性的作用。

我国民事答辩书主要包括以下几个方面的内容：

第一部分，首部：

① 标题。写明"民事答辩状"。

② 答辩人的情况。写明答辩人的姓名、性别、年龄、民族、籍贯、职业及住址。如果是法人答辩，写明法人全称和法定代表人。

③ 答辩案由。写明对何人起诉或对上诉的何案提出答辩。

第二部分，答辩理由和案由：

① 答辩的理由。答辩理由是对原告或上诉人的诉讼请求及其所依据的事实与理由进行反驳与辩解。答辩的内容可以分为两种：一种是承认对方的诉讼请求，包括全部承认和部分承认。另外一种则是反驳诉讼请求，即在答辩中提出充分的理由和证据，从实体和程序上等反驳原告或上诉人的请求，也可以否定原告或上诉人所提出的证据。

② 答辩请求。具体的答辩请求包括：

要求人民法院驳回起诉，不予受理；

要求人民法院否定原告请求事项的全部或一部分；

提出新的主张和要求；

提出反诉请求。

答辩理由及请求写完，应该列举出有关证据、证据来源和证人姓名、住址，以供人民法院审理使用。

第三部分，尾部：写明答辩书致送的人民法院单位名称、副本数和答辩人签名或盖章，并注明制作的日期。

范例 5：

答辩书 答辩人：武汉仁爱医院 住址：武汉市解放路七号 主要负责人：张建新 职务：院长 因陈乐要求武汉仁爱医院人身损害赔偿一案，现提出答辩意见如下： 答辩人与陈乐之间不存在直接的合同关系，答辩人 2003 年 6 月 10 日与瑞安国际建筑安装工程公司订立了一份口头合同，由瑞安国际建筑安装工程公司负责把答辩人的一个高压电表柜拆除，陈乐是受瑞安第二建筑安装工程公司的委托来拆除高压电表柜的，与答辩人之间不存在直接合同关系。 陈乐的伤害赔偿应由瑞安国际建筑安装工程公司负责，其一，根据我国法律和有关司法解释规定，瑞安国际建筑安装工程公司对其职工在履行合同的范围内所受到伤害应负责任，陈乐的伤害并不是由于合同客体以外的事物造成的。其三，受瑞安国际建筑安装工程公司委托的陈乐在拆除高压电表柜的过程中，存在着严重违反操作程序的行为，未尽一个电工应尽的注意。 答辩人对陈乐伤害赔偿不应承担责任。根据《中华人民民法通则》的规定，从事高度危险作业的人致他人损害的，应负赔偿责任。而本案中答辩人与瑞安国际建筑安装工程公司订有合同，高度危险来源已通过合同合法地转移给瑞安国际建筑安装工程公司。瑞安国际建筑安装工程公司成为该危险作业物的主体，陈乐在操作过程中受到伤害，这是瑞安国际建筑安装工程公司在履行合同过程中，合同客体造成自己员工的伤害行为，与答辩人无关。 综上所述，武汉仁爱医院为不适合被告，陈乐将我方列入被告是错误的，我方不承担与瑞安国际建筑安装工程公司的连带责任，请贵院依法驳回陈乐的起诉。 此致 武汉市中级人民法院 答辩人：武汉仁爱医院 日期：2006 年 9 月 3 日	**ANSWER TO COMPLAINT** Respondent：Wuhan Charity Hospital Address：No 7，Jiefang Road，Wuhan City Principal：Zhang Jianxin Position：the director of Wuhan Charity Hospital The following answer is hereby given to the claim of Chen Le for compensation by Wuhan Charity Hospital for personal injuries： 1. The respondent does not have a direct contractual relationship with Chen Le. The respondent entered into an oral contract with Ryan International Construction and Installation Company on June 10，2003，whereby Ryan International Construction and Installation Company shall be responsible for removing the high-voltage meter cabinet. Chen Le was engaged in removing the high-voltage meter cabinet as entrusted by Ryan International Construction and Installation Company and therefore has no direct contractual relationship with the respondent. 2. The liabilities for compensating Chen Le for the damage shall be born by Ryan International Construction and Installation Company for the following reasons. Firstly, pursuant to PRC laws and relevant judicial interpretations, Ryan International Construction and Installation Company shall be liable for any injuries suffered by its employees to the extent of the contract performance. The injuries of Chen Le were not caused by anything other than the object of the contract. Thirdly, Chen Le, who was entrusted by Ryan International Construction and Installation Company, seriously violated the operational procedure in removing the high-voltage meter cabinet and failed to pay due attention thereto. 3. The respondent shall not be liable for compensating the injuries of Chen Le. In accordance with *the General Principles of the Civil Law*, any person engaged in highly dangerous operation shall be liable for compensation in the event of any damages. In this case, however, the respondent entered into a contract with Ryan International Construction and Installation Company, whereby the source of high danger shifted to Ryan International Construction and Installation Company legitimately. Ryan International Construction and Installation Company became the subject of the dangerous operation, and therefore any damages caused in the contract performance by Ryan International Construction and Installation Company has no connection with the respondent. By reason of the foregoing, Wuhan Charity Hospital is not legible for becoming the defendant. Chen Le erroneously included Wuhan Charity Hospital as a defendant in this case. We should not be held jointly liable with Ryan International Construction and Installation Company. We hereby request the court to reject the Chen Le's action according to law. Respectfully submitted to： Wuhan City Intermediate People's Court Respondent：Wuhan Charity Hospital Date：September 3，2006

英美国家的民事答辩状 answer 也称 responsive pleading，通常指民事诉讼中被告针对原告的起诉书做出的书面回应。首先，答辩状必须针对诉状中提出的每个主张 allegation 做出回应，回应的方式有三种：① 承认 admit 原告提出的某些主张；② 否认 deny，既可以个别否认，也可以概括否认，然后提出否认的理由；③ 除了采用"多否认，少承认"的策略外，还可以称自己对原告所主张的事实不太清楚或者没有充分的信息相信原告所述的事实以达到"否认"的效果。其次，答辩人在回应诉状的每个主张后，必须做出法律或事实的抗辩。法律抗辩 legal defense 既可以针对程序上的失误也可以针对实体问题进行抗辩。事实抗辩是针对原告提出的事实情况提出的，即 a factual defense。另外，答辩人针对原告的起诉书提出答辩内容后，可以进行"积极抗辩" affirmative defense，积极抗辩是选择性的，它并非每份答辩状必需的内容。

范例 6：

Case No. Dr. 64.879　　　　　　　　　　　　　　案号：Dr. 64.879
Dept. No. 6　　　　　　　　　　　　　　　　　　庭号：6

FIRST JUDICIAL DISTRICT COURT
THE STATE OF VIRGINIA, RICHMOND,
CIVIL DIVISION

弗吉尼亚州里士满第一司法区法院
民事审判庭

Wilson Lee,
Plaintiff,
Vs.　　　　　　　　　　　　　　　Answer
Nan Chen
Defendant,

原告　威尔逊·李
诉　　　　　　　　　　　　　　　答辩状
被告　陈楠

Comes now, Nan Chen, Defendant in the above mentioned action, in answer to the Complaint, Dated June 3, 2007, alleges as follows:	被告陈楠现就上述案件，针对 2007 年 6 月 3 日的起诉状提出答辩如下：
I	一
Denies the allegations in Paragraph 1 of Plaintiff's Complaint, Defendant alleges that Plaintiff Wilson Lee is, and has at all relevant times been, a resident of Nassau County, the State of Florida. He is now and at all relevant times has been employed as a manager in a trading company.	被告否认原告诉状第一段的主张。被告认为，原告林东一直住在佛罗里达州拿骚县。他以前和现在都在加州担任一家贸易公司的主管。
II	二
Alleges that Plaintiff has falsely and fraudulently asserted that he is a resident of Virginia for the purpose of initiating a divorce action in Virginia for the sole purpose of obtaining a quick Virginia divorce.	被告认为，原告虚假并欺骗性地声称他是弗吉尼亚州居民，其目的是为了在该州提起离婚诉讼，这样做的唯一目的是想快速地获得弗吉尼亚州的离婚判决。

(续)

Ⅲ	三
Alleges that there is no jurisdiction basis for this divorce proceeding as neither Plaintiff nor Defendant, as husband and wife or otherwise, have ever been a lawful resident of the State of Virginia, nor is any community property of the marriage located in Virginia.	被告认为,这起离婚诉讼没有管辖权依据,因为无论是原告还是被告,无论是作为丈夫还是妻子或以其他身份,都不曾是弗吉尼亚州的合法居民,也没有任何共同婚姻财产位于该州。
Ⅳ	四
Admits the allegation contained in paragraph Ⅱ and Ⅲ of the Complaint.	被告承认原告诉状第二段和第三段的事实陈述。
Ⅴ	五
Alleges that the State of Virginia has no jurisdiction over the res of the marriage, as to decide the division of community property, as the marriage was contracted in Shanghai, China, Defendant's home, prior to marriage, and Plaintiff lives and has acquired community property in Nassau, Florida, and only the State of Florida and Shanghai City has the jurisdiction over the marriage.	被告认为,弗吉尼亚州对此婚姻事项及其共同财产的分割没有管辖权。原因在于:原告和被告之间的婚姻是在被告婚前的家乡中国上海市缔结的,而且原告住在佛罗里达州拿骚县,并在那里获得共同财产。因此只有佛罗里达州和中国上海市才可能对该婚姻有管辖权。
Ⅵ	六
Admits the allegation contained in paragraph Ⅵ of the Complaint.	被告承认原告诉状第六段的事实陈述。
Ⅶ	七
Defendant alleges that, even if jurisdiction exist, which Defendant denies, Virginia is an inconvenient forum for this action because all evidences and witnesses to this matter are located either in Shanghai China or Florida and that the costs of traveling to the United States, to defend this action are impossible barrier to Defendant, for as now the cost of a round trip ticket to the United States equals one full years salary.	被告认为,即使弗吉尼亚州对本案有管辖权,该州法院也不是适于审理本诉讼的地点,因为本案的所有证据及证人都在中国上海与佛罗里达州,而且前往美国进行本诉讼的旅行和应诉花费,对被告而言,是不可逾越的障碍,因为现在去美国的来回机票费用相当于被告全年的薪水。
Ⅷ	八
Alleges that paragraph Ⅳ and Ⅴ of Plaintiff's Complaint are improperly listed as allegations that are really prayers for relief and incapable of admission or denial.	被告认为原告诉状第四段和第五段所列举的主张不适当,它们其实是原告请求法院给予法律救济的部分。对原告诉状的这两段无法予以承认或否定。
Wherefore, defendant prays judgment as follows:	基于以上理由,被告请求法院做出如下判决:
1. That this Court dismiss the action for lack of personal and subject matter jurisdiction, or, in the alternative on grounds of forum non convenience.	1. 法院以缺乏对人管辖权和对物管辖权为由,或者基于不便审理原则驳回原告的起诉。
2. That in the event this Court assumes jurisdiction that a judgment of divorce absolute be denied for failure to meet the grounds of incompatibility.	2. 如果法院对本案行使管辖权,那么应以不符合夫妻感情不和这一离婚条件为由,拒绝做出准许无条件离婚的判决。
3. That this Court issue an order requiring Plaintiff to pay to Defendant immediately three thousand dollars ($3,000), to cover the costs of travel to Virginia, to defend this action, and food and lodging while in the United States, and five thousand dollars ($5,000) to cover the cost of attorney fees in defense of this action.	3. 法院发布一道命令,要求原告立即向被告支付三千美元,用于被告前往弗吉尼亚州应诉的旅行费和在美国的食宿开销,另外再支付五千美元作为被告因应诉本案而花费的律师费。
4. That in the event this Court determines to assume jurisdiction and grant a judgment of divorce absolute, that Defendant be awarded as her sole and separate property fifty-percent (50%) of all community property, including residences, vehicles, and shares of community property business, and all property which Defendant possessed prior to the marriage and all personal jewelry, belongings, and effects.	4. 如果法院认定其对本案有管辖权,并最终做出无条件离婚判决,那么法院应将所有共同财产的50%判给被告,作为她个人的单独财产,包括住所、汽车和共同财产经营盈利的份额,以及被告婚前所拥有的所有财产、个人珠宝、所有物和财物。

(续)

5. That Defendant further be granted permanent spousal support in the amount of one thousand five hundred ($1,500) per month, in the alternative a lump sum support payment of distributive award in the amount of $50,000 (fifty thousand dollars). 6. That Defendant shall be awarded all reasonable attorney fees, court costs, and other reasonable costs and expenses of this action. And, such other and further relief as this Court may deem just and proper. Date: June 9, 2007 Signature: Lin Nan Address: 242 Xujiahui Road, Shanghai, China	5. 此外,判令原告向配偶支付永久性的配偶抚养费,数额为每月一千五百美元,或者一次性支付五万美元的抚养费。 6. 判令原告向被告支付全部合理的律师费、诉讼费和其他因本诉讼而花费的合理支出。以及判给被告法院认为正当、合适的其他补偿。 日期:2007年6月9日 签字:林楠 地址:中国上海市徐家汇路242号

民事答辩书的翻译要点:

(1) 熟悉民事答辩书中经常使用的法律术语的翻译。在答辩书中经常看到辩护律师 defense attorney/lawyer,辩护人 defender,辩护证据 exculpatory evidence;defense evidence,补充答辩 supplementary answer,反诉 counterclaim,律师费 attorney fees,诉讼费 court costs,等等,这些词的翻译要求准确规范。

(2) 同其他诉讼文书类似,民事答辩书中也会经常使用一些惯用语,例如在中文的答辩书中会经常说道:

① "因……一案,现提出答辩意见如下:"可翻译为 The following answer is hereby given to the claim of... 或 By reason of the dispute based on which... sued..., the defense hereby answers as follows:...

② "为原告与被告因……纠纷起诉一案,被告现提出答辩如下:"可翻译为 With respect to the Complaint in relation to the dispute arising out of... between Plaintiff and Defendant, Defendant hereby responds as follows:...

③ "我们认为:该案与本公司无关,请法院依法撤销原告对我方的诉讼请求"可翻译为 We believe that this case is of no relevance of this company and request that the Plaintiff's claims against this company be dismissed.

④ "鉴此,被告请求法院在查明事实的基础上,驳回原告的诉讼请求"可翻译为 Accordingly, Defendant pleads that the Court deny Plaintiff's requests based on its fact finding.

⑤ "综上所述,请贵院依法驳回原告的起诉。"可翻译为 By reason of the foregoing, we hereby request the court to reject the Plaintiff's action according to law.

英美国家民事答辩书中会经常有出现这样的话:

① Now comes Defendant... by and through his or her attorney..., and answers the Plaintiff's Complaint as follows: 可翻译为 "兹有被告,……,经由他或她的律师,……,就原告的起诉书作如下答辩:……"。

② Paragraph... of the Plaintiff's Complaint states a legal conclusion to which no response is required. 可翻译为"原告起诉书第……段所陈述的法律结论,不要求做出回应"。

③ Defendant has no knowledge or information sufficient to form a belief as to the truth of each and every allegation contained in the paragraph... of the plaintiff's Complaint. 可翻译为"被告对原告起诉书第……段所包含的每一项事实和主张,都没有足够的信息使被告确定其的真实性"。

④ In response to the paragraph... of the plaintiff's Complaint, Defendant lacks sufficient knowledge, information, or belief to admit or deny the allegations in this paragraph, and, basing his or her denial on that ground, Defendant denies generally and specifically each and every allegation of this paragraph. 可以翻译为"针对诉状第……段,被告缺乏足够的认知、信息、或信念对这一段的主张予以承认或否认,据此,被告全面地特定地对这一段所有主张予以否认"。

⑤ Wherefore, Defendant prays that the Complaint of the Plaintiff be dismissed in its entirety and that no relief be afforded whatsoever thereunder. 可翻译为"由此,被告请求法院驳回原告的所有请求事项,不给予原告任何救济"。

⑥ As a separate affirmative defense to all purported claims for relief, Defendant are informed and believed, and on that basis allege that... 可翻译为"对所有要求的救济请求,被告独立的积极抗辩认为,被告得知并据此主张……"。

⑦ I hereby strongly protest and object to the said Application entered as Case on the following grounds: 可翻译为"本人在此强烈抗议和反对将前述申请立案,理由如下:……"。

⑧ In view of the grounds stated above, I respectfully submit that... 可翻译为"综上所述,本人认为……"。

(四) 涉外民事判决书的翻译

涉外民事判决书是法院在审理涉外案件过程中,适用民事法律法规,确认民事权利义务关系,解决涉外民事案件争议,就案件的实体问题和程序问题依法制作的具有法律效力的法律文书。在我国,按现行《民事诉讼法》的规定,人民法院在审理涉外案件过程中有特别规定的适用特别规定,没有特别规定的,适用民事诉讼法的其他有关规定。英美国家的民事判决书称 Civil Judgment,包括衡平法院的判决和允许上诉的命令或裁定。我国与英美国家的民事判决书格式上有较大差异,在翻译的过程中应当注意各自的固定格式。

我国民事判决书一般由四部分部分组成:

第一部分,首部。主要写明三项内容:

① 标题及案号。在文书顶端居中写明:

××人民法院

民事判决书

(年)×民初字第×号

② 当事人身份事项。按顺序写明以下各栏目情况:首先,原告和被告。如自然人的,注明其身份事项;如是法人的,写明法人名称和所在地址,写明法定代表人及其姓名和职务;如果是外国人或外国法人的,应当注明其自然人国籍或法人国籍。其二,诉讼代理人。写明其身份事项,并在姓名后括注与当事人的关系。中国法院有权进行审理的涉外案件中,诉讼代理人如果以律师身份参加诉讼的,必须是中国律师。外国律师不能以律师身份参加诉讼。

③ 案由。按固定格式规定,写明:"原告××(姓名)诉被告××(姓名)××(案由)一案,本院受理后,依法组成合议庭(或依法由审判员××独任审判),公开(或不公开)开庭进行了审理。本案现已审理终结。"

第二部分,事实。涉外民事判决书的事实应包括下面两方面内容:

① 用"原告××诉称:……、被告人××辩称:……、第三人××述称:……"的格式概述当事人双方争议的事实理由及各自的诉讼请求、答辩意见。

② 人民法院审理后查明的事实部分。法院认定的事实在整个案件事实中占有重要地位,是判决书说理性的基础。

第三部分,理由。理由是在事实叙述的基础上,对涉外案件进行的分析认定。主要应写明两项内容:一是判决的理由。即根据认定的事实和证据,阐明法院经审理后的观点,重点是指出事实和理由之间的因果关系。对当事人合法的诉讼请求予以支持;不合法的诉讼请求予以驳回。二是判决所依据的法律、法规。

第四部分,尾部。在涉外民事判决书最后写明:"如不服本判决,可在判决书送达之日起 30 日内,向本院递交上诉状,并根据对方当事人的人数提出副本,上诉于××人民法院。"(注意,涉外民事诉讼中的期限与非涉外民事诉讼期间不同,前者如果当事人在我国领域内没有住所,不服第一审人民法院判决,有权在判决书送达之日起 30 天内提起上诉,如果当事人在我国领域内有住所,则使用民诉法关于期间的一般规定,即 15 天的上诉期。)下方有审判人员、书记员署名、日期、印章等。

范例 7：

中华人民共和国福建省厦门市中级人民法院民事判决书 （1997）厦民三初字第 20 号 原告：厦门赣东实业有限公司 住所：厦门市三湾路 25 号 法定代表人：陈志坚，总经理 原告：新加坡 KALIO 机械公司 住所：新加坡科技大道 837 号 法定代表人：金志河，该公司总裁 委托代理人：刘克添，福建省方正律师事务所律师 被告：三亚市安易实业有限公司 住所：海南省三亚市赤屿路 23 号 法定代表人：叶轩河，该公司总经理 委托代理人：许可东，福建远东律师事务所律师 原告厦门赣东实业有限公司（以下简称赣东公司）、新加坡 KALIO 机械公司（以下简称 KALIO 公司）与三亚市安易实业有限公司（以下简称安易公司）合同纠纷一案，本院受理后，依法组成合议庭，公开开庭进行了审理。原告赣东公司法定代表人陈志坚，KALIO 公司委托代理人刘克添，被告安易公司委托代理人许可东到庭参加诉讼。本案现已审理终结。 原告厦门赣东公司、新加坡 KALIO 公司诉称： 1998 年 5 月 6 日，赣东公司、KALIO 公司共同作为乙方与作为甲方的安易公司签订了纺织机买卖合同。合同约定：甲方向乙方订购 730 部新加坡产开泰牌 Z61 型编织机；交货时间从 1998 年 5 月 8 日起至 1999 年 1 月 8 日止；价格按 FOB（新加坡）每台 20 000 元人民币；交货地点为厦门港；付款方式为机器运抵厦门港后付清全部货款；运输方法及费用负担：海运费用由甲方负担；违约责任，如单方违约，违约方必须向对方赔偿标准为未执行部分合同总额的 10% 的违约金。合同签订后，原告方按约定给被告发运了价值为 900 000 元的全自动编织机及部分配件。安易公司陆续给付了原告机款 500 000 元，现尚欠原告方机款 400 000 元未付。另外，为履行合同，赣东公司为安易公司发运编织机已垫付运费 5 000 元。	**Civil Judgment by Xiamen Intermediate People's Court of Fujian Province, People's Republic of China** Case No.：1997，Xia Minsanchuzi No. 20 Plaintiff：Gandong Industrial Co., Ltd. Domicile：25 Sanwan Road of Xiamen City. Legal Representative：Chen Zhijian, General Manager. Plaintiff：KALIO Machinery Company. Domicile：No. 837 Technology Avenue, Singapore. Legal representative：Jin Zhihe, president of the company. Attorney：Liu Ketian, lawyer of Fujian Fangzheng Law Firm. Defendant：Anyi Industrial Co., Ltd. Domicile：No. 23 Chiyu Road of Sanya City, Hainan Province. Legal representative：Ye Xuanhe, general manager of the company. Attorney：Xu Kedong, lawyer of Fujian Yuandong Law Firm. In respect of the dispute of sales contract of knitting machine between the plaintiffs Gandong Industrial Co., Ltd. of Xiamen City (hereafter referred to as Gandong Company) and KALIO Machinery Company (hereafter referred to as KALIO Co.) and the Defendant Anyi Industrial Co., Ltd. of Sanya City (hereafter referred to as Anyi Co.), the Court has accepted this case as filed and formed a collegial panel and opened a court session publicly. Legal representative Chen Zhijian of Gandong Company, attorney agent Liu Ketian, authorized by KALIO Co. and attorney agent Xu Kedong, authorized by the defendant Anyi Co, participated the court session and made their arguments. This case is decided now. Plaintiffs, Gandong Company and KALIO Co., claimed as follows： Parties B Gandong Company and KALIO Co. made and entered into the sales contract of knitting machine with Party A Anyi Co. on May 6, 1998. The contract stipulated that：Party A shall order 730 sets of Kaitan Z61 type knitting machines made in Singapore from Parties B (for the detailed plan of supply, refer to the fax from Singapore); the time of delivery was from May 8, 1998 to January 8, 1999; the price is RMB 20,000 per set FOB (Singapore); place of delivery: Xiamen Port; full payment on delivery after arrival of the targets at Xiamen; the freight fee shall be borne by Party A; in case either party breaches the contract, the party breaching the contract shall compensate the other party with 10% of the total price of the part of the contract that is not performed as fine for breach of contract. After the contract was signed, the plaintiff delivered automatic knitting machines and parts worth RMB 900,000 to the defendant. Anyi Co. paid RMB 500,000 to the plaintiff for the knitting machines and owes the plaintiff RMB 400,000. In addition, to fulfill the contract, Gandong Company paid Anyi Co. RMB 5,000 of freight in advance for the shipment of the knitting machine.

(续)

二原告提出如下诉讼请求： 1．要求被告给付 400 000 元及违约金 90 000 元，运费 5 000 元； 2．要求被告二原告赔偿 100 000 元人民币损失； 3．诉讼费用由被告承担。 二原告向法院提交了以下证据材料： 1．原被告签订的纺织机买卖合同。该合同由甲方安易公司加盖单位公章、法定代表人叶轩河签名，乙方赣东公司代理人陈志坚签名，KALIO 公司加盖单位公章、代表人金志河签名。由此证明二原告与被告所签订的纺织机合同为有效合同，被告方应给付拖欠的货款并承担违约责任。 2．厦门海关进口关税专用缴款书及厦门边境贸易公司代理进口证明。由此证明：1998 年 5 月 10 日，由厦门边境贸易公司代赣东公司从新加坡进口 57 台纺织机，赣东公司于 1998 年 8 月 12 日向厦门边境贸易公司交纳了 7 700 元的纺织机的代理费、办证费、商检费、口岸费等。 3．在合同履行期间，安易公司的法定代表人叶轩河与赣东公司的委托代理人陈志坚的多次往来信件。由此证明：原告已按照上述购销合同实际履行。 4．被告对于原告提交的三项证据都没有异议。 本法院认为： 二原告与被告所签订的纺织机购销合同为有效合同，被告方应给付拖欠的货款并承担违约责任。二原告要求被告给付 400 000 元及违约金 90 000 元，运费 5 000 元的主张本院予以支持；二原告要求被告赔偿 100 000 元人民币损失的主张无事实依据，本院不予支持。 依照《中华人民共和国经济合同法》第 6 条、第 29 条第 1 款、第 31 条、第 32 条、《中华人民共和国民法通则》第 106 条、第 61 条第 1 款之规定，判决： 1．安易公司于本判决生效之日起十日内偿付赣东公司、KALIO 公司纺织机机及配件款 400 000 元，运费 5 000 元，并支付违约金 90 000 元，合计 495 000 元；	The two plaintiffs pray as follows: 1. The defendant shall pay RMB 400,000, RMB 90,000 of fine for breach of contract and RMB 5,000 of freight; 2. The plaintiffs claim for compensation of damages of RMB 100,000 on the defendant; 3. The court fee shall be borne by the defendant. The following evidentiary documents were submitted by Plaintiffs: 1. Sales contract of knitting machine signed by plaintiffs and defendant. The contract was sealed by Party A and signed by Ye Xuanhe, legal representative of Party A, Chen Zhijian, agent of Party B Gandong Company, sealed by KALIO Co. and signed by Jin Zhihe, representative of KALIO Co. The contract proves that the sales contract of knitting machines singed by and between the two plaintiffs and defendant was valid and the defendant shall pay the money owed for purchase the goods and take the liability for breach of contract. 2. The special import duty pay-in warrant of Xiamen Customs and the agent import certificate of Xiamen Border Trade Company can certify that: Xiamen Border Trade Company which acted as an agent of Gandong Company imported 57 sets of knitting machines from Singapore on May 10, 1998 and Gandong Company paid on August 12, 1998 Xiamen Border Trade Company RMB 7,700 for agency commission, certification, commodity inspection, port management and others. 3. The correspondence between Ye Xuanhe, legal representative of Anyi Co. and Chen Zhijian, authorized agent of Gandong Company, during performance of the contract. This evidence can certify that plaintiffs have actually fulfilled the sales contract. 4. Defendant has no objection to the above evidences. The Court concluded that: The sales contract of knitting machines signed by and between the two plaintiffs and defendant was valid and the defendant shall pay the money owed for purchase the goods and take the liability for breach of contract. The two plaintiffs' claim that the defendant shall pay RMB 400,000 and RMB 90,000 of fine for breach of contract and RMB 5,000 of freight is supported by the Court; the plaintiffs' claim for compensation of damages of RMB 100,000 on the defendant has no factual evidence, and cannot be supported by the Court. In accordance with the stipulation of Article 6, Article 29 Section 1, Articles 31 and 32 of *the Economic Contract Law of the People's Republic of China* and the stipulation of Article 106 and Article 61 Section 1 of *General Principles of the Civil Law of the Peoples Republic of China*, it ordered as follows: 1. Anyi Co. shall pay the Gandong Company and KALIO Co. RMB 400,000 for the knitting machines and fittings, 5,000 RMB of freight and 90,000 RMB of fine for breach of the contract, totaling RMB 495,000 within ten days from the date of effectiveness of the judgment;

(续)

2. 案件受理费20 000元,由被告负担。	2. The total court acceptance fee is RMB 20,000, and shall be borne by the defendant.
如不服本判决,可在判决书收到之日起十五日内,向本院递交上诉状,并按对方当事人的人数提出副本,上诉于福建省高级人民法院。	Appeal shall be brought by the dissatisfying party to Fujian Superior People's Court via this court within 15 days from the service of the decision in the number of copies correspondent to the number of opponents.
审判长:刘国选 审判员:张俊中 审判员:马俊男 年月日:1999年3月3日 书记员:江南 (厦门市中级人民法院章)	Presiding Judge:Liu Guoxuan Judge:Zhang Junzhong Judge:Ma Junnan Dated:March 3,1999 Clerk:Jiang Nan (Official Chop of Xiamen Intermediate People's Court)

英美国家的民事判决书主要包括四部分:第一部分,首部。依次包括做出判决的法院,原被告姓名,判决做出的日期,审理法官的姓名;第二部分,对案件事实和背景进行陈述;第三部分,审理法官对案情的分析;第四部分,做出判决。在美国有些州使用一种表格式的判决书,但多用于离婚案件。

范例8:

Superior Court of Connecticut, Judicial District of Windham. Jon W. BAKER, Plaintiff. vs. Carroll E. SPINNEY, Defendant. Debra J. SPINNEY, Defendant. **No. CV075001737S.** June 2, 2008 *FACTS* On January 3, 2008, the plaintiff, Jon W. Baker (Baker) filed a complaint against the defendants, Carroll E. Spinney and Debra J. Spinney. The complaint alleges the following facts. The plaintiff and Judith M. Nilan (Nilan), who were husband and wife, lived on English Neighborhood Road in Woodstock, Connecticut. The defendants resided on Brickyard Road, also in Woodstock. The defendants hired Scott J. Deojay (Deojay) in 2002 to trim the lawn and run errands for the defendants. Before he was hired by the defendants, Deojay had been convicted of burglary in the third degree and larceny in the third degree. After Deojay had been hired, Kevin J. Rothwell (Rothwell), a handyman employed by the defendants, became aware of Deojay's previous criminal behaviors, the fact that Deojay had previously used marijuana, and that Deojay had attempted suicide. Further, after he was hired by the defendants, Deojay was arrested for various offenses on August 26, 2005.	康涅狄格州高级法院 温德汉姆司法区 原告:琼·W.贝克 诉 被告:卡罗尔 E. 司宾尼 狄波拉 J. 司宾尼 案号:CV075001737S. 日期:2008年6月2日 案件事实: 2008年1月3日,原告琼·W.贝克(以下简称贝克),起诉被告卡罗尔 E.司宾尼和狄波拉 J.司宾尼。原告在起诉中诉称:原告与茱迪 M.尼兰系夫妻关系,居住于康涅狄格州伍德斯托克市英区路。两位被告住在伍德斯托克市石园路。2002年,两名被告雇佣了斯科特 J.德加(以下简称德加)为其打理花园,办理日常琐事。 被告雇佣德加之前,德加就曾被指控犯有三级入室盗窃罪以及三级盗窃罪。德加为被告雇佣之后,被告雇佣的另外一名杂工,凯文 J.罗斯威尔(以下简称罗斯威尔),就得知了德加之前的犯罪行为,并了解到德加曾吸食大麻并曾试图自杀。此外,在德加被被告雇佣之后,德加又于2005年8月26日因多种违法行为被逮捕。

	(续)
On December 12, 2005, Nilan was jogging on Redhead Hill Road in Woodstock. Deojay, who had completed his work for the day at the defendants' property, approached Nilan in his motor vehicle. Deojay subsequently assaulted and kidnapped Nilan, taking her to the defendants' property. While on the defendants' property, Deojay viciously beat Nilan, causing severe injuries that ultimately caused her death. The plaintiff brought the instant action against the defendants in six counts. Counts one and two allege the defendants were negligent in that they knew or should have known of Deojay's violent criminal tendencies and failed to warn Nilan thereof. Counts three and four allege the defendants negligently hired Deojay. Counts five and six allege negligent supervision. On January 14, 2008, the defendants filed the present motion to strike, supported by a memorandum of law. **DISCUSSION** The defendants strike the plaintiff's complaint on the ground that it fails to state a legally sufficient claim for negligence as the defendants did not owe Nilan a duty of care. Because the defendants did not have a duty to protect Nilan from the criminal acts of Deojay, they argue, they cannot be held liable for negligence, negligent hiring, supervision or under the facts alleged. The defendants also argue that because the plaintiff's loss of consortium claims are derivative of the primary negligence claims, they must fail as well. The plaintiff contends that given Deojay's criminal background, history of bizarre and violent behavior, and the defendants' knowledge thereof, his later conduct toward Nilan was foreseeable. Therefore, the plaintiff maintains, the defendants had a duty of care toward Nilan. A. *Count 1: Foreseeability* The initial step in the court's analysis is to determine whether the harm suffered by the plaintiff's decedent was reasonably foreseeable to the defendants. The plaintiff alleges that the defendants knew at some point that Deojay: had a criminal background; had been convicted of burglary in the third degree, larceny in the third degree and disorderly conduct; had used marijuana at some point; had attempted suicide; and had exhibited violent and self-abusive behavior. It is not reasonably foreseeable that a person convicted of burglary and disorderly conduct will later commit assault, battery and murder. Similarly, it is not foreseeable that a person who has used marijuana or attempted suicide will subsequently commit such brutal, violent acts.	2005年12月12日,尼兰在伍德斯托克的红头山路慢跑。在被告住所完成一天工作的德加,骑摩托车遇到了尼兰。德加随后对尼兰施加暴力并将其绑架至被告的住所。在被告的住所,德加猛烈殴打尼兰,造成尼兰重伤并最终导致其死亡。 原告随即基于六点理由对两被告提起诉讼。第一点和第二点提出,被告事先已经发现或本应发现德加严重的犯罪倾向,然而却未能告知尼兰,因此,被告存在过失。第三、四点认为被告雇佣德加存有过失。第五、六点认为被告在对德加的监管中存在过失。 2008年1月14日,被告提交答辩状予以了抗辩,并附法律意见书一份。 **法庭讨论:** 被告对原告的起诉予以了反驳,理由如下:由于被告对于原告妻子尼兰并不负有照看义务,因此原告起诉被告存在过失的理由在法律上并不充分。被告辩称,由于被告并不负有保护尼兰免受德加刑事侵害的义务,他们也就无需承担原告所主张的"察觉过失""雇佣过失""监管过失"等责任。被告还辩称,由于原告的"丧失亲权赔偿请求"源于"过失赔偿请求",因而被告同样无需承担赔偿责任。原告认为,由于德加有犯罪前科,日常行为怪癖、极端,而被告对德加上述特点已经了解,因此,德加后来对尼兰的所作所为完全是可以为被告所预见的。因此,被告对尼兰负有看护义务。 A. 第一点:可预见性 法庭分析的第一步是确定被告是否应当合理预见原告已故妻子所遭遇的损害。原告认为,被告对德加有一定程度了解:有过犯罪前科;曾被指控犯有入室盗窃、盗窃罪行;曾吸食大麻并曾试图自杀;有暴力、自虐行为。然而,对于一个被指控犯有入室盗窃以及行为失常的人,他人并无法合理预见到他会实施伤害、殴打以及谋杀行为。同样,对于一个曾吸食大麻并曾试图自杀的人,他人也无法预见他会实施这种残忍的暴力行为。

(续)

The plaintiff's allegation that Deojay exhibited violent and self-abusive behavior is not enough to support a finding that his later acts towards Nilan were foreseeable by the defendants. While the complaint alleges Deojay behaved violently, it does not allege that Deojay had been violent toward another person. Because the defendants could not have anticipated Deojay's criminal acts toward Nilan, they could not have had a duty to protect her from such harm.	原告诉称,德加经常实施暴力、自虐行为;然而,这也不足以认定被告能够预见到德加会杀害尼兰。虽然原告诉称德加向来行为偏激,但是原告却也并未举例说明德加曾对其他人施过暴力。由于两位被告无法预见到德加对尼兰的犯罪行为,他们也就不负有保护尼兰不受侵害的任务。
B. Counts 3 and 5: *Negligent Hiring, Retention and Supervision*	B. 第三、第五点:雇佣过失、容留过失、监管过失
Liability for negligent hiring "extends to any situation where a third party is injured by an employer's own negligence in failing to select an employee fit or competent to perform the services of employment." <u>Shore v. Stonington, 187 Conn. 147, 155, 444 A. 2d 1379 (1982)</u>. The claim of negligent retention has been recognized by the Superior Court, but not by the appellate courts of the state. Negligent retention requires a plaintiff to "prove that an employer, during the course of employment, became aware of problems that indicate a lack of fitness for the position, that the unfitness was likely to cause the sort of harm incurred by the plaintiff; and that the employer failed to take action." Finally, to state a claim for negligent supervision, "a plaintiff must plead and prove that he suffered an injury due to the defendant's failure to supervise an employee whom the defendant had a duty to supervise." <u>Abate v. Circuit-Wise, Inc., 130 F. Sup. 2d 341, 344 (D. Conn. 2001)</u>.	"由于雇主过失从而使雇佣的雇员并不适合或难以胜任该职位,最终给第三方造成了损害",此时便可适用雇佣过失责任。州高等法院同样认可了容留过失责任,然而州上诉法院却仍未予认可。"容留过失责任"要求原告能够证明在雇主雇佣期间已经认识到雇员与其岗位不适,而这种不适可能会造成诸如给原告所造成的损害;而于此情形下,被告却并未采取相应举措。最后,原告若要主张"监管过失责任",就必须"主张并证明自己遭受的损害是由于被告对于雇员的监管不力造成的,而被告对雇员又负有监管义务。" Abate v. Circuit-Wise 集团 130 F. Sup. 2d 341, 344 (D. 康涅狄格州 2001年)。
The plaintiff's revised complaint fails to set forth legally sufficient causes of action for negligent hiring, retention or supervision because, as already determined, the defendants did not owe a duty of care toward Nilan, as the harm she suffered at the hands of Deojay was not foreseeable and public policy does not support enforcing a duty. "Whether the claim is for negligent hiring, negligent supervision or negligent retention, a plaintiff must allege facts that support the element of foreseeability." *Elbert v. Connecticut Yankee Council, Inc.*, Superior Court, judicial district of New Haven, Docket No. CV 01 0456879 (July 16, 2004, Arnold, J.) Accordingly, the defendants' motion to strike counts three and five is granted.	原告的修订版起诉书未能就"雇佣过失""容留过失""监管过失"提出具有充分的法律说服力的起诉理由。被告在前文已经认定,尼兰被德加侵害致死,而这对于被告并不可预知,因此,被告对于尼兰并不负有保护义务。原告主张被告承担"雇佣过失责任""容留过失责任"以及"监管过失责任",必须提出足以支撑"可预见性"的事实(*Elbert v. 康涅狄格州扬基理事会*,2004 年 7 月 16 日,纽海文司法区康涅狄格州高等法院,卷号 No. CV 01 0456879)。因此,本法院对被告针对原告理由三、五的答辩予以认可。
C. Counts 2, 4 and 6: *Loss of Consortium* In counts two, four and six, Baker brings claims for loss of consortium of his wife, Nilan, due to the defendants' alleged negligence. Loss of consortium is a derivative cause of action... That is to say, if an adverse judgment bars the injured spouse's cause of action, any claim for loss of consortium necessarily fails as well." <u>*United Services Automobile Ass'n. v. Kaschel*, 84 Conn. App. 139, 147 n. 9, 851 A. 2d 1257</u>, cert. denied,). The court has determined that counts one, three and five must be stricken for failure to state a legally sufficient claim. Thus, counts two, four and six are stricken as well.	C. 理由二、四、六:原告丧失亲权 在理由 2、4、6 中,贝克主张,由于被告的过失而使自己妻子尼兰遇害,于是请求丧失亲权赔偿。"丧失亲权"是起诉原因的衍生,"即如果法院某一与原告主张相反的结论否定了原告的起诉理由,那么任何有关丧失亲权的主张都将同样被驳回"。美国汽车服务协会 v. Kaschel,康涅狄格州 2004 年 271 Conn. 917, 859 A.2d 575。法院认为,第 1、3、5 点因法律说服力不足而予以驳回。第 2、4、6 点同样予以驳回。

(续)

CONCLUSION 　　For the foregoing reasons, the defendants' motion to strike counts one through six of the revised complaint is granted. Conn. Super., 2008. Baker v. Spinney	结论 　　基于以上理由，本法院对被告针对原告起诉书中六点理由的答辩予以认可。 康涅狄格州高等法院，2008年 贝克 v. 斯宾尼

民事判决书的翻译要点：

第一，熟悉民事判决书中经常出现的法律英语词汇。例如，"公开审理"可译为 hear cases in open court session，"不公开审理"可译为 trial in camera，"合议庭"可译为 collegial panel，"独议庭"可译为 sole-judge bench，"驳回请求"译为 dismiss or reject the claims，等等。

第二，我国的民事判决书标题一般译为 Civil Judgment 或者 Civil Case Decision，而人民法院的民事裁定书则翻译为 Civil Order。

① 在判决书第一部分陈述案由的时候，通常将"原告××（姓名）诉被告××（姓名）损害赔偿纠纷一案，本院受理后，依法组成合议庭（或依法由审判员××独任审判），公开（或不公开）开庭进行了审理。本案现已审理终结。"翻译为"In respect of the damages claims filed by Plaintiff,..., against Defendant,..., this court has accepted the case as filed and formed the tribunal by law that heard the case in open court sessions. The legal representative and the authorized legal counsels of the above Plaintiff and Defendant attend the trail. The case is tried and closed. 或者 In respect of the dispute of... between Plaintiff... and Defendant..., the Court has accepted this case as filed and formed a collegial panel and opened a court session publicly. The legal representative and the attorney agent authorized by Plaintiff and Defendant participated the court session and made their arguments. This case is decided now."

② 第二部分包括"原告××诉称：……。被告人××辩称：……。第三人××述称：……"等内容，可以分别译为：Plaintiff,..., claimed as follows:...; Defendant... defended as follows...; the third party...stated that....

③ 原被告向法庭提交证据材料也是事实的一个重要组成部分（The following evidentiary documents were submitted by Plaintiff），如果被告对原告所提供的证据没有异议（Defendant has no objection to the above evidences），法院将认定原告提交的证据材料具有证据效力（the court holds that the Exhibits submitted by Plaintiff are valid evidence）如果被告对原告的证据材料提出异议，则 Defendant objects to Exhibit... submitted by Plaintiff in that it calls into question the verity of the evidence and hold that it is not admissible as evidence，并且原告也没有其他证据予以佐证（Plaintiff has no other evidence to prove the issue),故法院认定原告提供的证据不具有证据效力(the court holds that Exhibit...submitted by Plaintiff is not valid evidence)或者 the court shall not uphold the verity of Exhibit...。

④ 根据上述的有效证据,本院认定以下事实(On the basis of the above valid evidence, this court makes the following of facts),在此基础上,法院针对原告提出的诉讼请求给予支持或否定(Plaintiff's claim that or for...can or cannot be supported by the court)。

⑤ 最后法院依据相关的具体法律法规,做出判决(In accordance with the relevant laws and regulations, it ordered as follows)或者(Under the relevant laws and regulations, the following decision is made);如不服本判决,可在判决书送达之日起十五日内,向本院递交上诉状,并按对方当事人的人数提出副本,上诉于××中级人民法院(Appeal shall be brought by the dissatisfying party to...intermediate People's Court via this court within 15 days from the service of the decision in the number of copies correspondent to the number of opponents.)

⑥ 如果法院正在审理的案件是上诉案件,上诉法院做出的判决通常有四种情况:维持原判(The judgment of the first-instance court is affirmed);推翻下级法院的判决(The judgment of the first-instance court is overruled);改变下级法院的判决(The appellate court modifies the judgment of the lower court);将案件发回重审(the case is remanded for retrial)。

第三,英美国家的民事判决书主要涉及管辖权,案件背景和事实的陈述,以及法院的判决等内容,有些判决书翻译成 Decree,一般指衡平法院的判决,即法院通过审理和听取诉讼各方的辩论后,根据公平和良知的原则确定各方的权利义务而做出的命令和判决。通常将判决书翻译成 Judgment,因为 Judgment 也包括 Decree。

① 判决书介绍完当事人身份等基本内容后,便是简要的说明案由,(This cause came on the day of...to be heard on the Claim that..., and the Court being fully advised in the premises find the following to be facts),本案于××(日期)进行审理,本案是应××纠纷一案审理的,本法院在充分考虑了各有关事项之后裁定下列事实。

② 管辖权问题在案件判决的过程中很重要,必须首先加以说明(This Court has jurisdiction over the subject matter and all necessary parties are properly before this Court)本法院对审议的问题有管辖权,而且所有需要出庭的当事人均已出庭。

③ 在判决部分,通常会说:(The Court orders, good cause appearing)本法院有充足理由裁定;或者(It is, therefore, ordered, adjudged and decreed that this Court has full and complete jurisdiction of the subject matter and of the parties and that all necessary parties are properly present at this Court; that all of the enumerated findings are determined to be facts.)因此，本法院裁决，本院对本案审议的问题及当事人享有完全的管辖权，所有必须出庭的当事人都已正当出庭，所有列举事项都被裁定为事实。

④ 法院的进一步判决（The Court further orders），(Jurisdiction is reserved to make other and further orders necessary to carry out this judgment)保留为执行本判决之需做出其他的和进一步裁定的管辖权；(Jurisdiction is reserved over all other issues and all present orders remain in effect)保留对所有其他问题的管辖权，而且一切现有的裁定仍然有效；This judgment shall be entered nunc pro tunc as of (date)...本判决追溯至××（日期），nunc pro tunc 为法律英语中保留的拉丁文，意思是可"溯及既往"。

⑤ 英美国家的民事上诉案件的判决书也有几种不同的结论：维持原判 It can **affirm** the judgment of the trial court, meaning that it approves of this judgment；改判 It can **reverse** that judgment and directly issue the judgment for the opposing side；撤销原判并发回重审 The appellate court will **vacate** the trial court's judgment and **remand** the case to the trial court for the further proceedings consistent with its opinion if the implication of the appellate court's opinion depend on development of further facts。

（五）涉外民事上诉书的翻译

涉外民事上诉书是诉讼当事人及其法定代理人不服地方法院的第一审民事判决，向上一级法院提出上诉，请求撤销、变更原审裁判或重新审判而提出的诉状。

我国涉外民事上诉书的写法最重要的是写明上诉理由、上诉要求，并分别论证其合理合法性，以便第二审人民法院接受并进行改判。涉外民事上诉书主要的内容包括：

（1）上诉人姓名。当事人是法人或其他组织的，还应当写明法人和其他组织的全称，法定代表人或主要负责人的姓名和职务。

（2）原审法院的名称、案件编号和案由。

（3）上诉理由。上诉理由必须针对原审判决的错误所在，是上诉人向上诉法院对一审法院在认定事实和使用法律方面持有异议的全面陈述。上诉的请求和理由决定着二审法院对案件的审理范围。针对原审判决适用法律不当及诉讼程序上的错误，提出予以纠正的法律依据。

（4）尾部。分两行写明"此致""××人民法院"，左下角写出附项：本上诉书副本×份。右下角由上诉人签名，注明上诉日期。

范例 9：

上诉书	**Appeal**
上诉人(一审被告)：浙江青城贸易有限公司 住所地：浙江省杭州市航天路342号 法定代表人：苏秦 职位：总经理	Appellant (Defendant in the first-instance trial)：Qingcheng Trading Limited Company Zhejiang Domicile：No.342 Hangtian Road, Hangzhou, Zhejiang Legal Representative：Su Qin Position：General Manager
	vs.
被上诉人(一审原告)：诺顿工程公司 住所地：美国康涅狄格州哈特福德市诺顿路223号 法定代表人：布兰顿·罗伊 职位：经理	Respondent (Plaintiff in the first-instance trial)：Norton Engineering Company Domicile：No. 223 Norton Street, Hartford, State of Connecticut, America Legal Representative：Brandon Roy Position：Manager
上诉人因房屋租赁合同一案，不服杭州市中级人民法院(2008)杭初字第6号《民事判决书》，现依法提起上诉。	Appellant hereby files an appeal from *the Civil Judgment* with the case number 2008.6. issued by Hangzhou Intermediate People's Court of PRC in respect of the lease contract case, and hereby files the appeal according to law.
上诉请求： 1. 撤销杭州市中院杭2008初字第6号《民事判决书》并发回重审或直接改判。 2. 判决被上诉人承担诉讼费用。	Claims of the Appeal： 1. To reverse the Judgment and remand the case for retrial or to modify the Judgment； 2. To order the cost to be borne by the Respondent.
事实和理由： 首先，上诉人对本案的基本和主导观点：	Facts and Reasons： Firstly, the Appellant's basic and leading opinions about the case follow：
上诉人认为，根据《中华人民共和国合同法》倡导的当事人意识高度自治和契约自由的理念，以及目前司法实践中的主流执法观念，上诉人与被上诉人之间共存在三份合同，均应认定为有效合同。该三份合同的主体、标的物、价款基本一致。	The Appellant maintains that in accordance with the mentalities of highly autonomous expression of intentions and contract freedom called for in *the Contract Law*, as well as the mainstream law-enforcing mentalities in judicial practice at present, there exist three contracts between the Appellant and the Respondent, which shall be deemed to be valid. The subjects, matters and considerations involved in the three contracts are basically identical.
一、一审法院认定2005年5月14日上诉人与被上诉人签订的租赁合同为无效合同，与法无据。 二、法院以被上诉人已履行了合同大部分义务，上诉人在双方订立合同时已在使用租赁房屋为由认定上诉人先履行抗辩权不能成立，这明显违反了《中华人民共和国合同法》有关先履行抗辩权的规定。	I. The first-instance court ascertained that the house lease contract executed between the Appellant and the Respondent on May 14, 2005 was invalid. This ruling is not law-based. II. The court ascertained that the Appellant's exercise of the right to avoid performing the contract as a defense against the Respondent's breach by reason that the Respondent has performed a majority of the contractual obligations and the Appellant was using the lease house when the parties entered into the contract. This ruling is in material violation of the provision of *the Contract Law* in respect of the defensive refusal to perform the contract.

(续)

其次，上诉人基于并不完全认可的一审法院判决的几点抗辩观点：	Secondly, the following are some defensive opinions of the Appellant based on the first-instance judgment which cannot be fully accepted:
一、一审法院以2006年后，上诉人与被上诉人之间存在事实租赁关系为由，判决上诉人比照2005年合同的租金标准承担租金，与法无据。	I. The ruling of the first-instance court ordering the Appellant to pay the rental according to the rental standard prescribed in the contract of 2006 by reason that the Appellant was in an actual lease relationship with the Respondent subsequent to 2005 is not law-based.
二、一审法院对被上诉人未履约的2 200平米问题的判决，存在明显的执法错误。	II. The first-instance judgment on the 2,200 square meters in respect of which the Appellant failed perform the contract is explicitly wrong in law implementation.
三、鉴于一审法院孤立执法（只处理2005年合同）的情况，则上诉人在2005年度以后已经给付的租金就不止贰拾万元。	III. Given the isolated law execution by the first-instance court (i.e. it only considered the contract of 2005), the Appellant has paid more than RMB 200,000 in rental following 2005.
四、即便按照在一审法院只处理2005年合同的情形下，对有关装潢不予补偿，亦不公平。	IV. Even under the circumstance of only handling the contract of 2005 by the first-instance court, no compensation has been given to decoration, which is unfair either.
综上所述，上诉人认为，上诉人与被上诉人之间共存在三份合同。被上诉人和一审法院对该三份合同在明知和已经查明的情况下，却有意割裂当事人之间的完整民事法律关系。从而造成一审判决存在片面、孤立执法，加重当事人的讼累。以及一审判决存在执法尺度、执法理念的不统一、不协调（如对2 200平米未追究违约责任）。还有一审判决存在越权司法、违法裁量等问题。	In view of the foregoing, the Appellant maintains that there have existed three contracts between the Appellant and the Respondent. The Respondent and the first-instance court has intentionally isolated the complete set of civil juristic relationships between the parties, thereby leading to one-sided judgment in the first instance and adding burden to the parties' litigation efforts. Meanwhile, the criteria for law-enforcement were unbalanced and unharmonious in the first instance, coupled with other problems including entitled law application and illegal ruling.
为此，上诉人恳请二审法院，能在基于依法查明本案全部事实的基础上，均衡执法，做出公正的裁判！	Therefore, the Appellant requests the second instance court to make a fair judgment on the basis of ascertaining all facts of this case.
上诉人：浙江青城贸易有限公司 日期：2008年3月6日	Appellant: Qingcheng Trading Limited Company Zhejiang Date: March 6, 2008

英美国家上诉书有几种表达，如 Appeal Petition, Appellant's Factum, Appellate Paper, Appellate Brief, Instrument of Appeal 等。通常认为，英美民事诉讼实行的是三审终审制；而就上诉审的审理对象而言，第二审原则上为法律审，一般不涉及事实问题，但在特定情形下亦涉及事实，第三审为法律审。因此翻译英文上诉书的时候要注意整体把握，例如该上诉书与下一级法院判决书（包括一审和二审）的内在联系，以及该上述书中上诉人和被上述人与一审中原告和被告的对应关系，弄清这些复杂的关系是翻译好整篇文书的前提。

范例 10：

Appellate Court of Connecticut Appeal on Judgment from Superior Court, judicial district of Waterbury Kimberly Gamble-Perugini, Defendant-Appellant, v. Mandy Zhang, Perugini, Plaintiff-Respondent No. 93-2992 **APPELLANT's FACTUM** PART Ⅰ STATEMENT OF FACTS This is an appeal from the judgment of Superior Court, judicial district of Waterbury, the State of Connecticut dated January 5th, 2008, abusing its broad discretion and issuing improper orders on alimony, property disposition and educational support. PART Ⅱ ERRORS IN JUDGMENTS FROM It is respectfully submitted that the learned trail Judge, erred as follows: 1. In assessing the parties' respective incomes and the value of assets, the court did not credit Appellant's testimony, and improperly accepted Respondent's proposed property division without modification. 2. The court abused its discretion in awarding Respondent $100 a week in alimony for a term of ten years. 3. The court improperly ordered Appellant to assume 75 percent of the children's private school tuition costs, given the substantive income shift from Appellant to Respondent resulting from the court's allocation of properties. Part Ⅲ ARGUMENT 1. The court improperly refused to consider evidence Appellant provided regarding the income stream from the rental properties in determining the property allocation. Appellant had to transfer to Respondent all of his right, title and interest in the following real estate: 67 Dallas Terrace, Waterbury; 50 Spring Brook Road, Waterbury; 62 Jacobs Street, Bristol; and 73 Race Street, Bristol. As a consequence of the court's allocation of property, Appellant is left with insufficient income to pay the court orders of child support, education costs and alimony. [General Statutes], "When assigning the parties' property in a marriage dissolution, in relevant part requires the court to consider 'the length of the marriage, the age, health, station, occupation, amount and sources of income, vocational skills, estate. The court shall also consider the contribution of each of the parties in the acquisition, preservation or appreciation in value of their respective estates." At the time of trial, Respondent is thirty-nine years old and Appellant is fifty-four. Therefore, Respondent still has enough time and energy to acquire income, while there is not much time left for Appellant. Furthermore, even though Appellant acquires several properties from which rental income was earned. But as a result of world financial crisis, the rental income reduced greatly recently. Appellant's personal properties also shrink greatly. Therefore, the court's division of the parties' real estate constitutes an abuse of discretion.	**康涅狄格州上诉法院** 就沃特伯里司法区高等法院所做判决提起上诉 上诉人（一审被告）：金伯利·盖博·帕鲁基尼 被上诉人（一审原告）：张曼丽·帕鲁基尼 案号：93-2992 **上诉人陈诉书** 一、事实陈述 本上诉因康涅狄格州沃特伯里司法区高等法院2008年1月5日所做判决而提起，法官在该判决中滥用了自由裁量权，在配偶生活费、财产划分及幼子教育费分担方面的判决并不适当。 二、本上诉所依据原判决的错误之处 初审法官阁下所犯的错误如下： 1. 在评估当事人双方收入及资产时，法院并未采信被告提供的证据，并且未加任何变动的采用了原告单方提出的财产分配方案。 2. 初审法院不适当地判决被告依100美元/周的标准支付原告为期十年的生活费，由此滥用了自由裁量权。 3. 由于法院的财产分配方案，上诉人的大量财产被分配给被上诉人，因此，初审法院判决被告承担孩子就读私立学校学费的75%，并不公平。 三、论据 1. 初审法院在分配财产的过程中并未采信上诉人提供的有关出租房产的收入数额的证据。上诉人必须将下列四处房产的全部权益移交给被上诉人：沃特伯里市达拉斯路67号、春溪路50号以及布列斯托市雅各布街62号和雷斯路73号。由此致使上诉人没有足够的收入支付孩子抚养费、教育费以及生活费用。 而根据《康涅狄格州一般法令》§第46b-81（c），"离婚案件中，法院在分配财产时，必须考虑婚姻维系时间，当事人年龄，健康状况，社会地位，职业，收入来源及数目，职业技能，房产情况。法院还需考虑当事人双方对于他们各自财产的获取、保管、升值所做的贡献。" 目前，被上诉人仅39岁而上诉人已有54岁。因此，被上诉人仍有足够的时间和精力取得收入，而上诉人的时间已所剩无几。上诉人虽然有几处资产可收取租金，但是由于受国际金融危机影响，租金收入锐减。上诉人的个人资产也严重缩水。

(续)

2. In dissolution proceedings, the court must fashion its financial orders in accordance with the criteria set forth in *General Statutes* § 46b-82, which governs awards of alimony. "In particular, rehabilitative alimony, is alimony that is awarded primarily for the purpose of allowing the spouse who receives it to obtain further education, training, or other skills necessary to attain self-sufficiency." There is evidentiary support for Appellant's claim that Respondent received properties from which she will earn rental income and that she also works as a real estate agent. Testimony regarding the parties' marriage also revealed that her earnings from employment were considerable: she earned $37,594 in 2006 and $14,700 in 2005. Therefore, there is no legal or factual rationale to justify the periodic alimony. 3. Finally, the obligation of the education fee imposed on Appellant is disproportionately high in light of the property allocation. The parties' older son attends the Taft School and the younger son attends Chase Collegiate School. The children's education costs a total of $55,000 per year, and Appellant has to assume 75 percent. In that case, Appellant will have not sufficient money to maintain his own life. PART Ⅳ ORDER SOUGHT The Appellant respectfully submits that this appeal should be allowed and that the judgment in favor of the Respondent be reversed. Waterbury, January 15, 2008. Louis. Berry of Council for the Appellant.	2. 在离婚诉讼中，法院涉及金钱的判决必须符合《康涅狄格州一般法令》第46b-82条有关抚养费的规定。即"复原抚养费主要是为使接受费用的配偶一方将来能够获得接受教育、培训以及获得其他生活上能够自给自足的技能。"有确凿的证据证明被上诉人可以从她所分得的房产中赚取租金，此外她还是一名地产中介。有关婚姻的部分证据同样显示她从这份工作中收入颇丰：她在2005年收入了14 700美元，2006年则收入了37 594美元。因此，这笔生活费无论在法律上还是事实上都是不合理的。 3. 最后，上诉人承担的孩子教育费的比例与财产分配相比是极不相称的。当事人双方的长子在塔夫特私立学校读书，幼子切斯克莱格私立学校读书。两人每年的教育开支总计为55 000美元，而上诉人必须承担75%。这样，上诉人便无法维持自己的生活了。 四、上诉请求 上诉人恳请准予上诉，并撤销初审法院判决。 沃特伯里市，2008年1月15日 上诉人律师：路易斯·宾利

民事上诉书的翻译要点：

（1）熟悉上诉书中专业术语的表述。例如：在我国的上诉书中"上诉人"翻译为 appellant；"被上诉人"译为 respondent 或者 appellee；"一审法院"译为 the first-instance court；"二审"译为 the trial of second instance；"抗辩权"译为 defensive right；"孤立执法"译为 the isolated law execution；"违法裁量"译为 illegal ruling；"越权司法"可译为 entitled law application 等。在英美国家的上诉书中经常出现 discretion 译为"自由裁量权"，dismiss the appeal 译为"驳回起诉"。

（2）我国的民事案件中的当事人提起上诉，往往先说明上诉的原因，然后列举事实，表明己方的观点，陈述上诉理由。翻译上诉书的时候会经常用到在文中起到过渡作用的表达方式，如：

①"上诉人因××一案，不服××市中级人民法院第×号《民事判决书》，现依法提起上诉"可翻译为 Appellant hereby files an appeal from the Civil Judgment with the case number... issued by... Intermediate People's Court of PRC in respect of the case that..., and hereby files the appeal according to law.

②在上诉书中表达己方观点，"首先，上诉人对本案的基本和主导观点："通常翻译为 Firstly, the Appellant's basic and leading opinions about the case follow：；"其次，上诉人基于并不完全认可的一审法院判决的几点抗辩观点："可以翻译为 Secondly, the following are some defensive opinions of the Appellant based on the first-instance judgment which cannot be fully accepted:....。

③ 上诉书中对原一审法院所做的判决持有异议的表述。如:一审法院以……为由,判决上诉人……与法无据。The ruling of the first-instance court ordering the Appellant to do... by reason that... is not law-based;又如:一审法院对……的判决,存在明显的执法错误。The first-instance judgment on that... is explicitly wrong in law implementation.

④ 上诉人在表达请求的时候,常常会说"为此,上诉人恳请二审法院,能在基于依法查明本案全部事实的基础上,均衡执法,做出公正的裁判!"

Therefore, the Appellant requests the second instance court to make a fair judgment on the basis of ascertaining all facts of this case.

(3) 英美上诉书主要包括四部分,事实陈述,原判决的错误之处,上诉人提出的论据,上诉请求等,各部分中间也有一些惯用的表达方式。

① 事实陈述部分常用 This is an appeal from the judgment of... dated... 本上诉因××法院某年某月某日所做判决而提起。

② 在表达某种请求时常用:It is respectfully submitted that the learned trail Judge, erred as follows:"一审法官阁下所犯的错误如下:";又如 The Appellant respectfully submits that this appeal should be allowed and that the judgment in favor of the Respondent granted at the trial court be reversed. 译为"上诉人恳请准予上诉,并撤销初审法院判决。"

二、涉外刑事诉讼文书的翻译

刑事诉讼法律文书是指公民,法人或者其他组织在参与刑事诉讼活动中制作和使用的具有法律意义的文书的总称。翻译刑事诉讼法律文书除了遵循一般法律英语的翻译原则外,还必须知晓在刑事诉讼活动中涉及的专业术语,如刑事罪行和刑罚的名称和概念。例如,adultery 通奸罪,battery 殴打罪,money laundry 洗钱,extortion 勒索,arson 纵火,smuggling 走私,manslaughter 误杀,等等。下面就重点介绍涉外刑事起诉书和判决书的翻译。

(一) 涉外刑事起诉书的翻译

我国刑事起诉书是人民检察院依照法定的诉讼程序,代表国家向人民法院对被告人提起公诉的法律文书。因为它是以公诉人的身份提出的,所以也叫公诉书。除首尾部分外,主要是三大部分,其中"犯罪事实和证据"一般是起诉书的主体。对不同性质案件要写出法律规定的犯罪特征;有关犯罪事实必须写清时间、地点、手段、目的(动机)、经过、后果等要素。要注意前后事实、时间之间的一致性,注意保护被害人名誉。叙述犯罪事实,要针对案件特点,详细得当,主次分明。

英国在传统上是由警察机关向法院提起公诉,检察官在刑事诉讼中的权限和作用较小。1985年5月英国议会通过了《犯罪起诉法》,强化了检察官在公诉中的作用,即警察机关在案件侦查终结以后,认为应该起诉的案件,必须移送检察机关,由检察官独立做出是否起诉的决定,这明显是吸收大陆法系的制度和做法。

美国起诉有两种形式,(1)经大陪审团(由16至23人组成)审查后批准的控诉书(indictment);(2)检察官提出的告发书(information)。联邦和半数的州规定重罪案件必须由大陪审团决定是否批准起诉。

范例11:

赤山市人民检察院 起 诉 书 赤检刑诉字(2000)第081号	People's Procuratorate Of Chishan City Criminal Indictment No. 081 ChiJianxingsu (2000)
被告人李玉书,男,1970年8月2日生,汉族,农民,赤山市人,住赤山市龙安村,2000年9月8日因强奸(未遂)、故意杀人、盗窃罪被赤山市公安局刑事拘留,2000年9月15日被赤山市人民检察院批准逮捕,2000年9月15日被赤山市公安局执行逮捕。 被告人李玉书强奸(未遂)、故意杀人、盗窃一案经赤山市公安局侦查终结,移送本院审查起诉,本院于2000年9月20日收到,经本院审查查明,被告人的犯罪事实如下: 2000年9月7日下午,被告人李玉书路经赤山市郊区时,见被害人Nancy Lorraine(女,34岁,来自加利福尼亚)一人在湖边拍照,便上前搭话。 由于双方语言不通,Nancy Lorraine对被告人李玉书未予理睬。被告人李玉书此时产生了强奸邪念,便上前将Nancy Lorraine拉入附近树林并按倒在地,强行撕扯Nancy Lorraine的裤子欲行强奸。Nancy Lorraine极力反抗,大声呼救。李玉书怕罪行暴露,掏出随身携带的匕首向徐的腹部猛刺一刀。Nancy Lorraine继续呼救,李玉书一手卡住Nancy Lorraine的脖子,另一只手向Nancy Lorraine的腹部猛刺数刀,致Nancy Lorraine当场死亡。李玉书随后取下Nancy Lorraine身上带的手表、相机、信用卡和身上的800元人民币和100美元,并将Nancy Lorraine的尸体移到附近掩埋。	The accused, Li Yushu, Male, born in Chishan City, on August 2, 1970, Han nationality, a farmer residing in Longan Village of Chishan City, was detained for committing the crime of rape (attempted), intentional homicide and theft on September 8, 2000. And he was arrested by Bureau of Chishan Municipal Public Security on September 15, 2000 with the arrest warrant issued by the People's Procuratorate of Chishan City. The Bureau of Chishan Municipal Public Security has ended the investigation and transferred this case to this Procuratorate for review before prosecution on September 9, 2000. After detailed examination, this Procuratorate found the facts of this case are as follows: On the afternoon of September 7, 2000, the victim, Nancy Lorraine (Female, thirty-four years old, from California) was taking pictures on the lakeside alone, when the accused Li Yushu passed by, and he went forward to speak to her. As they cannot communicate in the same one language, Nancy Lorraine did not show any interest in the accused, Li Yushu. The accused instantly had an evil thought of raping Nancy Lorraine. He subsequently dragged Nancy Lorraine into a forest nearby and pressed her down, and then ripped the victim's trousers so as to rape her forcefully. Nancy Lorraine resisted vehemently and cried for help. Li Shuyu was afraid of been detected and pulled a knife and stabbed into the victim's stomach. Nancy Lorraine still kept crying. Li Shuyu then held Nancy Lorraine's neck with one hand and stabbed the knife into Nancy Lorraine's stomach with the other hand, which resulted in Nancy Lorraine's immediate death. Li Shuyu subsequently took away Nancy Lorraine's watch, camera, credit card, 800 Yuan and 100 dollars in her pocket, and dragged Nancy Lorraine's body to another place and buried her.

(续)

上述犯罪事实,有被告人供述、物证、勘验检查笔录等证据。事实清楚,证据确实充分。 综上所述,第一,被告人李玉书,违背妇女意志,使用暴力手段欲与被害人 Nancy Lorraine 发生性关系但因被害人的极力反抗并未得逞。其行为已经触犯了《中华人民共和国刑法》第 236 条和第 23 的规定,构成强奸罪(未遂)。 第二,被告人李玉书,在强奸未遂后怕自己罪行暴露,用匕首将被害人 Nancy Lorraine 杀害。其行为已经触犯了《中华人民共和国刑法》第 232 条的规定,构成了故意杀人罪。 第三,被告人李玉书,以非法占有为目的,将 Nancy Lorraine 身上带的手表、相机、信用卡及被害人口袋里的 800 元人民币和 100 美元窃为己有。其行为已经触犯了《中华人民共和国刑法》第 264 条的规定构成盗窃罪。 被告人李玉书的犯罪情节极其严重、社会影响极其恶劣、造成的危害极其严重。本院为维护法律的尊严、维护社会秩序、保护广大人民群众的利益,根据《中华人民共和国刑事诉讼法》第 141 条规定,提起公诉,请依法严惩。 此致 赤山市中级人民法院 检察员:王大名 2000 年 9 月 25 日 (院印) 1. 证据目录 2. 主要证据复印件	The above facts are supported by the confession of the accused, the material evidences, and the record of inquisition and examination, etc.. The facts are true and evidences are verified. Wherefore, firstly, the accused Li Yushu violated the female's will and attempted to have sexual relationship with the victim Nancy Lorraine in violent manner, but failed because of the victim's resistance, which is in violation of Article 236 and Article 23 of *Criminal Law of the People's Republic of China*, committing the crime of rape (attempted). Secondly, the accused, Li Yushu, after failing to rape the victim, murdered the victim Nancy Lorraine with a knife afraid of being detected, which has violated Article 232 of *Criminal Law of the People's Republic of China* and constituted the crime of intentional homicide. Finally, the accused took away the victim's watch, camera, credit card and 800 Yuan and100 dollars in her pocket for unlawful seizure, which has violated Article 264 of *Criminal Law of the People's Republic of China* and constituted the crime of larceny. The extremely serious circumstances of the offence have brought abominable influence and server hazard to the whole society. To safeguard the sanctity of law and the social order and protect the interest of the public, this Procuratorate filed the case in accordance with Article 141 of *Criminal Procedural Law of the People's Republic of China*, and requests the Court punish the accused in accordance with law. Respectfully Submitted To: Chishan Intermediate People's Court Prosecutor:Wang Daming Date:September 25,2000 Seal of the Procuratorate 1. Evidence List 2. Copies of the Major Evidences

范例 12:

United States District Court FOR THE EASTERN DISTRICT OF WATERFORD Grand Jury Sworn in June 16,2001 UNITED STATES OF AMERICA 01-309-01-Cr v. 01-309-02-Cr Jim Green Indictment Frank Chou	美国地区法院 Waterford 东部地区大陪审团 于 2001 年 6 月 16 日宣誓 美利坚合众国 01-309-01-Cr 诉 01-309-02-Cr Jim Green 控诉书 Frank Chou

(续)

The Grand Jury charges: FIRST COUNT: On or about November 4, 2001, defendants Jim Green and Frank Chou unlawfully, knowingly, and intentionally distributed approximately 36 ounces (1,023 grams) of cocaine, a controlled substance, in violation of Title 21 U.S.C §§ 841(b)(1)(B). SECOND COUNT: From on or about November 1, 2001, and continuing thereafter up to an including November 4, 2001, the exact dates being unknown to the Grand Jury, defendants Jim Green and Frank Chou unlawfully, knowingly, and intentionally combine, conspire, confederate and agree together and with other persons known and unknown to the Grand Jury to distribute quantities of cocaine, a controlled substance, in violation of Title 21 U.S.C §§ 841(a)(1), 841(b)(1)(B). Objects Of The Conspiracy It was a part of said conspiracy that to obtain cash and other property, the defendants and others would acquire, repackage, and distribute for profit quantities of cocaine, a controlled substance. It was a further part of said conspiracy that to obtain cash and other property, the defendants and others, directly and indirectly, would unlawfully prepare, dilute, and package quantities of cocaine for sale and distribution within the Waterford area. The means and methods utilized during the course of this conspiracy included, among others, cooking the cocaine, giving the cocaine to street sellers for distribution, collecting money, and providing protection for individuals distributing cocaine in the Waterford area. Overt Acts During the course of and in furtherance of the conspiracy and to effect the objects thereof, the defendants and others in various combinations, did commit the following overt acts, among others, within the Waterford area, the exact dates being unknown to the Grand Jury: (1) Frank Chou and others directed the preparation, dilution, packaging, and distribution of a quantity of cocaine; (2) Frank Chou recruited individuals to distribute cocaine; (3) Frank Chou, at various times, armed himself with weapons. (4) Frank Chou employed Jim Green and others as distributors of cocaine. (5) On or about November 4, 2001, within Waterford, Jim Green and Frank Chou possessed with intent to distribute a quantity of cocaine.	大陪审团指控： 第一罪项： 在或约在2001年11月4日，被告人Jim Green和Frank Chou明知、故意地非法销售约36盎司(1 023克)可卡因(严禁流通物资)，违反了《美国法典》第21册第841条第(a)(1)款，第841条第(b)(1)(B)款。 第二罪项： 自或约自2001年11月1日起，并持续直至2001年11月4日，大陪审团尚不知道确切的日期，被告人Jim Green和Frank Chou不法、明知、故意地联合、合谋、勾结并商定一起向大陪审团已知或未知的其他人大量销售可卡因(严禁流通物资)，违反了《美国法典》第21册第841条第(a)(1)款，第841条第(b)(1)(B)款。 合谋的目的 为了获取现金和其他财物，被告人与其他人合谋的方式之一便是设法获得大量的可卡因这种严禁流通物资，随后对其再包装再而销售。 此外，为获取现金和其他财产，被告人共同犯罪的另一种方式便是，被告人和他人，直接或间接地非法准备、稀释并包装大量的可卡因以便在Waterford出售和经销。 在此共同犯罪的过程中所使用的手段和方法主要包括，蒸煮可卡因、为经销的目的向街头毒贩供应可卡因、收取金钱并为在Waterford贩卖可卡因的毒贩提供保护。 公开行为 在此共同犯罪的过程中，为促进共同犯罪和实现其目标，被告人及其他多人以多种联合方式实施了下列公开行为，特别是在Waterford，虽然下列行为发生的确切日期暂不为大陪审团所知： 1. Frank Chou和其他人指挥了准备、稀释、包装和分销大量可卡因的工作。 2. Frank Chou招收多人分销可卡因。 3. Frank Chou多次携带枪支。 4. Frank Chou雇佣Jim Green和其他几人作为可卡因经销人。 5. 在2001年11月4日左右，在Waterford，Jim Green和Frank Chou持有大量可卡因以待销售。

(续)

(6) On or about November 4, 2001, within Waterford, Jim Green and Frank Chou distributed 36 ounces (1023 grams) of cocaine, a controlled substance. All in violation of Title 21, U.S.C § 846. THIRD COUNT: On or about November 26, 2001, defendant Frank Chou unlawfully, knowingly, and intentionally possessed with intent to distribute approximately 70.5 ounces (2000 grams) of cocaine, a controlled substance, in violation of Title 21 U.S.C §§ 841(b)(1)(B), 841(b)(1)(B). Ranten B. Hall United States Attorney for the Eastern District of Waterford A TRUE BILL: Mainful Fissetle Foreperson.	6. 在 2001 年 11 月 4 日左右，在 Waterford 之内，Jim Green 和 Frank Chou 销售了 36 盎司(1023 克)可卡因这种严禁流通物资。 上述行为均触犯《美国法典》第 846 页第 21 条。 第三罪项: 在 2001 年 11 月 26 日左右，被告人 Frank Chou 明知、故意非法持有大约 70.5 盎司(2000 克)可卡因(严禁流通物资)以待销售，由此违反了《美国法典》第 21 册第 841 条(a)(1)款，第 841 条第(b)(1)(B)款。 Ranten B. Hall Waterford 东部地区检察官 成立诉状 Mainful Fissetle(签名) 陪审团团长

刑事起诉书的翻译要点：

（1）刑事指控中出现罪名和刑罚的翻译，如前面提到的，必须熟悉这些专业词汇的翻译，此外，还必须清楚地知道类似的刑事罪名之间的细微差别，不能张冠李戴。如 assault 和 battery，译成中文都可以是"殴打，攻击"，但事实上 Assault shall be distinguished from battery, in that assault is the threat of violence, whereas battery is actual violence. 用暴力威胁侵犯他人身体犯罪行为应与殴打罪区别开来。其区别是，前者是用暴力相威胁而后者是实际上的使用暴力。又如英美国家的杀人罪分很多种，murder 谋杀，manslaughter 误杀，homicide 杀人，infanticide 杀婴，等等。这些罪名虽然都是杀人，但是有区别的，译者在翻译的时候最大的困难就是不熟悉这些词汇及其确切的法律概念，因此平时必须注意学习和积累。

（2）我国的刑事起诉书和英美国家的刑事起诉书虽然在结构上存在较大差别，但内容上大体相同，即对犯罪事实的指控及所依据的法律。我国的刑事起诉书中经常会说道：

① "被告××(姓名，性别，籍贯，出生日期)因犯某罪于××(日期)被公安机关刑事拘留"可译为 The accused... was detained for committing the crime of... on... by Bureau of the Public Security.

② "被告人××一案经公安机关侦查终结，移送本院审查起诉，经本院审查查明，被告人的犯罪事实如下:"可翻译为 The Bureau of the Public Security has ended the investigation and transferred this case to this Procuratorate for review before prosecution. After detailed examination, this Procuratorate found the facts of this case are as follows:

③ "上述犯罪事实，有被告人供述、物证、勘验检查笔录等证据。事实清楚，证据

确实充分。"可译为 The above facts are supported by the confession of the accused, the material evidences, and the record of inquisition and examination, etc. The facts are true and evidences are verified.

④ "被告人××的犯罪情节极其严重、社会影响极其恶劣、造成的危害极其严重。本院为维护法律的尊严、维护社会秩序、保护广大人民群众的利益,根据《中华人民共和国刑事诉讼法》第……条规定,提起公诉,请依法严惩。"可翻译为 The extremely serious circumstances of the offence have brought abominable influence and server hazard to the whole society. To safeguard the sanctity of law and the social order and protect the interest of the public, this Procuratorate filed the case in accordance with Article...of *Criminal Procedural Law of the People's Republic of China*, and requests the Court punish the accused in accordance with law.

(二) 涉外刑事判决书的翻译

刑事判决书,是法院正式宣告的,对已经认罪或者被证明有罪的刑事被告处以法定刑罚的裁决,作为审判机关最为重要的法律文书,不仅是刑事诉讼侦查、起诉、审判程序的休止符,更是体现司法公正与法律尊严的"裁决金哨"。刑事判决书可翻译为 Sentence, Criminal Sentence 或者 Criminal Judgment。

我国的刑事判决书基本内容包括公诉机关和被告人的基本情况,被告人的犯罪事实,法院意见及所依据的法律,最后做出判决。

范例 13:

| 北京市第一中级人民法院
刑事判决书
(2001)京一中刑初字第 204 号

公诉机关:北京市人民检察院第一分院

被告人尤卡·奥拉多(Yoka Olado),男,1984 年 2 月 23 日出生,肯尼亚籍,北京语言大学留学生,住北京市海淀区上地十街 23 号。因涉嫌盗窃犯罪于 2001 年 9 月 27 日被刑事拘留,10 月 12 日被逮捕。现羁押于北京市海淀区看守所。

辩护人刘付利,北京市海淀区法律援助中心律师。

北京市人民检察院第一分院以京一中刑初字(2001)第 204 号起诉书指控被告人尤卡·奥拉多犯盗窃罪,于 2001 年 11 月 23 日向本院提起公诉。本院于同日立案,依法适用简易程序,实行独任审判,因被告人尤卡·奥拉多系未成年人,不公开开庭审理了本案。被告人尤卡·奥拉多、辩护人刘付利均到庭参加诉讼。现已审理终结。 | First Intermediate People's Court, Beijing City
Criminal Judgment
Case Number:(2001)Jingyizhongxingchuzi No. 204
Prosecutor:First People's Subsidiary Procuratorate of Beijing City

The accused, Yoka Olado, male, was born on February 23, 1984, Kenya nationality, an overseas student of Beijing Foreign Language College, residing in No 23 Shangdi Tenth Street, Haidian District of Beijing City, was detained on September 27, 2001 because of the suspicion of theft, arrested on October 12 the same year, and currently detained at the Haidian District Detention Center of Beijing City.

The accused's lawyer, Liu Fuli, lawyer of Legal Aid Center of Haidian District, Beijng City.

First People's Subsidiary Procuratorate of Beijng City brought this criminal charge〔(2001) Jingyizhongxingchuzi No. 204〕against the accused, Yoka Olado for theft, and filed the charge with this court on November 23, 2001. This court applied the simple proceeding pursuant to law and conducted the trial by a sole judge in camera as the accused was minor. The accused, Yoka Olado, and his lawyer Liu Fuli all appear for the trial. The case is now tried and closed. |

(续)

经查明,被告人尤卡·奥拉多于2001年9月24日,窜至北京市海淀区鑫泰饭店,窃取现金420元及价值5 400余元的钱江125的电动车1辆。盗窃财物总价值5 800余元。案发后,绝大部分赃物被追缴,发还失主。上述事实,有失主王桂刚陈述、证人孙传燕的证言、钱江125电动车的合格证和被告人尤卡·奥拉多的学籍证明、涉案物品价值认定书、现场勘查笔录等证据予以证实,被告人尤卡·奥拉多亦供认不讳,足以认定。	It is found that the accused, Yoka Olado, went to Xintai Restaurant in Haidian District of Beijing City on September 24, 2001, and stole 420 yuan in cash and a Qianjiang-125 electric motor car worthing more than 5,400 yuan. The total property worth more than 5,800 yuan. After the offence, most of the stolen property had been pursued and returned to the loser. The fact of the case is verified by the following evidences: statement of the victim, Wang Guigang, testimony from the witness, Sun Chuanyan, certificate of the Qianjiang-125 electric motor car, the accused's study certificate, value certificate of the stolen property, record of on-site investigation and examination. The accused, Yoka Olado, admits to the facts contained in the public prosecutor's charge. The above evidence is true to verify the charge.
另查明:被告人尤卡·奥拉多平时表现较好,与同学相处关系良好,有较强集体责任感,其所在的北京市海淀区上地十街23号邻居和所在学校北京语言大学师生对其评价较高。首次盗窃的诱因是被告人曾在北京市海淀区鑫泰饭店勤工俭学,而该饭店又欠其工资,随着年龄的增长,因爱慕虚荣,又进行了盗窃。庭审中,被告人尤卡·奥拉多非常后悔,决心改过自新,争做一个对社会有用的人。	The court further found that, the accused, Yoka Olado performed good in his daily life and get along well with his students. Yoka Olado also has a strong sense of collectivity, and the people in his residence and workplace, the neighbours living in No. 23 Shangdi Tenth Street, Haidian District and Beijing Foreign Language College respectively have a high evaluation for him. And the direct cause of the offence is that Yoka Olado once worked in Xintai Restaurant as a part-time job and that restaurant arreared his wages. And with the increase of his ages, his vanity led him to commit larceny. During the trial, the accused Yoka Olado regretted deeply for his misdeed, and is determined to correct his previous behavior and to be an useful person for society.
本院认为,被告人虽为肯尼亚国籍,但在中国境内进行犯罪活动,应适用我国法律。尤卡·奥拉多以非法占有为目的,秘密窃取公民财物,数额较大公诉机关指控其犯盗窃罪成立。被告人尤卡·奥拉多犯罪时不满18周岁,依法应当从轻或者减轻处罚。被告人尤卡·奥拉多归案后,积极坦白罪行,认罪态度较好,退赔绝大部分赃物,依法可以酌情从轻处罚。对其辩护人的被告人尤卡·奥拉多系未成年人、积极坦白罪行、认罪态度较好、是初犯等辩护意见,全部予以采纳。依照《中华人民共和国刑法》第264条、第17条第1、3款、第72条第1款之规定,判决如下:	This court finds that even though the accused Yoka Olado has the nationality of Kenya, he had committed crime in the territory of China; therefore this case shall be under the jurisdiction of China's law. Yoka Olado has stolen a relatively large amount of private property for the purpose with unlawful seizure, the charge of committing larceny is well founded. As the accused was under the age of eighteen years while committing the crime, he shall be given lighter sentence. After the accused was brought to justice, he had a good attitude and confessed his criminal act frankly, besides, most of the stolen property was also returned to the owner; consequently, the accused may be given a lighter punishment. This court also accept all the following defense opinions raised by the accused's lawyer: the accused is a minor; had a good attitude and confessed his criminal act frankly, and it was the accused's first offence. In accordance with Article 264, Section One and Three of Article 17, and Section One of Article 72, it is ordered that:
被告人尤卡·奥拉多犯盗窃罪,判处有期徒刑六个月缓刑一年(缓刑考验期,从判决确定之日起计算),并处罚金1 000元(限判决生效之日起十五日内缴纳)。	The accused Yoka Olado be sentenced to six month imprisonment for the crime of larceny with a probation of one year (Term of the probation period commences from the date of enforcement of the sentence) and be fined 1,000 Yuan as penalty. (the fine shall be paid within fifteen days after the sentencing takes effect).
如不服本判决,可在接到判决书的第二日起十日内,通过本院或者直接向北京市高级人民法院提出上诉。书面上诉的,应提交上诉状正、副本各一份。	Any appeal to this sentence shall be submitted to this court or directly to the Supreme Court of Beijing City, within ten days from the second day of receipt of the sentencing document. In case, the appeal is made in writing, one original and one copy of the appellate brief shall be submitted.
审判员 崔红 二○○一年十一月三十日 书记员 刘延飞	Judge Cui Hong Date November 30, 2001 Clerk Liu Yanfei

英美国家的判决书包括 opinion: stating the issue raised, describing the parties and facts, discussing the relevant law, and rendering judgment, 即法律争议（Issue）、事实经过、判决采用的相关法律以及判决结果。在普通法系国家，法官执笔的判决意见书同样具有法律效力。

范例14：

HUTCHINSON v. MIKE, 443 U.S. 111 (2005) HUTCHINSON v. MIKE STONE CERTIORARI TO THE UNITED STATES COURT OF APPEALS FOR THE SEVENTH CIRCUIT. No. 48-680. Argued April 17, 2005. Decided June 26, 2005.	哈金森 诉 迈克 原告：哈金森检察官 被告：迈克·斯通 向联邦上诉法院第七巡回审判庭的调卷令（案号48-680） 辩论于2005年4月17日 判决于2005年6月26日
Justice Black delivered the opinion of the Court. Respondent Mike Stone, 22 years old, came to the house of the victim, Carlos, sought to rob the new car of the house owner that was parking in front of the house on January 20, 2005. He pounded on the heavy wooden front door of the home and Carlos answered. Mike was pointing a stolen pistol at the door when Carlos arrived. As Mike demanded his car keys, Carlos slammed the door. At this moment Mike's gun went off. The bullet traveled through the wooden door and into the Carlos's chest, killing him. Seconds later the gun fired again. The second bullet traveled upward through the door and into the ceiling of the residence. Hearing the shots, the victim's wife entered the front door. Mike entered the house, demanded the car keys from the victim's wife, and added the threat "I might as well kill you." When she did not provide the keys, however, he made no effort to thwart her escape. Mike then stepped outside and encountered the victim's adult daughter. He repeated his demand for car keys but made no effort to stop the daughter when she refused the demand and fled. Failing to obtain a car, Mike left and remained at large until nightfall.	大法官布莱克发表法院判决： 被告迈克·斯通，现年22岁，2005年1月20日那天来到被害人卡洛斯家中，企图抢劫该屋主停在家门前的一辆新轿车。迈克敲打这栋房屋沉重的木制大门，卡洛斯上前开门。当门打开的时候，迈克用一把偷来的手枪指着卡洛斯。迈克向被害人索要小汽车的钥匙，于是被害人随即摔门。此时迈克手中的枪突然走火，子弹穿过木门，进入卡洛斯的胸部，致使他当场死亡。几秒钟之后，枪声再度响起，第二发子弹向上穿过木门射向房子的天花板。 听到枪声后，被害人的妻子来到大门前，被告进入屋内向被害人的妻子索要小汽车的钥匙，并恐吓她说"我会杀了你"。但被害人的妻子并没有交出车钥匙，被告也没有试图阻止她逃跑。被告随后走出屋子并正在此时撞见了被害人已成年的女儿。被告还是继续向被害人的女儿索要车钥匙，但是当被害人的女儿拒绝交出车钥匙并跑走的时候，被告也没有试图阻止其逃跑。被告并没有如他所愿得到小汽车，于是直到夜幕降临被告才离开现场。
Shortly after being captured, Mike made a formal statement to the authorities in which he admitted that he had shot the victim but emphatically denied that he did so voluntarily or intentionally. He claimed that the shots were fired in accidental response to the slamming of the door. He was tried in the Superior Court of Ogemaw County, Michigan, on charges of malice murder and attempted robbing. His sole defense to the malice murder charge was a lack of requisite intent to kill. To support his version of the event Mike offered substantial evidence tending to show a lack of intent. He defended that the circumstance surrounding the firing of the gun, particularly the slamming of the door and trajectory of the second bullet supported the hypothesis of accident. He also argued that his treatment of every other person encountered during the event indicated a lack of disposition to use force.	被捕之后，被告很快向当局做了一份正式的陈述：被告承认曾向被告人开枪，但是强调自己并非自愿或是有意向被告开枪。被告称开枪是对被害人摔门这种行为的条件反射。该案在密歇根州奥格莫县高等法院进行初审，该法院指控被告蓄意谋杀和企图抢劫两项罪行。被告唯一的辩护就是自己无意杀人，并提供了大量的证据予以支持。被告辩称开枪时的情景，特别是摔门的行为还有第二颗子弹射出的轨迹都证明开枪致人死亡系意外事故。被告还指出在该事件发生的过程中他如何对待其他人的行为也说明被告并没有使用暴力的倾向。

(续)

On the dispositive issue of the intent, the trial judge instructed the jury as follows: "A crime is a violation of the statute of this State in which there shall be a union of joint operation of act or omission to act, and the intention or criminal negligence. A person shall not be found guilty of any crime committed by misfortune or accident where it satisfactorily appears there was no criminal scheme or undertaking or intention or criminal negligence. The acts of a person sound mind and discretion are presumed to be the product of the person's will, but the presumption may be rebutted. A person of the sound mind and discretion is presumed to intend the natural and probable consequences of his acts but the presumption may be rebutted. A person will not be presumed to act with criminal intention but the facts, that is, the Jury, may find criminal intention upon a consideration of the words, conduct, demeanor, motive and all other circumstances connected with the act for which the accused is prosecuted." The jury returned a verdict of guilty after deliberation and the next day Mike was sentenced to death for murder conviction. Held: In light of the instructions on intent given in this case, the presumptions "may be rebutted" could reasonably be read as telling the jury that it was required to infer intent to kill as the natural and probable consequence of the act of firing the gun unless the defendant persuaded the jury that such an inference was unwarranted. The very statement that the presumption "may be rebutted" could have indicated to a reasonable juror that the defendant bore an affirmative burden of persuasion once the State proved the underlying act giving rise to the presumption. It is undeniable that the burden-shifting presumption has unconstitutionally violated the Due Process Clause of the Fourteenth Amendment which prohibits the State from making use of jury instructions that have the effect of relieving the State of the burden of proof on the critical question of intent in a criminal prosecution. For the reasons above mentioned, the judgment of the Superior Court of Ogemaw County, Michigan that charges the defendant the crime of malice murder is reversed, and the case is remanded for retrial consistent with this opinion. It is so ordered.	在开枪致人死亡是有意还是无意的问题上，初审法官给陪审团的指示是： "犯罪是指违反一国法律规定的行为，包括共同犯罪的行为，负有作为义务而不作为的行为和故意及犯罪性过失。因灾难或意外而导致的犯罪行为，如果发现并无犯罪计划或者不存在有意和犯罪性过失，任何人不得被判有罪。精神正常和有辨别能力者的行为均假定是其意愿所致，但可以反驳这一假定。假定任何精神正常和有辨别能力者均有意造成其行为的自然结果和极可能发生的后果，但可以反驳这一假定。一个人的行为不能通过他的犯罪意图来假定，而必须通过事实来推定。陪审团可通过考虑与犯罪行为有关的话语，行为，举止，动机及其他后果来判定是否是故意犯罪。" 陪审团审议之后提交了被告有罪的裁决，次日迈克因谋杀罪被判死刑。 本院认为：根据初审法官所给指示中"可以反驳"的假定，陪审团可以理解为杀人意图是被告人开枪行为自然且合理的推论，除非被告能说服陪审团这样的推断是没有根据的。这样的假设使一个通常的陪审员认为在检察官证明有开枪行为，并提出假设后，被告有推翻该假设的责任。 很显然，在这个案件中，这种举证责任的转换违反了美国宪法第十四条修正案正当法律程序条款，在宪法上是站不住脚的。该条款旨在防止国家利用陪审团指示减轻刑事指控中对有争议的故意犯罪的举证责任。 基于上述理由，本院撤销密歇根奥格莫县高等法院对被告蓄意谋杀的判决，并将案件发回按本意见重新审理。 特此判决。

刑事判决书的翻译要点：

（1）刑事判决书中常用法律词汇的翻译。例如，"刑事审判庭"译为 criminal tribunal，"审判长"可译为 presiding judge，"公诉人"译为 prosecutor，"刑事强制拘留"译为 criminal coercive measure，"追究刑事责任"译为 investigate for criminal responsibility，"无罪判决"可译为 acquittal 或者 finding of "not guilty"，"有罪判决"译为 sentence 或者 finding of "guilty"，"司法复核"可译为 judicial review，"从重处罚"heavier punishment，"主犯"principal offender，"从犯"accessory，等等。

（2）我国的刑事判决书首先介绍公诉机关及被告人的基本情况，然后由检察机关提出指控的事实并出示证据，法院依法做出判决。判决书的各部分论述严谨，逻辑严密，有一些固定表达法，如：

① ××市人民检察院以检刑诉×号起诉书指控被告××犯何等罪行，于某年某月某日向本院提起公诉。例句：Haidian District People's Procuratorate of Beijing City brought criminal charge No.... against the Accused... for arson. The charge was filed with this court on May 12，2003.

② 本院依照《中华人民共和国刑事诉讼法》相关程序，公开开庭审理本案，this court used the relevant proceeding pursuant to Criminal Procedure Law of People's Republic of China and conducted the trial through the public hearing.

③ 被告人××及其辩护人到庭参加诉讼，现已审理终结，the Defendant and his or her lawyer all appeared for the trial and the case is now adjudicated and closed.

④ 公诉机关提出指控，并请求法院依法判决。例句：The charges by the People's Procuratorate of... City are as follows：... as such, the court shall find Defendant guilty under the law. 上述事实，有公诉机关提供的证据证实，the above facts are supported by the following evidence provided by the public prosecutor：...

⑤ 被告人对公诉机关指控的事实供认不讳，或者予以否认。例句：Defendant admits or denies the facts contained in the public prosecutor's charge. 被告的律师或者辩护人也可以向法院申请从轻处罚，例如：The lawyer of Defendant asserts that Defendant is an accessory in this case and thus pleads for lighter sentence.

⑥ 上述事实，有公诉机关提供的以下证据证实：……，以上证据取证程序合法，并经法庭查证属实且相互印证，足以认定。例句：The above facts are supported by the following evidence provided by the public prosecutor：... All the above evidence were legally collected. This court, having examined and verified the evidence and found them to be true and collaborating, rules that they are admissible.

⑦ 本院认为，被告人无视国家法律，情节严重，其行为构成……罪，依照《中华人民共和国刑法》第……条，现判决如下：…… 例句：This court finds that the defendant ignored the laws of the country. The defendant's conducts are grave and have constituted the crime of.... Pursuant to Article... of the Criminal Law of the People's Republic of China, it is ordered：...

⑧ "如不服本判决，可在接到判决书的第二日起十日内，通过本院或者直接向北京市高级人民法院提出上诉。书面上诉的，应当提交上诉状正、副本各一份。"这句话经常出现在我国判决书的末尾，可翻译为"Any appeal to this sentence shall be submitted to this court or directly to the Supreme Court of... City, within ten days from the second day of receipt of the sentencing document. In case, the appeal is made in writing, one original and one copy of the appellate brief shall be submitted."

（3）英美国家的刑事判决书的基本结构可参考范例2，翻译的时候要结合英美国家有关刑事诉讼的法律知识，特别要注意其中特有的词汇，如 burden of proof 举证责任，beyond a reasonable doubt 排除合理怀疑，等等，前者是依据美国刑法，被告在审判开始前要被假定无辜，检察官有责任毋庸置疑地证明犯罪构成的每一因素；后者则是指在刑事诉讼中陪审团认定被告人有罪时适用的证明标准，即只有控诉方提出的证据对被告人有罪的事实证明达到无合理怀疑的确定性程度时，陪审团才会裁决被告人有罪。

第四节 本章小结

本章介绍了涉外诉讼文书的概念、特点、功能、分类等内容。在此基础上，总结了诉讼文书的语言特点及文体风格。除此之外，详尽分析了中英文诉讼文书的不同之处及其互译技巧。

 课后习题

请将下面一份英文起诉书的正文部分翻译成中文。
TO THE HONORABLE JUDGE OF SAID COURT：
Your Plaintiff, JANE DOE, respectfully represents unto Your Honor：

I

That she is a bona fide resident of Braxton County, West Virginia, and is and has been a bona fide resident of West Virginia for more than one (1) year last past, continuously, immediately preceding the filing of this Complaint.

II

That the Defendant is a resident of the State of West Virginia, and that his last known address is P. O. Box ABC, Heaters, West Virginia 26627.

III

That she and the Defendant, John Doe, were duly and legally married on the 11th day of June, 1967, in Lewis County, West Virginia.

IV

That there were two (2) living children born of the marriage of the Parties hereto, namely, Phillip Doe, born November 21, 1978, age sixteen (16); and Bethany Doe, born December 28, 1980, age thirteen (13), who are presently in the custody of the Plaintiff, the primary caretaker of said infants.

V

That from the date of said marriage until June, 1992, Plaintiff and Defendant lived together as man and wife.

VI

That Plaintiff and Defendant last lived and cohabited together as man and wife at P. O. Box DEF, Burnsville, Braxton County, West Virginia, until June, 1992, when they separated and their separation has been continuous and uninterrupted since that date.

VII

That the Plaintiff and the Defendant have irreconcilable differences resulting from their marriage which said differences make a continuing marriage relationship between the Parties impossible.

VIII

That the Defendant has been guilty of cruel and inhuman treatment toward the Plaintiff, which has been such as to destroy or tend to destroy her mental and physical well being, happiness and welfare and which renders continuous cohabitation unsafe and unendurable.

IX

That the parties have lived separate and apart in separate places of abode without any cohabitation and without interruption for one year next preceding the institution of this action, and such separation was the voluntary act of the parties hereto as set forth in West Virginia Code, Chapter 48, Article 2, Section 4, Sub-Section (a) (7).

X

That the Defendant has willfully abandoned or deserted the Plaintiff for a period in excess of six (6) months.

XI

That the Defendant has been guilty of adultery with one Snow White, which said adulterous acts on the part of the Defendant were not and have not been condoned by the Plaintiff.

XII

That regarding the child custody jurisdiction of the Court in this action, the Plaintiff says that the children of the marriage have resided only with one or both of the Parties since the birth of said children; that the Plaintiff has not participated in any other litigation concerning the custody of the children in this or any other state; that the Plaintiff has no information of any custody proceeding concerning the children of the marriage pending in a court of this or any other state; that the Plaintiff knows of no other person who has had physical custody of the children of the marriage or claims to have custody or visitation rights with the children, who is not a party hereto.

XIII

That the Plaintiff is entitled to equitable distribution of all marital assets for her economic contributions provided over the duration of the marriage herein sought to be dissolved, and she is entitled to reasonable compensation for homemaker services.

PRAYER

WHEREFORE, Plaintiff prays that she be awarded a divorce from the bonds of matrimony now existing between her and said Defendant; that she be awarded temporary and permanent alimony; that she be awarded her attorney fees and costs in this behalf expended; that she be awarded temporary and permanent care, custody and control of the infant children born of the marriage of the Parties hereto; that she be awarded temporary and permanent child support; that she be awarded hospitalization insurance coverage to be maintained at the Defendant's expense from a reputable carrier; that Defendant be ordered to assume primary responsibility for all debts and liabilities incurred jointly by the Parties hereto during covertures; that she be awarded equitable distribution of all marital property as defined by West Virginia Code 48-2-1 (e); that she be awarded all of her separate property as provided under West Virginia Code 48-2-1 (f); that she be awarded a reasonable sum for homemaker services rendered over the seventeen (17) year marriage herein sought to be dissolved; that she be awarded exclusive possession of the former marital home, situate at Burnsville, West Virginia, and all appurtenances thereunto belonging; and, that she may have such other, further and general relief as the Court may find proper.

第九章

涉外公证书翻译

第一节 概 述

一、概念及文体

随着全球化进程的加快,各国人员之间的联系也越来越紧密,商务、公务等交流活动日益频繁。同时随着我国经济的迅速发展,我国公民的收入也迅速增加,很多人选择出国留学、旅游、工作或者探亲。在这些活动中,公证书是必不可少的文件。

公证(notary)一词来源于拉丁语 nota 一词。"nota"指的是古罗马"书记"们用来迅速抄录文书的一种速记符号。后来,"公证"被用来表达为国家或为社会公证的证明活动。在我国,公证是指国家专门设立的公证机关代表国家进行证明活动,公证制度是国家司法制度的重要组成部分。《中华人民共和国公证暂行条例》第 2 条规定:"公证是国家公证机关根据当事人的申请,依法证明法律行为、有法律意义的文书和事实的真实性、合法性,以保护公共财产、保护公民身份上、财产上的权利和合法权益。"当前,有必要借助经济分析法学对中国公证进行研究,如何把有限的公证资源在相抗衡的目标之间进行配置。

公证书是国家公证机关根据当事人的申请,依照法定程序,对其法律行为及其有法律意义的文件、事实,证明其真实性、合法性的文书。

所谓涉外公证书就是我国公证机关对发生在国内的法律行为及有关法律意义的文件或事实向国外出具的公证文书。涉外公证是国际间交往必不可少的工具和法律武器,对发展对外经济和民事交往、保护国家利益和公民、法人合法权益等方面均具有重大意义。为了使用方便,大多数发往国外的公证书均要附英译文,有的国家还要求对涉外公证文书出具"中文与译文相符"的证明文件,以证明其内容的真实和可靠。所以能否准确地翻译涉外公证书,直接影响我国对外开放政策的落实和我国公民、法人在域外的合法权益。

为了能被各国相关人员准确的理解,在文体风格、词语运用、语法手段、辞格上属于法律公文一类的涉外公证文书有其鲜明的特点,即准确严密、庄重得体以及程式的规范化,这是由法律的社会职能决定的,也是法律语体区分于其他功能文体的根本特征。

(一) 准确严密

准确严密的含义是指忠实原文,准确透彻地理解原文的精神实质,对原文的内容既不歪曲,也不随意增减,译文中的意思必须正确无误。如果流畅和准确发生矛盾时,必须首先遵循准确的原则。

首先,对公证书中的词语选择要准确无冗余。例如,对"涉外公证书"的翻译,有人把它译为"foreign related notary certificates","foreign related"属于多余之词。对于目的语国家的读者来说,他们关注的焦点是"notarial certificate(s)";至于"foreign related"则是不言自明的事情,无须赘述。

其次,就是专业术语的应用要准确无误。涉外公证书像其他应用文体一样,有其特定的术语。涉外公证书的术语有相当一部分属于法律词汇,如:产权证书:Certificate of Title;住所:domicile;抵押:Mortgage;委任书:Power of Attorney;担保契约:Warranty Deed 等。如译成普通词汇,虽然目的语读者也能明白,但不是规范的翻译。

再次,对于某些特定的名称、机构、职位、头衔等都有成型的固定翻译,翻译时要采纳之,不能闭门造车。例如:北京大学:Peking University;清华大学:Tsinghua University;中国人民大学:Renmin University of China;北京第二外国语学院:Beijing International Studies University 等,而不能相应译为:Beijing University;Qinghua University;People's University of China;Beijing No. 2 Foreign Languages Institute。即使有些翻译值得商榷,但因为已经约定俗成,在翻译时也要沿袭。如"中南大学"译为"Central South University"虽显生硬,但无奈已获官方认定而约定俗成为 CSU,倘若按英语习惯改为"South Central University"反而与该校对不上号,故遵从原译不变。

此外,要保证语法的严密性。例如:

汉语文本	英语文本
兹证明王平(男,1985 年 5 月 12 日出生)于 2004 年 9 月入山东大学物理系学习,学制 4 年,于 2008 年 7 月毕业。	This is to certify that Wang Ping, male, born on May 12, 1985) was enrolled in the Physics Department of Shandong University (4 year course) in September 2004 and **was graduated** in July 2008.

此例中大学毕业用"graduate"是毫无疑问的,但是文中使用了被动语态显然是犯了严重的语法错误,这一点应该引起注意。

最后,从表述上应该做到明晰,不含混,不模棱两可,请看下例:

汉语文本	英语文本
公证书(90 鲁公证字第 1130 号) 兹证明赵强文先生持有的山东大学于 1980 年发给他的 064 号毕业文凭上的学校印鉴和校长周永森签字属实。 中华人民共和国 山东省济南市公证处 公证员:王芳 2000 年 5 月 2 日	Certificate (90)Lu Zi,No.1130 This is to certificate that Mr. Zhao Qiangwen holds a diploma issued to him in July, 1980 by Shandong University (Diploma No.064) and that we have carefully checked the seal of the University and the signature by President Zhou Yongsen. Jinan Notary Public Office Shandong Province the People's Republic of China Notary:Wang Fang May 2,2000

本例中的词语错误是"certificate"应为"certify";特定名称的错误是"the People's Republic of China"应为"People's Republic of China";例中的"we have carefully checked the seal of the University and signature by President Zhou Yongsen."这样的说法太模糊了:既然认真检查了,那么检查的结果怎么样呢?

对于文凭这类证件的公证,公证员也只是凭直觉和多年的办证经验去证明(公证员要一件一件去调查也不现实),因为公证处并没有这些文书的版本去核查、验证,更不可能把所有学校和校长的印鉴以及有关单位的印章留存下来。

有些公证处为了降低风险,也采取了一些办法。比如,只证明当事人提供的材料复印件与原件相符,不证明印章属实;这样就失去了公证的意义,也不是解决问题的根本办法。因为原件顾名思义应是原始证件,即原单位所发应是真实的、有效的。毋庸置疑,公证员要证明复印件与原件相符,就要保证所证明的文件的真实性,即原件的真实性。在此基础之上,翻译时要做到行文准确,不能模棱两可。否则,就难以保证公证书在使用国的法律效力。

(二)庄重得体

作为法律文书的一种,涉外公证书的语言也应该像法律文书一样庄重得体。如果找来一些英语国家的证书(如毕业证书、学位证书、公证书、营业执照等)和奖状加以研究,我们可以看到,其中的文字都十分庄重、严谨、贴切,并且都有一些特定的表达方法。法律语言是英语各种语体中正式程度最高的一种。它的句子复杂,个别地方仍然保持着古英语的形式。例如,下面这份香港大学的博士学位证书。

THE UNIVERSITY OF HONGKONG
Having fulfilled all the requirements of the University and having satisfied the examiners×××(人名,中英文)has this day been admitted to the degree of DOCTOR OF PHILOSOPHY.
Given under our hands this Eleventh day of January, One Thousand Nine Hundred and Ninety-five.
              Chancellor
Register   Vice-chancellor

整份证书所使用的词语都是书面语,采用分词短语结构,日期用单词(大写字母)书写,以一句贯穿全段,使得整段文字庄重、严肃,适合作为法律文书的语体风格。

(三) 程式的规范化

程式的规范化也就是所谓"行业性归化"问题。许多公文类翻译都涉及这个问题。如获奖证书的翻译:

发明创造科技之星奖

为表彰在科学技术发明创新方面做出的卓越成绩颁发此证书。

获奖项目:

获奖者:

联合国技术信息促进系统

发明创新科技之星评审委员会

如果只传递基本信息,可以译为:

Diploma

This is to award for the remarkable achievements In science & technology innovation Awarded by National Bureau in China Technological Information Promotion System.

United Nation

但是要符合目的语程式结构,必须彻底"改写"。改译如下:

The China Office of the United Nations System For the Promotion of Technical Information

Diploma

This certificate of award is presented to STAR

of scientific/technological

invention/ innovation

_____

(name o recipient)

for the outstanding accomplishment

_____

(name of project)

Signed by _____ Date

The Apprising Committee of the Star Award For Scientific/Technological Invention/Innovation

---

涉外公证书也有其固定的格式,如《无刑事处分公证书》的格式通常是:

> 无刑事处分公证书
>
> （　）×字第××号
>
> 兹证明张×（男，1966年6月6日出生）至2015年12月20日在中国居住期间没有受过刑事处分。
>
> 中华人民共和国××省××市(县)公证处
>
> 公证员：×××（签名）
>
> ××××年××月××日

译文：

> Notarial Certificate of Non-criminal Punishment
>
> （　）× ZI. NO. ××
>
> This is to certify that ×× (male, born on June 6, 1966) hadn't had any record of committing offences against the criminal laws during the period of his residence in China until December 20, 2015.
>
> Notary：(signed)
>
> ×× Notary Public Office of
>
> ×× Province
>
> The People's Republic of China
>
> ××/××/××××

《遗嘱公证书》的格式通常是：

> 遗嘱公证书
>
> （　）×字第××号
>
> 兹证明张×（男，1945年3月15日出生）于2010年1月7日来到我处，在我的面前，在前面其本人所立的遗嘱上签名。
>
> 中华人民共和国××省××市(县)公证处
>
> 公证员：×××（签名）
>
> ××××年××月××日

译文：

> Notarial Certificate of Testament
>
> （　）× ZI. NO. ××
>
> This is to certify that ××（male, born on March 15, 1945）came to my office on Jan. 7, 2010 and affixed his signature in my presence to the testament made by himself which is attached hereto.
>
> Notary：(signed)
> ×× Notary Public Office of
> ×× Province
> The People's Republic of China
> ××/××/××××

二、公证书的目的和意义

所谓公证目的，顾名思义就是指自然人、法人或者其他组织借助于公证制度，证明或合法、或不合法、或真实、或不真实、或真实而不合法、或合法而不真实。这是因为，从本身的动机、经济、利益、效力等出发来求助于公证制度，则无论是站在社会学、法律体系学，还是我国《公证法》的角度上来加以判断，不同的主体应当分别有着相应的公证目的。提出公证申请的自然人、法人或其他组织有着本身的公证目的，接受公证申请的公证机构及其公证员有着自己的公证目的，主观与客观上申请启动公证程序的利害关系人（也可以被列入自然人、法人或其他组织）也有着自己的公证目的，如此等等，展现了公证目的的多元性与社会性。诸多公证目的的冲突与妥协直至平衡的过程实际上就是国家公证法律法规不断完善的过程。

社会化与专业化的基本原理告诉我们，对于社会中最为普遍的主体即自然人、法人或其他组织的公证目的的最大保护成为国家在其法律体系范围内通过各种公证法律规范来对于公证目的加以授权与制约的最为基本的着眼点。换句话说，作为提出公证申请的不特定的社会人的自然人、法人或其他组织的公证目的，才是最为基本或根本的公证目的。因此，为我国《公证法》所接受的公证目的，是指自然人、法人或者其他组织向公证机构申请启动公证程序的实体法、证据法或诉讼法（包括公证法以及仲裁法）意义上的真实目的。

涉外公证直接关系到公民和法人在国（境）外的合法权益，是利用法律来保证他们在继承财产、留学、定居、探亲等活动中的权利和利益。对于签发签证的外方，它是是否批准发给签证的法律依据；对于申办签证的中国公民来说，它是能否取得合法签证的有力证明。

三、涉外公证书与国内公证书的异同

涉外公证是指国家公证机关对含有涉外因素的公证事项,依法证明其真实性、合法性的活动。涉外公证和国内公证是我国全部公证活动的两个组成部分。

涉外公证和国内公证的共同之处是:他们都代表国家行使公证权,并根据当事人的申请,依照法定程序,对法律行为、有法律意义的事实和文书的真实性、合法性加以确认并予以证明,以保护当事人的合法权益。

与国内公证相比,涉外公证又有不同之处:

(1) 申请公证的当事人不同。涉外公证的申请人除我国公民外,还有华侨、归侨、侨眷及外国人;而国内公证的申请人,只能是我国公民。

(2) 提出申请公证的地点不同。涉外公证既可以在我国境内提出申请,也可以在境外提出申请;而国内公证只能在我国境内提出申请。

(3) 公证文书发往使用的地域和效力不同。涉外公证文书主要在国外或其他地区使用,其目的是在域外发生法律效力;国内公证书只在我国国内使用并发生法律效力。

(4) 办理公证的程序有所不同。涉外公证一般要通过认证,并附有译文。

(5) 保护的合法权益所受的法律约束不同。涉外公证所保护的合法权益,往往受所在国或地区的法律约束,有的甚至还要通过判决,才能得到保护,有的公证文书如不符合该国法律规定的,则被认为无效而退回;而国内公证就不存在此类问题。

由此可见,涉外公证涉及面广,办证难度高,质量要求严,涉外公证员必须牢固树立质量第一的业务指导思想,怀着强烈的质量意识去工作,只有严格认真,一丝不苟地公证,才能满足社会的需要。

四、分类及结构

我国《公证暂行条例》定义了公证书的类型。公证书可以分为四个类型:一是证明法律行为的公证书,如委托、遗嘱、继承权、合同、财产赠与和分割、收养关系等;二是证明有法律意义事实的公证书,如出生、死亡、婚姻状况、亲属关系、健康状况等;三是证明有法律意义文件的公证书,如学历、学位、经历等;四是文件的执行、保管等事项的公证书,如追偿物品、清款的文件等。

目前,我国公证处经常办理的涉外公证文书主要有学历、成绩单公证、学位证书公证、婚姻公证、亲属关系公证、未受刑事处分公证、出生公证、银行存款公证、经济担保公证等。由于每个人的目的不同,所需要的涉外公证书也就不同。

自费留学一般需要提供与学历有关的公证,如毕业证、学位证、成绩单公证、出生和未受刑事制裁等公证。在校生要提供在校证明,还要有家庭财产的有关公证。

准备移民国外的人,根据技术移民和投资移民的不同情况,所办理的公证又有区别。办理技术移民,要把与本人工作技能有关的公证文书尽量办理齐全,如工作经历公证、职称证书或专业资格证书公证等。办投资移民除学历证明公证和无刑事制裁等一般公证外,更多的则需要办理与本人财产有关的公证书,如营业执照公证、纳税证明公证、存款证明公证、住房甚至股票等有价证券的公证等。

出国探亲,需要提供与国外亲属有关的公证。

出国定居则需提供出生、未受刑事制裁、婚姻状况等全套公证书。

《公证暂行条例》第 20 条:"公证员应当按照司法部规定或批准的格式制作公证文书。"《公证程序规则(试行)》第 38 条规定:"公证书按司法部规定或批准的格式制作。公证书中应包括以下内容:(1) 公证书编号;(2) 当事人的基本情况;(3) 公证证词;(4) 承办公证员的签名(签名章)、公证处印章和钢印;(5) 公证日期。有强制执行效力的公证书应在公证证词中注明,并注明债务人履行债务的期限、强制执行标的名称、种类、数量等。公证词中注明的文件是公证书的组成部分。公证书不得涂改、挖补,必须修改的应加盖公证处校对章。

公证书除了在内容上要遵从以上所说的五点外,在结构上也有其特定的要求:公证书的结构分为首部,正文(证词)和尾部三部分。

(一) 首部

(1) 文书名称。在文书的上部正中写"公证书"

(2) 文书编号。在"公证书"的右下方用阿拉伯数字写年度的全称。接着写公证机关简称和编号。如:"(20××)×公证字第×号"。

在首部,一般不写当事人的身份和基本情况;但是,继承、收养亲属关系的公证书的首部应写明当事人的姓名、性别、出生年月日、住址等身份事项。

(二) 正文

正文也叫证词,是公证书的核心部分和主要内容。证词应根据证明事项来写,当事人申请公证的事项不同,因而其证词的写法也不尽相同。但不论公证何种事项,都应写得清楚、准确、真实、合法。

公证证明事项的具体内容,有些全部体现在公证书的证词里,如:出生、生存、死亡、收养、婚姻关系、亲属关系公证等。至于法律行为公证,公证书的公证词文字只是寥寥数语。例如:"兹证明×××于××××年×月×日来到我处,在我的面前,在前面的赠与书上签名(或盖章)。"因此,这类公证可以印成填空式的文书用纸。但收养子女、财产继承等类公证书,则应根据具体情况,逐件制作。

成批的公证事项(内容同一),如供电局与农村乡镇全面签订《供用电合同》,可以把填空式的公证词拟好,附印到合同(协议后)的后面,这样办证时就大大简化了手续。

（三）尾部

（1）制作文书的机关名称。如写"中华人民共和国××省××市（县）公证处"，是哪个公证机关出具的公证书便落款该公证机关，但必须冠以"中华人民共和国"字样，因为它是代表国家公证。

（2）文书签署人的职务和签名。先写"公证员"然后由公证员签名或盖章。

（3）文书签发的年月日，并加盖公章。

第二节　常用涉外公证书的翻译

各类涉外公证书的翻译有其特定的格式和需要注意的事项，下面我们一一予以解释。

一、毕业证公证书

由前一节的讨论我们知道，毕业证公证书是出国留学人员必须办理的公证书之一。所谓"毕业证公证书"，就是指公证机关证明当事人的毕业证书的真实性，合法性的法律文书。在进行毕业证公证书的翻译时，要注意一下常用到的但是经常被我们所忽视的地方。例如，翻译"入学"时，"to be enrolled in"是针对大学以上的学历而言的，而"to start school"主要指"开始进入小学学习"，"to enter a school"一般指"进入中等学校学习"；另一个是"毕业"。一般我们说到"毕业"，就会想到用"graduate"，但"graduate"一词的意思是"to complete a university degree course"，所以只有大学毕业才能用"graduate"。如果是中学毕业则直接用"to finish school"就可以了。

首先，来看一份毕业证书的翻译：

普通高等学校
毕　业　证　书

学生 李娜，性别 女，一九八五年十二月二十二日生，于二〇〇四年九月至二〇〇八年七月在本校英语专业四年制本科学习，修完教学计划规定的全部课程，成绩合格，准予毕业。

校名：东北师范大学　　　　　　　　　　　　　　　　　　　　校长：马淑远

证书编号：136621200805000034　　　　　　　　　　　　　　　二〇〇八年七月一日

译文：

General Institution of Higher Education
Graduation Certificate

Student Li Na, female, born on 22 December 1985, studied four-year English undergraduate program in our college from September 2004 to July 2008. She has successfully completed all the courses stipulated in our teaching plan, and is therefore permitted to leave with this graduation certificate.

School Name：Northeast Normal University（seal）
Certificate No. 136621200805000034
President：Ma Shuyuan（seal）
1 July 2008

毕业证公证书的一般格式如下所示：

其一：

毕业证公证书

（　）×字第××号

兹证明前面××大学于××（日期）发给李平编号为0123的毕业证书与原文一致。该毕业证书上所盖的××大学印章属实。并证明前面所附的英文译本与中文文本内容一致。

中华人民共和国××省××市（县）公证处
公证员：×××（签名）
××××年××月××日

译文：

Notarial Certificate of Diploma

（　）× ZI. NO.××

This is to certify that the above duplicate copy of diploma with No. 0123 issued to Li Ping on ×× （date of issue） by ×× University is in conformity with the original. The seal of ×× University affixed to the above mentioned diplomas found to be authentic. And this is also to certify that the English translated copy attached hereto is in conformity with the content of the Chinese original.

Notary：（signed）
×× Notary Public Office of
×× Province
The People's Republic of China
××／××／××××

在翻译上面这份公证书时，需要注意以下几点：

1. "与……一致"一般译为"in conformity with…"，使用名词化结构，语体严谨庄重。

2. "属实"翻译为"authentic",因其是比较正式的词汇,体现法律语言严肃庄重的特点。

3. "前面所附的"译为"the copy attached hereto",其中的"hereto"是古英语词汇,在日常生活中极少用得到,却在英语法律文本中很常见。其使用是为保证译入语能够原汁原味,并符合文体要求。

其二:

毕业证公证书

( )×字第××号

兹证明王平(男,1985年5月30日出生)于2003年9月入××大学化学系学习,学制4年,于2007年7月毕业。

中华人民共和国××省××市(县)公证处

公证员:×××(签名)

××××年××月××日

译文:

Notarization of Diploma

( )× ZI. NO.××

This is to certify that Wang Ping (male, born on May 30, 1985) was enrolled in the Chemistry Department of ××University (4-year course) in September 2003 and graduated in July 2007.

Notary:(signed)

×× Notary Public Office of

×× Province

The People's Republic of China

××/××/××××

二、学位证公证书

学位证公证书和毕业证公证书一样,是出国留学人员必不可少的公证书之一。"学位证公证书"指的是公证机关证明当事人的学位证书的真实性,合法性的法律文书。

对于学位证公证书的翻译,除了毕业证中应该注意的问题外,我们还应了解一下各种学位的表达。如:"理学学士"应翻译为"B. S.—Bachelor of Science","文学学士"为"B. A.—Bachelor of Arts","工程学学士"则为"B. Eng.—Bachelor of Engineering"。学位证公证书的翻译格式与毕业证公证书的一样。有时对于出国留学人员,除了需要学位公证书外,还需要学位证书的英译版,下面就是一个学位证书的样本:

学士学位证书

_____（男/女，_____出生）于_____年九月到_____年七月在我校_____系学习期间，圆满完成学业，被准予毕业。同时被授予_____学士学位。

证书编号：_____　　　　　　　　　　　　　　　_____大学

　　　　　　　　　　　　　　　　　　　　学位评定委员会主席_____

　　　　　　　　　　　　　　　　　　　　　　××××年××月××日

译文：

Certificate of Bachelor's Degree

Certificate No.：_____

_____, male / female, native of _____, born on _____, has been majoring in the specialty of _____ at our university/ institute from September _____ to July _____. Upon completion of all the courses specified by the four-year undergraduate teaching program with qualified score, he/she is qualified for graduation. In conformity with the articles of the Regulations Regarding Academic Degrees of the People's Republic of China, he/she has been conferred to the degree of Bachelor of _____.

　Chairman _____（signature）

　Committee of Degree Accreditation

　_____ University（seal）

　××/××/××××

学位证公证书

（　）×字第××号

兹证明×××（男/女，××××年××月××日出生）于 2003 年 9 月入××大学化学系学习，学制 4 年，于 2007 年 7 月毕业，并获得学士学位。

　　　　　　　　　　　　　　　中华人民共和国××省××市（县）公证处

　　　　　　　　　　　　　　　　　　公证员：×××（签名）

　　　　　　　　　　　　　　　　　　××××年××月××日

译文：

> Notarization of Degree Certificate
>
> ( ) ×ZI. NO.××
>
> This is to certify that ×××（male/female，born on ××/××/××××）was enrolled in the Chemistry Department of×× University (4-year course) in September 2003 and graduated in July 2007 and was awarded baccalaureate.
> Notary：(signed)
> ×× Notary Public Office of
> ×× Province
> The People's Republic of China
> ××/××/××××

三、成绩单公证书

在联系留学过程中，成绩单是重要的申请材料之一。成绩单中显示出来的分数基本上就是申请人在校的学习成果，从中可以判断出该申请者有无学习上的实力和潜力。我国大学一般由学校教务处、档案馆或外事办公室负责开具成绩单。

成绩单的形式与办理方法因学校而异，但通常在成绩单上显示的项目有：

（1）学校名称、教务长、档案馆馆长签名（盖章）；
（2）学生姓名、性别、出生日期和申请人照片；
（3）系别、专业、学业年限、毕业后授予的学位；
（4）各学期所修课程、学分数（或学时数）及分数；
（5）在英文成绩单上应有分数换算的公式。

下面是南京大学的一份学生成绩单：

Student Transcript of Nanjing University				
Name：Wei Xiaoming			Grade & Class：Class 1 Grade 2000	
Department：Information Engineering			Major：Computer & its application	
Second Semester of 1996				
Subject		Category	Hours	Score
FORTRAN Programming		Basic	51	95
Advanced Mathematics		Basic	96	78
Physics		Basic	68	67
Principle of Philosophy		Basic	68	82
Public Labor		Basic	30	85
Law Basis		Basic	17	65
Foreign Language		Basic	64	74
Physical Education		Basic	34	82
Military Theory		Basic	32	87

成绩单公证书也有其特定的格式，以下就是其中英文的格式：

成绩公证书
（　）×证外字第××号
兹证明前面×××持有的成绩单的复印件与原件相符，原件上所盖的"××××大学"印章属实。
中华人民共和国××省××市×××公证处
公证员：×××
××××年××月××日

译文：

Notarization of Academy Transcription
（　）×．ZI．NO．××
This is to certify that the foregoing copy of Transcripts held by ××× is in conformity with the original. The seal of ×××× University affixed on the original is found to be authentic.
Notary：×××（signed）
××× Public Office of
×× City，×× Province（sealed）
The People's Republic of China
××／××／××××（date）

四、亲属关系公证书

亲属关系是指以婚姻为基础、血缘为纽带，以及收养而形成的相互关系。凡是法律上承认的亲属，彼此间就产生权利义务。比如，我国婚姻法规定，夫妻、父母和子女负有互相扶养的义务。

亲属关系公证是指有涉外业务权公证处，根据当事人的申请，依法证明申请人与关系人之间亲属关系的真实性、合法性。亲属关系公证书，主要用于出入境签证，我国公民到国外定居、探亲、留学、继承遗产、申请劳工伤亡赔偿、领取抚恤金等事项。

对于亲属关系公证书，其一般格式的中英文对照如下：

亲属关系公证书
（　）×字第××号
申请人：×××，男或女，于××××年××月××日出生，现住＿＿＿＿＿＿＿＿＿＿。
关系人：×××，男或女，于××××年××月××日出生，现住＿＿＿＿＿＿＿＿＿＿。
×××，男或女，于××××年××月××日出生，现住＿＿＿＿＿＿＿＿＿＿。
兹证明申请人×××是关系人×××的××（关系称谓）；是关系人×××的××（关系称谓）。
中华人民共和国××省××市×××公证处（盖章）
公证员：×××（签名）
××××年××月××日

译文：

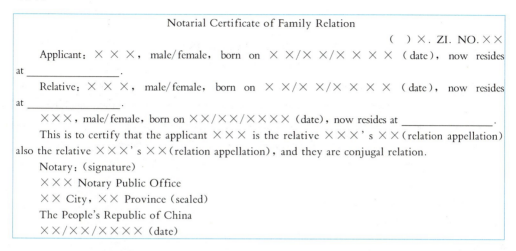

五、婚姻状况公证书

在办理结婚手续,申请到国外探亲,定居,或是申请领养孤儿时,婚姻状况公证书是必不可少的。

婚姻状况指的是当事人结婚、未婚、离婚以及丧偶的情况。而婚姻状况公证是指公证机关根据当事人的申请,依照法定程序,对当事人现存的婚姻状况这一法律事实的真实性予以证明的活动。对一些涉外活动,证书需要翻译成英语。下面是结婚证书的样本：

中华人民共和国
结婚证书

×××和×××的结婚申请,符合《中华人民共和国婚姻法》规定,予以登记,发给此证。
中华人民共和国民政部(印章)
北京海淀区民政局婚姻登记处(印章)
婚姻登记员:×××
持证人:×××
登记日期:××/××/××××
结婚证字号:( )×市结字×××

姓名:
性别:
国籍:中国
出生日期:
身份证件号:

姓名:
性别:
国籍:中国
出生日期:
身份证件号:

译文：

PEOPLE'S REPUBLIC OF CHINA
MARRIAGE CERTIFICATE

×××and ×××applied for marriage registration. After being examined, their application conforms to the Marriage Law of the People's Republic of China. We give them the permission to register and hereby issue this marriage certificate. Ministry of Civil Affair of the People's Republic of China(seal)

Special Seal for Marriage Register of Haidian District, Beijing Civil Affairs Bureau

Marriage Register：(signature) ×××

Certificate Holder：×××

Registration Date：××/××/××××

Marriage Certificate No. ×××××××

Name：

Sex：

Nationality：Chinese

Date of Birth：

ID Card：

Name：

Sex：

Nationality：Chinese

Date of Birth：

ID Card：

各种婚姻状况公证书的格式如下所示：

1.

结婚公证书

（　）××字第××号

兹证明×××(男，××××年××月××日出生)与×××(女，××××年××月××日出生)于××××年××月××日在×××(地点)登记结婚。

中华人民共和国××省××市(县)公证处

公证员：×××(签名)

××××年××月××日

译文：

> Notarial Certificate of Marriage
>
> （　）××.ZI. NO.××
>
> This is to certify that ××× (male, born on ××/××/××××) and ××× (female, born on ××/××/××××) have been married at Registry ×××× on ××/××/××××.
>
> Notary：(signed)
>
> ×× Notarial Public Office
>
> ×× City，×× Province
>
> The People's Republic of China
>
> ×× /××/ ××××

2.

> 未婚公证书
>
> （　）××字第××号
>
> 兹证明×××(男/女，××××年××月××日出生)，现在××××(住址)，至今未曾登记结婚。
>
> 中华人民共和国××省××市(县)公证处
>
> 公证员：×××(签名)
>
> ××××年××月××日

译文：

> Notarial Certificate of Being Single
>
> （　）××.ZI. NO.××
>
> This is to certify that ××× (male/female, born on ××/××/××××)，now resides at ×××，has never been married at a registry.
>
> Notary：(signed)
>
> ×× Notarial Public Office
>
> ×× City，×× Province
>
> The People's Republic of China
>
> ×× / ×× / ××××

3.

> 离婚公证书
>
> （　）××字第××号
>
> 兹证明×××(男，××××年××月××日出生)与×××(女，××××年××月××日出生)于×年×月×日在×××(地点)登记结婚，于×年×月×日在×××(原婚姻登记机关名称，或者经人民法院判决)离婚。其夫妻关系自该日终止(登记离婚之日或者判决之日)。
>
> 中华人民共和国××省××市(县)公证处
>
> 公证员：×××(签名)
>
> ××××年××月××日

译文：

> Notarial Certificate of Divorce
>
> （　）××.ZI. NO.××
>
> This is to certify that ×××（male, born on ××/××/××××）and ×××（female, born on ××/××/××××）, married at a registry at ×××× on ××/××/×××, divorced at ×××× on ××/××/×××, and the conjugal relation shall spontaneously terminate.
>
> Notary：（signed）
> ×× Notarial Public Office
> ×× City, ×× Province
> The People's Republic of China
> ××/ ××/ ××××

在翻译上述离婚公证书时，特别需要引起注意的是"terminate"。法律英语要求严谨庄重，所以使用非常正式的词汇。

4.

> 夫妻关系公证书
>
> （　）××字第××号
>
> 根据×××（调查材料、当地人证等），兹证明×××（男，××××年××月××日出生）与×××（女，××××年××月××日出生）于××××年××月××日在×××（地点）按照当地民族传统风俗习惯结婚，是夫妻关系。
>
> 中华人民共和国××省××市（县）公证处
> 公证员：×××（签名）
> ××××年××月××日

译文：

> Notarial Certificate of Conjugal Relation
>
> （　）××.ZI. NO.××
>
> This is to certify that ×××（male, born on ××/××/××××）and ×××（female, born on ××/××/××××）, according to ×××, married at ××× in accordance with Chinese traditional custom, and that the conjugal relation is established.
>
> Notary：（signed）
> ×× Notarial Public Office
> ×× City, ×× Province
> The People's Republic of China
> ××/ ××/ ××××

六、无刑事犯罪记录公证书

当我们出国留学,探亲或是定居时,接收国希望我们没有刑事犯罪记录。特别是现今,整个社会在恐怖组织威慑下人心惶惶,各国对入境人员是否犯罪前科的监察愈加严格。因此,《无刑事犯罪记录公证书》就成为出国人员必须提交的申请材料。一般说来,《无刑事犯罪记录公证书》的格式如下:

无刑事犯罪记录公证书

( )××字第××号

兹证明王×(男,1988年8月8日出生)至2008年12月20日在中国居住期间没有受过刑事处分。

中华人民共和国××省××市(县)公证处

公证员:×××(签名)

××××年××月××日

译文:

Notarization of No Record of Criminal Offense

( ) ×× ZI. No. ××

This is to certify that ×× (male, born on August 8, 1988) hadn't had any record of committing offences against the criminal laws during the period of his residence in China until December 20, 2008.

Notary:(signed)

×× Public Office of

×× City, ×× Province

The People's Republic of China

××/××/××××

七、收养公证书

收养是拟制血亲的亲子关系借以发生的法定途径。收养制度是婚姻家庭制度的重要组成部分。领养他人的子女为自己的子女。收养人称为养父、养母,被收养人称为养子、养女。收养须符合法律规定的条件和程序。我国保护合法的收养关系。养父母与养子女之间的权利和义务,适用婚姻法对父母子女关系的规定。当执行收养行为时,必须办理收养公证书,对于涉外收养,则要求有中英文两个版本的收养公证书。

首先，看一下有关收养的一些常用词汇的翻译：汉语的"养父"有两种意思，一种是如同"继父"，无"养父"的身份；另一种是"享有养父的收养权利和义务"。在涉外收养公证中，"养父"是后者，应译成"adoptive father"；而不是前者，故不能译成"foster father"。因为在《牛津现代高级英汉双解词典》中，adopt 是"take（sb.）into one's family as a relation，esp. as a son or a daughter，with legal guardianship（以合法监护人的身份将某人收入家中为亲属；尤指收养某人为养子或养女）"，而 foster 是"care for；help the growth and development of；nature（照顾、抚育、培养）"。另外"收养人"不能简单地译成"adopter"或"consignee"，因为在法律上"收养关系"成立后，收养人与被收养人之间便发生了父母子女关系，即"养父母与养子女"的关系，故"收养人"译为"adoptive parents"。

收养公证书可以分为两种，一种是事实收养公证，另一种是弃婴的事实收养公证。其具体格式如下：

1.

收养公证书

（　）××字第××号

收养人：×××，男，××××年××月××日出生，现住××省××市××街××号。
　　　　×××，女，××××年××月××日出生，现住××省××市××街××号。

被收养人：×××，男(或女)，××××年××月××日出生，现住××省××市××街××号。

送养人：×××，男，××××年××月××日出生，现住××省××县××乡××村。
　　　　×××，女，××××年××月××日出生，现住××省××县××乡××村。

兹证明收养人×××、×××与被收养人×××的生父母×××、×××于××××年××月××日商定,收养×××为养子(女)。同时征得×××（被收养人）的同意。自该日起，×××、×××（收养人）与×××共同生活，相互以父母子女相称，并履行抚(扶)养义务，已形成事实收养关系。×××是×××的养父，×××是×××的养母。

中华人民共和国××省××市××公证处

公证员：×××（签名）

××××年××月××日

译文：

> Notarial Certificate of Adoption
>
> ( )×× ZI. NO.××
>
> Adoptive parents：×××, male, born on ××/××/××××, now resides at NO.××, ×× Street, ×× City, ×× Province.
>
> ×××, male, born on ××/××/××××, now resides at NO.××, ×× Street, ×× City, ×× Province.
>
> Adoptee：×××, male/female, born on ××/××/××××, now resides at NO.××, ×× Street, ×× City, ×× Province.
>
> Adoptee's Guardian：×××, male, born on ××/××/××××, now resides at ×× Village, ×× Town, ×× County, ×× Province.
>
> ×××, female, born on ×/×/××, now resides at ×× Village, ×× Town, ×× County, ×× Province.
>
> This is to certify that the adoptive parents ×××, ××× and the adoptee's guardian ×××, ××× come to an agreement on ××/××/×××× that they adopt ××× as their adoptive son/daughter. And since then ×××, ××× (adoptive parents) will live together with ××× (adoptee) with first securing ×××'s agreement, in addition, they will call each other by the name of parents and children and will fulfill their duty determined by law. Since then the adoptive relationship has been eradicated, and ××× is ×××'s adoptive father, ××× is ×××'s adoptive mother.
>
> Notary：(signed)
> ×× Public Office of
> ×× City, ×× Province
> The People's Republic of China
> ××/××/××××

2.

> 收养公证书
>
> ( )××字第××号
>
> 收养人：×××,男,××××年××月××日出生,现住××省××市××街××号。
>
> ×××,女,××××年××月××日出生,现住××省××市××街××号。
>
> 被收养人：×××,男(或女),××××年××月××日出生,现住××省××市××街××号。
>
> 兹证明收养人×××、×××于××××年××月××日在××××(何处)收养弃婴×××。双方共同生活,相互以父母子女相称,并履行抚养义务,已形成事实收养关系。×××是×××的养父,×××是×××的养母。
>
> 中华人民共和国××省××市公证处
> 公证员：×××(签名)
> ××××年××月××日

译文：

> Notarial Certificate of Adoption
>
> ( ) ××ZI. NO.××
>
> Adoptive parents：×××, male, born on ××/××/××××, now resides at NO.××, ×× Street, ×× City, ×× Province.
>
> ×××, female, born on ××/××/××××, now resides at NO.××, ×× Street, ×× City, ×× Province.
>
> Adoptee：×××, male/female, born on ××/××/××××, now resides at NO.××, ×× Street, ×× City, ×× Province.
>
> This is to certify that the adoptive parents ×××, ××× adopted the abandoned infant ××× at ×××× on ××/××/××××. And since then ×××, ××× (adoptive parents) will live together with ××× (adoptee) with first securing ×××'s agreement, also they will call each other by the name of parents and children and will fulfill their duty determined by law. Since then the adoptive relationship has been eradicated, and ××× is ×××'s adoptive father, ××× is ×××'s adoptive mother.
>
> Notary：(signed)
> ×× Public Office of
> ×× City, ×× Province
> The People's Republic of China
> ××/××/××××

八、经历公证书

对于一些出国工作的人员来说，要想找到一份合适的工作并不是一件很容易的事情，特别是在现阶段金融危机的影响下，愈加困难。但是，如果你有一份经历公证书来证明自己以前工作的性质和经验，就很有可能使得原本困难的事情变得简单。那么，经历公证书所要求的格式是什么呢？下面举例加以说明：

> 经历公证书
>
> (2000)××证字第×××号
>
> 兹证明×××（男，一九××年×月××日出生）于一九九八年八月至二零零零年三月在××科技处工作；二零零零年四月至二零零一年一月借调在××科技处从事计算机软件开发工作；二零零一年一月至二零零一年八月在××工作。
>
> 中华人民共和国××省××市××公证处
> 公证员：×××
> 二零零一年九月十三日

译文：

> NOTARIAL CERTIFICATE OF EXPERIENCE
>
> (2001)××ZI. No. ×××
>
> This is to certify that (male, born on ××, 19××) had worked in the Department of Science and Technology of ×××× from August 1999 to March 2000, that he was temporarily transferred to work in the Department of Science Technology of ××××× in the work of Computer software Development from April 2000 to January 2001; and that he had worked in ××× from January 2001 to August 2001.
>
> Notary: ×××
> ×× Notary Public Office
> ×× City, ××× Province
> the People's Republic of China (Seal)
> September 13, 2001

九、合同公证书

随着世界经济的全球化，各国之间的合作日益频繁。这不仅体现在跨国公司的出现，而且还体现在劳务输出上。为了保证合作双方以及出国务工人员的利益，合同公证书是必不可少的。所谓合同公证书，是指公证机关对签订合同的双方在自愿的前提下所签订的合同内容，双方代表的资格等进行认真审核后，而出具的公证书。

请看以下合同书的样本：

> 合　　同
>
> 日期：　　　　　　　　　　合同号码：
> 买　方：　　　　　　　　　卖方：
> 兹经买卖双方同意按照以下条款由买方购进，卖方售出以下商品：
> (1) 商品名称：　　　　　　(2) 数量：
> (3) 单价：　　　　　　　　(4) 总值：
> (5) 包装：　　　　　　　　(6) 生产国别：
> (7) 支付条款：　　　　　　(8) 保险：
> (9) 装运期限：　　　　　　(10) 起运港：
> (11) 目的港：
> (12) 索赔：在货到目的口岸45天内如发现货物品质，规格和数量与合同不附，除属保险公司或船方责任外，买方有权凭中国商检出具的检验证书或有关文件向卖方索赔换货或赔款。
> (13) 不可抗力：由于人力不可抗力的缘由发生在制造，装载或运输的过程中导致卖方延期交货或不能交货者，卖方可免除责任，在不可抗力发生后，卖方须立即电告买方及在14天内以空邮方式向买方提供事故发生的证明文件，在上述情况下，卖方仍须负责采取措施尽快发货。
> (14) 仲裁：凡有关执行合同所发生的一切争议应通过友好协商解决，如协商不能解决，则将分歧提交中国国际贸易促进委员会按有关仲裁程序进行仲裁，仲裁将是终局的，双方均受其约束，仲裁费用由败诉方承担。
> 买方：　　　　　　　　　　　　　　　　　卖方：
> （授权签字）　　　　　　　　　　　　　　（授权签字）

译文：

CONTRACT

Date: Contract No.:

The Buyers: The Sellers:

This contract is made by and between the Buyers and the Sellers; whereby the Buyers agree to buy and the Sellers agree to sell the under-mentioned goods subject to the terms and conditions as stipulated hereinafter:

(1) Name of Commodity:

(2) Quantity:

(3) Unit price:

(4) Total Value:

(5) Packing

(6) Country of Origin :

(7) Terms of Payment:

(8) Insurance:

(9) Time of Shipment:

(10) Port of Lading:

(11) Port of Destination:

(12) Claims:

Within 45 days after the arrival of the goods at the destination, should the quality, Specifications or quantity be found not in conformity with the stipulations of the contract except those claims for which the insurance company or the owners of the vessel are liable, the Buyers shall, have the right on the strength of the inspection certificate issued by the C. C. I. C and the relative documents to claim for compensation to the Sellers

(13) Force Majeure:

The sellers shall not be held responsible for the delay in shipment or non-deli-very of the goods due to Force Majeure, which might occur during the process of manufacturing or in the course of loading or transit. The sellers shall advise the Buyers immediately of the occurrence mentioned above the within fourteen days thereafter. The Sellers shall send by airmail to the Buyers for their acceptance certificate of the accident. Under such circumstances the Sellers, however, are still under the obligation to take all necessary measures to hasten the delivery of the goods.

(14) Arbitration :

All disputes in connection with the execution of this Contract shall be settled friendly through negotiation. In case no settlement can be reached, the case then may be submitted for arbitration to the Arbitration Commission of the China Council for the Promotion of International Trade in accordance with the Provisional Rules of Procedure promulgated by the said Arbitration Commission. The Arbitration committee shall be final and binding upon both parties, and the Arbitration fee shall be borne by the losing parties.

The Buyers: (signed)   The Sellers: (signed)

合同公证书的样板：

合同公证书

　　　　　　　　　　　　　　　　　（年）_____证字第_____号

兹证明甲方的代表人_____与乙方的代表人_____于_____年_____月_____日签订_____合同。

　　　　　　　　　　　　　　　　中华人民共和国_____公证处
　　　　　　　　　　　　　　　　　　　公证员：_____
　　　　　　　　　　　　　　　　　_____年_____月_____日

译文：

Notary of Contract Certificate

　　　　　　　　　　　　　　　　（year）_____ ZI. No. _____

This is to certify that _____, acting on behalf of the Party A, and _____, acting on behalf of the Party B, signed on _____/_____/_____, the contract "_____" attached here.

　　　　　　　　　　　　　　　　　　Notary: _____
　　　　　　　　　　　　_____ Notary Public Office
　　　　　　　　　　　　　The People's Republic of China
　　　　　　　　　　　　　_____/_____/_____

十、商标注册公证书

中国企业走向国际化，碰到了最现实的商标被注册的尴尬。以民族品牌——联想（Legend）为例，据了解，Legend商标此前在很多国家已经被注册。如果联想想要打入国际市场，就面临一个商标侵权问题。因为在别国Legend商标已经被本国所公证为合法的品牌，而中国的联想则就成了盗用商标，造成侵权。由此可以看到商标注册公证的必要性。当然，现在的联想商标改为Lenovo。

商标注册公证书的格式：

商标注册公证书

　　　　　　　　　　　　　　　　　　　　（　　）字第××号

兹证明我国××厂(或公司)生产的××(货名)的××商标注册证(编号或登记号为××号)系我国工商行政管理总局出具。该商标的专有权属于我国××厂(或公司)。

　　　　　　　　　　　　　　中华人民共和国××省××市公证处
　　　　　　　　　　　　　　　　　公证员：×××(签名)
　　　　　　　　　　　　　　　　××××年××月××日

译文：

>
> **NOTARIAL CERTIFICATE OF**
> **REGISTRATION OF TRADE MARK**
>
> （　　）ZI, No.［　　］
>
> This is to certify that No. ×× Trademark Registration Certificate, identifying the ×× Trademark on ××(the name of the goods) produced by ×× Factory(or Company), is issued by the General Administration for Industry and Commerce of the People's Republic of China. The patent right of the Trademark Registration belongs to ×× Factory (or Company).
>
> Notary: ×××（Signature）
> ××× Notary Public Office（Seal）
> ××× Province
> The People's Republic of China

十一、企业法人资格公证书

法人是相对于自然人而言的，它是具有民事权利能力和民事行为能力，依法独立享有民事权利和承担民事义务的组织，是社会组织在法律上的人格化。自然人是以生命或血缘为其存在特征的单个人，依法享有民事权利和承担民事义务，我们每个人都是自然人。

法人作为民事法律关系的主体，是与自然人相对称的，两者相比较有不同的特点：(1) 法人是社会组织在法律上的人格化，是法律意义上的"人"，而不是实实在在的生命体，其依法产生、消亡。自然人是基于自然规律出生、生存的人，具有一国国籍的自然人称为该国的公民。自然人的生老病死依自然规律进行，具有自然属性，而法人不具有这一属性。(2) 虽然法人、自然人都是民事主体，但法人是集合的民事主体，即法人是一些自然人的集合体。例如大多数国家（包括我国）的公司法都规定，公司法人必须由两人以上的股东组成。对比之下，自然人则是以个人本身作为民事主体的。(3) 法人的民事权利能力，民事行为能力与自然人也有所不同。

根据《民法通则》第37条规定，法人必须同时具备四个条件，缺一不可。

(1) 依法成立。即法人必须是经国家认可的社会组织。在我国，成立法人主要有两种方式：① 根据法律法规或行政审批而成立。如机关法人一般都是由法律法规或行政审批而成立的。② 经过核准登记而成立。如工商企业、公司等经工商行政管理部门核准登记后，成为企业法人。

(2) 有必要的财产和经费。法人必须拥有独立的财产，作为其独立参加民事活动的物质基础。独立的财产，是指法人对特定范围内的财产享有所有权或经营管理权，能够按照自己的意志独立支配，同时排斥外界对法人财产的行政干预。

(3) 有自己的名称、组织机构和场所。法人的名称是其区别于其他社会组织的标志符号。名称应当能够表现出法人活动的对象及隶属关系。经过登记的名称，法人享有专用权。法人的组织机构即办理法人一切事务的组织，被称作法人的机关，由自然人组成。法人的场所是指从事生产经营或社会活动的固定地点。法人的主要办事机构所在地为法人的住所。

(4) 能够独立承担民事责任。指法人对自己的民事行为所产生的法律后果承担全部法律责任。除法律有特别规定外，法人的组成人员及其他组织不对法人的债务承担责任，同样，法人也不对除自身债务外的其他债务承担民事责任。

根据《民法通则》的规定，我国的法人主要有四种：机关法人、事业法人、企业法人和社团法人。

因此，要想成为法人必须具备上述条件，还需得到公证处的公证，才能依法享有法律所规定的权利和义务。

其公证书的格式如下所示：

机关(事业)法人资格公证书

（　）××字第××号

兹证明××××(单位全称)于××××年××月××日经××××(批准机关名称)批准成立。根据《中华人民共和国民法通则》第50条之规定，具有法人资格。〔其法定代表人是××(职务)×××(姓名)，法人住所在××××××。〕

中华人民共和国××省××市(县)公证处

公证员：×××（签名）

××××年××月××日

译文：

Notarial Certificate

（　）×× ZI, No. ××

This is to certify that ×××× was registered as a corporation at ×××× on ××/××/××××. Under the Article 50 of "General Principles of the Civil Law of the People's Republic of China", it has the qualification as a legal person.

The corporate executive is ××××（title）××××（name）, now resides at ××××.

Notary：×××（Signature）

××× Notary Public Office（Seal）

××× City, ××× Province

The People's Republic of China

××/××/××××

企业法人资格公证书

（　）××字第××号

兹证明×××（企业名称）于×年×月×日经××工商行政管理局核准登记,取得工商××第××号《企业法人营业执照》,具有法人资格。（××××系××经济性质的企业,注册资金××元,法人住所在×市×街×号,法定代表人是××（职务）×××（姓名）,其经营范围是）。

中华人民共和国　××省××市公证处

公证员：×××（签名）

××××年××月××日

译文：

NOTARIAL CERTIFICATE OF BUSINESS ENTITY

（　）×× ZI, No. ××

This is to certify that ×××（Name of the Enterprise）registered as a corporation at the Industry and Commerce Administration Bureau on ×（day）, ×（month）, ××（year）, and accepted corporate status (×××, located in ×××, is an enterprise engaging in with RMB ××× as its registered capital. ×××（Name）, ×××（Post and Title）, is its corporate executive whose business covers...）

Notary：（Signature）

×× Notary Public Office（Seal）

×× City, ×× Province

Peoples Republic of China

××/××/××××

十二、赠与公证书

一般情况下,赠与行为通常发生在特定的场合或时日,比如,逢年过节,人们为增进感情,相互之间属于礼尚往来的礼节性的财产馈赠等。因此,赠与财产的价值通常都比较小,一般无须用书面形式予以固定。

但对于价值较大的财产,若仍以口头形式作为建立赠与法律关系的表现形式,则对赠与双方当事人都不利。对受赠人而言,由于没有书面的赠与合同,受赠人若要证明已合法设立的赠与法律关系有很大的难度,其接受所赠财产的权益完全取决于赠与人能否承认该赠与法律关系并能够守约。

为保护赠与双方的合法权益,对于超过一定价值的财产的赠与应当以书面形式做出表示,从我国目前的国民收入来看,建议立法或司法解释对价值超过人民币2 000元的财产的赠与,应当签订书面赠与合同,否则,该赠与行为无效。

那么在什么条件下订立的赠与合同才有效呢？按照我国现行的法律,应该具备以下条件：

(1) 赠与人应当具有民事行为能力。

《最高人民法院关于贯彻执行〈中华人民共和国民法通则〉若干问题的意见》(简称《民通意见》)第 6 条规定:"无民事行为能力人、限制民事行为能力人接受奖励、赠与、报酬,他人不得以行为人无民事行为能力、限制民事行为能力为由,主张以上行为无效。"第 129 条规定:"赠与人明确表示将赠与物赠给未成年人个人的,应当认定赠与物为未成年人的个人财产。"《合同法》第 185 条规定:"赠与合同是赠与人将自己的财产无偿给予受赠人,受赠人表示接受赠与的合同。"由此可见,赠与行为涉及双方当事人,系双方民事法律行为,但考虑到赠与人处分财产的无偿性特征,法律并未要求受赠人必须具备意思表示能力;对于无民事行为能力人或限制民事行为能力人,不管其是否做出接受赠与的意思表示,皆视为接受。因此,受赠人是否具有民事行为能力不影响赠与行为的法律效力。

(2) 赠与人与受赠人应当就赠与财产无偿转移给受赠人达成一致意见,但受赠人为无民事行为能力人或限制行为能力人除外。

(3) 赠与财产系赠与人有权处分且为可以合法流通的财产。

(4) 赠与行为所涉及的内容不违反我国法律、行政法规的强制性规定。

赠与合同样本:

甲方:_____(赠与方)

乙方:_____(受赠方)

双方根据《中华人民共和国合同法》的规定,就赠与事项达成协议如下:

赠 与 合 同

1. 甲方将_____赠与乙方

(赠与物的名称、数量、质量)

2. 甲方将于_____(时间)在_____(地点)将赠与物交付给乙方

3. 甲方承担_____的责任义务

4. 甲方享有_____权利

(明确甲方的撤销权及行使撤销权的情形)

5. 乙方应于_____(时间)之前做出是否接受赠与的意思表示,否则,赠与不生效力。

6. 其他

甲方:_____ 签字:_____ 盖章:_____

住址:_____ 电话:_____

乙方:_____ 签字:_____ 盖章:_____

住址:_____ 电话:_____

_____年_____月_____日

对于所订立的赠与合同要得到公证部门的公证才能拥有法律效力,赠与公证书的一般格式如下:

```
┌─────────────────────────────────────────────────────────────┐
│                    赠与公证书                                 │
│                                   （ ）××字第××号           │
│    兹证明_____于_____年_____月_____日来到我处,在我的面前,在前面的赠 │
│ 与书上签名(或盖章)。                                          │
│              中华人民共和国_____省_____（县）公证处   │
│              公证员：_____（签名）                  │
│              _____年_____月_____日                         │
└─────────────────────────────────────────────────────────────┘
```

译文：

```
┌─────────────────────────────────────────────────────────────┐
│              NOTARIAL CERTIFICATE BESTOWAL                   │
│                                    （ ）×× ZI, No. ××       │
│   On this day of _____ (date), _____ (name) personally appeared before me. │
│ Mr. _____, known to me to be the person whose signature is subscribed to the foregoing │
│ Deed of Gift.                                                │
│   IN WITNESS WHEREOF, I have hereunto set my hand and official seal on the day and year │
│ first written above.                                         │
│                              Notary：(signed)                │
│                              _____ Notary Public Office │
│                              _____ Province            │
│                              the People's Republic of China  │
│              _____ (Day) _____ (Month) _____ (Year)    │
└─────────────────────────────────────────────────────────────┘
```

十三、有关继承的公证书

继承分为遗嘱继承和法定继承。为了防止不必要的争抢现象和篡改,伪造遗嘱等活动的发生,遗嘱和继承的公证成为必要。

首先,注意这类公证书中常用到的词汇短语的翻译:

(1)"继承人",有人译为"successor",这是不妥的。因为"successor"主要指"a person who takes an office or position formerly held by another",如:"王位的继承人"译为"the successor to the Throne"。涉外公证书的"继承人"是指"a person who has the lawful right to receive the property of one who dies",故应选用"heir"。

(2)"遗产"一词是很重要的。汉英词典上有 legacy, estate, inheritance,但这几个词是有很大区别的:"legacy"主要指遗产中的动产部分;"estate"指被继承人死后留下尚未被继承的全部遗产,既包括动产也有不动产;"inheritance"指已被当事人继承了的遗产。因此,"遗产"一词应译成"estate"。

(3)"遗嘱"一词在汉英词典上有 testament,will,dying words 和 devise。其中,will 是一般用语,指立遗嘱人按照法律规定的方式处分遗产或其他事物并于其死亡时发生效力的行为,其所处分的遗产可以是不动产也可以是动产。testament 作为"遗嘱"时有两种用法,一种是作为一般用语,相当于 will;另一种用法,和 devise 相对应,作为"处分动产的遗嘱"(a will disposing of personal property);devise 是"处分不动产的遗嘱"(a will disposing of real property),或指"遗嘱中处分不动产的条款"(a clause in a will disposing of property and esp. real property)。在公证书中,"遗嘱"一词一般指正式的"书面遗嘱",选用"will"较妥:"生前立有遗嘱",有人译成"made a will"就不如"had a will",因为"made a will"只强调当时的行为,而公证机关出具的公证书是根据当事人提供的、经公证机关审查的真实、合法的书面遗嘱,所以这里强调的是结果。

(4)"遗产应由×××继承"应译成"estate is to be inherited by ×××","to be to do"表示按遗嘱安排一定要实行的行为。

下面我们来看一下遗嘱继承的相关内容:所谓遗嘱就是指遗嘱人生前在法律允许的范围内,按照法律规定的方式对其遗产或其他事务所做的个人处分,并于遗嘱人死亡时发生效力的法律行为。遗嘱共有以下几个特征:

(1)遗嘱是单方法律行为,即遗嘱是基于遗嘱人单方面的意思表示即可发生预期法律后果的法律行为。

(2)遗嘱人必须具备完全民事行为能力,限制行为能力人和无民事行为能力人不具有遗嘱能力,不能设立遗嘱。

(3)设立遗嘱不能进行代理。遗嘱的内容必须是遗嘱人的真实意思表示,应由遗嘱人本人亲自做出,不能由他人代理。如是代书遗嘱,也必须由本人在遗嘱上签名,并要有两个以上见证人在场见证。

(4)紧急情况下,才能采用口头形式,而且要求有两个以上的见证人在场见证,危急情况解除后,遗嘱人能够以书面形式或录音形式立遗嘱的,所立口头遗嘱因此失效。

(5)遗嘱是遗嘱人死亡时才发生法律效力的行为。因为遗嘱是遗嘱人生前以遗嘱方式对其死亡后的财产归属问题所做的处分,死亡前还可以加以变更、撤销,所以,遗嘱必须以遗嘱人的死亡作为生效的条件。

遗嘱的形式：

遗　嘱

立遗嘱人［中文姓名（英文姓名）］［婚姻状况/职业］（香港身份证号码：××××××（×）），兹郑重声明，将本人所有以前订立之遗嘱、遗嘱修订附件及遗嘱性质的产权处置，尽行作废，并立此嘱书为本人最后之遗嘱。

（一）本人指定及委派本人之［与阁下的关系，如"丈夫"］［中文姓名（英文姓名）］（香港身份证号码：××××××（×））住［居住地址］为本人此遗嘱之唯一的遗嘱执行人及受托人。

（二）本人将本人名下位于［不可动财产，如物业，请列明详细地址］之物业遗赠本人之［受益人与阁下的关系，如"儿女"］［受益人中文姓名（英文姓名）］承受及享用。

（三）本人将本人名下的［可动财产：如珠宝首饰，为清楚鉴别，请列明财产，如财产所在地］遗赠本人之［受益人与阁下的关系，如"儿子"］［受益人中文姓名（英文姓名）］承受及享用。

（四）本人将本人名下的［现金财产，如港币］遗赠本人之［受益人与阁下的关系，如"孙儿"］［受益人中文姓名（英文姓名），如受益人人数超过一人，请列明各人关系及姓名］平均承受及享用，并免除此遗赠之任何遗产税项责任。

（五）除上述第二、三及四段的产业外，本人将本人名下在各处所有之不动产及动产产业，除清付本人丧葬费及其他费用（包括债项在内）外，全部尽行遗赠本人之［受益人与阁下的关系，如"丈夫""女儿"］［受益人中文姓名（英文姓名）］）［如受益人人数超过一人，请列明各人关系及姓名］平均承受及享用。

（六）本人以香港为本人之永久居留地，本遗嘱乃根据香港法律处理，此嘱。

立遗嘱人亲签
［日期：　年　月　日］

上开遗嘱，经×××等人在场见证，由该立遗嘱人［立遗嘱人姓名］亲自签署，作为其最后遗嘱；同时×××等人应其所请，为之见证，于签署名字作见证人时，该立遗嘱人与×××等两人均同时在场，此证。

第一见证人×××

姓名：

香港身份证号码：

签署：

第二见证人×××

姓名：

香港身份证号码：

签署：

＊注意：因遗嘱内是否列明有关遗赠现金的所有地或详细事项将可引致不同法律效果，立遗嘱人须考虑是否因其意愿而加以列明，有关法律效果可向阁下的律师查询。

＊＊注意：遗嘱的受益人不应同时作为遗嘱的见证人，以避免因嫌疑影响立遗嘱人的意愿以致令遗嘱的有效性受到质疑。

译文：

WILL

[name of testator]([Chinese name]) (Holder of Hong Kong Identity Card No. [HKID No.]) of [Address], [martial status / occupation], hereby revoke all former wills codicils and testamentary dispositions made by me and declare this to be my last Will and Testament.

1. I APPOINT [the relationship of beneficiary e.g. my husband] [name] [Chinese name] (Holder of Hong Kong Identity Card No. [HKID No.]) of [address] be the sole Executor and Trustee of this my Will (hereinafter called "my Trustee" which expression shall include the trustee or trustees for the time being hereof whether original or substituted)。

2. I GIVE all my share and interest of and in the landed property situate lying and being at [the description of immovable property e.g. address] to [the relationship of beneficiary e.g. my son] [name] [Chinese name] for his/her own use and benefit absolutely.

3. I GIVE my [movable property e.g. jewellery / necklace etc.] [for identification purpose, the place of the property e.g. in my safe deposit box with ×××Bank Limited at [address]] to [the relationship of beneficiary e.g. my son] [name] [Chinese name] for his/her own use and benefit absolutely.

4. I GIVE the sum of HK $[amount] to my [the relationship of beneficiary] [name] [Chinese name] (if more than one, their relationship and names etc.) in equal shares for their own use absolutely free of any duty payable on or by reason of my death.

5. I GIVE DEVISE AND BEQUEATH all my estate real and personal of whatsoever nature and where so ever situate (excluding my property hereto before disposed of) subject to and charged with the payment thereout of my funeral and testamentary expenses just debts taxes and estate duty to my Trustee UPON TRUST to sell call in and convert the same into money with power to postpone such sale calling in and conversion for so long as he shall in his absolute discretion think fit without being liable for loss and after payment thereout of my debts funeral and testamentary expenses TO HOLD the residue ("my Residuary Estate") on trust to divide such residue into [the number of shares] equal shares to be distributed in the following manner:—

(a) as to one of such shares for [the relationship of beneficiary] [name] [Chinese name] for his/her own use and benefit absolutely;

(b) as to one of such shares for [the relationship of beneficiary] [name] [Chinese name] for his/her own use and benefit absolutely;

(c) etc.

PROVIDED THAT if any of the above beneficiary or beneficiaries shall die before me then his or her or their share or shares shall be divided and paid to the other surviving beneficiaries in equal shares.

6. I declare that Hong Kong is the place of my domicile and that the law in force in Hong Kong at the time of my death shall be the law of this my Will.

IN WITNESS whereof I the said [name of testator] have hereunto set my hand this day of two thousand.

(续)

> SIGNED by the above named [name of testator] as her/his last Will in the presence of us both present at the same time who at her/his request in her/his presence and in the presence of each other have hereunto subscribed our names as witnesses:
> WITNESS:[names of two witnesses]
> INTERPRETER BY:[name of interpreter]
> * Note: whether the details of property, e.g. the location and description, is specified in the Will shall have different legal effect, the testator should consider how to specify the property in accordance with his/her intention. You may contact your lawyer for legal advice for the legal effect.
> ** Note: in order to avoid the suspicion of undue influence by the Beneficiary to the testator affecting the validity of the Will, the Beneficiary should not be signed the Will as witness.

常见的遗嘱公证书的格式如下:

> 遗嘱公证书
>
> （　）××字第××号
>
> 兹证明×××(应写明姓名、性别、出生年月日和现住址)于×年×月×日在×××(地点或者公证处)，在我和×××(可以是其他公证员，也可以是见证人)的面前，立下了前面的遗嘱，并在遗嘱上签名(或者盖章)。
> 经查，遗嘱人的行为和遗嘱的内容符合《中华人民共和国继承法》第16条的规定，是合法有效的。
>
> 中华人民共和国××省××市(县)公证处
> 公证员(签名)
> ××××年××月××日

译文:

> Notarial Certificate of Will
>
> （　）×× ZI. NO.××
>
> This is to certify that ×××, (male/female, born on ××/××/××××) came to this ××× on the day of ××/××/×××× and sign the foregoing statement before ××× and me.
>
> Notary: (signed)
> ×× Notarial Public Office
> ×× Province
> The People's Republic of China
> ××/××/××××

由于种种原因被继承人未立遗嘱的，其财产要按照《继承法》的相关规定予以继承。

首先，应按照国家要求的遗产继承顺序办理。《继承法》规定遗产要按以下顺序继承：

第一顺序：配偶、子女、父母。

第二顺序：兄弟姐妹、祖父母、外祖父母。

继承开始后，由第一顺序继承人继承，第二顺序继承人不继承。没有第一顺序继承人继承的，由第二顺序继承人继承。

本法所说的子女，包括婚生子女、非婚生子女、养子女和有抚养关系的继子女。

本法所说的父母，包括生父母、养父母和有抚养关系的继父母。

本法所说的兄弟姐妹，包括同父母的兄弟姐妹、同父异母或者同母异父的兄弟姐妹、养兄弟姐妹、有扶养关系的继兄弟姐妹。

其次，我们要看以上所说的继承人是否有继承的权利。继承权包括两种涵义：

(1) 客观意义上的继承权。它是指继承开始前，公民依照法律的规定或者遗嘱的指定而接受被继承人遗产的资格，即继承人所具有的继承遗产的权利能力。即享有客观意义上的可能性继承权。

(2) 主观意义上的继承权。它是指当法定的条件（即一定的法律事实）具备时，继承人对被继承人留下的遗产已经拥有的事实上的财产权利，即已经属于继承人并给他带来实际财产利益的继承权。这种继承权同继承人的主观意志相联系，不仅可以接受、行使，而且还可以放弃，是具有现实性、财产权的继承权。继承权的实现以被继承人死亡或宣告死亡时开始。

以上所说的涉及继承权公证书和放弃继承权公证书两种，其形式如下：

继承权公证书

( )××字第××号

被继承人：×××（应写明姓名、性别、生前住址）

继承人：×××（写明姓名、性别、出生年月日、住址、与被继承人的关系）

继承人：×××（同上，有几个继承人应当写明几个继承人）

经查明，被继承人×××于××××年××月××日因×××（死亡原因）在×××地（死亡地点）死亡。死后留有遗产计：×××（写明遗产的状况）。死者生前无遗嘱。根据《中华人民共和国继承法》第5条和第10条的规定，被继承人的遗产应当由其×××、×××（继承人名单）共同继承。（如果有代位继承的情况应当写明继承人先于被继承人死亡的情况；如果放弃继承，应当写明谁放弃了继承，放弃部分的遗产如何处理的内容）

中华人民共和国××省××市（县）公证处

公证员：×××（签名）

××××年××月××日

放弃继承权公证书

（　）××字第××号

兹证明×××(姓名)于××××年××月××日来到我处，在我面前，自愿在前面的放弃遗产继承权的证明上签名。

中华人民共和国××省××市(县)公证处
公证员(签名)
××××年××月××日

译文：

Notarial Certificate

（　）×× ZI. NO. ××

This is to certify that ××× came to this ××× on the day of ××/××/×××× and sign before me the foregoing statement.

Notary：(signed)
×× Notarial Public Office
×× Province
The People's Republic of China
××/××/××××

对于一些特殊情况的遗产继承还要用到出生公证书或死亡公证书。比如继承人先于被继承人死亡的，则继承人的亲属有权利继承被继承人的财产，这时就需要出示继承人的死亡公证书。对于另一些情况，如被继承人失散的亲属或是收养的子女在其死亡后想要继承其财产就必须出示其出生证明。这两种公证书的一般格式如下：

死亡公证书

（　）××字第××号

根据××××(写明调查的材料，包括档案记载、知情人证明等)兹证明×××，男(或者女)，于××××年××月××日在××××(地点)因××(死亡原因)死亡。

中华人民共和国××省××市(县)公证处
公证员：×××(签名)
××××年××月××日

译文：

Notarial Certificate of Death

　　　　　　　　　　　　　　　　　　　　　（　）××ZI. NO.××

　　This is to certify that×××, male (or female), died of (from)×× at××× on××/××/××××, according to××××.

　　　　　　　　　　　　　　　　　　Notary：(signed)
　　　　　　　　　　　　　　　　　　×× Notarial Public Office
　　　　　　　　　　　　　　　　　　×× Province
　　　　　　　　　　　　　　　　　　The People's Republic of China
　　　　　　　　　　　　　　　　　　××/××/××××

出生公证书

　　　　　　　　　　　　　　　　　　　　　（　）××字第××号

　　根据××省××市（或县）××户籍管理机关档案记载（或××省××市医院出生证明或知情人××提供的材料），兹证明×××，男（或女），于××××年××月××日出生。于××××年××月××日被遗弃在××省××市××（地点），被送到××社会福利院抚养后，于××××年××月××日被收养，×××的养父是×××，×××的养母是×××。收养公证书（或收养证）的编号是××××××。

　　　　　　　　　　　　　　　　　　中华人民共和国××省××市（县）公证处
　　　　　　　　　　　　　　　　　　公证员：×××（签名）
　　　　　　　　　　　　　　　　　　××××年××月××日

译文：

Notarial Certificate of Birth

　　　　　　　　　　　　　　　　　　　　　（　）××ZI. NO.××

　　According to the record of the domicile management department of×× City, ×× Province, this is to certify that×××, (male/ female), born on××/××/××××), was abandoned at×× City of×× Province on××/××/××××, and then was adopted by××× and××× after being fostered by social welfare institute, and the number of the notarial certificate of adoption is××××××.

　　　　　　　　　　　　　　　　　　Notary：(signed)
　　　　　　　　　　　　　　　　　　×× Public Office of
　　　　　　　　　　　　　　　　　　×× City, ×× Province
　　　　　　　　　　　　　　　　　　The People's Republic of China
　　　　　　　　　　　　　　　　　　××/××/××××

十四、委托公证书

当我们自己不能亲自办理某项业务时可以委托他人代做。为了保证我们委托别人的这个事实和保护双方的利益，可以签订委托协议书，然后再由公证处公证所签订的协议是有法律效力的。根据我们所委托的事情的性质，委托书可以分为两类：一种是指被委托人是律师，另一种则对被委托人的身份没有特殊的要求。这两类委托书的一般格式如下：

一般授权委托书

我，×××（姓名），××××（地址等），在此指定×××（姓名），××××（地址或律师事务所名称等），为我的律师，以我的身份履行一切实践中我通过律师所能从事的合法行为。本权利在以下载明日期全权生效并一直持续到××或持续到双方当事人规定的延展期或提前撤销期。

日期：××××/××/××

地址：××××

州名和县名：××××

GENERAL POWER OF ATTORNEY

I, ×××, of ×××, hereby appoint ×××, of ×××, as my attorney in fact to act in my capacity to do every act that I may legally do through an attorney in fact. This power shall be in full force and effect on the date below written and shall remain in full force and effect until ×× or unless specifically extended or rescinded earlier by either party.

Dated: ××/××/××××

STATE OF ××××

COUNTY OF ××××

委托书

兹有我，×××（姓名），为×××（公司名称及性质）的以下署名股东，在此任命和指定×××（姓名）为我的事实和合法授权代理人，为我和以我的名义、职位和身份，在上述公司于××（日期）召开的或就此延期召开的股东大会上作为我的代理人对与会前合法提交大会讨论的任何事项进行表决，且为我和以我的名义，在大会上全权履行我的职责；在此我撤销此前所做的任何其他授权委托。

于20××年××月××日签字盖章，特此为证

译文：

PROXY

BE IT DNOWN, that I, ×××, the undersigned Shareholder of ×××, a ××× corporation, hereby constitute and appoint ××× as my true and lawful attorney and agent for me and in my name, place and stead, to vote as my proxy at the Meeting of the Shareholders of the said corporation, to be held on ×× or any adjournment thereof, for the transaction of any business which may legally come before the meeting, and for me and in my name, to act as fully as I could do if personally present; and I herewith revoke any other proxy heretofore given.

WITNESS my hand and seal this ×× day of ××, 20××.

委托公证书

（　）×字××号

　　兹证明，×××于××××年××月××日来我处，在我面前，在前面的委托书上签名(或盖章)。

中华人民共和国××省××市公证处
公证员：×××(签章)
××××年××月××日

译文：

Notarial Certificate

（　）×× ZI. NO.××

This is to certify that ×××, came to this ××× on the day of ××/××/×××× and sign before me the foregoing statement.

Notary：(signed)
×× Notarial Public Office
×× Province
The People's Republic of China
××/××/××××

十五、其他公证书

在有些情况下，在国外生活多年的人员回国定居，或者是华侨放弃外国国籍回归祖国，抑或是留学人员回国创业。如果国外的政府部门想知道这样一些人的去向，工作和职位等信息时，以下的几种公证书就派上用场了。

生存公证书

（　）××字第××号

　　兹证明×××,(男或女,于××××年××月××日在××省××市出生)尚健在,现住××省××市××街××号。

中华人民共和国××省××市××公证处
公证员：×××
××××年××月××日

译文：

> Notarial Certificate
>
>   （ ）××ZI. NO.××
>
> This is to certify that×××,（male/female, born at ×× City,×× Province, on ××/××/××××）is alive and living at NO.×× of ×× City,×× Province.
>
>   Notary：(signed)
>   ×× Notarial Public Office
>   ×× Province
>   The People's Republic of China
>   ××/××/××××

> 职务公证书
>
>   （ ）××字第××号
>
> 兹证明×××,(男或女,××××年××月××日出生)，现担任××省××市××××（职务名称,可有多个）。
>
>   中华人民共和国××省××市××公证处
>   公证员：×××
>   ××××年××月××日

译文：

> Notarial Certificate of Position
>
>   （ ）×× ZI. NO.××
>
> This is to certify that×××,（male/female. Born on ××/××/××××），now assume the ×××× of ×× City,×× Province.
>
>   Notary：(signed)
>   ×× Notarial Public Office
>   ×× Province
>   The People's Republic of China
>   ××/××/××××

> 定居公证书
>
>   （ ）××字第××号
>
> 兹证明原旅居法国华侨×××,(又名×××,男或女,××××年××月××日出生)，于××××年××月××日回国定居,现住××省××市××街××号。
>
>   中华人民共和国××省××市××公证处
>   公证员：×××
>   ××××年××月××日

译文：

> Notarial Certificate of Settlement
>
>   ( )××ZI. NO.××
>
> This is to certify that ×××, (another name ×××, male/female, born on ××/××/××××), once living in France, returned to China for settlement on ××/××/××××, now residing at NO.××, ×× Street, ×× City, ×× Province.
>
>   Notary: (signed)
>   ×× Public Office of
>   ×× City, ×× Province
>   The People's Republic of China
>   ××/××/××××

第三节 翻译中应注意的问题

涉外公证书证词译文质量的优劣不仅对涉外公证书效力的正常发挥和我国公证的形象产生重要影响，而且因译文质量问题也引发过公证赔偿，因此，公证处出具涉外公证书在注重程序和证明对象的真实、合法的同时，也应把译文的质量要求放到重要的位置。

根据司法部颁布的《公证程序规则（试行）》，公证书存在下列任何一个问题，即被视为无效：（1）未按照规定附外文译文的；（2）公证员的中文姓名与外文姓名不一致的；（3）外文译文不正确、不规范或有错误的；（4）外文译文未译成公证书使用国要求的相应文字的。在这四项要求中，第（2）、（3）、（4）项是我们在翻译时应特别注意的事项。下面就公证书翻译过程中经常遇到的问题逐一加以讨论。

一、标题的翻译（Translation of Headings）

公证书的标题就如一个人的名字一样，如果连自己的名字都写错的人，又怎么能够赢得别人的信任与尊重呢？同样，公证书标题的翻译也是至关重要的。

公证书可译作"Notarization"或"Notarial Certificate"，而且一旦某一特定公证处采用其中的一种译法，一般不应做改动。

就像上一节中所列举的，通常所遇到的公证书的翻译主要有毕业证公证书（Notarization of Diploma）、学位证公证书（Notarization of Degree Certificate）、成绩单公证书（Notarization of Academic Transcription）、亲属关系公证书（Notarization of Family Relation）、婚姻状况公证书（Notarization of Marital Status）、无刑事犯罪记录公证书（Notarization of No Record of Criminal Offense）、及（涉外）收养公证书（Notarization of Adoption）、经历公证书（Notarial Certificate of Experience）、合同公

证书(Notary of Contract Certificate)、企业法人资格公证书(Notarial Certificate of Business Entity)等等。当然,在实际工作中可以笼统地将公证书译为"Notarization"或者"Notarial Certificate",这要根据具体的工作性质来加以取舍。

由于公证书是法律文书的一种,所以其标题的写法与翻译都要与其他的法律文书相一致,即应该注意以下问题:

(1) 标题要在公证书上方中央位置(Center Top);

(2) 标题中不用引号(Quotation Marks)及句号(Periods);

(3) 公证书标题必须全部大写(Capitalize All Letters)或大写标题中每个单词的第一个字母(Capitalize the Very First Letter of Each Word);

(4) 标题中的冠词(Articles)及少于5个字母的连词(Conjunctions)、介词(Prepositions)不应大写,除非位于句首;受公证书类型限制,在公证书标题中一般不会出现像"Between"这样长的连词或介词。

此外,公证书标题的翻译应追求准确、简洁。比如有的公证员将"毕业证"译作"Graduation Certificate",这就不如用"Diploma"简洁;有的公证员将"亲属关系"译为"Relationship",但是用"Relationship"不如用"Domestic Relation"或"Family Relation"准确。还有,在译"学位证公证书"时如采用《英汉—汉英双向法律字典》中"学位证书(Diploma)"的译法显然会造成与毕业证表达上的混乱。那么,能否区别对待?答案是肯定的,比如说具体称之为"理科学士学位公证书"(Notarization of B. S. Degree)或"文工科硕士学位公证书"(Notarization of M. A. Degree)或者是直接称之为"学士学位公证书"(Notarization of Degree Certificate)等等。"婚姻状况公证书"(Notarial Certificate of Marital Status)的翻译也应依据具体情况分别作"离婚公证书"(Notarization of Divorce)及"未婚公证书"(Notarization of Being Single)等诸如此类的细分。

二、公证书正文即公证词的翻译(Translation of the Body Part)

(一)"兹证明"的翻译

我国公证书公证词多以"兹证明……"开头,"证明"一词的主要的英语翻译有:prove,testify,certify等等,那么,对于"兹证明……"我们应该选择哪一个呢?首先我们来看一下各个词的释义:"prove"是指"to show that something is true by providing facts, information etc.";"testify"是指"to make a formal statement of what is true, especially in a court of law";而"certify"是指"to state that something is correct or true, especially after some kind of test"。在这里,公证书显然是经过一系列证明之后所得出的结论,因此"兹证明……"的英文翻译(English Equivalent)应该是:"This is to certify that..."。

(二) 公证书中姓名、地址的翻译

公证书中姓名翻译按照司法部的统一要求需使用普通话发音的拼音拼写,对于我国南方大部分地区的居民来说,其发音与普通话相差很大,在翻译人名和地名时经常混淆不清。sh与h、ch与c、zh与z常常混淆,"老师"变成"老四"或"老死"。尤其是有些地方h和f分不清,"头发"经常发音成"头花","软软的"说成"暖暖的","女子"变成"驴子",还有把exam发音成[ig'dzem]。因此,人名或地名的拼音可以查阅《现代汉语词典》《中国地图册》或《中国地名词典》等工具书。

有关我国地名的翻译,《中国翻译》杂志(1999年第3期)刊登了一篇文章:《中国地名英译的几点注意事项》(作者:连益)可供参考。对香港、澳门地名的翻译,包括中译英和英译中,我们可参考中英文对照的《香港特别行政区地图册》《澳门特别行政区地图册》。但如当事人在申办公证时已办妥护照,公证机关出具的公证书翻译可以与其护照上的拼写一致。

对地址的翻译通常除行政区域名称用特定的单词写法外,其他地名部分均可按汉语拼音拼写。如河北省承德市围场满族蒙古族自治县围场镇新兴街建设小区3号楼1单元201室,可译为:Room 201, Entrance 1, Building 3, Jianshe Subdistrict, Xinxing Street, Weichang Town, Weichang Manzu & Mongolian Autonomous County, Chengde City, Hebei Province。对于街、路、村等因属非行政区域,根据国际通行作法,均可以拼音拼写,如:Jie, Lu, Cun等。还有一个情况需注意的是我国的山西和陕西两省汉语拼音相同,为区别,通常将陕西省拼写成"Shannxi Province"。

对于从国外寄来的邀请信,入学通知书等文件翻译成汉语时,一定要当事人提供中文姓名,这是因为这种姓名只有汉语拼音而没有声调,我们很难拿准到底是怎么写的。例如"Li Ming"这个姓名的汉字可以是李明,李铭,黎明等,到底是哪个,只有当事人才知道,我们不能凭空想象。

另外,在翻译个人经历、毕业证书、学位证书等公证文书的时候,要注意单位名称、学校名称等专有名词的翻译,尤其是某些校名有其习惯译法,我们必须按照其固定译法,而不能凭自己的经验乱译。关于这一点,我们在前面谈公证书语言特点的时候已经进行了详尽的谈论,在这里就不再赘述了。

(三) 公证书中专业术语的翻译

正确使用专业术语。要求我们不但要精通法律,还要精通专业英语。举常见几个法律术语为例,我们可以分析其与一般含义的区别,如诉讼,action(行动);合同等的签订,excution(执行);未成年人,infant(婴儿);时效,limitation(限制);应当,shall(将);mansion在法律意义上指住宅及其附近并不连接一体的建筑,如车库等;acknowledgement在公证书中指身份证明,conveyance为产权转让证书,attestation为证词等。这就要求我们在平常的翻译工作中要注意这种小知识点的积累与总结。

(四) 公证书中标点符号的正确应用

中文的标点符号不能糊乱用在英文中,而有些公证员在翻译诸如经历证明等公证书时,将《经历证明》等按照中文的习惯在翻译中加上书名号,使人觉得十分滑稽。我们知道在英语中是没有书名号的,在严肃的公证文书翻译中出现这样的错误是会很可笑的。正确的方法是将汉语中应该加书名号的部分斜写、加下划线或大写。还有一个比较容易犯的错误就是省略号的应用,中文中的省略号"……"有六个点,而英文中的省略号"..."有三个点,有些公证员就想当然的把中文的省略号直接挪用到英文当中,让人一看就知道此公证员的业务水平有限。因此,我们在平常的翻译实践中一定要注意这些小的细节,因为一个公证员的水平是从细节表现出来的。

(五) 公证词翻译应忠实于原文(Conformity)

公证书作为法律文件,它的翻译与一般报刊文章的翻译不同,与文学翻译的差别就更大了。要求公证文书翻译一定要忠实于原文,翻译者不得随意发挥或进行任何形式的修饰。对所证明的事实情况要准确反映出来,一定要符合公证书的准确严密的语言特点。例如下面是一个结婚公证书正文的翻译:

> This is to certify that Wang, who is male and was born on May 1, 1964, and Hao, who is female and was born on October 19, 1965, **registered** marriage on October 1, 1992 at the registration office of Civil Affairs Department, Hohhot, Inner Mongolia.

这篇译文的缺陷之一在于时态。译文中"Registered"一词为动词的过去式,表明的是过去发生这一登记结婚的事实而不能证明现在的婚姻状况是离异(Divorced)、丧偶(Widowed)还是分居(Separate)。这样便不能满足公证书语言的严密性、准确性要求。因此,应该将时态改为现在完成时态"have been married",以表达"一直持续到现在的状态"要严谨一些。

缺陷之二在于译文不够简洁,建议改为:

> This is to certify that Wang **(male, born on May 1, 1964)** and Hao **(female, born on October 19, 1965) have been married** since October 1, 1992 at the registration office of Civil Affairs Department, Hohhot, Inner Mongolia.

三、涉外公证书的落款(Close)

任何司法类文书都必须有落款,有了落款才能证明所签立的司法文书的当事人或单位,以及签订的时间,才能使得司法文书拥有法律效力。公证书也不例外,其落款主要分为以下几项内容:

(1) 公证员(Notary)姓名和签名(Signature)或盖章(Seal);
(2) 公证处名称及盖章;
(3) "中华人民共和国"(People's Republic of China)字样;
(4) 日期。日期的格式一般为月/日/年。

此外,在出国留学经济担保(Affidavit of Financial Support)中通常有担保人(Financial Sponsor)如下誓词:

> I certify that I will provide tuition fees, living expenses for my son Lee during his stay in the United States. If he requires any further monetary assistance, I will provide this as well.

通常,公证处需要担保人出具财产证明或银行存款证明(Bank Savings Statement)。所有这些均附于公证材料后。在涉及财产证明时,有时会遇到个体工商户(Individual Business)的营业执照(Business License)。在逐项翻译中会遇到如"某某市/县工商行政管理局"印章。笔者认为不应译作"Commercial and Industrial Administration Bureau of City (Prefecture)/County x",而应译为"x City (Prefecture)/County Administration of Industry and Commerce"。因为,"Administration"一词本身便有"executive branch of a government"的意思,即"行政机关、局(署)等"。

有时,公证机关还对材料的译本的真实性和可靠性予以公证,即"翻译件与原件一致公证"(Notarization of the Conformity of Translated Copy and the Original)。最后一点,在涉及"毕业证书公证"时,最后一句通常是:"原件上的校长某某某和毕业学校某某大学之印鉴均属实"。周帮友老师的实用英语应用文大全中将"属实"二字译为"Genuine"。笔者认为通译该是"Authentic"。因为"Authentic"一词在法律英语中常用。比如:"作准证书"是"Authentic Instrument","作准文件"是"Authentic Document"。《麦克米伦字典》中将"Authentic"一词解释为:"being what it purports to be",并且给出了一个搭配例子即:"an authentic document";而且,还有的书中,将"公证书"译为:"Authentic Deed"或"Authentic Act"。由此可见,用"Authentic"一词更准确一些,更与公证书语言靠近一些。现将上面一句汉语译出以供参考:"Both the signature of President ××× and the seal of the graduation School ××× University are found to be authentic."

四、公证书中英美翻译的不同

(一) 产生方法不同

两国公证员的产生方法不同,可以公证的文件范围不同,公证员的公证管辖区域不同。英国选择公证员非常严格,大都是有丰富经验,受过特殊培训的合格律师,终身制。公证员有三类：一类是 scrivener notaries，是伦敦市区合法公证员，他们精通一两门外语，熟悉国外法律，并且有 5 年的实习期。另外两种分别是 qualified solicitors（在伦敦城外工作）和 non-legally qualified persons（对法律有一定了解，经坎特博雷大主教任命）。公证书上必须有公证员的个人签名章，而且还得备案。英式公证书一般由律师事务所出具。这些律师一般是 The Notaries Society 成员，如 SONI & CO Notaries 律师事务所（伦敦一家为商务机构和个人提供广泛法律服务的公司），其公证服务有：法庭辩护律师权利证明（powers of attorney for worldwide use）、国际证词（international Affidavits, Sworn Statements and Depositions）、商业文件（commercial documents for worldwide use）、翻译证明（certified translations）、语言证书（language certificates）、版权文件（copyright documentation for worldwide use）、财产文件（property documents for worldwide use）、指印确认（fingerprinting confirmation）、彩票（lottery conduct notarizations）、受教育类证书（Education Certificates for worldwide use）。相比于美国公证员只能对当事人的签名（signature）公证，英国还能对财产交易进行公证。

美国各州有各州的公证条例，加州有 California Notary Law，但大部分管理比较松散，一般是州政府（大部分是州内政大臣 Secretary of State，但新泽西州是州财长，弗吉尼亚州是州长）任命公证员，有一定任职年限。有的州做公证员非常容易，甚至不需要什么专业知识。各州公证员权利不同，如原法属殖民地的路易斯安那州公证员权利较大，加州也是，权利大到可以接受票据（bills of exchange）。公证书要求也不同，如新泽西和弗吉尼亚州的公证文件不用公证员签名章，但经当事人要求可以加盖。弗吉尼亚州的公证员甚至不用自己的签名，还可以收取 5 美元小费。

各州公证书种类不同，加州有两类：acknowledgements（身份证明）和 Jurat（文件证明）。得克萨斯州有：acknowledgements, Jurat verifications, oath or affirmation, statement of officer, deposition, protests, certified copy of non-recordable documents，弗吉尼亚州的公证处不证明婚姻状况，由牧师或教堂证明，可以 acknowledge signatures, take oaths, certify copies of non-government documents。根据宾夕法尼亚州公证法，公证书有 acknowledgements, oath depositions, affidavits, certificates 等形式。从以上可以看出，美式和英式公证可以对法庭的证词公证。美国公证员管理较松散，公证书法律效力不高。

（二）语言选择

一般来讲，公证书语言比较固定，有时使用古英语，文辞古奥，多长句。同时，英国英语习惯使用保守的陈述，美国英语则简单明了。如：英国一份译者证明译文与原文一致的翻译公证：

(1) Sample translation certification

"I (name) a qualified translator fluent in (source & target language) registered with the institute of linguist number ×××working on behalf on Nettranslation ltd, declare that to the best of my knowledge, the attached document in (target language) is a true and accurate translation of (name of document and source language)"

Signed or attested before me on date by

(name/s of person/s).

(Signature of notary public/solicitor) (seal)

而美式英语中一份证明文件真实性的公证则简单明了：

(2) Sample Certificate

State of Texas County of _____

This instrument was acknowledged before me on (date) by (name or names of person or persons acknowledging).

_____ Notary Public Signature

也可以是以下形式：

(3) SAMPLE ACKNOWLEDGMENT（个人身份证明）

Commonwealth of Pennsylvania ( ) SS: County of ( ). On this, the day of, 19, before me a notary public, the undersigned officer, personally appeared, known to me (or satisfactorily proven) to be the person whose name is subscribed to the within instrument and acknowledged that he executed the same for the purposes therein contained.

In witness hereof I hereunto set my hand and official seal ××× Notary Public.

(三) 词语选择

两种语言由于两个国家地理和文化传统的差异，很多词义有差别。如公证员两国都可以用 notary public, public notary，但英国还用 notary 一词。return ticket 在英国英语中，它指的是往返票，在美式英语中，只有返程票之意。美国用 round-trip ticket 来表示往返票。（以下都是先英式英语后美式英语）Crib（婴儿床，大一些的床），Cricket（板球，蟋蟀），Torch（手电筒，火把），table（提交法案，搁置法案），rubber（橡皮，避孕套），裤子(trousers, pants)，电梯(lift, elevator)，商店(shop, store)，超市购物车(trolley, cart)，收银员(cashier, teller)，足球(football, soccer)，租用(hire, rent)，公寓(flat, apartment)，有(have got, have)，临时工(holiday jobs, temporary jobs)，上课(go on a course, take a course)，样本(specimen, sample)。数字类：billion（万亿，十亿），gallon(4.56 升，3.785 升)，pint(20 液量盎司，16 液量盎司)，零(naught, zero)。

尤其是在财产证明中数字的差异更是不可小觑,英美对于数字的表达有差别,英国英语百位和十位数之间通常用 and 连接,而美国则常省略,如下例:

This is to certify that Mr. Bryant Frank has maintained a deposit account with ×× Bank, New York, USA through A/C No. 4632-9 with a balance of US Dollars $74,642.50 SAY SEVENTY FOUR THOUSAND SIX HUNDRED AND FORTY TWO AND FIFTY CENTSONLY as of September 21, 1999.

上例中 only 一词在两国用的频率都不高,一般表示出数字即可,我们中文中说到的多少元整,可以不译。

(四) 格式差异

格式上,两种文体都有三个部分:标题、正文、署名和日期。但在顺序等方面有些不同。美式公证中用 before me,或 I certify 开头者多,日期一般在正文的前半部分。而英国的公证日期一般在公证正文的后半部分。英国英语的日期表达为日月年方式,而美国英语的日期表达方式为月日年方式。另外英国姓名与美国姓名的顺序也稍有差别。

另外,美国公证书还经常看到 to whom it may concern,表示对有关人士的称呼。一般是个人在公证员面前的证词,例如下例中:

FINANCIAL GUARANTEE
TO WHOM IT MAY CONCERN

I hereby certify that I, the mother/father of _____ will support my son/daughter with a monthly allowance of _____ US dollars while he/she is in France studying, and that I am financially responsible for any emergency which may arise.

SIGNATURE

NAME:

ADDRESS:

Sworn to before me, a notary public this day:

SIGNATURE of PUBLIC NOTARY

通过以上的介绍我们知道,当涉及英国和美国的公证书时,要给予不同的对待。如果是发往英国的就要按照英国公证书的习惯与规范予以翻译;如果是发往美国的就要按照美国公证书的习惯与规范予以翻译。只有这样才能真正发挥公证书应有的效力,也才能体现我们对对方的重视,才能更好地促进国与国之间的交流与合作!

五、公证书中的有所译有所不译

虽然说我们在翻译公证书时要忠于原文,但是当遇到一些没有用处或者会造成接受方理解困难的地方我们可以选择不译或者意译。比如,在我们的成绩单是通常会有老师的评语如"此学生热爱祖国,拥护共产党的领导……"等等之类几十年没有变化的套话,我们在遇到翻译这种地方时可以选择不译。因为如果我们直译出来会让接受方不知所云,而西方国家大部分是资本主义国家,价值观的差异让他们无法理解这样的语句。故而在翻译这类话语时要有所选择的翻译。

近年来,由于我国国民收入的迅速增加,父母对孩子教育的投入也随之飞速增长。这就使得出国留学迅速升温,特别是近年来中学生的出国浪潮更是一浪高过一浪。对于中学生出国留学所需要的公证书就会涉及一些获奖证书公证,九年义务教育证书公证,或者是一些诸如《中学生守则》的翻译等问题。在这些文书的翻译中往往会遇到像"遵守纪律,尊敬老师,团结同学,热爱班集体","政治上要求进步","希今后继续努力,争取更大成绩"等老师的评语。那么对于这些具有中国特色的东西我们在翻译成英语时应该怎么处理呢?是依照忠实原文的原则直译过去还是意译或者干脆摒弃不译呢?在笔者看来应该采取"有所译有所不译"的原则,摒弃形式上的对等,只译实质性的东西。

综上,对于上面所提到的问题需要译者在翻译时仔细斟酌,反复推敲,力求翻译的准确规范。

第四节 本章小结

本章首先系统地介绍了公证书和涉外公证书的概念、文体、分类、结构、目的和意义。然后,介绍了常用涉外公证书的格式,翻译以及翻译中需要注意的问题。通过以上的学习,读者可以对涉外公证书有一个全面的了解和认识,这对以后的深入学习是十分有益的。

 课后习题

1. 什么是涉外公证书?
2. 涉外公证书的语言特点有哪些?
3. 涉外公证书的有哪几类?
4. 涉外公证书的结构是怎样的?
5. 将下列公证书翻译成英语:

(1)

学历公证书

(2008)鲁济证外字第 1986 号

兹证明张三,(男,于 1984 年 9 月 14 日出生)于 2004 年 9 月 1 日入山东大学计算机系学习计算机工程专业,学制四年,于 2008 年 7 月毕业。

中华人民共和国山东省济南市公证处

公证员:王大明

2008 年 12 月 20 日

(2)

结婚公证书

(2009)京海证外字第 0512 号

兹证明李野,(男,1986 年 3 月 12 日出生)与章小惠,(女,1986 年 4 月 4 日出生)于 2009 年 1 月 12 日在北京市海淀区结婚。

中华人民共和国北京市海淀区公证处

公证员:尚迪

2009 年 1 月 20 日

(3)

遗嘱公证书

(2007)豫洛证外字第 1473 号

继承人:李健仁,男,1974 年 6 月 24 日出生,现住河南省洛阳市黄河路 134 号。

被继承人:李大富,男,1950 年 4 月 11 号出生,生前住河南省洛阳市黄河路 134 号。

查李大富于 2007 年 11 月 13 日在洛阳市人民医院死亡,死亡后在家中留有遗产。死者生前立有遗嘱。根据死者遗嘱,死者李大富的遗产应由李健仁继承。

中华人民共和国河南省洛阳市公证处

公证员:李如花

2007 年 3 月 24 日

(4)

经历公证书

(2008)吉吉证外字第 1456 号

兹证明王蔷,(女,于 1978 年 4 月 25 日出生)于 2000 年 9 月至 2003 年 6 月在吉林省吉林市实验中学任英语老师,2003 年 9 月至 2007 年 6 月在吉林省双阳县中学任英语老师。

中华人民共和国吉林省长春市公证处

公证员:李华

2008 年 4 月 14 日

(5)

企业法人公证书

(2009)京海证外字第 0203 号

兹证明无边落木图书销售有限公司于 2008 年 12 月 16 日取得工商第 02030512 号《企业法人经营执照》,具有法人资格。(其法定代表是董事长伍小小,注册资金 500 万,法人住所北京市海淀区中关村大街 23 号,其经营范围是图书经销,经营方式是跨国经营)。

本公证有效期至 2019 年 1 月 12 日止。

中华人民共和国北京市海淀区公证处

公证员:尚迪

2009 年 1 月 12 日

附录一

合同翻译中的常用词汇

INQUIRIES

1. potential business 潜在业务
2. prospective customer 潜在顾客
3. customers of long standing 长期顾客
4. potential supplier 潜在供应商
5. trade fair 贸易博览会
6. the latest issue of 最新一期……
7. integrated software package 完整软件包
8. substantial order 大宗订单
9. quantity discount 数量折扣
10. cash discount 现金折扣
11. list price 标价、目录价格
12. export terms 出口条件
13. pictured/illustrated catalog 带插图的商品目录
14. article number / Art. No. 货号
15. bulk buyer 大买户
16. business concern 商行
17. business relations / relationship 业务关系
18. business status 业务状况
19. commercial counselor 商务参赞
20. commercial counselor's office 商务参赞处
21. means of packing 包装方法
22. parent company 母公司
23. sales literature 促销资料

24. trading association 贸易关系
25. trade journal 行业刊物
26. firm offer 实盘
27. non-firm offer：offer without engagement 虚盘
28. trade discount 同业/批发折扣
29. bill of exchange（bill / draft；B/E）汇票
30. documents against payment：D/P 付款交单
31. shipping documents 装运单据
32. line of business 业务/经营范围
33. specific inquiry 具体询价

REPLIES AND QUOTATIONS

1. regular customer 老顾客
2. be in a position to do 能够
3. for your consideration/reference 供你方考虑/参考
4. promotional novelties 促销小礼品
5. profit margin 利润赚头/幅度
6. by separate post/mail/cover：separately 另邮/函
7. bathroom fittings 浴室设备
8. building contractor 建筑承包商，营造商
9. net price 净价
10. cash with order：CWO 订货付款，随订单付现
11. sample cutting 剪样
12. ceiling price 限价
13. consumer goods 消费品
14. counter-offer 还盘
15. counter-bid 还价
16. current/prevailing price 现价
17. durable goods：durables 耐用品
18. fancy goods 花俏商品
19. gross price 毛价，总价
20. lead time 从订货到交货的间隔时间
21. offer sheet 报盘单
22. quotation sheet 报价单
23. retail price 零售价

24. rock-bottom price 最底价
25. make an offer / a quotation 报盘/价
26. offer firm 报实盘
27. quote a price 报价
28. credit status 资信状况
29. correspondent bank 往来行
30. publicity brochure 宣传小册子
31. down payment 预订金
32. find a ready sale/market for 畅销
33. end-user 最终用户
34. Ex Works：EXW 工厂交货（价）
35. Cost & Freight：CFR 成本加运费
36. Cost，Insurance and Freight：CIF 成本加保险费运费
37. Carriage & Insurance Paid to：CIP 运费保险费付至……
38. Carriage paid to：CPT 运费付至……
39. Delivered At Frontier：DAF 边境交货
40. Delivered Duty Paid：DDP 完税后交货
41. Delivered Duty Unpaid：DDU 未完税交货
42. Delivered Ex Quay：DEQ 目的港码头交货
43. Delivered Ex Ship：DES 目的港船上交货
44. Free Alongside Ship：FAS 船边交货
45. Free Carrier：FCA 货交承运人
46. Free On Board：FOB 装运港船上交货

ORDERS AND ACKNOWLEDGEMENT

1. captioned order 标题所述订单
2. by courier 由快递公司传递
3. make out a contract 缮制合同
4. make up the order 备货
5. please sign and return one copy for our file 请签退一份供我方存档
6. bulk delivery 大宗货物的交付
7. replenish stocks 补充库存 / 进货
8. maximum discount 最大折扣
9. contractual obligation 合同义务
10. counter-sign 副署，会签

11. counter-signature 连署签名

12. general terms and conditions 一般交易条件

13. import license：I/L 进口许可证

14. mode of payment 付款方式

15. Proforma invoice：P/I 形式发票

16. prompt shipment 即期装运

17. provisional order 临时订单

18. purchase confirmation：P/C 购货确认书

19. purchase contract 购货合同

20. purchase order：P/O 订单

21. regular order 经常订单, 定期订单

22. regular purchase 定期购货

23. repeat order 重复订单, 翻单

24. sales contract：S/C 销售合同

25. trial order 试销订单

26. accept an order 接受订单/订货

27. acknowledge an order （卖方）确认订单

28. arrive at / come to an agreement 达成协议

29. book an order 接受订单/货

30. cancel an order 撤销订单/货

31. complete an order 处理订单, 备货

32. confirm an order （买方）确认订单

33. decline an order 谢绝订单

34. deliver an order 交付订货

35. draft a contract 起草合同

36. enter into a contract 订立合同

37. fill / fulfill / make up an order 处理订单, 备货

38. meet an order 备货

39. place an order 下/放订单, 订货

40. process an order 处理订单, 备货

41. refuse / reject an order 拒绝订单

42. supply an order （根据订单）供货

43. unit price 单价

INSURANCE

1. obtain indemnity 获得赔偿
2. a cover note 承保单
3. a marine policy 海洋运输保单
4. a floating policy 全额保单
5. an open policy 预约保单
6. a valued policy 定值保单
7. declaration form 启运通知书
8. a claims form 索赔申请书/表
9. be for the buyers' account 由买方付款
10. assessor's report 估损报告
11. survey report 货物检验报告
12. insurance certificate 保险凭证
13. insurance claim 保险索赔
14. insurance surveyor （保险公司）货物检查员
15. a complete write-off 报废东西
16. at your end 在你地
17. the People's Insurance Company of China：PICC 中国人民保险公司
18. the state-owned company/enterprise 国有公司/企业

PACKING

1. bar code 条形码
2. bulk cargo 散装货；统装货
3. bulky cargo （体大质轻的）泡货
4. bulky parcel 大宗包裹
5. color assortment 颜色搭配
6. country of origin 原产地国
7. customary packing 习惯包装
8. equal assortment 平均搭配
9. flexible container 集装包/袋
10. gunny bag 麻袋
11. iron drum 铁桶
12. lot number 批号
13. metric ton 公吨

14. open-top container 开顶式集装箱
15. state-of-the-art 最先进的
16. gross weight 毛重
17. net weight 净重
18. indicative mark 指示性标志
19. shipping mark 装运标志；唛头
20. warning mark 警告性标志
21. neutral packing 中性包装
22. nude cargo 裸装货
23. packing list 装箱单
24. paper bag 纸袋
25. long ton 长吨
26. short ton 短吨
27. seller's usual packing 卖方习惯包装
28. size assortment 尺寸搭配
29. trade mark 商标

TRANSPORTATION

1. ETA：Estimated Time of Arrival 估计到达时间
2. ETD：Estimated Time of Departure 估计离开时间
3. Secure the vessel 弄到船只
4. Cargo capacity 载货能力
5. Charter party 租船合同
6. Air waybill 空运提单
7. Carrying vessel 运货船
8. Direct steamer 直达船
9. Dock receipt 码头收据
10. Document of title 产权单证
11. Freight prepaid 运费已付
12. Freight to collect 运费到付
13. General cargo vessel 杂货船
14. Negotiable instrument 可流通/转让票据
15. Sailing schedule 船期表
16. Sailing date 起航日期
17. Shortlanded memo 短卸单

18. Take delivery of 取货
19. Make delivery of 发货
20. Dispatch money 速遣费，快装费
21. Freight ton 运费吨
22. Measurement ton 尺码吨
23. Weight ton 重量吨
24. Weight memo 重量单
25. Ocean transportation 海洋运输
26. Full container load：FCL 整箱货
27. Less than container load：LCL 拼箱货
28. Bill of lading：B/L 海运提单
29. Partial / part shipment 分批装运
30. Port of destination 目的港
31. Port of shipment 装货港
32. Shipping advice 已装船通知
33. Shipping order 装船通知单，装货/运单
34. Shipping space 舱位
35. Storage cost/charges 仓储费
36. Time charter 定期租船
37. Voyage charter 定程租船
38. Time of shipment 装运/船期

PAYMENT BY L/C；OTHER MODES OF PAYMENT

1. aggregate amount 总价/金额
2. L/C amendment advice 信用证修改通知书
3. accepting bank 承兑行
4. days of grace 宽限期
5. expiry date 失效期
6. extension of the L/C 信用证展期
7. operative instrument 有效票据
8. waiver of legal rights 放弃合法权利
9. banking/bank charges 银行手续费
10. cash against documents 凭单付现/款
11. cash against documents on arrival of goods 货到后凭单付现/款
12. conversion rate 兑换率

13. exchange rate 外汇率
14. financing of projects 项目融资
15. fine bank bill 有信用的银行汇票
16. first class bill 信誉好的汇票
17. foreign exchange：外汇
18. protest for non-payment 拒付证书
19. protest note 拒付通知书
20. finance a project 为项目提供资金
21. honor a draft 承兑汇票
22. dishonor a draft 拒付汇票
23. protect a draft 备妥货款以支付汇票
24. clean shipped on board bill of lading 清洁的已装船提单
25. opening / issuing bank 信用证开证行
26. correspondent bank 往来行
27. advising/notifying bank 通知行
28. blank endorsement 空白背书
29. more or less clause 溢短装条款
30. bona fide holder 善意真诚持有人
31. accompanying documents 随附单据
32. L/C 远期信用证
33. without recourse 无追索权
34. mail transfer：M/T 信汇
35. telegraphic transfer：T/T 电汇
36. demand draft：D/D 票汇
37. debit note 索款通知书
38. D/P after sight 远期付款交单
39. financial standing 财务状况
40. status inquiry 资信调查

COMPLAINTS & ADJUSTMENT

1. short-open (信用证)少开
2. arbitration body 仲裁机构
3. arbitration clause 仲裁条款
4. breach of the contract 违反合同；违约
5. color deviation 色差

6. compulsory arbitration 强制性仲裁
7. faulty goods/packing 有毛病的货物/包装
8. force majeure 不可抗力
9. legal action 诉讼
10. non-conformity of quality 质量不符
11. non-performance of the contract 不履行合同
12. settlement of claims 理赔
13. shoddy goods 次货
14. voluntary arbitration 自愿仲裁
15. slip up 出错
16. wear and tear 磨损；损耗
17. customs examination 海关检查
18. fair average quality：FAQ 中等品，大路货
19. commodity inspection bureau：商品检验局

AGENCIES

1. confirming house 保付商行
2. opportune moment 恰当时机
3. please ignore this letter 不必复函
4. authorized agent 指定代理人
5. channel of distribution 销售渠道
6. exclusive distribution 总经销
7. exclusive / sole agency 独家代理
8. exclusive sales 包销
9. exclusive sales agreement 包销协议，独家经销协议
10. general agency 总代理，一般代理
11. forwarding agent：forwarder 货运代理，运输代理商
12. procurement authorization：P/A 采购授权书
13. salesmen's traveling and entertainment expenses 销售员旅费及交际费
14. volume discount 总购量折扣
15. trade volume 贸易额；交易额
16. volume of business 营业/交易额
17. advertising agency 广告公司
18. advertising agent 广告代理商/人
19. agency commission 代理佣金

20. annual turnover 年营业额,年成交量
21. buying agent 采购代理商/人
22. commission house 佣金商行
23. insurance agent 保险代理商/人
24. sales room 拍卖场,售货处

附录二

中外法律名言英汉对照

英文	中文
A sage punishes not because a crime has been committed, but rather to prevent its being committed; because the past cannot be revoked, but the future is being forestalled. —Plato	智者非因犯罪已然发生才去惩罚,实乃为了防止犯罪而施刑责;其原因在于,过去无法逆转,而未来则可以预防。 ——柏拉图
The law is the last result of human wisdom acting upon human experience for the benefit of the public. —Samuel Johnson	法律是人类为公众利益所做实践中探索出的人类智慧最终结晶。 ——塞缪尔·约翰逊
In civilized life, law floats in a sea of ethics. —Earl Warren	在文明的生活中,法律漂浮在道德的海洋上。 ——厄尔·沃伦
The law seems like a sort of maze through which a client must be led to safety, a collection of reefs, rocks and underwater hazards through which he or she must be piloted. —John Mortimer	法律看起来就像某种迷宫委托人要想通过,肯定需要他人引导其通过种种暗礁。 ——约翰·莫蒂默
The verdict acquits the raven, but condemns the dove. —Juvenal	裁决认定掠夺者无罪,而给主张和平的人判刑。 ——尤维纳利斯
The law often allows what honor forbids. —Bernard Joseph Saurin	法律允许的而道义上常常禁止。 ——伯纳德·约瑟·莎伦
Unnecessary laws are but traps for money. —Hobbes	无用的法律不过是捞钱的陷阱。 ——霍布斯
Arms and laws do not flourish together. —Julius Caesar	武力与法律不能同时兴盛。 ——尤利乌斯·凯撒
It is safer that a bad man should not be accused, than that he should be acquitted. —Titus Livy	不指控坏人较宣告他无罪更稳妥。 ——泰特斯·李维
The prince is not above the laws, but the laws above the prince. —Pliny the Younger	不是君主高于法律,而是法律高于君主。 ——小普林尼
The strictest law sometimes becomes the severest injustice. —Terence	最严厉的法律有时会变成最大的不公平。 ——泰伦斯

(续表)

英文	中文
The judge is condemned when the guilty is acquitted. —Publilius Syrus	如果犯罪之人被判无罪，法官应该判刑。 ——普布里利亚斯·西拉斯
He who decides a case without hearing the other side, though he decide justly, cannot be considered just. —Lucius Annaeus Seneca	偏听一方而对案件做出判决不可能公正，虽然他自认为很公正。 ——卢西乌斯·阿纽斯·塞内加
I do not know the method of drawing up an indictment against an whole people. —Edmund Burke	我不知道如何起草控告所有人的方法。 ——埃德蒙·伯克
No written law has been more binding than unwritten custom supported by popular opinion. —Carrie Chapman Catt	由民众意见支持的不成文习惯法比成文法更具约束力。 ——卡丽·查普曼·凯特
Law is mind without reason. —Aristotle	法律是无由的理念。 ——亚里士多德
Necessity has no law. —William Langland	"必要"不受制于法。 ——威廉·朗格兰
Let us consider the reason of the case. For nothing is law that is not reason. —Sir John Powell	让我们来搜寻本案的理由，因为没有理由不成其为法律。 ——约翰·鲍威尔爵士
I know of no method to secure the repeal of bad or obnoxious laws so effective as their stringent execution. —Ulysses S. Grant	我知道取缔有害或讨厌的法律最有效的方法是严厉地去执行它。 ——尤利塞斯·S.格兰特
At least in the law of the jungle, you've survival of the fittest. In Congress, you've just got survival. —Robert W. Packwood	至少在法律丛林中，适者生存。在国会中，你得生存。 ——罗伯特·W.帕克伍德
He found law dear and left it cheap. —Ulysses S. Grant	他对法律一见钟情，随即又见异思迁。 ——尤利西斯·辛·格兰特
There is a point beyond which even justice becomes unjust. —Sophocles	公平与不公平仅一线之隔。 ——萨福克里斯
The law exists to protect us all, whether we are union members, union leaders, employers or merely long-suffering members of the public. We cannot do without it. But the law is not a one-way street. Part goes our way, part goes against us. We have either to accept it all or else to opt bor anarchy. —Sir John Donaldson	法律保护我们所有人，不管你是工会成员、工会领导人、职员还是长期受苦的公众成员。没有法律我们一事无成。但是法律不是一条单行道，有些是我们的方向，而有些与我们反向。我们要么全部接受，要么选择无政府状态。 ——约翰·唐纳森爵士
The question is, not what may be supposed to have been intended, but what has been said. —Lord Halsbury	问题不是推定的意图，而是曾经说过什么。 ——赫斯布里勋爵
It is found by experience that admirable laws and right precedents among the good have their origin in the misdeeds of others. —Cornelius Tacitus	经验告诉我们绝妙的法律及正确的先例来源是他人的犯罪。 ——科尼利厄斯·塔西佗

(续表)

英文	中文
People say I've had brushes with the law. That's not true. I've had brushes with overzealous prosecutors. —Mark Duffy	人们说我与法律有过冲突,其实是不准确的。我只是同那些过分热心的检举人有过冲突。 ——马克·达菲
There can be no really pervasive system of oppression... without the consent of the oppressed. —Florynce R. Kennedy	没有被压迫者的同意,就不会有真正的压迫制度。 ——弗洛里恩斯·R.肯尼迪
The strongest bulwark of authority is uniformity; the least divergence from it is the greatest crime. —Emma Goldman	权力最有力的保障是一致性;最小的分歧就是最大的犯罪。 ——爱玛·戈德曼
The grandest of all laws is the law of progressive development. —John Christian Bovee	法律最重要的是法律随着时代不断改革发展。 ——约翰·克里斯蒂安·波夫
There are so many lawyers with their hands in the till there isn't room for money. —Howard Engel	抽屉内到处都是律师的手,以致没有放钱的空间。 ——霍华德·恩格
It is often thought that the police represent the law. It would be more accurate to say that they represent the force behind the law. —J. Ricker and J. Saywell	经常有人认为警察代表法律。更准确来讲,他们代表法律背后的强制力。 ——J.雷克 & J.塞维尔
Senility has it's privileges. —Edward Farrer	老人应享有特别待遇。 ——爱德华·法拉
Plant a kernel of wheat and you reap a pint; plant a pint and you reap a bushel. Always the law works to give you back more than you give. —Anthony Norvell	种下一粒麦种你可以收获一品脱;种下一品脱你可以收获一蒲式耳。通常法律回报你的总比你给予的多。 ——安东尼·诺维尔
Laws were made to be broken. —Christopher North	制定法律用于被人破坏。 ——克里斯托弗·诺斯
HOMICIDE, n. The slaying of one human being by another. There are four kinds of homicide: felonious, excusable, justifiable, and praiseworthy, but it makes no great difference to the person slain whether he fell by one kind or another — the classification is for advantage of the lawyers. —Ambrose Bierce	杀人:名词,一个人被另一个人杀死。一般分为四种情况:重罪的、可免除的、有理由的及值得称颂的,但是对于被杀者没有任何区别。而这种分级只对于律师有用。 ——安布罗斯·比尔斯
Reason is the life of the law; nay, the common law itself is nothing else but reason. —Coke	法律的生命是推理,不仅如此,而且普通法本身除了推理外别无他物。 ——科克
Discourage litigation. Persuade your neighbors to compromise whenever you can. As a peacemaker the lawyer has superior opportunity of being a good man. There will still be business enough. —Abraham Lincoln	阻止诉讼。随时说服你的邻居采取折中措施去避免诉讼,律师作为调节人,不但有很好的机会成为一个好人,而且总是有许多生意上门。 ——亚伯拉罕·林肯

（续表）

英文	中文
The illegal we do immediately. The unconstitutional takes a little longer. —Henry Kissinger	违法一瞬间即可完成，但违宪则需更长一点时间。 ——亨利·基辛格
With every civil right there has to be a corresponding civil obligation. —Edson Haines	每一个民事权利必须有对应的民事义务。 ——埃德森·海恩斯
We are creating the kind of society where the criminal is out of jail before his victim is out of hospital —Richard J. Needham	我们正在建设一种受害者尚未出院而罪犯却已出狱的社会。 ——理查德·J.尼达姆
The law gives a dog more rights than the person he bites —J. C. McRuer	法律给予狗的权利比被它咬的人多。 ——J. C.麦克鲁尔
It may be true that the law cannot make a man love me, but it can keep him from lynching me, and I think that's pretty important. —Martin Luther King	事实上，法律不能让一个人爱上我，但可以阻止他对我动私刑。我认为这是最重要的。 ——马丁·路德·金
Lawyers are operators of the toll bridge across which anyone in search of justice has to pass. —Jane Bryant Quinn	律师就像收费桥的工作人员，任何搜寻公平的人都必须由此经过。 ——简·布莱恩特·奎因
There are not enough jails, not enough policeman, not enough courts to enforce a law not supported by the people. —Hubert Humphrey	就是再多的监狱、再多的警察及法庭也无法实施民众不支持的法律。 ——休伯特·汉弗莱
Lawyers are men whom we hire to protect us from lawyers. —Elbert Hubbard	律师是我们聘来用以应付其他律师的。 ——埃尔伯特·哈伯德
It is the spirit and not the form of law that keeps justice alive. —Earl Warren	法律的本质就是保持正义不灭。 ——沃伦伯爵
A lawyer cannot be made honest by an act of the Legislature. You've got to work on his conscience, and his lack of conscience is what made him a lawyer. —Will Rogers	立法机关的法令不可能使律师变得诚实。你必须凭良心做事，而正是缺乏良心才使他成为律师。 ——威廉·罗杰斯
A law-suit is like an ill-managed dispute, in which the first object is soon out of sight, and the parties end upon a matter wholly foreign to that on which they began. —Edmund Burke	诉讼就像失控的争斗，开始争夺的目标很快淡出视野，而双方结束时的目标已与之毫无关联。 ——埃德蒙·伯克
As soon as laws are necessary for men, they are no longer fit for freedom. —Pythagorus	一旦法律成为人们的必需品，自由就不再适合他们。 ——毕达哥拉斯
You have to lead people gently toward what they already know is right. —Philip Crosby	你必须带领人民慢慢地向他们认为正确的方向发展。 ——菲力普·克罗斯比
What power has law where only money rules. —Gaius Petronius	金钱统治的地方权力就是法律。 ——盖厄斯·佩特罗尼乌斯

(续表)

英文	中文
Our defense is not in our armaments, nor in science, nor in going underground. Our defense is in law and order. 　　　　—Albert Einstein	我们的防御不在于我们的军备,不在于科技,也不在于地下活动,而就是法律和秩序。 　　　　——阿尔伯特·爱因斯坦
Good laws have their origins in bad morals. 　　　　—Ambrosius Macrobius	好的法律来源于道德的沦丧。 　　　　——安波罗休·玛克罗比乌斯
The body of the law is no less incumbered with superfluous members, that are like Virgil's army, which he tells us was so crowded, many of them had not room to use their weapons. 　　　　—Joseph Addison	法律的躯体因为过量的成员而妨碍其正常运作,就如维吉尔的军队,他告诉我们,他们因为拥挤而没有空间使用武器。 　　　　——约瑟夫·阿狄森
A law is something which must have a moral basis, so that there is an inner compelling force for every citizen to obey. 　　　　—Chaim Weizmann	法律必须有一个道德基础,所以需要一个内部强制力让每一个公民去遵守。 　　　　——杰姆·魏茨曼
Pity is the virtue of the law, and none but tyrants use it cruelly. 　　　　—William Shakespeare	怜悯是法律的美德,只有暴君残酷地使用它。 　　　　——威廉·莎士比亚
To see what is right, and not to do it, is want of courage or of principle. 　　　　—Lisa Alther	知道是对的但不去做,不是缺乏勇气就是丧失原则。 　　　　——丽莎·奥尔瑟
Truth is the summit of being; justice is the application of it to affairs. 　　　　—Ralph Waldo Emerson	真理是生命的制高点,正义是其实践者。 　　　　——拉尔夫·沃尔朵·爱默生
A multitude of laws in a country is like a great number of physicians, a sign of weakness and malady. 　　　　—Voltaire	在一个国家里,众多的法律就如众多的医生,虚弱和疾病的标志。 　　　　——伏尔泰
There is no such thing as justice—in or out of court. 　　　　—Clarence Seward Darrow	无论法庭内外都没有公正这类东西存在。 　　　　——克拉伦斯·苏厄德·达罗
Organized crime constitutes nothing less than a guerilla war against society. 　　　　—Lyndon Baines Johnson	有组织犯罪不亚于组织反社会的游击战争。 　　　　——林顿·贝恩斯·约翰逊
Pray: To ask that the laws of the universe be annulled in behalf of a single petitioner confessed unworthy. 　　　　—Ambrose	祈祷:请求废除世界法则以利于个别无疑不足道的请求者。 　　　　——安布罗斯
Every kind of peaceful cooperation among men is primarily based on mutual trust and only secondarily on institutions such as courts of justice and police. 　　　　—Albert Einstein	人们之间的每种和平协作首先是建立在相互信任的基础之上,其次才是公共机构比如法庭、警察。 　　　　——阿尔贝特·爱因斯坦
Laws are like sausages. It's better not to see them being made. 　　　　—Bismarck	法律如香肠,大家最好不要看它的制作过程。 　　　　——俾斯麦
Banning gun shows to reduce violent crime will work about as well as banning auto shows to reduce drunken driving. 　　　　—Bill McIntire	禁止枪支以减少暴力犯罪就如禁止汽车以减少酒后驾驶一样可笑。 　　　　——比尔·麦金太尔

(续表)

英文	中文
To live outside the law you must be honest. —Bob Dylan	生活在法律范围之外,你必须诚实。 ——鲍勃·迪伦
As with forms of government, so with forms of law; it is the national character which decides. —Herbert Spencer	有什么样的政府就有什么样的法律;这是由国家的性质决定的。 ——赫伯特·斯宾塞
Even a clock that does not work is right twice a day. —Polish Proverb	即使是坏了的钟一天也能对两次。 ——波兰谚语
The strictest law often causes the most serious wrong. —Cicero	最严苛的法律经常导致最严重的冤屈。 ——西塞罗
The welfare of the people is the ultimate law. —Cicero	人民的幸福是法律的根本。 ——西塞罗
When men are pure, laws are useless; when men are corrupt, laws are broken. —Benjamin Disraeli	当人类思想纯洁时,法律显得无用;当人类思想腐败时,法律则不被遵守。 ——本杰明·迪斯雷利
Even when laws have been written down, they ought not always to remain unaltered. —Aristotle	即使法律已经写下,它们也不必须保持一成不变。 ——亚里士多德
Persecution is the first law of society because it is always easier to suppress criticism than to meet it. —Howard Mumford Jones	迫害是社会的第一部法,因为抑制批评问题比迎合批评要容易。 ——霍华德·芒福德·琼斯
Too much sensibility creates unhappiness; too much insensibility leads to crime. —Talleyrand	过于关注易产生不快;过于漠视易导致犯罪。 ——塔列朗
How many crimes are committed simply because their authors could not endure being wrong. —Albert Camus	许多人犯罪仅仅是因为不能忍受不公正(的待遇)。 ——阿尔贝特·卡缪
Injustice anywhere is a threat to justice everywhere. —Martin Luther King	无论何处的不公平都是对公平的威胁。 ——马丁·路德·金
The successful revolutionary is a statesman, the unsuccessful one a criminal. —Erich Fromm	成功的革命者是政治家,而失败的则为罪犯。 ——艾里克·弗洛姆
Time is the great legalizer, even in the field of morals. —Henry Louis Mencken	时间是伟大的法律判定者,即使在道德领域。 ——亨利·路易斯·孟肯
War does not determine who is right — only who is left. —Bertrand Russel	战争不能决定谁是正确的,只能决定谁离去。 ——伯特兰·罗素
There can be no justice so long as rules are absolute. —Patrick Stewart	只要有专制的规章就没有公平可言。 ——帕特里克·斯图尔特
For most men the love of justice is only the fear of suffering injustice. —Francois Duc de la Rochefoucauld	对大多数人来说,对公平的热爱仅仅因为对遭受不公平的恐惧。 ——佛朗克斯·德·拉·罗希夫格

(续表)

英文	中文
Next in importance to Freedom and Justice is popular education, without which neither Freedom nor Justice can be permanently maintained. —James Abram Garfield	全民教育的重要性仅次于自由与公平，没有它自由与公平就得不到永久的维持。 ——詹姆斯·亚伯拉罕·加菲尔德
Behind every great fortune there is a crime. —Honoré de Balzac	每个巨额财富背后都包含着犯罪。 ——奥诺德·巴尔扎克
The triumph of justice is the only peace. —Robert Green Ingersoll	公正的胜利才是唯一的和平。 ——罗伯特·格林·英格索尔
Without justice courage is weak. —Benjamin Franklin	缺乏公平的勇气是虚弱的。 ——本杰明·富兰克林
Comedy is allied to justice. —Aristophenes	喜剧与司法是同类的。 ——阿里斯多芬尼士
Change is the law of life. And those who look only to the past or present are certain to miss the future. —John Fitzgerald Kennedy	变革是法律的生命。那些只关注过去或现在的人必然会错过将来。 ——约翰·菲茨杰拉德·肯尼迪
Let us have justice, and then we shall have enough liberty! —Joseph Joubert	我们维护正义，我们将会得到更多的自由。 ——约瑟夫·儒贝尔
Only the winners decide what were war crimes. —Gary Wills	只有战胜者才有权判定什么是战争犯罪。 ——加里·维尔
Rigid justice is the greatest injustice. —Thomas Fuller	呆板的公平其实是最大的不公平。 ——托马斯·福勒
Where there is no law, but every man does what is right in his own eyes, there is the least of real liberty. —Henry Martyn Robert	如果没有法律，但每个人都做着自认为对的事情，那他们至少享受着真正的自由。 ——亨利·马丁·罗伯特
A lean agreement is better than a fat lawsuit. —German Proverb	一份不公平的合同也好过一场冗长的官司。 ——德国谚语
The law is in another world; but it thinks it's the whole world. —John Mortimer	法律存在于另一个世界，但它自认为它是整个世界。 ——约翰·莫蒂默
He who commits injustice is ever made more wretched than he who suffers it. —Plato	制造冤屈的人比遭受冤屈的人更可怜。 ——柏拉图
Laws describe constraint. Their purpose is to control, not to create. —Tom Robbins	法律记述着约束。他们的目标是控制而不是创造。 ——汤姆·罗宾斯
You never, but never, go to litigation if there is another way out...Litigation only makes lawyers fat. —Wilbur Smith	如果有另外的出路的话，你千万不要提起诉讼……提起诉讼只会养肥律师。 ——威尔伯·史密斯
One of the greatest delusions in the world is the hope that the evils of this world can be cured by legislation. —Thomas B. Reed	世界上最严重的错觉之一就是希望立法可以拯救世间的罪恶。 ——托马斯·B.里德

(续表)

英文	中文
When Mr Justice was a counsellor, he would never take less than a guinea for doing anything, nor less than half a one for doing nothing. He durst not if he would; among lawyers, moderation would be infamy. —Jeremy Bentham	如果法官做律师,他不会因为多给钱而多做事;也不会因为少给而少做。对其而言是两难,因为对于一般律师,立场不明是败笔。 ——杰里米·边沁
I am ashamed the law is such an ass. —George Chapman	我以法律如此愚蠢为耻。 ——乔治·查普曼
The law is of much interest to the layman as it is to the lawyer. —Lord Balfour	对法律而言,外行比律师能获更多的利益。 ——巴尔弗爵士
A lawyer starts life giving $500 worth of law for $5, and ends giving $5 worth for $500. —Benjamin H. Brewster	一个律师开始其职业生涯付出500元只能得到5元的回报;而结束时5元能值500元。 ——本杰明·H.布鲁斯特
A British lawyer would like to think of himself as part of that mysterious entity called The Law; an American lawyer would like a swimming pool and two houses. —Simon Hoggart	英国律师愿意把自己认为是被称为神秘实体的法律的一部分;而美国律师愿意(拥有)一个游泳池、两栋别墅。 ——西蒙·霍加特
A man without money, needs no more fear a crowd of lawyers, than a crowd of pickpockets. —William Wycherley	一个穷光蛋不用害怕律师也不用害怕扒手。 ——威廉·威彻利
Please remember that law and sense are not always the same. —Jawaharlal Nehru	请记住法律与观念并不总是一致的。 ——贾瓦哈拉尔·尼赫鲁
There are limits to permissible misrepresentation, even at the hands of a lawyer. —John Maynard Keynes	律师的手中恰当地把握着虚假陈述在法律允许范围内的限度。 ——约翰·梅纳尔·凯恩斯
I should regret to find that the law was powerless to enforce the most elementary principles of commercial morality. —Lord Herschell	我应该为发现法律无力保护商业道德的基本原则而遗憾。 ——荷斯彻尔爵士
Lawyers cannot remain empty of head and pure of heart.... A lawyer has a duty to investigate or take some steps to inform himself in a situation where he believes that there is client perjury. —Barry S. Alberts	律师不能让脑袋与心灵处于空白状态……一个律师如果认为他的客户在作伪证,他有义务去调查或采取一些措施去让自己确认它。 ——巴里·S.艾尔伯斯
I hope ever to see America among the foremost nations of justice and liberality. —George Washington	我希望永远看到美国是最公正、公平的国家。 ——乔治·华盛顿
One man's justice is another's injustice; one man's beauty another's ugliness; one man's wisdom another's folly. —Ralph Waldo Emerson	对一个人公平意味着对另一个人不公平;一个人的美丽意味着另一个人的丑陋;一个人的睿智意味着另一个人的愚昧。 ——拉尔夫·沃尔多·爱默生

(续表)

英文	中文
We hold these truths to be self-evident, that all men are created equal, that they are endowed by their Creator with certain unalienable Rights, that among these are Life, Liberty and the pursuit of Happiness. ——The Declaration of Independence	我们认为下述真理是不言而喻的：人人生而平等，造物主赋予了他们若干不可让渡的权利，其中包括生命权、自由权和追求幸福的权利。 ——独立宣言
Law must be stable, and yet it cannot stand still. ——Pound	法律应该是稳定的，但不能停止不前。 ——庞德
Law is the reason free from passion. ——Aristotle	法律是一种远离激情的理智。 ——亚里士多德
Lawyer's houses are built on the heads of fools. ——George Herbert	律师的房子建在傻子的头上。 ——乔治·赫伯特
I know you lawyers can, with ease, Twist words and meanings as you please; That language, by your skill made pliant, Will bend to favour ev'ry client. ——John Gay	我知道你们律师可以毫不费力地根据自己的喜好扭曲词汇和意义；通过技巧使语言顺从于每一个顾客的喜好。 ——约翰·盖伊
The law is only a memorandum. ——Ralph Waldo Emerson	法律仅仅是一个备忘录。 ——拉尔夫·沃尔朵·爱默生
Fools and obstinate men make lawyers rich. ——Thomas Fuller	傻子及固执的人使律师变得富有。 ——托马斯·福勒
The practice of the law is a perfectly distinct art. ——Sir Frederick Pollock	法律实践是一门很独特的艺术。 ——弗雷德里克·波洛克爵士
The lawyer's is a manifold art. ——Sir Frederick Pollock	律师是一门多方面的艺术。 ——弗雷德里克·波洛克爵士
That ignorant, blundering, blind thing, the law. ——Elbert Hubbard	法律，无知、笨拙及盲目的事物。 ——埃尔伯特·哈伯德
Lawyers Can Seriously Damage Your Health. ——Michael Joseph	律师能严重损害您的健康。 ——迈克尔·约瑟夫
A man's house is his castle. ——Sir Edward Coke	一个人的房子就是他的城堡。 ——爱德华·科克爵士
Every lawyer should be a conciliator. ——Elbert Hubbard	每一个律师应该是一个调和人。 ——埃尔伯特·哈伯德
Words are the lawyers tools of trade. ——Lord Denning	言语是律师从业的工具。 ——丹宁勋爵
Where there is hunger, law is not regarded; and where the law is not regarded, there will be hunger. ——Benjamin Franklin	饥饿的地方通常不关心法律；同时，法律不被关心的地方通常是饥饿的地方。 ——本杰明·富兰克林
Lawyers are brought up with an exaggerated reverence for their system and, apart from a few, they don't see what's wrong with it. ——Tom Sargeant	律师在培养过程中对自己的体系有着夸张的敬畏，除了少数人以外，他们发现不了体系的问题所在。 ——汤姆·沙吉恩
Lawyers generally prefer not to rush things. ——Justice Kirby	律师通常不喜欢匆忙行事。 ——柯尔比法官

(续表)

英文	中文
That which is law to-day is none to-morrow. —Robert Burton	今天的法律,明天什么也不是。 ——罗伯特·伯顿
Fee: A contingency fee is an arrangement in which if you lose, your lawyer gets nothing — and if you win you get nothing. —George M. Palmer	费用:风险代理律师费是这样安排的:如果你输了官司,你的律师将一无所获;而如果你赢了,你将一无所获。 ——乔治·M.帕尔默
Credit: A system whereby a person who can't pay gets another person who can't pay to guarantee that he can pay. —Charles Dickens	信用:一个不能支付的人让另一个不能支付的人保证他能支付的体系。 ——查尔斯·狄更斯
Laws, like houses, lean on one another. —Edmund Burke	法律像房子一样,彼此相依。 ——埃德蒙·伯克
Law is a bottomless pit, it is a cormorant, a harpy, that devours everything. —John Arbuthbit	法律是个无底洞,它贪得无厌、掠夺成性、吞食所有的东西。 ——约翰·阿布斯比特
Seventy per cent of the members of all our law-making bodies are lawyers. Very naturally, lawyers making laws favour laws that make lawyers a necessity. —Elbert Hubbard	我们所有立法机构成员中有70%是律师。很自然,立法的律师们偏爱以律师为重要元素的法律。 ——埃尔伯特·哈伯德
Nothing is more subject to change than the laws. —Michel de Montaigne	法律是最需要变革的。 ——米哈伊·德·蒙田
Debt: Blessed are the young, for they shall inherit the national debt. —Herbert Hoover	债:为年轻人祈福,因为他们将继承国债。 ——赫伯特·胡佛
Lawful, adj. Compatible with the will of a judge having jurisdiction. —Ambrose Bierce	合法的:形容词,符合行使裁判权法官意愿的。 ——安布罗斯·比尔斯
That whether you're an honest man or whether you're a thief Depends on whose solicitor has given me my brief. —Sir W. S. Gilbert	你是一个诚实的人还是一个小偷,取决于辩护律师已交与我的答辩状。 ——W.S.吉尔伯特爵士
Will: A man left the bulk of his fortune to his lawyers. If every body did this, a lot of time would be saved. —Anonymous	遗嘱:一个人留下大量财富给他的律师。如果每个人都这么做,将会省下大量的时间。 ——佚名
Lawyers' fingers, who straight dream on fees. —William Shakespeare	律师一直梦着数钱(律师费)。 ——威廉·莎士比亚
A lawyer's a man well trained in memory of cases, precedent, repartee, speeches. —Stephen Spender	律师是在案例、判例、应答、演讲方面受过良好训练的人。 ——斯蒂芬·斯彭德
Lawyers are always more ready to get a man into troubles, than out of them. —Oliver Goldsmith	律师总是准备将当事人拖入麻烦之中,而不是将其从中救出。 ——奥利弗·戈德史密斯
Lawyers don't love beggars. —Thomas Fuller	律师不喜欢乞丐。 ——托马斯·富勒

(续表)

英文	中文
Bigamy: Two rites making a wrong. ——Bob Hope	重婚:两次仪式导致一次错误。 ——鲍勃·霍普
I cannot resist saying that I regard our profession [the law] as one of the obstacles to national reform. ——Lord Hailsham	我不禁说,我把我的专业(法律)作为国家改革的阻力之一。 ——希斯曼勋爵
The laws I love, the lawyers I suspect. ——Charles Churchill	我热爱法律,但我怀疑律师。 ——查尔斯·丘吉尔
Laws for the regulation of trade should be most carefully scanned. That which hampers, limits, cripples and retards must be done away with. ——Elbert Hubbard	调节贸易的法律应该经过最仔细的检查,对于那些妨碍、限制、削弱及延迟其发展的规定必须废除。 ——埃尔伯特·哈伯德
Judgement: Good judgement comes from experience; and experience — well, that comes from bad judgement. ——Anonymous	判决:好的判决来自于经验;而经验又来自于坏的判决。 ——佚名
The most enlightened judicial policy is to let people manage their own business in their own way. ——Oliver Wendell Holmes	最开明的司法政策是让人民用自己的方法管理自己的事。 ——奥利弗·温德尔·霍姆斯
It is when merchants dispute about their own rules that they invoke the law. ——Judge Brett	商人们为他们自订的行规争执不下时,通常他们会引用法律。 ——布雷特法官
Every law has its loophole. ——Anonymous	任何法律都有漏洞。 ——佚名
The language of laws should be simple; directness is always better than elaborate wording. ——Montesquieu	法律语言应该简单;直接好过繁杂的措词。 ——孟德斯鸠
We dedicated ourselves to a powerful idea — organic law rather than naked power. There seems to be universal acceptance of that idea in the nation. ——Supreme Court Justice Potter Stewart	我们致力于一个强有力的观念——有组织的法律胜于无保护的权力。这个观念看起来在全国普遍接受。 ——最高法院波特·斯图尔特法官
Justice, though due to the accused, is due to the accuser too. ——Justice Benjamin N. Cardozo	公平(的产生)虽然应归于被告,也应归于原告。 ——本杰明·N.卡多索法官
When we neither punish nor reproach evildoers... we are ripping the foundations of justice from beneath new generations. ——Alexander	当我们既不惩处也不责备经常为恶者时,……我们将从新一代开始撕裂公正的基础。 ——亚历山大
Reason is the life of the law; nay, the common law itself is nothing else but reason. ——Coke	推论是法律的生命;而且,习惯法本身除了推论以外并没什么东西。 ——科克
Every law is an evil for every law is an infraction of liberty. ——J. Bentham	所有的法律都是邪恶的,因为它们都侵害人们的自由。 ——J.本杰明

(续表)

英文	中文
Justice is incidental to law and order. 　　—J. Edgar Hoover	公平是伴随着法律和法令而来的。 　　——J.埃德加·胡佛
The great object of the law is to encourage commerce. 　　—Judge Chambre	法律的主要目标是鼓励商业发展。 　　——尚布尔法官
Listening to both sides does not necessarily bring about a correct judgment. 　　—Donald Rumsfeld	听取两方的意见并不一定能做出正确的判决。 　　——唐纳德·拉姆斯菲尔德
Lawyers cannot remain empty of head and pure of heart.... A lawyer has a duty to investigate or take some steps to inform himself in a situation where he believes that there is client perjury. 　　—Barry S. Alberts	律师们不能保证自己的纯洁……他有义务研究或采取步骤使自己相信客户所讲的一切甚至伪证。 　　——巴里·S.艾伯特斯
The law, as manipulated by clever and highly respected rascals, still remains the best avenue for a career of honorable and leisurely plunder. 　　—Gabriel Chevallier	法律由聪明的且受人尊敬的混蛋所控制，它仍然是取得可以从容掠夺的荣耀事业的最佳途径。 　　——加百列·谢瓦列
Perhaps the adage that hard cases make bad law should be revised to cover easy cases. 　　—Justice John Paul Stevens	也许谚语"难办的案件引出坏法律"应修改为简单案件同时适用。 　　——约翰·保罗·史蒂文斯大法官
When there are too many policeman, there can be no liberty; when there are too many soldiers, there can be no peace; when there are too many lawyers, there can be no justice. 　　—Lin Yutang	警察过多，可能会失去自由； 战士过多，可能会失去和平； 律师过多可能会失去公正。 　　——林语堂
Singularity is almost invariably a clue. The more featureless and commonplace a crime is, the more difficult is it to bring it. 　　—Sir Arthur Conan Doyle	奇特几乎总能提供一种线索。一种犯罪越是普通，越是不具特点，就越难以查明。 　　——柯南·道尔爵士
Every kind of peaceful cooperation among men is primarily based on mutual trust and only secondly on institutions such as courts of justice and police. 　　—Einstein	人类一切和平合作的基础首先是相互信任，其次才是法庭和警察一类的机构。 　　——爱因斯坦
If we only had some God in the country's laws, instead of beng in such a sweat to get him into the Constitution, it would be better all around. 　　—Mark Twain	如果我们国家的法律中只有某种神灵，而不是殚精竭虑将神灵揉进宪法，总体上来说，法律就会更好。 　　——马克·吐温
Pubic officers are the servats and agents of the people, to execute the laws which the people have made. 　　—Cleveland	政府官员是人民的公仆和代理人，应执行人民制定的法律。 　　——克利夫兰
I will not accept if nominated, and will serve if selected. 　　—William Sherman	如果被任命，我不愿接受，但是如果被选上，将效力。 　　——威廉·谢尔曼
An incompetent attorney can delay a trial for months or years. A competent attorney can delay one even longer. 　　—Evelle J. Younger	一个不合格的律师可以把审判拖上几个月或几年；而合格的律师甚至可以拖更长。 　　——伊夫林·J.扬格

(续表)

英文	中文
Really, what we want now, is not laws, against crime, but a law a-gainst insaity. —Mark Twain	实际上,我们想要的不是针对犯罪的法律,而是针对疯狂的法律。 ——马克·吐温
Law can nerver be enforced unless fear supports it. —Sophocles	如果法律没有恐惧支撑,它绝不能生效。 ——索福克勒斯
The laws of Nature, that is to say the laws of God, plainly made every human being a law unto himself, we must steadfastly refuse to obey those laws, and we must as steadfastly stand by the conventions which ignore them, since the statutes furnish us peace, fairly good government and stability, and therefore are better for us than the laws of God, which would soon plunge us into confusion and disorder and anarchy if we should adopt them. —Mark Twain	自然法即神灵法,只是用来约束每一个个体的法律,我们必须坚定地拒绝遵守。我们应该坚定地遵守忽视神灵法的规章制度,因为规章制度赋予我们和平、比较好的政府和稳定,因而对我们来说,规章制度比神灵法更好,因为如果我们采用神灵法的话,他会将我们陷入迷惑、无序和无政府状态。 ——马克·吐温
The law cannot make all men equal, but they are all equal before the law. —Frederick Pollck	法律不能使人人平等,但是在法律面前人人是平等的。 ——弗雷德里克·波洛克
One of the laws of paleontology is that an animal which must protect itself with thick armor is degenerate. It is usually a sign that the species is on the road to extinction. —John Steinbeck	生物进化的规律之一就是:如果一种动物必须用厚厚的装甲来保护自己,表明它正在退化。这通常是一个物种走向消亡的标志。 ——约翰·斯坦贝克
My daddy is a movie actor, and sometimes he plays the good guy, and sometimes he plays the lawyer. —Malcolm Ford	我爸爸是个电影演员,有时他演好人,但有时他也演律师。 ——马尔科姆·福特
There is no better way of exercising the imagination than the study of law. No poet ever interpreted nature as freely as a lawyer interprets the truth. —Jean Giraudoux	没有比学习法律更能锻炼人的想象力。没有一个诗人能像律师解释事实一样自由地解说阐释事实。 ——让·吉兰多恩克斯
Concepts such as truth, justice, compassion are often the only bulwarks which stand against ruthless power. —Aung San Suu Kyi	诸如真理、公平及同情等观念通常是抵制暴力的唯一屏障。 ——翁山苏姬
There are not enough jails, not enough policemen, not enough courts to enforce a law not supported by the people. —Hubert H. Humphrey	如果一项法律没有人民的支持,那么即使再多的监狱,再多的警察,再多的法庭也不能去执行它。 ——休伯特·霍·汉弗莱
There is no American right to loot stores, or to burn buildings, or to fire rifles from the rooftops. That is crime — and crime must be dealt with forcefully and swiftly, and certainly — under the law. —Lyndon Baines Johnson	任何美国人都没有权利去犯罪,如抢掠商店或到大厦纵火或从屋顶随便开枪。犯罪必将在很短的时间内受到法律严厉的制裁。 ——林登·贝恩斯·约翰逊
Most of the trouble in the world is caused by people wanting to be important. —T. S. Eliot	世界上大部分的麻烦都是要想成为伟大人物的人搞出来的。 ——艾略特

(续表)

英文	中文
The objector and the rebel who raises his voice against what he believes to be the injustice of the present and the wrongs of the past is the one who hunches the world along. —Clarence Darrow	反对者和反抗者以自己的声音反对自认为现实的不公平和过去的错误,通常他们都是世界发展的推动者。 ——克拉伦斯·达罗
The danger of success is that it makes us forget the world's dreadful injustice. —Jules Renard	成功的危险在于使我们忘记世界上可怕的不公正。 ——朱尔斯·勒纳尔
In my time I have seen truth that was anything under the sun but just, and I have seen justice using tools and instruments I wouldn't want to touch with a 10-foot fence rail. —William Faulkner	在我的有生之年,我已经看见了真理,但它决非正义。我已经看见正义正在使用各种工具,我非常不愿意接触它们,即使在我们之间有一条10英尺长的防护栏存在。 ——威廉·福克纳
Man's capacity for justice makes democracy possible; but man's inclination to injustice makes democracy necessary. —Reinhold Niebuhr	人类维护正义的能力使民主政治成为可能;但人类非正义倾向使民主政治成为必需。 ——雷恩霍德·尼布尔
In the little world in which children have their existence, whosoever brings them up, there is nothing so finely perceived and so finely felt, as injustice. —Charles Dickens	在儿童生活的世界里,不管谁抚养他们,他们都不会敏锐地感觉到不公平。 ——查尔斯·狄更斯
The world's history is constant, like the laws of nature, and simple, like the souls of men. The same conditions continually produce the same results. —Friedrich von Schiller	世界的历史是恒定的,就如法律的本质;又是单纯的,就如人类的灵魂。相同的条件总是产生相同的结果。 ——弗雷德里希·冯·席勒
We live in a stage of politics, where legislators seem to regard passage of laws as much more important than the results of their enforcement. —William Howard Taft	我们生活在政治舞台上,在这里立法者把法律的通过看得比其实施结果重要得多。 ——威廉·霍华德·塔夫脱
Envy, among other ingredients, has a mixture of love of justice in it. We are more angry at undeserved than at deserved good fortune. —William Hazlitt	在其他因素中的嫉妒包含了对正义的热爱。与理所当然的好运相比,我们更憎恨不正当的好运。 ——威廉·哈兹里特
Few of us have enough wisdom for justice or enough leisure for humanity. —Rex Stout	我们很少有人有足够的智慧思考公平或有足够的时间体验人性。 ——雷克斯·斯托特
The biggest gap in the world is the gap between the justice of a cause and the motives of the people pushing it. —John P. Grier	世界上最悬殊的差距就是目标的正确性与推动目标实现的人的动机之间的差距。 ——约翰·P.格瑞尔
All ambitions are lawful except those which climb upward on the miseries or credulities of mankind. —Joseph Conrad	所有的野心都是合法的,除非它是建立在人类的不幸或轻信基础之上。 ——约瑟夫·康拉德

(续表)

英文	中文
It's a good thing justice is blind; she might not like some of the things done in her name if she could see them. —Joe Moore	正义(女神)盲了是件幸运的事。因为如果她能看见的话,她可能不喜欢看见一些以她的名义所做的事情。 ——乔·摩尔
Lawyers as a group are no more dedicated to justice or public service than a private public utility is dedicated to giving light. —David Melinkoff	作为一个群体,律师并未像私营公共事业公司致力于提供光源一样致力于司法公正或公用事业。 ——大卫·麦林科夫
The Constitution of the United States is not a mere lawyers' document; it is a vehicle of life, and its spirit is always the spirit of the age. —Woodrow Wilson	美国宪法不仅仅是律师们起草的文件。它是生活的工具,通常是时代的灵魂。 ——伍德罗·威尔逊
Cruelty is the law pervading all nature and society; and we can't get out of it if we would. —Thomas Hardy	残忍是一种无所不在的规律,我们不能避开它。 ——托马斯·哈代
Justice was born outside the home and a long way from it; and it has never been adopted there. —Walter Cronkite	正义诞生在遥远的国外,从来没有被国内采纳过。 ——沃尔特·克朗凯特
Justice is too good for some people, and not good enough for the rest. —Norman Douglas	对一部分人而言,司法是非常公正的,而对其他的人来讲,司法的公正程度还远远不够。 ——诺曼·道格拉斯
The police must obey the law while enforcing the law. —Earl Warren	警察在执法时必须守法。 ——厄尔·沃伦
Laws too gentle are seldom obeyed; too severe, seldom executed. —Benjamin Franklin	法律如果太温和,很少有人去遵守它;如果太严厉,很少有人去执行它。 ——本杰明·富兰克林
Corn can't expect justice from a court composed of chickens. —African proverb	谷粒不可能指望从由鸡组成的法庭上得到公平。 ——非洲谚语
Laws and institutions must go hand in hand with the progress of the human mind. —Thomas Jefferson	法律制度必须与人类智力发展同步。 ——托马斯·杰斐逊
Every law is an evil, for every law is an infraction of liberty. —Jeremy Bentham	任何法律都有害,因为每项法律都侵犯自由。 ——杰里米·边沁
The slave begins by demanding justice and ends by wanting to wear a crown. He must dominate in his turn. —Albert Camus	奴隶的身份由要求公正开始,在渴望王冠时结束。他必须处于统治地位。 ——阿尔贝特·卡缪
Military justice is to justice what military music is to music. —Groucho Marx	军事司法与司法的关系正如同军乐同音乐的关系。 ——格罗克·马克思

(续表)

英文	中文
Crime is contagious. If a government becomes a lawbreaker, it breeds contempt for the law; it invites every man to become a law unto himself. ——Justice Louis D. Brandeis	犯罪是会传染的。如果一个政府成为犯法者,那么它将会四处传播轻视法律的种子,导致每个人将自己置于法律之上。 ——路易斯·德·布兰德斯法官
It is better to be a mouse in a cat's mouth than a man in a lawyer's hands. ——Spanish proverb	在猫嘴里的老鼠的境遇好过在律师手中的人。 ——西班牙谚语
Let all the laws be clear, uniform and precise; to interpret laws is always almost to corrupt them. ——Voltaire	让所有的法律都清晰、一致和准确,解释它们通常都是破坏它们。 ——伏尔泰
Believe in no other God than the one who insists on justice and equality among men. ——George Sand	只信仰坚持公正与平等的上帝。 ——乔治·桑
Liberty is obedience to the law which one has laid down for oneself. ——Jean-Jacques Rousseau	自由是遵守人们自己制定的法律。 ——让—雅克·卢梭
If you have ten thousand regulations you destroy all respect for the law. ——Winston Churchill	如果你有一万条法规,那么你将毁掉所有对法律的尊敬。 ——温斯顿·丘吉尔
In a democracy only those laws which have their basis in folkways or the approval of strong groups have a chance of being enforced. ——Abraham Myerson	在民主社会,法律只当它建立在公序民俗基础上或得到强力集团的首肯,才有机会付诸实施。 ——亚伯拉罕·梅耶森
What do you get in place of a conscience? Don't answer. I know: a lawyer. ——Detective Story	你用什么替代良心?不用说我也知:律师。 ——《侦探的故事》
Parents are not quite interested in justice, they are interested in quiet. ——Bill Cosby	父母(那一辈人)并不在意公平,只对安宁感兴趣。 ——比尔·考斯贝
Two farmers each claimed to own a certain cow. While one pulled on its head and the other pulled on its tail, the cow was milked by a lawyer. ——Jewish parable	两个农夫分别宣布拥有某头牛,当他们一个抓着牛头另一个抓着牛尾(相持不下)时,牛奶最后都会被律师挤走。 ——犹太格言
It is not what a lawyer tells me I may do; but what humanity, reason, and justice tell me I ought to do. ——Edmund Burke	不是律师告诉我可以做,而是人性、理智及正义告诉我必须做。 ——埃德蒙·伯克
Every society gets the kind of criminal it deserves. What is equally true is that every community gets the kind of law enforcement it insists on. ——Robert F. Kennedy	什么样的社会就有什么样的罪犯。同理,任何社会都会坚持其固有的执法程序。 ——约翰·F.肯尼迪
The laws of conscience, which we pretend to be derived from nature, proceed from custom. ——Michel de Montaigne	法律的道德准则,我们自称取自自然,实际上出自传统习俗。 ——米哈伊·德·蒙田

（续表）

英文	中文
Of course, people are getting smarter nowadays; they are letting lawyers instead of their conscience be their guides. ——Will Rogers	当然,现在人们已变得越来聪明,总是以自律师而不是良心作为处理事情的向导。 ——威·罗杰斯
When I hear any man talk of unalterable law, the only effect it produces on me is to convince me that he is an unalterable fool. ——Sydney Smith	当我听到别人谈论不可变更的法律时,给我的唯一的印象就是他是一个不折不扣的傻瓜。 ——西德尼·史密斯
Human law may know no distinction among men in respect of rights, but human practice may. ——Frederick Douglass	人为的法律在人权方面没有区别,但是法律实践在人权方面有区别。 ——弗雷德里克·道格拉斯

课后习题参考答案

第二章

1. 翻译下列法律术语。

active capacity 民事行为能力	返还财产 restitution
rights of the person 人身权	名义当事人 nominal party
court of arbitration 仲裁庭	临终遗嘱 deathbed will/testament
judgment of last resort 终审判决	养父母 adoptive parents
final judgment 终局判决	避税 tax avoidance
citation of authorities 对法律权威的引证（援引，引用）	上诉法院 appellate court
legal fiction 法律拟制	司法审查 judicial review
doctrine of constitutional supremacy 宪法至上原则	颁布一部法律 promulgate a law
bona fide mortgage 善意抵押	欧洲人权委员会 European Commission of Human Rights
a case tried *de novo* 重新审理的案件（*de novo*＝anew，重新）	立法解释 legislative interpretation
body corporate 法人	具结悔过 make a statement of repentance
in light of the specific conditions of the case 根据案件具体情况	传闻证据 hearsay; hearsay evidence
demurrer to the jurisdiction 管辖权异议	区域自治 regional autonomy
delivery by installments 分期交货（交付）	普遍选举权 universal suffrage
notarial will 公证遗嘱	世界人权宣言 Universal Declaration of Human Rights
action *in rem* 对物（物权）诉讼	资产负债表 balance sheet
bailiff 法庭事务官（执达官）	以剥夺财产相胁迫 duress of/to goods (or property)

(续表)

actionable nuisance 可起诉的妨害（妨害行为）	初审法院 court of first instance; trial court
forcible felony 暴力性重罪	公诉人 public prosecutor
false imprisonment 非法拘禁	司法协助 judicial assistance
trespass to chattels 侵害他人动产	对领土无可争辩的主权 indisputable sovereignty over the territory
tort liability for negligence 过失侵权责任	法律冲突 conflict of laws
insurance premium 保险费	从合同 accessory /collateral contract
coercion in fact 事实上的胁迫	共同共有权 joint ownership
general average contribution 共同海损分担	原始取得 original acquisition
pecuniary damages 金钱损害赔偿	双边条约 bilateral treaty
extort confessions by torture 刑讯逼供	不当得利 unjust enrichment
parol contract 口头合同	民事责任 civil liability/ responsibility
consensus *ad idem* 合意（*ad idem*，相当于 identical，一致的，相同的）	合同的期满 expiry/expiration of a contract
contempt of court 藐视法庭（罪）	互惠贸易协定 reciprocal trade agreement

2. 请翻译以下段落，请注意画线部分的翻译。

（1）经众议院和参议院通过的法案，在正式成为法律之前，须呈送合众国总统；总统如批准，便须签署，如不批准，即应连同他的异议把它退还给原来提出该案的议院，该议院应将异议详细记入议事记录，然后进行复议。倘若在复议之于，该议院议员的三分之二仍然同意通过该法案，该院即应将该法案连同异议书送交另一院，由其同样予以复议，若此另一院亦以三分之二的多数通过，该法案即成为法律。但遇有这样的情形时，两院的表决均应以赞同或反对来定，而赞同和反对该法案的议员的姓名，均应由两院分别记载于该院的议事记录之内。如总统接到法案后十日之内（星期日除外），不将之退还，该法案即等于曾由总统签署一样，成为法律。当国会休会因而无法将该法案退还时，该法案才不得成为法律。（《美利坚合众国宪法》第1章第7款）

（2）All nationalities in the People's Republic of China are equal. The state protects the lawful rights and interests of the minority nationalities and upholds and develops the relationship of equality, unity and mutual assistance among all of China's nationalities. Discrimination against and oppression of any nationality are prohibited; any acts that undermine the unity of the nationalities or instigate their secession are prohibited.

The state helps the areas inhabited by minority nationalities speed up their economic and cultural development in accordance with the peculiarities and needs of the different minority nationalities.

Regional autonomy is practiced in areas where people of minority nationalities live in compact communities; in these areas organs of self-government are established for the exercise of the right of autonomy. All the national autonomous areas are inalienable parts of the People's Republic of China.

The people of all nationalities have the freedom to use and develop their own spoken and written languages, and to preserve or reform their own ways and customs.

(*The Constitution of the People's Republic of China*，Article 4)

3. 翻译下列合同文本节选部分。

第三章　价格和支付

（适用于一次总支付）

考虑到许可方全面且适当履行其合同义务，被许可方同意向许可方支付总价为_____（币种）_____（大写：_____整），该款项以电汇方式通过被许可方银行转至许可方银行。具体分项如下：

　　A. 许可费：_____（大写：_____整）；

　　B. 设计费：_____（大写：_____整）；

　　C. 技术资料费：_____（大写：_____整）；

　　D. 技术服务费：_____（大写：_____整）；

　　E. 技术培训费：_____（大写：_____整）。

上述合同总价为固定价格，包括了技术资料的交付、技术服务和技术培训的提供等所有支出和费用，其技术资料价格为DDU目的地机场交付价。

本章3.1条A、B、C、E项所规定的合同价格将由许可方依照下列方式和比例支付给被许可方：

3.3.1　该款的_____%，即_____（大写：_____整）在被许可方收到许可方提交的下列单据并经审核无误后_____天内支付给许可方：

　　A. 许可方国家有关当局出具的有效的出口许可证或不需出口许可证的证明文件，正本一份，副本两份；

　　B. 许可方银行出具的金额为_____元（大写：_____整）以被许可方为受益人的对预付款的不可撤销保函正本一份，副本一份，保函格式件合同附件；

　　C. 金额为合同总价的形式发票一式五份；

　　D. 签发的标明支付金额的商业发票一式五份；

　　E. 即期汇票一式二份。

3.3.2　该款的_____%，即_____（大写：_____整）在被许可方收到许可方提交的下列单据并经审核无误后_____天内支付给许可方：

　　A. 标明"运费已付"的技术资料空运提单或交付技术资料的空运挂号收据，正本一份，副本三份；

B. 签发的标明支付金额的商业发票一式五份；

C. 即期汇票一式二份。

本章第 3.1 条 D 项规定的技术服务费在许可方的第一批技术人员到达工作现场后每_____月且被许可方收到许可方提交的下列单据并审核无误后_____天内支付给许可方：

A. 双方授权代表签署的"工时卡"一份；

B. 签发的标明支付金额的商业发票一式五份；

C. 即期汇票一式二份。

如果依据合同许可方应支付预提税、违约金和/或赔偿金，被许可方有权从应支付给许可方的款项中扣除。

所有在被许可方银行发生的费用均由被许可方承担，所有在被许可方银行外发生的银行费用均由许可方承担。（李克兴、张新红，2006：256—257）

第三章

1. 根据所学法律英语的翻译原则，改正下列各句画线部分在原译文中的错误或不妥之处。

(1) 原句的 negotiation，collection 此处准确的含义分别是"议付"和"托收"。

改译：卖方必须将下列单据提交银行议付或托收。

(2) 原句的 acceptance 翻译为"承兑"更精确

改译：如为远期汇票，持票人应在汇票到期前交由付款人提示承兑。

(3) 原译文没有体现法律合同翻译的严谨和准确，此处 upon 一词含有"后一个动作将在前一个动作之后随即或马上发生之意"，原译文存在漏洞，不精确。

改译：余款应在货物到达目的港后随行支付。

(4) 原译中对介词 on or before 翻译得不够精确和严密，改译的译文则不会导致曲解。

改译：装船：2007 年 2 月 28 日前（含 28 日）装船。

(5) 原句中 claim 在这里的意思是"索赔"，而不是一般意义上的"主张"。

改译：买方对于装货的任何索赔，必须于货到提单规定的目的地 15 天内提出，并须提供卖方同意的公证机构出具的检验报告。

(6) 原文中的 physically 这里应该译为"外界条件"，即认为以外的条件。

改译：除法律或外界条件不允许的情况之外，承包商应严格按合同施工和竣工，并改正工作中的任何缺陷，达到工程师满意的程度。

(7) 原文中的 hidden 被翻译成"收藏"不精确，可改译为"藏匿"；plaintiff 被翻译成"原告人"也不符合法律规范，可改译为"原告"。

改译：若该等证据被销毁或藏匿，则原告在该法院案件中取得胜诉更为困难。

(8) 原句中的 depreciate, jeopardize, prejudice the value 分别被翻译成"损耗""妨害""妨碍……的价值",这样的译文显然用词不当,不符合法律翻译的专业化原则,可改译为"贬低""危及""损害……的价值"。

改译:借款人将不会做出或促使或准许他人做出可能在任何方面贬低、危及或以其他方式损害代理人在本契据项下之抵押品的价值的任何事情。

(9) 原文中的"attorney"此处的确切含义应该是"受权人、代理人"而不是"律师"。

改译:借款人特此按照第13条规定作出一项不可撤消的委任,委任代理人及破产管理人作为其受权人。

(10) 原文中的"one of the Parties"在原译文中被翻译为"任何一方",而根据原文的逻辑关系,此处应翻译为"另一方"。

改译:如果一方破产、结束营业或在法律上或事实上直接或间接地被第三方所接管,另一方可立即终止本协议,任何一方无须就此做出赔偿。

2. 根据法律英语的翻译原则,改正或改进下列各句原译文的错误或不妥之处。

(1) 原译行文拖沓、有失简洁,与法律文本要求有一定距离。"management"强调"管理人员;经营才能;管理部门",而"governance"强调"管理方法",所以此处用"governance"较好。

改译:The new company shall establish an office for its daily governance.

(2) 原译文语句不够精炼,"export"就有"export products"之意,即"出口产品";"exempt from Customs duty"可用更简洁的词"duty-free"代替;"除……另有规定外",原文"except..."共有6个单词,而改为("unless...")只需要3个单词。

改译:Exports manufactured by foreign-invested enterprises in the New Area are duty-free, unless otherwise regulated by the State.

(3) 原文的"维护职工的合法权益"意为"维护职工的合法正当权益",因此译文用 lawful 欠准确,应译为"legitimate"。

改译:The staff and workers of a company organize a trade union in accordance with the law to carry out union activities and protect the legitimate rights and interests of the staff and workers.

(4) 英语中表示"要求"大致有3个,即 ask, request, require。ask 为泛指,request 和 require 为特指。request 是"请求某人做某事",是下对上的要求;而 require 表示 order, command,指上对下的要求,比如法律条款对当事人的要求,业主对雇员的要求。此句中人民法院对当事人的要求,应该是 require,原译文用 request 不准确。

改译:A People's court shall have the authority to require the parties to provide or supplement evidence.

(5) "经济责任"主要指合同当事人在违反合同时应承担的违约责任,主要形式有"赔偿损失""支付违约金""支付迟延支付金额的利息"等,所以经济责任应译为

"financial responsibility"而不应满足字面上的一致，译为"economic responsibility"。

改译：In case of losses caused by a breach of contract, the financial responsibility shall be borne by the party who has breached the contract.

（6）在补偿贸易合同项下，"偿付"指的是买方对卖方先行垫付的设备款项进行偿还，应译为"reimburse"如果译为"settle"则失去了"偿还"的意思。

改译：The buyers shall reimburse the sellers the total value of the entire equipment by installments in three years stating from June 1st, 1998.

第四章

1. 仔细阅读下列句子及其译文，分析各句中画线词语的含义与其在普通英语中含义的差异。

（1）原句中 swing, carry over and carry forward 是常用词和常用短语，分别解释为"摇摆""推迟""转换"，但是按照常用意义翻译，译文将无法理解。这些常用词语在该句中表达了不常用的含义，所以应该翻译为"调用""留用""借用"。

（2）原句中的 determination of injury, dumped imports, like products 不能望文生义而翻译成"损害的决心""堆放的产品"和"想象的产品"，这些常用词汇在该句中表达的是不常用的词义，因此分别翻译为"损害确定""倾销的进口产品"和"同类产品"。

（3）原句中 therewith 是指 connect with the high seas，使用这一古语，使得原句精炼、严谨和庄严。

（4）原句中由 shall 构成的谓语用来表示汉语的"应当"，表示法律义务或职责。

（5）原句中的 bona fide 是拉丁语，有"真诚的""善意的"的意思。句中使用拉丁语使该法律条款庄重、严肃。

（6）原句中的 publicly available 是赘言，法律一经颁布，当然就是公布于众，因此不需要再在译文中添加"可为公众获得的"之类的赘言。

（7）原句中的 jointly and severally 是法律用语，通常用于 jointly and severally liable（应承担连带责任）。在本句中，"binds them jointly and severally"表示"各人共同和分别受其约束"。

（8）原句中 department 和 concerned 在法律背景下的含义分别是"机构"和"承运的"，而不是一般意义上的"部门"和"有关的"。

（9）原文中的 elect 作为不及物动词，在法律文件中属于"正式"词 choose or decide to do something，这里应译为"决定"，而不是"选举"。句中 so elects 用来代替"to purchase the interest to be transferred at fair market value"，为避免重复，译文用"此等意向"表达"so"的含义。

（10）"material"一词，用作名词时解作"材料""物质"。该词在经贸法律等文本中可作形容词,表示"重大的""实质的"的意思。

2. 仔细阅读下列句子及其译文,找出译句中能体现相关法律英语词汇特点之处并加以分析。

(1)译文 there is no agreement 后面用了 therein 这一法律文件中常用的古体词语,为 agreement 下了明确的界说,指 agreement in the contract。因 therein 表示 in that, in that particular context, in that respect 之意,在此它指上文所指的范围。该词的运用,增加了译文的庄严感。

(2)译文中使用了法律文件中常用的古体词语 there from,表示 from the original article,准确指出 interest 的来源,同时也使译文显得严谨和正式。另外,译句中使用了表示法律义务的词汇 shall,表明当事人的法律义务。

(3)原句中的动词"遵守"在词典上可译为"observe","obey","comply with"表示"to act in accordance with a provision, rule, demand"。

(4)译文中的 convene 属于法律词语,比 call 正式。前者语义明确,指"召集,召开",没有其他联想意义;后者多为多义词,容易产生歧义。

3. 请写出表格中拉丁语的英文和中文含义,并将用法举例中的英文译成中文。

拉丁词语	英文含义	中文含义	用法举例
ab initio	from the beginning	从头,自始	trespass ab initio 自始非法侵入他人土地之诉
ad interim	for the time between	过渡的/地,临时的/地	an ad interim report 临时报告
ad litem	for the lawsuit	为了诉讼(而指定的)	agent ad litem 诉讼代理人
alibi	elsewhere (when the offence was committed)	不在犯罪现场	lodge a special defense of alibi 提出不在犯罪现场的特别辩护
bona fide	in good faith	真诚的/地,守信的/地,善意的/地	bona fide holder (= holder in due course) 善意持票人
			bona fide error 善意(造成的)错误
mala fide	in bad faith	不真诚的/地,不守信的/地,恶意的/地	mala fide business purpose 恶意商业目的
bona fides(用作单数)	good faith	真诚,守信,善意	a party whose bona fides is unshakable 一贯真诚的当事人
mala fides(用作单数)	bad faith	不真诚,不守信,恶意	the mala fides of the company 公司的恶意
de novo	anew	重新	a case tried de novo 重新审理的案件

(续表)

拉丁词语	英文含义	中文含义	用法举例
ex parte	from one part	单方面的	an ex parte testimony 单方面的证言
flagrante delicto	with the crime still blazing; in flagrant delict	在犯罪现场,当场	be caught flagrante delicto 被当场捕获
habeas corpus	you should have the body	人身保护令(传讯诉讼当事人出庭的令状,当事人据以请求法庭审查拘押的合宪性,而非是否有罪)	Habeas Corpus Act 1679《1679年人身保护法》
in personam	against the person	对人	in personam action (action in personam) 对人诉讼,债权诉讼(基于个人权利遭受侵害而对被告提起的、要求获得赔偿的诉讼)
in rem	against the matter	对物	in rem action (action in rem) 对物诉讼,物权诉讼(原告主张收回被他人占有之物,或确立其对某物权利的诉讼)
inter alia	among other things	除别的因素外,除了其他事项,特别是	The contract stipulates, inter alia, that the parties shall submit any dispute to arbitration. 除了其他事项,合同规定,当事人应将任何争议提交仲裁。
lex loci	law of the place	发生地法律,当地的法律	lex loci actus 行为地法
non obstante verdicto	notwithstanding the verdict	尽管陪审团已做裁断;不顾陪审团裁断	judgment non obstante verdicto (法庭做出的)与陪审团裁断相反的判决(一方当事人否定另一方当事人诉讼请求的事由为陪审团所确认,但不足以推翻该诉讼请求;上诉法院根据一方当事人的重审请求,认为陪审团裁断不当,而所有必需证据均已呈交法庭)
nunc pro tunc	now for then	溯及既往,事后补正	nunc pro tunc judgment 追溯性判决(修正以前判决记录的错误,其效力追溯至被修正判决做出之时)
per capita	by heads	人均;按人数	per capita consumption 人均消费
per curiam	by the court	依法院,由法庭一致同意	per curiam opinion/decision 法庭意见(全体法官的一致意见)

(续表)

拉丁词语	英文含义	中文含义	用法举例
per se	by itself	亲自，自身	negligence per se, per se negligence 法律上的当然过失（被告违反法定义务，对原告造成损害） nuisance per se, per se nuisance 本身妨害（某一行为（如危及他人生命，损害公德）、建筑物等本身构成妨害，为法律禁止）
pro rata	according to the rate	按比例，成比例	pro rata contribution（共同债务人之间）按比例分担债务
pro tem/tempore	for the time, for the time being	临时，暂时	pro tempore judge 临时法官（在正式法官缺席或因故不能履行职责等情形下，临时选任的法官）
seriatim	one after another	逐条，逐一	deliver their opinions seriatim 逐一发表看法
sui generis	of sb.'s/its own kind	独特的，自成一类的	sui generis qualities 独特品质
ultra vires	beyond the power	越权的/地	ultra vires act 越权行为
versus	against	对；诉	the plaintiff versus the defendant 原告诉被告

第五章

1. 汉译英，并分析其句法特征和涉及的典型句式。

(1) The Supreme People's Court will set up circuit courts, and the country will explore establishing cross-administrative region courts and procuratorates, and seek to allow prosecutors to initiate public interest litigations.

(2) Under the 4th plenary session of the 18th CPC Central Committee, the general target is to establish a system serving "the socialist rule of law with Chinese characteristics" and build a country under "the socialist rule of law."

(3) Under the 4th plenary session of the 18th CPC Central Committee, the major tasks are to improve a socialist system of laws with Chinese characteristics, in which the Constitution is taken as the core, and strengthen the implementation of the Constitution; to promote administration by law, and accelerate the building of a government under the rule of law; to safeguard judicial justice and improve judicial credibility; to promote the public awareness of rule of law, and enhance the building of a law-based society.

(4) Two or more obligees or obligors involved in one transaction are to enjoy their rights or do their duties respectively in specified shares.

2. 英译汉。

(1) 在不损害律政司权利的原则下,每名申诉人或告发人可进行其申诉或告发,并亲自或由代表律师讯问及盘问证人。

(2) 若一仲裁开始审理后,申请人未出庭,则仲裁处有权中止该仲裁的审理,但该决定不影响申请人以仲裁处认为合理的理由提出,要求恢复该仲裁的申请。

(3) 被许可方无权就上述任何行为起诉或要求许可方起诉,但许可方可自行决定并自付费用,以许可方和被许可方双方名义或任何一方名义,对实际发生或似将发生的商标侵权行为提起诉讼,或以其他方式阻止或防止该等侵权行为。无论许可方采取前述任何行动,被许可方均应提供许可方所要求的一切合理协助。

(4) 虽有第(4)款(a)项以及第(4)款、第(5)款除外条款规定,附着物出租人的权益,包括出租人的剩余权益,货物在建筑物建设完成之前成为附着物的,从属于不动产抵押权人根据建筑物抵押记录取得的冲突性权益。在建筑物抵押再融资的范围内,抵押权人的冲突性权益在相同范围内与建筑物抵押权人享有同等优先权。

(5) 除根据及按照本条的条文外,不得就裁判官在一项他在法律上并无司法管辖权或超越其司法管辖权的事项上所做的任何作为,在民事法庭提出针对裁判官的诉讼。

(6) 除非本条例另有规定,否则凡属仲裁处司法管辖权范围内的申索,不得在任何法庭进行诉讼。

(7) 除成文法另有规定外,对于因不缴付根据定罪裁定须缴付的款项(不论是罚款或就作为罪行主体的财物而须缴付的款项),或因犯罪者所造成的损害,或因无足够扣押物以抵偿此等款项,则行使简易程序审判权的裁判官,可判处其认为就案情而言是符合公正原则的监禁刑期,但无论如何不得超过下表所定的最长刑期……。

(8) 除了(c)中包括的背书外,如果票据载有使用下列词句的背书,即付款应向作为代理人、受托人的被背书人做出或向其他为了背书人或另一人的利益的受托人做出,就应适用下列规则:……

(9) 基于租务条例并基于这些通知,有关该楼宇的租金,如果未照合约第一条规定的那样提前缴付,应被视为是拖欠。

(10) 凡雇员获给予任何一段期间的年假,雇主最迟须于该段期间后的第一个发薪日付给该雇员该段期间的年假薪酬。

第六章

1. 请翻译下列文章标题。

(1) On Administration According to the Law 或 On Administration Upon Law Administration

(2) Make China An Innovative Nation

（3）Deepening Reform and Opening Wider to the out side World to Readjust Economic Structure

（4）Government Power Can Only Be Used for Public Good Not for Personal Gains

（5）Probe into the Verification and Compensation for Psychic Damage

（6）On the Law of the Development of Cultural and Ethical Progress

（7）Core Socialist Values Winning the Hearts and Minds of the People

（8）Communiqué of the Fourth Plenary Session of the 18th Central Committee of the Communist Party of China

（9）Humanistic Concept as a Necessity for Economic and Social Development During "the 10th Five-year Plan" 或 The Necessity of Humanism in Economic and Social Development During "the 10th Five-year Plan"

（10）National Debts Used as Starting Funds for the Economic Growth of Underdeveloped Areas

2. 请翻译中美两国宪法序言。

（1）PREAMBLE

In building socialism it is imperative to rely on the workers, peasants and intellectuals and unite with all the forces that can be united. In the long years of revolution and construction, there has been formed under the leadership of the Communist Party of China a broad patriotic united front that is composed of democratic parties and people's organizations and embraces all socialist working people, all patriots who support socialism and all patriots who stand for reunification of the motherland. This united front will continue to be consolidated and developed. The Chinese People's Political Consultative Conference is a broadly representative organization of the united front, which has played a significant historical role and will continue to do so in the political and social life of the country, in promoting friendship with the people of other countries and in the struggle for socialist modernization and for the reunification and unity of the country.

The People's Republic of China is a unitary multi-national state built up jointly by the people of all its nationalities. Socialist relations of equality, unity and mutual assistance have been established among them and will continue to be strengthened. In the struggle to safeguard the unity of the nationalities, it is necessary to combat big-nation chauvinism, mainly Han chauvinism, and also necessary to combat local-national chauvinism. The state does its utmost to promote the common prosperity of all nationalities in the country.

China's achievements in revolution and construction are inseparable from support by the people of the world. The future of China is closely linked with that of the whole world. China adheres to an independent foreign policy as well as to the five principles of mutual respect for sovereignty and territorial integrity, mutual non-aggression, non-interference in each other's internal affairs, equality and mutual benefit, and peaceful coexistence in developing diplomatic relations and economic and cultural exchanges with other countries; China consistently opposes imperialism, hegemonism and colonialism, works to strengthen unity with the people of other countries, supports the oppressed nations and the developing countries in their just struggle to win and preserve national independence and develop their national economies, and strives to safeguard world peace and promote the cause of human progress.

This Constitution affirms the achievements of the struggles of the Chinese people of all nationalities and defines the basic system and basic tasks of the state in legal form; it is the fundamental law of the state and has supreme legal authority. The people of all nationalities, all state organs, the armed forces, all political parties and public organizations and all enterprises and undertakings in the country must take the Constitution as the basic norm of conduct, and they have the duty to uphold the dignity of the Constitution and ensure its implementation.

(2) 序言

我们美利坚合众国的人民,为了组织一个更完善的联邦,树立正义,保障国内的安宁,建立共同的国防,增进全民福利和确保我们自己及我们后代能安享自由带来的幸福,乃为美利坚合众国制定和确立这一部宪法。

3.请翻译下列法条,尤其注意各条文之间的结构安排。

合同引致的法律责任

(1) 如立约一方以消费者身份交易,或者按另一方的书面标准业务条款交易,则本条适用于处理立约各方之间的问题。

(2) 对上述的立约一方,另一方不能借合约条款而——

(a) 在自己违反合约时,卸除或局限与违约有关的法律责任;或

(b) 声称有权——

(i) 在履行合约时,所履行的与理当期望他会旅行的有颇大的分别;或

(ii) 完全不履行其依约应承担的全部或部分法律义务,但在该合约条款(与本款上述的任何情况下)符合合理标准的范围内,则不在此限。

〔比照 1997 c. 50 s. 3 U. K.〕

4．请翻译下列法律条文。

Two months before the expiration of the term of office of a National People's Congress, its Standing Committee **must** ensure that the election of deputies to the succeeding National People's Congress is completed. Should exceptional circumstances prevent such an election, it **may** be postponed by decision of a majority vote of more than two-thirds of all those on the Standing Committee of the incumbent National People's Congress, and the term of office of the incumbent National People's Congress may be extended. The election of deputies to the succeeding National People's Congress **must** be completed within one year after the termination of such exceptional circumstances.

5．请翻译下列法条，尤其注意各句子结构的分析。

A mentally ill person who causes dangerous consequences at a time when he is unable to recognize or unable to control his own conduct is not to bear criminal responsibility; but his family or guardian shall be ordered to subject him to strict surveillance and arrange for his medical treatment.

A person whose mental illness is of an intermittent nature shall bear criminal responsibility if he commits a crime during a period of mental normality.

An intoxicated person who commits a crime shall bear criminal responsibility.

6．请将下列文本译成汉语。

（1）为求实现第一条所述各宗旨起见，本组织及其会员国应遵行下列原则：

① 本组织系基于各会员国主权平等之原则。

② 各会员国应一秉善意，履行其依本宪章所担负之义务，以保证全体会员国由加入本组织而发生之权益。

③ 各会员国应以和平方法解决其国际争端，避免危及国际和平、安全及正义。

④ 各会员国在其国际关系上不得使用威胁或武力，或以与联合国宗旨不符之任何其他方法，侵害任何会员国或国家之领土完整或政治独立。

⑤ 各会员国对于联合国依本宪章规定而采取之行动，应尽力予以协助，联合国对于任何国家正在采取防止或执行行动时，各会员国对该国不得给予协助。

⑥ 本组织在维持国际和平及安全之必要范围内，应保证非联合国会员国遵行上述原则。

⑦ 本宪章不得认为授权联合国干涉在本质上属于任何国家国内管辖之事件，且并不要求会员国将该项事件依本宪章提请解决；但此项原则不妨碍第七章内执行办法之适用。

（2）2-201 正式要求；反欺诈法

① 除本条另有规定外，价格为 500 或 500 美元以上的货物买卖合同经行为或抗

辩均不具有执行力,除非存在足以表明买卖合同已由双方当事人订立并由被执行人或其授权代表或经纪人签署的书面材料。一份书面材料并非不充分,如果其遗漏或不正确地描述经协商一致的条款,但是,如果一份合同超过上述材料所显示的数量,则在本节中不具有执行力。

②在商人之间,如果在合理时间内,一份确认合同且对于递送者而言是充分的书面材料被接收了,而且接收方有理由知道该材料的内容,则对上述当事人而言,该材料满足了(1)款的要求,除非在接收该材料后的10天内做过一份反对其内容的书面通知。

③一份不满足(1)款要求的合同若满足下列情况,则其仍可生效,

(i)如果货物是为买方特别制造,且在买方的一般商业过程中不适用与出售给其他人,而且在否认通知被收到之前,情况合理表明货物是为买方制造的,且卖方已经开始实质性地制造货物或承诺制造货物;或者

(ii)如果在其答辩、证言或法庭上,被要求履约方承认买卖合同已经成立,但是该合同若超过承认的货物数量,则在本条中不具有执行力;或者

(iii)对货物的支付已经做出并被接受或者货物已被接收和接受。

7. 请将下列文本译成英语。

It was stressed at the session that the Party's leadership is the most essential feature of socialism with Chinese characteristics and the most fundamental guarantee for socialist rule of law in China. The need to exercise the Party's leadership throughout the whole process and in every aspect of the law-based governance of the country is a basic lesson we have learned in developing socialist rule of law in China.

The position of leadership of the CPC is written into China's Constitution. Upholding the Party's leadership is fundamental to socialist rule of law; it is the foundation and lifeblood of both the Party and the country, affects the interests and wellbeing of people of all China's ethnic groups, and is an integral part of our efforts to comprehensively advance the law-based governance of the country. The Party's leadership is consistent with socialist rule of law: socialist rule of law must uphold the Party's leadership, while the Party's leadership must rely upon socialist rule of law.

Only through the law-based governance of China and insisting on the rule of law, both under the leadership of the Party, can we ensure that the people fully act as masters of the country, and can we steadily increase the level of rule of law in the country and in society. To exercise state power based on law, the Party not only has to govern the country in accordance with the Constitution and laws, but also has to ensure that its self-governance is in line with its own rules and regulations.

It was made clear at the session that the major tasks of comprehensively advancing the law-based governance of the country are as follows:

　　• to improve the socialist system of laws with Chinese characteristics, at the heart of which is the Constitution, and strengthen the implementation of the Constitution;

　　• to thoroughly advance the administration of government on the basis of the law and accelerate our efforts to build a rule of law government;

　　• to ensure judicial impartiality and improve judicial credibility;

　　• to strengthen the notion of the rule of law among all Chinese people and drive forward the development of a rule of law society;

　　• to raise the level of competence of rule of law professionals; and

　　• to strengthen and improve the Party's leadership over efforts to comprehensively advance the law-based governance of the country.

第七章

1. 将下列段落译成汉语。

（1）本合同的订立、效力、解释、执行及合同争议的解决，均受中华人民共和国法律的管辖。

（2）一方欲将其全部或部分注册资本出资额转让给第三方时，应向另一方提供书面通知。

（3）如果甲方实质性违反本合同，乙方或其权益继承人有权终止本合同或要求得到损害赔偿。如果乙方实质性违反本合同，甲方经发出书面通知，有权要求乙方在收到书面通知后十五（15）天内改正违约行为。如果乙方在十五（15）天期限内未予改正，甲方则有权解除合同并要求得到违约赔偿。

（4）装运船只按期到达装运港后，如卖方不能按时装船发生的空船费或滞期费由卖方负担。

（5）货到目的港后，买方将申请中国商品检验局（以下简称商检局）对货物的规格和数量/重量进行检验。

（6）凭不可撤销的即期信用证付款，并于上述装运期后15天内在中国议付有效。

（7）收到通知后，未履行责任方应自费迅速采取必要措施弥补这类失误，如不能弥补失误或不能立即弥补，不能在接到被侵害一方的通知后10天内采取有效措施改正失误，被侵害一方可终止协议。

（8）本合同由买卖双方缔结，用中英文写成，两种文本具有同等效力，按照下述条款，卖方同意购进以下商品：

（9）对公司提供的所有有关制造及其产品销售的信息，市场（调研）顾问有保密义务，未经授权，不能泄露。

（10）因退货或索赔引起的一切费用（包括检验费）及损失均由卖方负担。在此情况下，凡货物适于抽样者，如卖方要求，买方可将样品寄交卖方，但是，样品应属于可寄交的物品。

2. 将下列段落译成英语。

（1）After friendly consultations conducted in accordance with the principles of equality and mutual benefit, the Parties have agreed to enter into a distributorship relationship in accordance with the applicable laws and the provisions of this Contract.

（2）In order to protect knowledge transferred by the Supplier to the Distributor, the Distributor shall not manufacture, purchase, sell or resell goods that compete with products from the premises used by Distributor for a period of one year after the termination of this Contract.

（3）The prevented party shall notify the other party of the occurrence of a force majeure event by telex or e-mail within the shortest possible time and shall send by registered airmail, within 14 days thereafter, to the other party a certificate issued by the relevant competent authorities for the confirmation by the other party.

（4）The goals of the parties to the cooperative venture are to enhance economic cooperation and technical exchanges, to improve product quality, to develop new products, and to gain a competitive position in the world market in terms of quality and price by adopting advanced and appropriate technology and scientific management methods, so as to raise economic results and ensure satisfactory economic benefits for each Cooperator.

（5）Upon announcement of the termination of the Contract and/or the pending liquidation of the Joint Venture Company, the Board of Directors shall work out procedures and principles for liquidation and nominate candidates for the liquidation committee.

（6）Shipment during the period beginning April 1st and ending October 20th (both dates inclusive) is subject to the Buyer's Letter of Credit reaching the Seller on or before March 20th.

（7）Should the force majeure event last for more than one hundred and twenty consecutive days, both parties shall, through consultations, decide whether to terminate the contract or to exempt part of the obligations for implementation of the contract according to the effects of events on the performance of the contract.

（8）If an event of force majeure occurs, a Party's contractual obligations affected by such an event under this contract shall be suspended during the period of this delay caused by the force majeure and shall be automatically extended, without penalty or liability, for a period equal to such suspension.

(9) Should either of the parties to the contract be prevented from executing the contract by force majeure (such as earthquake, typhoon, flood, fire, war or other unforeseen events) and their occurrence and consequences are unpreventable and unavoidable, the prevented party shall notify the other party by telegram without delay, and within 15 days thereafter provide detailed information of the events and a valid document for evidence issued by the relevant public notary organization explaining the reason for its inability to execute or delay in the execution of all or part of the contract.

(10) If, on the expiry of a contract, the term for a patent relating to the imported technology has yet to expire, the case shall be handled in accordance with the relevant provisions.

(11) Both parties will solve any disputes arising from the execution of the contract or in connection with the contract through friendly consultation. In case an agreement cannot be reached, any party can submit the dispute to the court that has jurisdiction over the matter.

3. 请将下列文本译成英语。

(1) Chapter I General Provisions

Article 1 This Law is formulated and enacted in order to protect the lawful rights and interests of the parties to contracts, safeguard the social economic order and promote the progress of the socialist modernization drive.

Article 2 A contract defined in this Law refers to an agreement establishing, modifying and terminating the civil rights and obligations between subjects on an equal footing, that is, between natural persons, legal persons and other organizations.

Agreements involving personal status relationship such as on matrimony, adoption, guardianship, etc. shall apply within the provisions of other Laws.

Article 3 The parties to a contract shall have equal legal status. Neither party shall impose its will on the other party.

Article 4 The parties to the contract shall, in accordance with law, have the right to voluntarily conclude and enter into a contract. No unit or individual shall illegally interfere.

Article 5 The parties to the contract shall comply with the principle of fairness in defining the rights and obligations of the parties thereto.

Article 6 The parties to the contract shall, in accordance with the principle of good faith, execute the rights and perform the obligations thereof.

Article 7 The parties shall, in concluding and performing a contract, comply with the relevant laws administrative regulations, observe social ethics. Either party shall not disrupt the socio-economic order or damage the public interests.

Article 8 As soon as a contract is established in accordance with the law, it shall be legally binding on the parties. The parties shall perform their respective obligations in accordance with the terms of the contract. Neither party may unilaterally modify or rescind the contract.

The contract established in accordance with law shall be under the protection of law.

(2) Contracts for Intermediation

Article 424 An intermediation contract refers to a contract where-by the intermediator reports to the principal the opportunity for concluding a contract, and the principal pays the remuneration.

Article 425 The intermediator shall report truthfully to the principal the matters related to the conclusion of a contract.

Where the intermediator intentionally conceals the important facts relating to the conclusion of the contract or provides false information and harms the interests of the principal, the said party may not claim the payment of remuneration and shall be liable for damages.

Article 426 The principal shall pay the intermediator remuneration according to the terms of the contract if the intermediator has facilitated the establishment of a contract. Where there is no such agreement in the contract on remuneration or such agreement is unclear, nor can it be determined according to the provisions of Article 61 of this Law, the remuneration shall be determined reasonably according to the service rendered by the intermidiator. If the establishment of a contract has been facilitated by the intermediate service rendered by the intermediator, the remuneration shall be borne equally by the parties to the contract.

Where the intermediator has facilitated the conclusion of the contract, the expenses for the intermediate service shall be borne by the intermediator.

Article 427 Where the intermediator fails in facilitating the conclusion of a contract, the intermediator may not request for the payment of remuneration, but may request the principal to pay the necessary expenses for the intermediate service.

第八章

请将下面一份英文起诉书的正文部分翻译成中文。

原告简·杜特向西弗吉尼亚州布洛斯顿县巡回法院提出离婚诉讼请求：

一

原告系西弗吉尼亚州布洛斯顿县居民，并且在起诉前已连续在西弗吉尼亚州居住满一年。

二

被告系西弗吉尼亚州居民，其最近可知的通信地址为西弗吉尼亚州 26627，赫特斯，ABC 信箱。

三

原告与被告约翰·杜于 1967 年 6 月 11 日在西弗吉尼亚州刘易斯市结婚。

四

原被告婚后育有两子：菲利普·杜，生于 1978 年 11 月 21 日，现年 16 岁；贝特尼·杜，生于 1980 年 12 月 28 日，现年 13 岁。原告为两位孩子的监护人，同时也承担了主要的照顾责任。

五

结婚后，原被告便以夫妻名义共同居住直至 1992 年 6 月。

六

原被告便以夫妻名义共同居住在西弗吉尼亚州布洛斯顿县波斯维尔直至 1992 年 6 月。随后，原被告处于持续且未曾间断的分居状态。

七

原被告的婚姻存在着不可调和的矛盾，这种矛盾的存在使得本案原被告的婚姻关系无法继续维系。

八

被告长期残忍且毫无人道地对待原告，破坏了或即将破坏原告的精神和身体健康以及幸福、快乐的生活，原被告的同居状态也使原告毫无安全感并难以忍受。

九

原被告长期分居两地，截止到本诉讼提起之日，分居状态已持续不间断满一年。原被告的分居状态已符合了西弗吉尼亚州法典第 48 章第 4 节第 2 条第 7 款所做的自愿行为的规定。

十

被告已主动离开或抛弃原告超过六个月。

十一

被告与他人存在通奸行为,并且被告的这一行为一直未能得到原告的宽恕。

十二

本案中,就子女监护权的法院管辖权方面,原告称,原被告子女自出生起仅随一方或双方居住;原告未在本州或其他州提起任何有关子女监护权的诉讼;原告也并不知晓在本州或其他州法院是否存在有关本案子女监护权的诉讼;原告确信,除本案原被告外,再无其他人对原被告子女享有或主张享有监护权或探视权。

十三

对于所有的婚姻财产,考虑到在这段婚姻维系期间对家庭所做的贡献,原告享有平等分配的权利,此外,原告有权就其付出的家务劳动获得适当补偿。

请　　求

因此,原告特此提出如下请求:法院解除本案原被告的婚姻关系;被告给付原告临时性及永久性生活费用;被告给付原告诉讼代理费用及相应开支;原告临时及永久性子女的监护、抚养、照看权利;被告向原告支付临时及永久性子女抚养费用;由被告向某一知名保险商为原告购买医疗保险;就双方在婚姻期间所产生的一切债务及责任,由被告负主要承担义务;原告有权请求平均分配依西弗吉尼亚法典48-2-1(e)所定义的婚姻财产;原告有权获得依西弗吉尼亚法典48-2-1(f)所规定的个人独立财产;请求法院判决被告补偿原告17年婚姻维系期间所付出的家务劳动;原告获得位于西弗吉尼亚州波斯维拉的婚姻住所及其内部设施的专属所有权;给付法院认为适当的其他和进一步补偿。

第九章

1. 所谓涉外公证书就是我国公证机关对发生在国内的法律行为及有关法律意义的文件或事实向国外出具的公证文书。

2. 属于法律公文一类的涉外公证文书,有其鲜明的特点,即准确严密、庄重得体以及程式的规范化,这是由法律的社会职能决定的,也是法律语体区分于其他功能文体的根本特征。

(1) 准确严密。准确严密的含义是指忠实原文,准确透彻地理解原文的精神实质,对原文的内容既不歪曲,也不随意增减,译文中的意思必须正确无误。如果流畅和准确发生矛盾时,应选择后者。

(2) 庄重得体。作为法律文书的一种,涉外公证书的语言也应该像法律文书一样庄重得体。如果找来一些英语国家的证书(如毕业证书、学位证书、公证书、营业执照等)和奖状加于研究,我们可以看到,其中的文字都十分庄重、严谨、贴切,并且都有一些特定的表达方法。法律语言是英语各种语体中正式程度最高的一种。它的文辞古奥，句子复杂，个别地方仍然保持着古英语的残存形式。

（3）程式的规范化。程式的规范化也就是所谓"行业性归化"问题。涉外公证书有其固定的格式。

3.《中华人民共和国公证暂行条例》定义了公证书的类型。公证书可以分为四个类型：一是证明法律行为的公证书，如委托、遗嘱、继承权、合同、财产赠与和分割、收养关系等；二是证明有法律意义事实的公证书，如出生、死亡、婚姻状况、亲属关系、健康状况等；三是证明有法律意义文件的公证书，如学历、学位、经历等；四是文件的执行、保管等事项的公证书，如追偿物品、清款的文件等。

目前，我国公证处经常办理的涉外公证文书主要有学历、成绩单公证、学位证书公证、婚姻公证、亲属关系公证、未受刑事处分公证、出生公证、银行存款公证、经济担保公证等。由于每个人的目的不同，所需要的涉外公证书也就不同。

自费留学一般需要提供与学历有关的公证，如毕业证、学位证、成绩单公证、出生和未受刑事制裁等公证。在校生要提供在校证明，还要有家庭财产的有关公证。

准备移民国外的人，根据技术移民和投资移民的不同情况，所办理的公证又有区别。办理技术移民，要把与本人工作技能有关的公证文书尽量办理齐全，如工作经历公证、职称证书或专业资格证书公证等。办投资移民除学历证明公证和无刑事制裁等一般公证外，更多的则需要办理与本人财产有关的公证书，如营业执照公证、纳税证明公证、存款证明公证、住房甚至股票等有价证券的公证等。

出国探亲，需要提供与国外亲属有关的公证。

出国定居则需提供出生、未受刑事制裁、婚姻状况等全套公证书。

4.涉外公证书同非涉外的公证书一样，结构上分为首部，正文（证词）和尾部三部分。需注意的是，涉外公证书通常需要提供公证书的英译本。

（1）首部

① 文书名称

在文书的上部正中写"公证书"

② 文书编号

在"公证书"的右下方用阿拉伯数字写年度的全称。接着写公证机关简称和编号。如："(199×)×公证字第×号。

在首部，一般不写当事人的身份和基本情况；但是，继承、收养亲属关系的公证书的首部应写明当事人的姓名、性别、出生年月日、住址等身份事项。

（2）正文

正文也叫证词，是公证书的核心部分和主要内容。证词应根据证明事项来写，当事人申请公证的事项不同，因而其证词的写法也不尽相同。但不论公证何种事项，都应写得清楚、准确、真实、合法。

公证证明事项的具体内容，有些全部体现在公证书的证词里，如：出生、生存、死亡、收养、婚姻关系、亲属关系公证等。至于法律行为公证，公证书的公证词文字只是寥寥数语。例如："兹证明×××于××××年×月×日来到我处，在我的面前，在前面的赠与书上签名（或盖章）。"因此，这类公证可以印成填空式的文书用纸。但收养子女、财产继承等类公证书，则应根据具体情况，逐件制作。

成批的公证事项（内容同一），如供电局与农村乡镇全面签订《供用电合同》，可以把填空式的公证词拟好，附印到合同（协议后）的后面，这样办证时就大大简化了手续。

（3）尾部

① 制作文书的机关名称

如写"中华人民共和国××省××市（县）公证处"，是哪个公证机关出具的公证书便落款该 公证机关，但必须冠以"中华人民共和国"字样，因为它是代表国家公证。

② 文书签署人的职务和签名

先写"公证员"然后由公证员签名或盖章。

③ 文书签发的年月日，并加盖公章。

5.（1）

Notarization of Diploma

(2008) Lu. Ji. ZI. NO.1986

This is to certify that Zhang San（male，born on September 14，1984）was enrolled in the Computer Science Department of Shandong University（4-year course）in September 2004 and was graduated in July 2008.

Notary：Wang Daming

Jinnan Notary Public Office of

Shandong Province

People's Republic of China

12/20/2008

（2）

Notarial Certificate of Marriage

(2009)Jing. Hai NO.0512

This is to certify that Li Ye（male，born on March 12，1986）and Zhang Xiaohui（female，born on April 4，1986）have been married at Haidian District，Beijing on January 12，2009.

Notary：Shang Di

Haidian Notarial Public Office

City of Beijing

People's Republic of China

1/20/2009

(3)

Notarial Certificate of Testament

(2007) Yu. Luo ZI. NO.1473

Heir: Li Jianren, (male, born on June 24, 1974) now resides at NO. 134, Huanghe Lu, Luoyang, Henan Province.

Testator: Li Dafu, (male, born on April 11, 1950) once resided at NO. 134, Huanghe Lu, Luoyang, Henan Province.

This is to certify that Li Dafu died at Renmin Hospital of Luoyang on November 13, 2007. He had made a will which said that the estate is to be inherited by Li Jianren.

Notary: Li Ruhua

Luoyang Notary Public Office of

Henan Province

People's Republic of China

3/24/2007

(4)

NOTARIAL CERTIFICATE OF EXPERIENCE

(2008) Ji. Ji. ZI. No. 1456

This is to certify that Wang Qiang (female, born on April 25, 1978) had worked in the Experiment School of Jilin as an English Teacher from September 2000 to June 2003, that he was temporarily transferred to work in the Shuangyang School of Jilin as an English Teacher from September 2003 to June 2007.

Notary: Li Hua

Changchun Notary Public Office

Jilin Province

People's Republic of China (Seal)

April 14, 2008

(5)

NOTARIAL CERTIFICATE OF BUSINESS ENTITY

(2009)Jing. Hai ZI, No. 0203

This is to certify that Wubianluomu books sale Co., Ltd., registered as a corporation at the Industry and Commerce Administration Bureau on December 16,2008, and accepted corporate status (02020512, located in NO. 23, Zhongguancun Street, Haidian district, Beijing, is an enterprise engaging in with RMB 5million as its registered capital. Wu Xiaoxiao, President, is its corporation representative's business covers).

Notary: Shang Di

Haidian Notary Public Office

City of Beijing

Peoples Republic of China

January 12, 2009

参考文献

1. 曹叠云:《立法技术》,北京:中国民主法制出版社,1993年。
2. 曹永强:《法律英语解构》,陆文慧:《法律翻译:从实践出发》,香港:中华书局,2002年。
3. 陈炯:《法律语言学概论》,西安:陕西人民教育出版社,1998年。
4. 陈国崇:《关于涉外公证文书的翻译》,《广东工业大学学报》(社会科学版)2002,2(1)。
5. 陈建平:《法律文本翻译探索》,杭州:浙江大学出版社,2007年。
6. 陈忠诚:《悦读法律英语》,北京:法律出版社,2007年。
7. 丁江建:《文本类型理论与翻译》,《中国矿业大学学报》2003,5(3)。
8. 杜金榜、张福、袁亮:《中国法律法规英译的问题和解决》,《中国翻译》2004(3)。
9. 杜金榜:《法律语言学》,上海:上海外语教育出版社,2004年。
10. 傅伟良:《法律文本翻译教程》,北京:中国人民大学出版社,2013年。
11. 高战荣:《论法律翻译的等效性》,《科技信息》2007(30)。
12. 顾海根:《法律英语教程》,北京:北京大学出版社,2005年。
13. 何家弘:《法律英语》,北京:法律出版社,1997年。
14. 何家弘:《法律英语:中英文对照》,北京:法律出版社,2006年。
15. 何美欢:《香港合同法(上册)》,北京:北京大学出版社,1995年。
16. 胡庚申等:《国际商务合同起草与翻译》,北京:外文出版社,2003年。
17. 黄巍:《论法律翻译中译者的创造性》,《中国翻译》2002(3)。
18. 黄宁夏:《公证书语篇分析与翻译》,《国际关系学院学报》2004(3)。
19. 季益广:《法律英语文体特点及英译技巧》,《中国科技翻译》,1999年。
20. 江前良:《涉外经济合同范本》,北京:法律出版社,1999年。
21. 金朝武、胡爱平:《试论我国当前法律翻译中存在的问题》,《中国翻译》2000(3):45—50。
22. 邝江红:《关联翻译理论在我国发展的轨迹》,《绵阳师范学院学报》2008(7)。
23. 兰天:《国际商务合同翻译教程》(第3版),长春:东北财经大学出版社,2011年。
24. 李阳:《法律英语的文体特征及其翻译》,长沙:湖南出版社,1998年。
25. 李德凤、胡牧、李丽:《法律文本翻译》,北京:中央编译出版社,2007年。
26. 李德凤、胡牧:《法律翻译研究:现状与前瞻》,《中国科技翻译》2006(8)。
27. 李斐南、黄瑶、曾报春、任崇正:《法律英语实务》,广州:中山大学出版社,2005年。

28. 李剑波：《法律英语世界》，北京：法律出版社，1999年。
29. 李克兴、张新红：《法律文本与法律翻译》，北京：中国对外翻译出版社，2006年。
30. 李克兴：《法律翻译理论与实践》，北京：北京大学出版社，2007年。
31. 李文娟：《法律翻译的特性及发展现状研究》，《考试周刊》2008(40)。
32. 李振宇：《漫谈立法语言实现》，"应用语言学：法律语言与修辞国际研讨会"，上海，2000年。
33. 栗长江：《涉外公证书汉译英》，《中国科技翻译》2005，18(4)。
34. 梁可：《走进涉外公证》，《21世纪》2002(5)。
35. 林克敏：《中国律师实训经典：中英商务合同精选与解读》，北京：中国人民大学出版社，2013年。
36. 刘庆秋：《国际商务合同的文体与翻译》，北京：对外经济贸易大学出版社，2011年。
37. 刘润清、胡壮麟：《语言文化差异的认识与超越》，北京：外语教学与研究出版社，2000年。
38. 卢敏：《英语法律文本的语言特点与翻译》，上海：上海交通大学出版社，2008年。
39. 陆文慧：《法律翻译——从实践出发》，北京：法律出版社，2004年。
40. 吕昊等：《商务合同写作及翻译》，武汉：武汉大学出版社，2005年。
41. 潘庆云：《跨世纪的中国法律语言》，上海：华东理工大学出版社，1997年。
42. 邱贵溪：《论法律文件的翻译原则》，《中国科技翻译》2000(5)。
43. 曲新久：《民法学》，北京：中国政法大学出版社，2006年。
44. 屈文生、石伟：《论我国近代法律翻译的几个时期》，《上海翻译》2007(4)。
45. 宋德文：《国际贸易英文合同文体与翻译研究》，北京：北京大学出版社，2006年。
46. 宋雷：《法律英语同义·近义术语辨析和翻译指南》，北京：法律出版社，2004年。
47. 孙万彪：《汉英法律翻译教程》，上海：上海外语教育出版社，2006年。
48. 孙万彪：《英汉法律翻译教程》，上海：上海外语教育出版社，2003年。
49. 孙懿华、周广然：《法律语言学》，北京：中国政法大学出版社，1997年。
50. 汤维建、徐卉、胡浩成(译)：《美国联邦地区法院民事诉讼流程》，北京：法律出版社，2001年。
51. 陶博：《法律英语——中英双语法律文书制作》，上海：复旦大学出版社，2007年。
52. 滕超、孔飞燕：《英美实质性条款中解除条件的汉译研究》，《考试周刊》2008(10)。
53. 王春辉：《涉外法律文件的翻译》，《中国翻译》，1998年。
54. 王道庚：《英汉法律翻译教程》，杭州：浙江大学出版社，2006年。
55. 王卫国：《刑法学》，北京：中国政法大学出版社，2004年。
56. 王泽鉴：《民法学说与判例研究》，北京：中国政法大学出版社，1997年。
57. 温建平：《法律英语的特征与汉英翻译》，《国际商务研究》2001(2)。
58. 吴敏、吴明忠：《国际经贸英语合同写作》，广州：暨南大学出版社，1999年。
59. 谢爱林：《论法律语言的特点》，《南昌大学学报》2007(1)。
60. 谢桂梅：《英美公证书翻译之差异》，《语文学刊(高教·外文版)》2006(8)。
61. 熊先觉：《中国司法文书学》，北京：中国法制出版社，2006年。
62. 徐卉(译)：《美国联邦地区法院刑事诉讼流程》，北京：法律出版社，2003年。
63. 徐勤：《英文招标文件的文体特征及翻译》，《中国翻译》2005(1)。
64. 许国新：《英译经贸契约条款中 shall 的正确使用与滥用》，《中国科技翻译》2003(4)。
65. 杨俊峰、屈文生、夏元军：《法律英语案例探究》，北京：清华大学出版社，2007年。
66. 余文景：《法律翻译的理论和技术》，香港：香港大学出版社，1976年。

67. 曾育生:《涉外公证书的翻译》,《广东科技》2006(10)。
68. 张法连:《英美法律术语辞典》,上海:上海外语教育出版社,2014年。
69. 张凤英:《论长句在法律英语中的应用》,《安徽职业技术学院学报》2008(7)。
70. 张新红:《文本类型与法律文本》,《现代外语》2001(02)。
71. 赵元任:《汉语口语语法》,北京:商务印书馆,2002年。
72. 周玲:《如何翻译英语法律文献》,北京:对外经济贸易大学出版社,2006年。
73. 周文建:《怎样写公证书和海外公证书》,《新闻与写作》2003(9)。
74. 周雪婷:《法律英语翻译的模糊性与准确性》,《集美大学学报》2006(2)。
75. 《法学词典》编辑委员会:《法学词典》(增订版),上海:上海辞书出版社,1984年。
76. Bryan A. Garner, *Black's Law Dictionary*, *7th Edition*, Eagan: West Publishing Company, 1999.
77. Fung, S. & Watson-Brown, A., *The Template: A Guide for the Analysis of Complex Legislation*, London: Institute of Advanced Legal Studies, 1994.
78. Kenneth A. Adams, *A Manual of Style for Contract Drafting*, 3rd Edition, American Bar Association, 2013.
79. Lawrence Venuti, *The Translator's Invisibility: A History of Translation*, 2nd Revised Edition, Routledge, 2006.
80. Nida, E. A., *Toward a Science of Translating*, Bill Academic Publishers, 1964.
81. Nida, E. A., *Language, Culture and Translation*, Shanghai: Shanghai Foreign Language Education Press, 1993/2000.
82. O'Barr, William M., *Linguistic Evidence: Language, Power, and Strategy in the Courtroom*, New York: Academic Press, 1982.
83. Sager, T., Planning and the Liberal Paradox: A Democratic Dilemma in Social Choice, *Journal of Planning Literature* 1997, 12(1): 16—29.
84. Sarcevic, Susan, *New Approach to Legal Translation*, The Hague: Kluwer Law International, 1997, 243—246, 251.
85. Uwe Muegge, *Translation Contract*, Authorhouse, 2005.
86. Varo, E.A. & Brian Hughes, *Legal Translation Explained*, Manchester & Northampton: St. Jerome Publishing, 2002.